Epistemic Consequentialism

Epistemic Consequentialism

EDITED BY
Kristoffer Ahlstrom-Vij
and Jeffrey Dunn

OXFORD
UNIVERSITY PRESS

OXFORD
UNIVERSITY PRESS

Great Clarendon Street, Oxford, OX2 6DP,
United Kingdom

Oxford University Press is a department of the University of Oxford.
It furthers the University's objective of excellence in research, scholarship,
and education by publishing worldwide. Oxford is a registered trade mark of
Oxford University Press in the UK and in certain other countries

© the several contributors 2018

The moral rights of the authors have been asserted

First Edition published in 2018

Impression: 1

All rights reserved. No part of this publication may be reproduced, stored in
a retrieval system, or transmitted, in any form or by any means, without the
prior permission in writing of Oxford University Press, or as expressly permitted
by law, by licence or under terms agreed with the appropriate reprographics
rights organization. Enquiries concerning reproduction outside the scope of the
above should be sent to the Rights Department, Oxford University Press, at the
address above

You must not circulate this work in any other form
and you must impose this same condition on any acquirer

Published in the United States of America by Oxford University Press
198 Madison Avenue, New York, NY 10016, United States of America

British Library Cataloguing in Publication Data
Data available

Library of Congress Control Number: 2017958145

ISBN 978-0-19-877968-1

Printed and bound by
CPI Group (UK) Ltd, Croydon, CR0 4YY

Links to third party websites are provided by Oxford in good faith and
for information only. Oxford disclaims any responsibility for the materials
contained in any third party website referenced in this work.

Contents

List of Contributors   vii

   Introduction: Epistemic Consequentialism   1
   Jeffrey Dunn and Kristoffer Ahlstrom-Vij

Part I. Epistemic Consequentialism: The Right and the Good

  1. The Right in the Good: A Defense of Teleological Non-Consequentialism   23
    Clayton Littlejohn

  2. Adaptive Misbeliefs, Value Trade-Offs, and Epistemic Responsibility   48
    Nancy E. Snow

  3. The Naturalistic Origins of Epistemic Consequentialism   70
    Hilary Kornblith

  4. Epistemic Teleology: Synchronic and Diachronic   85
    Ralph Wedgwood

  5. The "Consequentialism" in "Epistemic Consequentialism"   113
    Julia Driver

  6. Good Questions   123
    Alejandro Pérez Carballo

Part II. Accuracy-First Epistemology: For and Against

  7. Can All-Accuracy Accounts Justify Evidential Norms?   149
    Christopher J. G. Meacham

  8. A Problem for Credal Consequentialism   182
    Michael Caie

  9. Making Things Right: The True Consequences of Decision Theory in Epistemology   220
    Richard Pettigrew

  10. Accuracy, Ratification, and the Scope of Epistemic Consequentialism   240
    James M. Joyce

Part III. Epistemic Consequentialism Applied

  11. Epistemic Value and the Jamesian Goals   269
    Sophie Horowitz

12. Epistemic Consequentialism and Epistemic Enkrasia 290
    Amanda Askell

13. Epistemic Free Riding 310
    Jeffrey Dunn

Index 333

List of Contributors

KRISTOFFER AHLSTROM-VIJ, Birkbeck College, University of London

AMANDA ASKELL, New York University

MICHAEL CAIE, University of Pittsburgh

JULIA DRIVER, Washington University, St Louis

JEFFREY DUNN, DePauw University

SOPHIE HOROWITZ, University of Massachusetts, Amherst

JAMES M. JOYCE, University of Michigan

HILARY KORNBLITH, University of Massachusetts, Amherst

CLAYTON LITTLEJOHN, King's College London

CHRISTOPHER J. G. MEACHAM, University of Massachusetts, Amherst

ALEJANDRO PÉREZ CARBALLO, University of Massachusetts, Amherst

RICHARD PETTIGREW, University of Bristol

NANCY E. SNOW, University of Oklahoma

RALPH WEDGWOOD, University of Southern California

Introduction
Epistemic Consequentialism

Jeffrey Dunn and Kristoffer Ahlstrom-Vij

0.1 Consequentialism: Moral and Epistemic

What makes an action right or wrong? One of the most influential answers over the past couple of centuries is that of the *consequentialist*. There are a variety of consequentialist views and there are a variety of ways of stating precisely what it is for a view to count as consequentialist. Nevertheless, consequentialists agree that, in some sense, rightness is to be understood in terms of goodness. Act utilitarianism is perhaps the most well-known version of consequentialism. According to such a view, an action is right if and only if no alternative to that action has a set of consequences with greater total value. The most familiar version of such a view is of the hedonist variety, where total value is understood as pleasure minus pain,[1] though of course there are other accounts of value. But no matter your account of value, it is value that comes first, and specifically the value of consequences, since rightness of actions on this view is determined by the value of the states of affairs that actions lead to.

Notice several other commitments of act utilitarianism. First, it maintains that rightness is determined not just by *some* of the consequences of actions but by the *total* set of consequences. Second, it maintains that right actions *maximize* the value of the consequences. Finally, it is, we might say, a *direct* version of consequentialism in that the rightness of an action is determined by *its* consequences (relative to alternatives). Not all views that have been said to be instances of consequentialism share these features. We can, for example, imagine a form of ethical egoism, where actions are right when maximizing the good *for the agent herself*. Such a view might not be particularly plausible as an ethical theory, but that doesn't prevent it from qualifying as a consequentialist view. As for the second point above, satisficing consequentialism does not require maximizing: right actions must have consequences that are valuable above some non-maximal threshold.[2] And as for the final point above, notice that

---

[1] See e.g., Mill (1861/2001) and Feldman (2004).   [2] See, e.g., Slote (1984).

rule consequentialism is not direct: rightness of actions depends on whether they conform to right rules, where the rightness of rules depends on the consequences of the widespread adoption of those rules.[3] It is controversial whether these variations render the corresponding views non-consequentialist.[4] But note that these views still agree that rightness is understood in terms of goodness, and the goodness of consequences in particular.[5]

Despite strong and frequent resistance from defenders of non-consequentialist moral theories, many have felt that consequentialism—specifically utilitarianism—has dominated the debate. Citing T. M. Scanlon's (1982) puzzlement over utilitarianism occupying such a central position, despite being 'wildly at variance with firmly held moral conviction' (p. 103), Philippa Foot (1985) famously wrote that 'it is remarkable how utilitarianism tends to haunt even those of us who will not believe in it. It is as if we for ever feel that it must be right, even though we insist that it is wrong' (p. 196). Indeed, according to Christine Korsgaard (1996), 'to later generations, much of the moral philosophy of the twentieth century will look like a struggle to escape utilitarianism' (p. 279).

Meanwhile, much of contemporary epistemology has been marked not so much by a struggle as by a tacit endorsement of *epistemic consequentialism*, the idea that epistemic rightness—denoted by terms such as 'justification' or 'rationality'—is to be understood in terms of conduciveness to epistemic goods. Many epistemologists, for instance, have been attracted to the idea that epistemic norms that describe appropriate belief-forming behavior ultimately earn their keep by providing us with some means to garner accurate beliefs. And accuracy is plausibly an important kind of epistemic good. Hence, we have epistemic rightness understood in terms of conduciveness to epistemic goodness.

However, it is important to be clear that nothing like act utilitarianism has gained any widespread adherents in epistemology, muddying the comparison between moral and epistemic consequentialism. An epistemic version of act utilitarianism would presumably be the following: a belief is justified (or rational) just in case the total causal consequences of holding or forming that belief contain more epistemic good than the total causal consequences of holding or forming any alternative belief (or lack of belief). This view would surely deserve to be an instance of epistemic consequentialism, but to our knowledge, no epistemologist

---

[3] See Hooker (2000).

[4] For example, some maintain that a view is only consequentialist if it defines what right or obligated in terms of what will maximize value (e.g., Smart and Williams 1973, Pettit 2000, and Portmore 2007).

[5] There are other ways to try to state what is distinctive about consequentialism. For example, some maintain that a consequentialist is one who is committed to only agent-neutral, rather than agent-centered prescriptions (e.g., McNaughton and Rawling 1991). Still others maintain that what is distinct about consequentialism is the lack of intrinsic constraints on action types (e.g., Nozick 1974, Nagel 1986, and Kagan 1997). For a general overview, see Driver (2012). For a discussion of these issues specifically with regard to epistemic consequentialism, see Dunn and Ahlstrom-Vij (2017).

has defended this position. So what kinds of consequentialist views *have* been held by epistemologists?

As we'll see, some evaluate processes of belief formation with reference to the processes' consequences, and then individual beliefs derivatively. Others seem to maintain that an account of justification can be rejected if justification is not in some way connected to accuracy, though the connection may be complex. Still others have maintained that the justification of a belief consists not in its *leading* to epistemic goodness but rather in virtue of *exemplifying* it. This last view might be thought to be better described as a *teleological approach* to epistemology: epistemic rightness is understood in terms of goodness, but not necessarily in terms of the goodness of *causal consequences*. If the epistemic version of act utilitarianism is clearly an instance of epistemic consequentialism, then where does epistemic consequentialism end and teleology begin? That is a contested question, as some of the contributors in this volume note.[6] It is nevertheless worth noting that some of the seeming tacit agreement in epistemology regarding epistemic consequentialism results from the fact that it is being thought of in slightly different ways.

Having noted this, it is probably most fruitful to examine particular epistemological views, and note ways in which they seem committed to some form of consequentialism, rather than formulating a grand and controversial theory about what makes an epistemological view genuinely consequentialist. In this spirit, it is particularly helpful to consider the debate over how to understand *justification*. The main theories that have dominated the debate over the past thirty years each have prominent proponents that seem to endorse an epistemic consequentialist line, as the following examples make clear.

The chief proponent of reliabilism has been Alvin Goldman. In his (1979) he maintains that beliefs are justified when they are produced by suitably reliable processes. Put another way, beliefs are justified when produced by the right kinds of processes, and the right kinds of processes are those that are truth-conducive. Notice that, since not evaluating the rightness of a belief in terms of *its* consequences, reliabilism thereby isn't analogous to act utilitarianism (which, as we shall see below, enables the reliabilist to avoid certain problems that some of her detractors have attempted to adapt from the ethical literature). According to Goldman (1986) himself, reliabilism is instead a kind of rule consequentialism for beliefs.

According to coherentism, a belief is justified if and only if it belongs to a coherent system of beliefs. One of its chief proponents is Laurence BonJour (although he has since changed his mind). In his (1985), he devotes a chapter to arguing that coherent systems of belief are likely to "correspond closely to independent reality" (p. 171). He calls this a *metajustification* for his version of coherentism. And why is such a metajustification required? He writes:

---

[6] See particularly Ralph Wedgwood's contribution. James Joyce and Richard Pettigrew also discuss this.

The basic role of justification is that of a *means* to truth, a more directly attainable mediating link between our subjective starting point and our objective goal.... If epistemic justification were not conducive to truth in this way, if finding epistemically justified beliefs did not substantially increase the likelihood of finding true ones, then epistemic justification would be irrelevant to our main cognitive goal and of dubious worth.... Epistemic justification is therefore in the final analysis only an instrumental value, not an intrinsic one. (BonJour 1985, pp. 7–8)

The fact that BonJour takes justification to be a means to truth strongly suggests that he thinks of justification in consequentialist terms.

Finally, consider evidentialism. As defended by Richard Feldman and Earl Conee (1985), the view is a kind of foundationalism where a belief is justified if and only if it is supported by the total evidence that the believer has. Is this a form of epistemic consequentialism? Less obviously so than in the cases considered above, but we think there's still a case for filing this kind of evidentialism under the heading of epistemic consequentialism. For one thing, Conee (1992) motivates this total evidence requirement with reference to an overriding goal of true belief. Thus, in Conee's version of the view, evidentialism agrees with reliabilism and with BonJour-style coherentism that justification is a matter of truth conduciveness. Feldman (2000), by contrast, motivates the total evidence requirement with reference to an overriding goal of *reasonable* belief (rather than true belief). Thus, on this reading of Feldman, evidentialism disagrees with reliabilism and BonJour-style coherentism about the nature of the relevant goal, but agrees that justification should be spelled out in consequentialist terms.

So here we have three competing views about the nature of justification whose main proponents, while disagreeing about many things, nevertheless are in agreement in endorsing the basic epistemic consequentialist idea that epistemic rightness should be understood in terms of the epistemic goodness of consequences.

0.2 Questions for Epistemic Consequentialists

Though saying that epistemic rightness should be understood in terms of the epistemic goodness of consequences gives one an idea of the epistemic consequentialist view, more needs to be said to understand it.

The first important question for the epistemic consequentialist concerns the nature of epistemic goodness, or as we'll refer to it henceforth, *epistemic value*. Here the question concerns *final epistemic value*, epistemic value that is not derived from something else. One popular answer among epistemic consequentialists is that true belief has final epistemic value, false belief has final epistemic disvalue, and nothing else has final epistemic value or disvalue. More succinctly, we might say that the final epistemic value is accuracy. Alvin Goldman (1999) calls this view *veritism*. Note two things about veritism. First, it is monistic: there is one dimension of value, not many dimensions that need to be combined, as the pluralist would have it.

Epistemic consequentialists need not be committed to monism about final epistemic value, though in practice many are. Second, we might say that according to veritism, epistemic value is *naturalistically acceptable* in that the property of being an accurate belief is not itself a normative property. Again, epistemic consequentialists need not be committed to this. After all, believing that accuracy or related concepts pick out non-natural properties—perhaps in a manner analogous to G. E. Moore's (1903) views in ethics—doesn't as such make you a non-consequentialist.

A second important question for the epistemic consequentialist concerns what is being evaluated for epistemic rightness. Often, as in the theories of justification mentioned above, individual beliefs are being evaluated. But this is not the only option. As we'll see shortly, a prominent version of epistemic consequentialism within formal epistemology evaluates sets of beliefs for rationality. Further, not everyone agrees about how to think about beliefs. Some represent beliefs as all-or-nothing, while others think of beliefs as coming in degrees. Epistemic consequentialism is (of course) not committed to either representation, and, indeed, in this volume there are contributions from both camps. Though most of the work in this volume focuses on instances of epistemic consequentialism that evaluate belief—we may refer to this as *doxastic epistemic consequentialism*—there are views that perhaps deserve the name but do not evaluate belief. Some work in the philosophy of science about the distribution of cognitive labor seeks to evaluate things like the communication structures of scientific communities, the cognitive biases of scientists, and the methodological strategies that scientists employ in order to see how truth-conducive such structures, biases, or strategies are. For example, Philip Kitcher (1990) adopts a consequentialist approach in order to argue that scientific communities containing a diversity of belief can be more epistemically productive than communities wherein each community member works on the same, most probable theory. We might refer to this as *methodological epistemic consequentialism*.

A third important question for the epistemic consequentialist concerns the nature of the relationship between the thing being evaluated and whatever has final epistemic value. To be a genuine instance of consequentialism (as opposed to teleology, perhaps) it would seem that the relationship must be some kind of *conducing* relation. But there are a variety of options here. One view says that the relation has to be such as to maximize value. This would be an analogue of utilitarianism in ethics. Another view says that right beliefs must instead lead to some *threshold* level of epistemic value. This is the view of the reliabilist—a process can generate justification while failing to be maximally reliable—and it is in this respect analogous to the satisficing consequentialist in ethics. Still another view says that right belief is belief that is not epistemic-value-dominated, where a belief state is epistemic-value-dominated just in case in every world there is some belief state that leads to more epistemic value than it does. Cutting across these distinctions about the conducing relation is a distinction concerning whether the conducing is *direct* or *indirect*. For example, the act utilitarian holds that conducing must be direct: whether an act is right depends on the value that *that* act leads to. The rule utilitarian, on the other hand, holds that conducing is indirect: whether an act is right depends on whether it conforms to a proper rule, and whether the rule is proper depends on the consequences of adopting such a rule. Reliabilism, as noted above, is an example of a view that has been thought of as an analogue of rule utilitarianism and thus an instance of *indirect* epistemic consequentialism: it's not the consequences of the belief itself that determine its rightness, but rather the reliability of the process from which it emanates.[7]

A final important question for the epistemic consequentialist concerns which consequences of a process, belief, or what have you matter for the rightness of belief. Focusing on the reliabilist, one natural answer is that the rightness of a belief is determined by the epistemic value of *all* the consequences of the process producing it. But many restrict this in various ways. For example, if a process by way of which I form a belief leads to lots of true belief for you further downstream, that's typically not taken to count in favor of that process, or the belief it produces in me. Moreover, reliabilists typically also hold that it is the value of the *direct* products of a process that matter. An example may make this clearer. Suppose you tell me that the WWII history book I was looking for is under the desk and that my auditory process leads to me believing this. Suppose that the book *is* under the desk, I find the book, and I am thus led to form many other true beliefs about WWII on account of reading the book. According to process reliabilism, we don't count these true beliefs about WWII as telling in favor of my auditory process. Only the true belief about the location of the book counts in its favor. There can be more radical restrictions on consequences, too. Some work in formal epistemology looks to have a consequentialist structure, but such views evaluate entire belief states for how well *that* belief state does with respect to accuracy.[8] So, the consequences that matter for the thing being evaluated (a total belief state) is just the thing itself. One might think that such views are no longer instances of consequentialism because nothing can be a *consequence* of itself. Indeed, one might think that *any* restriction on the consequences that matter is inconsistent with consequentialism. Perhaps. But even views that restrict the consequences in extreme ways still have a means–end structure to them that makes them worth considering as of a related family.

At any rate, it is not the purpose of this section to argue that *every* answer to the four questions here results in a defensible view that deserves to be called an instance of epistemic consequentialism. The point is rather to highlight several key decisions that must be made by those who hope to develop a view committed to the idea that the epistemic right is to be understood in terms of the epistemic good of consequences. In the next section, we'll highlight some prominent views in the literature and note how they answer some of these important questions.

---

[7] See also Chase (2004) and Firth (1981).   [8] See, e.g., Konek and Levinstein (forthcoming).

0.3 Extant Epistemic Consequentialist Views

0.3.1 Reliabilism

Process reliabilism about justification has already been mentioned above, but it is worth saying a bit more about the view here, since it has been singled out for criticism in a recent series of papers by Selim Berker (2013a and b). (More on this in Section 0.4.) As we have already seen, the standard process reliabilist, of the sort found in Goldman (1979), maintains that a belief is justified if and only if it is produced by a belief-forming process that is reliable over some threshold. Thus, it is an instance of *indirect doxastic epistemic consequentialism*. We evaluate processes of belief-formation in terms of whether those processes (directly) produce a ratio of true beliefs to false beliefs above some threshold. Then we evaluate individual beliefs indirectly by whether they were produced by processes that were evaluated positively in the first stage.

0.3.2 Epistemic utility theory

There has been a flurry of work in the last fifteen years following the lead of James Joyce's accuracy-based arguments for various norms of rationality.[9] According to this approach, one attempts to justify formal rationality constraints by defining a measure of accuracy for doxastic states, and then using the methods of decision theory to argue that those doxastic states that meet the formal constraints are to be preferred (e.g., they maximize expected accuracy, or dominate all other doxastic states in terms of accuracy). This looks to be committed to a consequentialist picture of epistemic normativity: conforming to the norms of rationality is required because conforming to those norms leads to accurate doxastic states. The general structure of epistemic utility theory does not require that accuracy is the sole thing of epistemic value, although this has been the dominant view in this literature. The subset of epistemic utility theory that does adopt this view of epistemic value can be usefully referred to as *accuracy-first epistemology*.

In this literature, beliefs are thought of as coming in degrees and represented by a *credence function*, a function that assigns to propositions real numbers in the interval [0,1]. Joyce (1998) proves that every credence function that violates *probabilism*, the thesis that rational credences are probabilities, is accuracy-dominated by some credence function that satisfies probabilism. A credence function, c, is *accuracy-dominated* by another, c^*, when in all possible worlds, the accuracy of c^* is at least as great as the accuracy of c, and in at least one world, the accuracy of c^* is greater than the accuracy of c. Joyce (2009) proves that no credence function that satisfies probabilism is accuracy-dominated in this way by a credence function that violates

---

[9] Joyce (1998) is seminal. Representative work in this area includes: Greaves and Wallace (2006), Leitgeb and Pettigrew (2010a, b), Easwaran (2013), Easwaran and Fitelson (2015), and Pettigrew (2016). For a nice survey of this project, see Pettigrew (2013).

8 INTRODUCTION

probabilism. This, together with some assumptions about how to measure accuracy, completes Joyce's argument.

Since several contributions to this volume respond to or build on this work, a short example of the style of argument might be useful. To keep things simple, suppose we are focused on credence functions that are defined only over the proposition q and its negation. Consider the following two credence functions:

$$c_1(q) = 0.75 \qquad c_2(q) = 0.8$$
$$c_1(\sim q) = 0.25 \qquad c_2(\sim q) = 0.3$$

Suppose that all we want to argue is that c_2 is an impermissible credence function to have. Here's how we would proceed. First we need to define an epistemic value function (sometimes called an 'epistemic utility function') that tells us how much epistemic value a credence function has at a world. In Joyce (1998) the epistemic value function is one according to which perfect accuracy in a world is obtained by a credence function that matches the truth-values of propositions in that world (that is, a perfectly accurate credence function is one that assigns 1s to the truths and 0s to the falsehoods).[10] To fully define the function, however, we must say more than just what makes for perfect accuracy. We also want the function to tell us the degree of accuracy for imperfect credence functions. In a world where q is false, though $c(q) = 0.8$ and $c(q) = 0.2$ are both inaccurate, the second is plausibly closer to perfect accuracy. The appropriate mathematical tool to use to calculate the distance a credence function is from perfect accuracy is a *scoring rule*. Scoring rules are functions that specify an accuracy score for credence x in a proposition relative to two possibilities: the possibility that the proposition is true and the possibility that it is false. There are many constraints that can be placed on scoring rules, but one popular constraint is that the scoring rule be *proper*. A scoring rule is proper if and only if the *expected* accuracy score of a credence of x in a proposition q, where the expectation is weighted by probability function P, is maximized at $x = P(q)$. Putting together a notion of perfect accuracy and a notion of distance to perfect accuracy yields a final epistemic value function that is sensitive solely to accuracy.

One proper scoring rule that is often used as a measure of accuracy is the Brier score. Let $v_w(q)$ be a function that takes value 1 if proposition q is true at possible world w and that takes value 0 if proposition q is false at possible world w. Thus, $v_w(q)$ merely tells us whether proposition q is true or false at possible world w. In addition, let $c(q)$ be the credence assigned to proposition q, and let Ω be the set of propositions to which our credence function assigns credences. Then the Brier score for that credence function at possible world w is:

$$\sum_{q \in \Omega} 1 - (v_w(q) - c(q))^2$$

---

[10] Though this is a natural choice, there are alternatives. For instance, one might think that a perfectly accurate credence function is one that matches the *chances*.

Consider how c_1 and c_2 fare according to the Brier score. There are only two possible worlds to consider: the world where q is true and the world where it is false. In the world (call it "$w1$") where q is true, the Brier score for each credence function is as follows:

Brier score for c_1: $[1 - (v_{w1}(q) - c_1(q))^2] + [1 - (v_{w1}(\sim q) - c_1(\sim q))^2]$
$= [1 - (1 - 0.75)^2] + [1 - (0 - 0.25)^2]$
$= [1 - .0625] + [1 - .0625]$
$= 1.875$

Brier score for c_2: $[1 - (v_{w1}(q) - c_2(q))^2] + [1 - (v_{w1}(\sim q) - c_2(\sim q))^2]$
$= [1 - (1 - 0.8)^2] + [1 - (0 - 0.3)^2]$
$= [1 - .04] + [1 - .09]$
$= 1.87$

As one can verify, c_1 has a higher score than c_2 in a world where q is true. Now, consider a world where q is false (call this world "$w2$"):

Brier score for c_1: $[1 - (v_{w2}(q) - c_1(q))^2] + [1 - (v_{w2}(\sim q) - c_1(\sim q))^2]$
$= [1 - (0 - 0.75)^2] + [1 - (1 - 0.25)^2]$
$= [1 - .5625] + [1 - .5625]$
$= .875$

Brier score for c_2: $[1 - (v_{w2}(q) - c_2(q))^2] + [1 - (v_{w2}(\sim q) - c_2(\sim q))^2]$
$= [1 - (0 - 0.8)^2] + [1 - (1 - 0.3)^2]$
$= [1 - .64] + [1 - .49]$
$= .87$

Again, as one can verify, c_1 has a higher score than c_2 in a world where q is false.

This takes care of the epistemic value function. Once this is in hand, the second step is to pick a decision rule that orders credence functions in terms of their epistemic value. For instance, in Joyce (1998) the decision rule is that (weakly) dominated options are impermissible. In our simple example, we can see that c_2 is dominated by c_1 because in every possible world, c_1 has a higher score than c_2.

In our simple example, the argument is complete. The algebra above proves that c_2 is dominated and our decision rule thus rules this credence function to be impermissible. In actual arguments of this form, there is more work to do in generalizing the result to show that, e.g., *all* incoherent credence functions are dominated in this way.

Others have altered or extended this basic Joycean framework in various ways. One alteration of Joyce's program is to use a different decision rule, for instance, the decision rule according to which permissible options maximize expected epistemic value. Leitgeb and Pettigrew (2010a, b) use this decision rule to prove that no incoherent credence function maximizes expected utility.

The results can be extended to other norms, too. For instance, conditionalization is a rule about how to update one's credence function in light of acquiring new information. Suppose that c is an agent's credence function and c_e is the agent's credence function after learning e and nothing else. Conditionalization maintains that the following should hold:

$$\text{For all } a, \text{ and all } e, c(a|e) = c_e(a), \text{ so long as } c(e) \neq 0.$$

In this expression, $c(a|e)$ is the conditional probability of a, given e. Greaves and Wallace (2006) prove that, with suitable choices for the epistemic value function, the updating rule conditionalization maximizes expected epistemic value in situations where the agent will get some new information from a partition (a simple case of this is where an agent will either learn p or learn $\sim p$). Leitgeb and Pettigrew (2010a, b) give an alternative proof that conditionalization maximizes expected utility.

The approach can also be extended to prove norms where all-or-nothing belief states are taken as primitive. Easwaran and Fitelson (2015) extend the approach in this way. Interestingly, their approach yields the result that some logically inconsistent belief states are permissible (for instance, in lottery cases). The approach has also been extended to comparative confidence rankings (where a comparative confidence ranking represents only certain qualitative facts about how confident an agent is in propositions—for instance, that she is more confident in p than in q). Williams (2012) has extended the approach in a different direction by examining cases where the background logic is nonclassical.

0.3.3 Other instances of epistemic consequentialism

Other areas of epistemology have displayed consequentialist tendencies, too. For example, in the growing field of social epistemology, Goldman (1999) makes clear that he wants to evaluate social institutions and policies in terms of their 'veritistic consequences', i.e., with reference to how these institutions or policies affect people's ability to form true beliefs. He writes:

> People have interest, both intrinsic and extrinsic, in acquiring knowledge (true belief) and avoiding error. It therefore makes sense to have a discipline that evaluates intellectual practices by their causal contributions to knowledge or error. This is how I conceive of epistemology: as a discipline that evaluates practices along truth-linked (veritistic) dimensions. Social epistemology evaluates specifically social practices along these dimensions. (Goldman 1999, p. 69)

Others have taken a similar approach in attempting to understand the structure of scientific inquiry. Aforementioned work by Kitcher (1990) on the division of cognitive labor is a good example here. Others, such as Zollman (2007), Muldoon and Weisberg (2009), and Mayo-Wilson et al. (2011), have followed Kitcher in this approach.

Miriam Solomon (1992) is another philosopher of science who adopts a consequentialist framework. She writes that the central normative question in the philosophy of science is "whether or not, and where and where not, our methods are conducive to scientific success... Scientific rationality is thus viewed instrumentally" (p. 443).

Larry Laudan is similarly attracted to the consequentialist picture. For Laudan, the things we are ultimately evaluating are methodological rules:

A little reflection makes clear that methodological rules possess what force they have because they are believed to be instruments or means for achieving the aims of science. More generally, both in science and elsewhere, we adopt the procedural and evaluative rules we do because we hold them to be optimal techniques for realizing our cognitive goals or utilities.

(Laudan 1984, p. 26)

Decision-theoretic accounts of theory acceptance in the philosophy of science, made popular by Levi (1967) and Maher (1993), also display consequentialist ideas. According to these accounts, the decision to accept a theory is rational when accepting that theory maximizes subjective expected cognitive utility. Cognitive utility is, in turn, understood as balancing two desiderata: accuracy and informativeness. This is similar in some ways to the project of epistemic utility theory described in the section above, but different in important ways, too. In particular, the things being evaluated are not credence functions, but rather acts of theory acceptance. And the value to promote is not merely accuracy, but rather some balance between accuracy and informativeness.

0.4 Trade-Off Objections to Epistemic Consequentialism

So should we all be epistemic consequentialists, then? Several people think that reflecting on ethical consequentialism should give us pause. Perhaps the most prominent objections to consequentialist views in ethics concern problematic trade-offs that consequentialists look forced to endorse. Consider the infamous surgeon case: the classic utilitarian seems to sanction cutting up a healthy person—even if against her will—if that saves the lives of five people in need of organs (Thomson 1976). Still, most of us find that clearly immoral. We have the same reaction in other well-known cases in the literature, such as that involving the framing of a perfectly innocent person to prevent a mob from starting a violent riot (McCloskey 1957), or a person being asked to shoot (Williams 1973) or torture (Foot 1985) one person to save a large number of people.

Structurally similar cases are by far the most common objections to epistemic consequentialism. Firth (1981) gives an early instance of such a trade-off objection, with reliabilism as the target. Fumerton (1995) gives a trade-off objection that nicely illustrates the basic structure of such objections. Suppose that you are applying for a research grant from a religious organization and they will only give grants to those who believe that God exists. You do not believe and find the evidence overwhelmingly in favor of atheism. However, you realize that (a) you won't be able to fool the organization unless you really believe, and (b) that if you receive the grant, you will learn many new and interesting things you wouldn't otherwise learn. Believing (against your evidence) that God exists looks as though it leads to more accuracy than not believing. And so a certain kind of consequentialist looks committed to saying that you epistemically should believe. But, Fumerton claims, this is mistaken. It's important to note that the temporal element in Fumerton's case is dispensable. As Jenkins (2007) notes, we can construct cases where the reward and the cost come at the same time. Let q be a proposition that you have no reason to believe and that is false. And suppose that a goddess has set things up so that if you believe q in the next moment, at that same moment you will be given a mass of true beliefs. According to Jenkins, it would be irrational to believe q in this case, though consequentialists look forced to say you should believe q.

One problem with these objections, however, is that they assume that epistemic consequentialism takes a form analogous to act utilitarianism in ethics. But, as noted above, the most prominent version of epistemic consequentialism, reliabilism, does not take that form; on reliabilism, the rightness of a belief is not a function of the goodness of its consequences, but of the reliability of the process that generates it. More recent trade-off objections to epistemic consequentialism are sensitive to this point. This includes Littlejohn (2012) and Berker (2013a, b). For an example, consider Berker's (2013b) objection to reliabilism.[11] Suppose there is a process of belief-formation that in response to a query about whether a number is prime, yields the belief that the number is not prime. Given the relative scarcity of primes in the natural numbers, this process is guaranteed to be highly reliable. But, Berker maintains one would not be justified in believing that, say, 7 is not prime on the basis of such a process. There is a kind of trade-off here. The process itself achieves overall high accuracy by getting certain obvious cases wrong. Note that this case is similar in certain ways to lottery beliefs. Though it is controversial, a number of epistemologists[12] hold that one is not justified in believing that a particular ticket in a fair lottery is a loser before the lottery is drawn. And yet one can gain a lot of accuracy by believing of each ticket that it is a loser. In this case, one is getting overall high accuracy, even though one can be certain that one is inaccurate about one ticket.

Greaves (2013) and Carr (2017) give structurally similar trade-off objections but with the target of epistemic utility theory rather than reliabilism. For an example, consider Greaves's Garden of Epistemic Imps. Suppose that there is one imp playing in the garden before me, who I clearly see. Five other imps are inside and will come out to play in the next moment with some probability. Let I_0 be the proposition that the imp in front of me is playing in the garden, and $I_1, I_2, \ldots, I_5$ be the propositions that each of the five other imps come out to play. Suppose the probability that $I_n (1 \leq n \leq 5)$

---

[11] For recent responses to Berker, see Ahlstrom-Vij and Dunn (2014) and Goldman (2015).
[12] For instance, BonJour (1980), Pollock (1995), Evnine (1999), Nelkin (2000), Adler (2005), Douven (2006), Kvanvig (2009), Nagel (2011), Littlejohn (2012), Smithies (2012), McKinnon (2013), and Locke (2014).

is true is $1 - (0.5 \times c(I_0))$. Thus, if I can get myself to set $c(I_0) = 0$ I will certainly have five perfectly accurate credences. If I follow my evidence and set $c(I_0) = 1$ then my overall expected accuracy is lower, since each of $I_1, I_2, \ldots, I_5$ is only 50 percent likely to be true. If the epistemic consequentialist says that one ought to maximize the expected accuracy of one's credences, then it looks as though she must say that I ought to ignore what is manifest to me and set $c(I_0) = 0$. But it might seem that I shouldn't ignore my evidence in a case like this—hence, the challenge for epistemic utility theory.

0.5 Contributions in this Volume

The previous sections will hopefully have given the reader an overview of the variety of considerations relevant to gauging the viability of epistemic consequentialism. One thing that this overview should make clear in particular is that the consequentialist common ground mentioned at the outset, and that not too long ago held sway in epistemology, is in the process of breaking up. One of the main motivations for this collection is to document this process—and to do so whether or not the common ground will ultimately be re-established, or be replaced by a new set of assumptions and projects.

That said, we should be clear up-front about an editorial choice we've made in putting together this volume. While we are looking to document a particularly interesting and productive period in discussions about epistemic consequentialism, we're not attempting to provide anything like a representative cross-section of the relevant debates. Rather, we have chosen to focus on collecting some of the most interesting but until now unpublished contributions to some of the most active parts of the relevant debates. Readers interested in reading up on what is already available in the literature should make use of the references provided in the previous sections.

Part I. Epistemic Consequentialism: The Right and the Good

The chapters in the first part of the volume are focused on what epistemic consequentialists say about epistemic value, and in particular on the relationship between the right and the good. Clayton Littlejohn and Nancy Snow both appeal to features of epistemic value to criticize the consequentialist. Hilary Kornblith, on the other hand, argues that considerations of epistemic value favor the consequentialist picture. Ralph Wedgwood distinguishes epistemic *teleology* from epistemic *consequentialism* and offers arguments in favor of the former. The section concludes with advice for would-be epistemic consequentialists. Julia Driver is interested in finding out what we might learn about epistemic consequentialism by exploring a more sophisticated theory about the relation between the right and the good while Alejandro Pérez Carballo argues that the consequentialist should expand her picture of epistemic value to include more than mere accuracy.

CHAPTER 1. CLAYTON LITTLEJOHN, 'THE RIGHT IN THE GOOD: A DEFENSE OF TELEOLOGICAL NON-CONSEQUENTIALISM'

In his contribution, Littlejohn considers and criticizes the value theory that underlies epistemic consequentialism, whether it is deployed to evaluate credences or full belief. Littlejohn first casts doubt on *veritism*, the view according to which accuracy and only accuracy is the final epistemic good. One might think that the consequentialist is unscathed by this: simply put in something else as the epistemic good. But Littlejohn argues that this fails, too. For whatever it is that the consequentialist says is the epistemic good, she cannot make sense of why such a good should be promoted.

CHAPTER 2. NANCY E. SNOW, 'ADAPTIVE MISBELIEFS, VALUE TRADE-OFFS, AND EPISTEMIC RESPONSIBILITY'

Snow focuses on a class of beliefs that have been called 'adaptive misbeliefs'—beliefs that are false or ungrounded, but nevertheless helpful for action—and argues that they are not justified by the greater value they accrue for the agent. She then argues that this verdict remains even if the greater value is *epistemic value* rather than *pragmatic value*. This work is consonant with Berker's (2013a, b) criticism of epistemic consequentialism, but adds to it by rendering it plausible that there are actual cases of adaptive misbelief that instantiate the kinds of fictional cases Berker imagines. Snow also adds that we should be able to not only judge whether an agent's *belief* is justified, but also whether the agent is believing *responsibly* or *irresponsibly*. If she's right about this, then it is a further challenge for the epistemic consequentialist to say something about this sort of epistemic verdict.

CHAPTER 3. HILARY KORNBLITH, 'THE NATURALISTIC ORIGINS OF EPISTEMIC CONSEQUENTIALISM'

In his contribution to this volume, Kornblith argues that epistemic consequentialism has several real advantages over non-consequentialist approaches. It is naturalistically acceptable in that normative properties are present at the ground floor, and it offers a real answer to why we might want beliefs that come highly recommended by an epistemic theory. That is, it not only tells us which beliefs are good, but also *explains* why those beliefs are good.

CHAPTER 4. RALPH WEDGWOOD, 'EPISTEMIC TELEOLOGY: SYNCHRONIC AND DIACHRONIC'

Wedgwood focuses his discussion around two evaluative concepts: *correctness* and *rationality*. Wedgwood proposes that these two concepts are related in the following way: one belief state is more rational than another if and only if the first has less expected inaccuracy than the former. As Wedgwood notes, this proposal is of a piece with Joyce's (1998) accuracy-based arguments for various norms of rationality and has it that rationality is grounded in correctness. The good is thus prior to the right. This view, however, should not be understood as a form of consequentialism since in Wedgwood's view it is not the *total* consequences of a belief state that determine its rationality. The view is rather a version of *epistemic teleology*. Wedgwood deploys this view to illuminate the difference between synchronic and diachronic evaluation of belief states and along the way responds to objections to epistemic consequentialism made by Berker (2013a, b), Greaves (2013), Caie (2013), and Carr (2017).

CHAPTER 5. JULIA DRIVER, 'THE "CONSEQUENTIALISM" IN "EPISTEMIC CONSEQUENTIALISM"'

Driver discusses a number of similarities and differences between ethical and epistemic consequentialism, for purposes of getting clearer on the latter's views on the relationship between the epistemic right—for example, justification—and the epistemic good. In so doing, her aim is to outline a form of epistemic consequentialism that is analogous to Railton's sophisticated consequentialism in ethics. While not endorsing the resulting view, Driver suggests that outlining it is helpful in two respects. For one thing, it offers a way to avoid some problems presented by Berker, discussed earlier in this introduction. For another, pursuing the analogy between consequentialism in ethics and epistemology helps shine the spotlight on some shortcomings of the epistemic version of that theory, and make clear that what the epistemic consequentialist is relying on is most likely not so much an analogy between epistemology and ethics, as between epistemology and prudence.

CHAPTER 6. ALEJANDRO PÉREZ CARBALLO, 'GOOD QUESTIONS'

Pérez Carballo adopts the epistemic utility theory picture of rational norms where epistemic utility functions measure the value of credences and rationality consists in maximizing expected epistemic utility. Within this framework he seeks to show that we can make sense of the intuitive idea that some true beliefs—say true beliefs about botany—are more valuable than other true beliefs—say true beliefs about the precise number of plants in North Dakota. To do so, however, Pérez Carballo argues that we must think of the value of epistemic states as consisting in more than simply accuracy. In this way, then, he breaks with the accuracy-first epistemologists.

Part II. Accuracy-First Epistemology: For and Against

In the second part of the volume are chapters focused on the accuracy-first version of epistemic utility theory mentioned above, constituting one of the most prominent versions of epistemic consequentialism in contemporary epistemology. Christopher Meacham and Michael Caie raise objections to the accuracy-first program, while James Joyce and Richard Pettigrew defend it.

CHAPTER 7. CHRISTOPHER J. G. MEACHAM, 'CAN ALL-ACCURACY ACCOUNTS JUSTIFY EVIDENTIAL NORMS?'

Meacham takes aim at the epistemic utility approach initiated by Joyce and expanded by Pettigrew. In particular, Meacham argues that scoring-rule-based arguments for various Bayesian norms are (i) not compatible with each other (so not all can be correct), (ii) not solely relying on accuracy considerations (so betraying the accuracy-first mantra), and (iii) not able to capture intuitive norms about how we ought to respond to evidence.

CHAPTER 8. MICHAEL CAIE, 'A PROBLEM FOR CREDAL CONSEQUENTIALISM'

Caie starts with the observation, noted above, that epistemic consequentialism—specifically of the epistemic utility theory variety—will face seemingly objectionable trade-offs. He seeks to show that the problem for epistemic consequentialism is greater than this, however. For, Caie argues, in a wide variety of cases epistemic consequentialism either entails that every credal state is rational, none is, or it issues no verdicts. This is, roughly, because an agent's credence function will often not encode the appropriate dependence hypotheses that are needed so that various beliefs have expected epistemic utility values. Caie thus argues that the unintuitive verdicts of epistemic utility theory are not limited to the byzantine examples of trade-offs, but are much more widespread.

CHAPTER 9. RICHARD PETTIGREW, 'MAKING THINGS RIGHT: THE TRUE CONSEQUENCES OF DECISION THEORY IN EPISTEMOLOGY'

In his contribution, Pettigrew considers a variant on the trade-off objection to epistemic consequentialism described above. In particular, he focuses on one of the objections given by Greaves (2013) against epistemic utility theory, which is a version of accuracy-first epistemology. Pettigrew's strategy is to accept that epistemic utility theory has some of the unintuitive verdicts her opponents have said it has, but to offer an error theory for why these intuitions do not show the theory to be false.

CHAPTER 10. JAMES M. JOYCE, 'ACCURACY, RATIFICATION, AND THE SCOPE OF EPISTEMIC CONSEQUENTIALISM'

Joyce focuses on objections to epistemic consequentialism, due to Michael Caie and Hilary Greaves, in which adopting an intuitively incorrect belief leads to a net gain in overall epistemic accuracy. Joyce argues that, while certain versions of epistemic consequentialism may succumb to these objections, they do not succeed against a version that incorporates a ratifiability principle. His argument turns on distinguishing between treating degrees of belief as *final ends* and treating them as a basis for future *estimation* of truth-values and other epistemically important quantities.

Part III. Epistemic Consequentialism Applied

The third part of the volume contains chapters that apply the consequentialist picture to different topics in epistemology. Sophie Horowitz investigates whether the consequentialist is able to capture the Jamesian idea that different believers can place different emphasis on the twin goals of believing truly and not believing falsely. Amanda Askell considers what the consequentialist framework allows us to say about epistemic enkrasia. Closing out the section, Jeffrey Dunn argues that the consequentialist framework allows for situations of epistemic free riding.

CHAPTER 11. SOPHIE HOROWITZ, 'EPISTEMIC VALUE AND THE JAMESIAN GOALS'

William James famously tells us that there are two main goals for rational believers: believing truth and avoiding error. In her contribution, Horowitz argues that epistemic consequentialism—in particular its embodiment in epistemic utility theory—seems to be well positioned to explain how epistemic agents might permissibly weight these goals differently. After all, *practical* versions of consequentialism render it permissible for agents with different goals to act differently in the same situation. Nevertheless, Horowitz argues that epistemic consequentialism doesn't allow for this kind of permissivism and goes on to argue that this reveals a deep disanalogy between decision theory and the formally similar epistemic utility theory. This raises the question whether epistemic utility theory is a genuinely consequentialist theory at all.

CHAPTER 12. AMANDA ASKELL, 'EPISTEMIC CONSEQUENTIALISM AND EPISTEMIC ENKRASIA'

In her contribution, Amanda Askell investigates what the epistemic consequentialist will say about *epistemic enkrasia principles*, principles that instruct one not to adopt a doxastic attitude that one takes to be irrational. She argues that a certain epistemic enkrasia principle for credences can be shown to maximize expected accuracy, and thus that a certain kind of epistemic consequentialist is committed to such a principle. But this is bad news for such an epistemic consequentialist, according to Askell, because epistemic enkrasia principles are problematic.

CHAPTER 13. JEFFREY DUNN, 'EPISTEMIC FREE RIDING'

Free riding occurs in the practical domain when some action is rational for each group member to perform but such that when everyone performs that action, it is worse overall for everyone. Overfishing a lake is a classic example of a free-riding scenario. In his contribution, Dunn argues that some surprising empirical evidence about group problem-solving reveals that groups will often face cases where it is epistemically best for each individual to do one thing, even though this is ultimately epistemically worse for the group. Dunn's work can thus be thought of as an extension of Kitcher's (1990) work on the distribution of cognitive labor and ways that group inquiry might differ from individual inquiry.

References

Adler, J. (2005). 'Reliabilist Justification (or Knowledge) as a Good Truth-Ratio'. *Pacific Philosophical Quarterly* 86: 445–58.

Ahlstrom-Vij, K. and Dunn, J. (2014). 'A Defence of Epistemic Consequentialism'. *Philosophical Quarterly* 64: 541–51.

Berker, S. (2013a). 'Epistemic Teleology and the Separateness of Propositions'. *The Philosophical Review* 122: 337–93.

Berker, S. (2013b). 'The Rejection of Epistemic Consequentialism'. *Philosophical Issues* 23: 363–87.

BonJour, L. (1980). 'Externalist Theories of Empirical Knowledge'. *Midwest Studies in Philosophy* 5: 53–74.

BonJour, L. (1985). *The Structure of Empirical Knowledge*. Cambridge, MA: Harvard University Press.

Caie, M. (2013). 'Rational Probabilistic Incoherence'. *Philosophical Review* 122: 527–75.

Carr, J. (2017). 'Epistemic Utility Theory and the Aim of Belief'. *Philosophy and Phenomenological Research* 95: 511–34.

Chase, J. (2004). 'Indicator Reliabilism'. *Philosophy and Phenomenological Research* 69(1): 115–37.

Conee, E. (1992). 'The Truth Connection'. *Philosophy and Phenomenological Research* 52(3): 657–69.

Douven, I. (2006). 'Assertion, Knowledge, and Rational Credibility'. *Philosophical Review* 115: 449–85.

Driver, J. (2012). *Consequentialism*. Abingdon: Routledge.

Dunn, J. and Ahlstrom-Vij, K. (2017). 'Is Reliabilism a Form of Consequentialism?' *American Philosophical Quarterly* 54: 183–94.

Easwaran, K. (2013). 'Expected Accuracy Supports Conditionalization—And Conglomerability and Reflection'. *Philosophy of Science* 80: 119–42.

Easwaran, K. and Fitelson, B. (2015). 'Accuracy, Coherence, and Evidence'. In T. S. Gendler and J. Hawthorne (eds.), *Oxford Studies in Epistemology, Volume 5*. Oxford: Oxford University Press, 61–96.

Evnine, S. (1999). 'Believing Conjunctions'. *Synthese* 118: 201–27.

Feldman, F. (2004). *Pleasure and the Good Life*. Oxford: Oxford University Press.

Feldman, R. (2000). 'The Ethics of Belief'. *Philosophy and Phenomenological Research* 60(3): 667–95.

Feldman, R. and Conee, E. (1985). 'Evidentialism'. *Philosophical Studies* 48: 15–34.

Firth, R. (1981). 'Epistemic Merit, Intrinsic and Instrumental'. *Proceedings and Addresses of the American Philosophical Association* 55: 5–23.

Foot, P. (1985). 'Utilitarianism and the Virtues'. *Mind* 94(374): 196–209.

Fumerton, R. (1995). *Metaepistemology and Skepticism*. Lanham, MD: Rowman & Littlefield.

Goldman, A. (1979). 'What Is Justified Belief?' In G. Pappas (ed.), *Justification and Knowledge*. Dordrecht: D. Reidel, 1–23.
Goldman, A. (1986). *Epistemology and Cognition*. Harvard, MA: Harvard University Press.
Goldman, A. (1999). *Knowledge in a Social World*. Oxford: Oxford University Press.
Goldman, A. (2015). 'Reliabilism, Veritism, and Epistemic Consequentialism'. *Episteme* 12: 131–43.
Greaves, H. (2013). 'Epistemic Decision Theory'. *Mind* 122: 915–52.
Greaves, H. and Wallace, D. (2006). 'Justifying Conditionalization: Conditionalization Maximizes Expected Epistemic Utility'. *Mind* 115: 607–32.
Hooker, B. (2000). *Ideal Code, Real World: A Rule-Consequentialist Theory of Morality*. Oxford: Oxford University Press.
Jenkins, C. S. (2007). 'Entitlement and Rationality'. *Synthese* 157: 25–45.
Joyce, J. (1998). 'A Nonpragmatic Vindication of Probabilism'. *Philosophy of Science* 65: 575–603.
Joyce, J. (2009). 'Accuracy and Coherence: Prospects for an Alethic Epistemology of Partial Belief'. In F. Huber and C. Schmidt-Petri (eds.) *Degrees of Belief*. Dordrecht: Springer, 263–300.
Kagan, S. (1997). *Normative Ethics*. Boulder, CO: Westview Press.
Kitcher, P. (1990). 'The Division of Cognitive Labor'. *The Journal of Philosophy* 87: 5–22.
Konek, J. and Levinstein, B. (*forthcoming*). 'The Foundations of Epistemic Decision Theory'. *Mind*.
Korsgaard, C. (1996). *Creating the Kingdom of Ends*. Cambridge: Cambridge University Press.
Kvanvig, J. (2009). 'Assertion, Knowledge, and Lotteries'. In P. Greenough and D. Pritchard (eds.), *Williamson on Knowledge*. Oxford: Oxford University Press, 140–60.
Laudan, L. (1984). *Science and Values*. Berkeley, CA: University of California Press.
Leitgeb, H. and Pettigrew, R. (2010a). 'An Objective Justification of Bayesianism I: Measuring Inaccuracy'. *Philosophy of Science* 77: 201–35.
Leitgeb, H. and Pettigrew, R. (2010b). 'An Objective Justification of Bayesianism II: The Consequences of Minimizing Inaccuracy'. *Philosophy of Science* 77: 236–72.
Levi, I. (1967). *Gambling with Truth*. Cambridge, MA: MIT Press.
Littlejohn, C. (2012). *Justification and the Truth Connection*. Cambridge: Cambridge University Press.
Locke, D. T. (2014). 'The Decision-Theoretic Lockean Thesis'. *Inquiry* 57: 28–54.
McCloskey, H. J. (1957). 'An Examination of Restricted Utilitarianism'. *The Philosophical Review* 66(4): 466–85.
McKinnon, R. (2013). 'Lotteries, Knowledge, and Irrelevant Alternatives'. *Dialogue* 52: 523–49.
McNaughton, D. and Rawling, P. (1991). 'Agent-Relativity and the Doing-Happening Distinction'. *Philosophical Studies* 63: 163–85.
Maher, P. (1993). *Betting on Theories*. Cambridge: Cambridge University Press.
Mayo-Wilson, C., Zollman, K., and Danks, D. (2011). 'The Independence Thesis: When Epistemic Norms for Individuals and Groups Diverge'. *Philosophy of Science* 78: 653–77.
Mill, J. S. (1861/2001). 'Utilitarianism'. In G. Sher (ed.), *Utilitarianism and the 1868 Speech on Capital Punishment*. Indianapolis: Hackett Publishing Company, Inc. Originally published in 1861.
Moore, G. E. (1903). *Principia Ethica*. Cambridge: Cambridge University Press.

Muldoon, R. and Weisberg, M. (2009). 'Epistemic Landscapes and the Division of Cognitive Labor'. *Philosophy of Science* 76: 225–52.

Nagel, J. (2011). 'The Psychological Basis of the Harman-Vogel Paradox'. *Philosophers' Imprint* 11: 1–28.

Nagel, T. (1986). *The View from Nowhere*. Oxford: Oxford University Press.

Nelkin, D. K. (2000). 'The Lottery Paradox, Knowledge, and Rationality'. *Philosophical Review* 109: 373–409.

Nozick, R. (1974). *Anarchy, State, and Utopia*. New York: Basic Books.

Pettigrew, R. (2013). 'Epistemic Utility and Norms for Credences'. *Philosophy Compass* 8: 897–908.

Pettigrew, R. (2016). *Accuracy and the Laws of Credence*. Oxford: Oxford University Press.

Pettit, P. (2000). 'Non-Consequentialism and Universalizability'. *The Philosophical Quarterly* 50: 175–90.

Pollock, J. (1995). *Cognitive Carpentry*. Cambridge, MA: MIT Press.

Portmore, D. (2007). 'Consequentializing Moral Theories'. *Pacific Philosophical Quarterly* 88: 39–73.

Scanlon, T. M. (1982). 'Contractualism and Utilitarianism'. In A. Sen and B. Williams (eds), *Utilitarianism and Beyond*. Cambridge: Cambridge University Press, 103–28.

Slote, M. (1984). 'Satisficing Consequentialism'. *Proceedings of the Aristotelian Society* 58: 139–63.

Smart, J. J. C. and Williams, B. (1973). *Utilitarianism: For and Against*. Cambridge: Cambridge University Press.

Smithies, D. (2012). 'The Normative Role of Knowledge'. *Noûs* 46: 265–88.

Solomon, M. (1992). 'Scientific Rationality and Human Reasoning'. *Philosophy of Science* 59: 439–55.

Thomson, J. J. (1976). 'Killing, Letting Die, and the Trolley Problem'. *The Monist* 59: 204–17.

Williams, J. R. G. (2012). 'Gradational Accuracy and Nonclassical Semantics'. *The Review of Symbolic Logic* 5: 513–37.

Williams, B. (1973). 'A Critique of Utilitarianism'. In J. J. C. Smart and B. Williams (eds), *Utilitarianism: For and Against*, Cambridge: Cambridge University Press, 77–150.

Zollman, K. (2007). 'The Communication Structures of Epistemic Communities'. *Philosophy of Science* 74: 574–87.

PART I

Epistemic Consequentialism: The Right and the Good

1

The Right in the Good
A Defense of Teleological Non-Consequentialism

Clayton Littlejohn

1.1 Introduction

Moore never said that the only possible reason that can justify any belief is that its formation would result in the greatest amount of what is good.[1] This omission is surprising. Given his interests in epistemology and his consequentialist instincts, we could have expected him to say just this.[2] Did Moore miss out on a good thing? Might our beliefs be right or rational because of the role that they play in promoting the epistemic good?

An increasing number of epistemologists seem to think so.[3] Starting from the idea that accuracy is the fundamental epistemic good, epistemic consequentialists try to determine which norms govern belief. If you wanted to know why we should be probabilistically coherent, epistemic consequentialism gives you a plausible answer. Given some plausible assumptions about how to score the accuracy of a set of credences, a coherent set can never be dominated by an incoherent alternative. Most

---

[1] For helpful discussion, I would like to thank audiences at Bristol, King's College London, LSE, and the University of Konstanz as well as the anonymous referees for this volume, Kristoffer Ahlstrom-Vij, Maria Alvarez, Jochen Briesen, Jennifer Carr, Charles Cote-Bouchard, Jeff Dunn, Julien Dutant, Kenny Easwaran, Anna-Maria Eder, Catherine Elgin, Branden Fitelson, John Hawthorne, Hilary Greaves, Mark Eli Kalderon, Jason Konek, Eliot Michaelson, David Papineau, Richard Pettigrew, Josh Schechter, Florian Steinberger, Ralph Wedgwood, and Jose Zalabardo.

[2] In *Principia Ethica*, Moore said, "The only possible reason that can justify any action is that by it the greatest possible amount of what is good absolutely should be realized" (1993: 153).

[3] See Ahlstrom-Vij and Dunn (2014), Dorst (forthcoming), Easwaran and Fitelson (2015), Goldman (1986), Greaves (2014), Joyce (1998, 2009, MS), Konek and Levinstein (MS), Pettigrew (2013a 2013b, 2015, 2016), and Talbot (2014) for discussions of epistemic norms that are (to varying degrees) sympathetic to the consequentialist idea that the epistemic good determines the epistemic right. These writers are all sympathetic to the idea that the fundamental epistemic good is true belief, so we can see some of the arguments here as challenges to some of the assumptions operative in their work.

people don't like to be dominated, so maybe this will move you to keep your credences in order even if you aren't moved by a fear of Dutch bookies. If you were struggling to decide whether it's possible to be rational and inconsistent because you were pulled in different directions by lottery and preface cases, you might think that it is interesting and important that the cost of conforming to some consistency norm is steep. In some situations, the way to maximize expected accuracy is to keep an inconsistent set of beliefs. Perhaps the wise person ought to proportion her beliefs to the evidence and ignore the putative principles people appeal to in an attempt to defend the virtues of consistency.[4]

While the current literature is filled with lots of interesting results about the costs and benefits of conforming to various (putative) epistemic norms, it suffers from two serious deficiencies. First, there hasn't yet been enough discussion of the value theory used by epistemic consequentialists. While the veritists are right that there's something bad about believing falsehoods and often something good about believing truths, their account doesn't capture what's bad or good about it. Second, there hasn't yet been enough discussion of whether the right and the good are related in the way the consequentialist takes them to be. Once we see why the veritists are wrong about the fundamental epistemic values, we will see why the consequentialist justifications of epistemic norms are problematic. The chapter concludes with a brief presentation of a teleological alternative to consequentialism.

1.2 Truth and Consequences

Suppose we were to pursue Moore's methods in epistemology. If we adopt Moore's basic theoretical orientation and try to identify the norms governing belief, we would have to assume that the epistemic good is prior to the epistemic right:

Priority Thesis: The good is metaphysically prior to the right.

To determine what makes right belief right or rational belief rational, we would have to identify the fundamental epistemic good or goods. The standard proposal about the epistemic good is a *veritist* proposal that says that truth or accuracy is the fundamental epistemic good. We would use this account of the good to give an account of the better and best.

If our consequentialists are veritists who see accuracy as the fundamental epistemic good, we should expect them to accept the following:

Necessity Thesis: Only accurate states are epistemically good.

---

[4] For interesting defenses of the virtue of consistency that appeal to principles of the sort we would expect consequentialists to attack, see Ryan (1996).

Sufficiency Thesis: Every accurate belief is epistemically good.[5]

Distinctiveness Thesis: The beliefs that are epistemically good are distinctively valuable.

Monism: The fundamental epistemic good is accuracy.

Roughly, this captures the idea that accuracy is the good-making feature of the beliefs that are good and that accurate belief plays a unique role in determining how well things are going. These theses all play important roles in consequentialist arguments for their favored epistemic norms because they tell us what does and does not matter when it comes to ranking options.

There are two further theses to consider when thinking about ranking options in terms of the value they contain and the kind of value such rankings are sensitive to:

Totalizing Thesis: The right is determined by comparing the total value that options would/could realize.[6]

Promotion Thesis: If an option is acceptable and an alternative is at least as valuable, it must also be acceptable.[7]

The Totalizing Thesis reminds us that the ranking of options that determines the rational status of our attitudes is done in terms of the total value that these options contain. The thesis plays an important role in justifications of consequentialism. As Foot (1985) observed, the reason that consequentialism seems so compelling is that when it comes to the good, the better, and the best, it *is* irrational to prefer some acknowledged lesser good to one that is greater. The Promotion Thesis tells us that the rational status of the attitudes contained in an option will be wholly determined by the value contained in those options. This rules out the possibility that there might be some principle that functions like a side-constraint, forcing us to opt for a suboptimal option by making it impermissible to opt for some superior alternative.[8]

Our epistemic consequentialists should agree to this much, but they might disagree about the kind or kinds of accuracy that matter. An epistemic consequentialist concerned with full belief might adopt this value theory:

---

[5] Strictly speaking, these claims are claims about final goodness. An anonymous referee reminded me that actual veritists (e.g., Goldman (1999)) think that the value realized by our beliefs depends upon things like the significance or importance of the relevant accurate states. I wanted to avoid these complications because they are orthogonal to the issues discussed here. None of the objections discussed below can be met by distinguishing interesting from uninteresting truths, for example.

[6] For discussion, see Carlson (1995). [7] For discussion, see Vallentyne (2006).

[8] Pettigrew (2013a) reads Easwaran and Fitelson's (2012) challenge as involving an appeal to side-constraints. I should mention that I don't think we need side-constraints in the fight against epistemic consequentialism. We only need to invoke them if we concede that certain options should be ranked in such a way that the best options strike us as inappropriate. If you don't see much good contained in the inappropriate options, the side-constraints become otiose. Like many consequentialists, I'm skeptical of side-constraints because they often seem to be ad hoc.

Categorical Veritism: True belief is intrinsically good, false belief is intrinsically bad, and these are the only intrinsic values that matter to inquiry. (Goldman 1999)

One concerned with partial belief might adopt this one:

Gradational Veritism: The categorical good of fully believing truths is replaced by the gradational good of investing high credence in truths (the higher the better); the categorical evil of fully believing falsehoods is replaced by the gradational evil of investing high credence in falsehoods (the higher the worse). (Joyce MS)

As stated, these are competing views about the bearers of epistemic value. The first view sees full belief as the only thing that could be epistemically good. The second says that partial beliefs can be good even if they don't constitute full beliefs and doesn't think it matters whether some partial belief is, *inter alia*, a full belief. My impression is that many of the leading consequentialists are open to a kind of hybrid view on which full belief and partial belief are both potential bearers of epistemic value. If we define 'accuracy' broadly enough, we can say that the fundamental veritist commitment is to the thesis that accurate states are the positive epistemic value atoms and that inaccurate ones are the negative value atoms.[9]

Not all consequentialists are maximizers, but it will simplify the discussion to speak as if they are.[10] According to maximizing epistemic consequentialism, it's only possible to say which beliefs are rational once we've found some way of ranking the agent's options and seen which options contain the relevant attitude. Roughly, an attitude is rational iff this attitude is included in the best feasible option(s). This requires two points of clarification. First, we will think of the outcome as the possible world that would be actual if the agent were to have the attitudes contained in the relevant option. Second, remember that some writers use 'best' to refer to the *objectively best* and others to refer to the *prospectively best* where the former is understood in terms of actual value and the latter in terms of expected value.

---

[9] I'm borrowing this talk of value atoms from Bradley (2009: 5). Think of the value atoms as the things that are most fundamentally good or bad. They are things that don't derive their value from the value contained in their proper parts and that incorporate all the properties involved in the realization of the value. Together, the value atoms determine how well or badly things are going for you. We might say that accurate states are to the veritist what hedons and dolors are to the hedonist.

[10] An anonymous referee observed (quite rightly) that this is an understatement as reliabilism appears to some to be the most popular form of consequentialism and reliabilists are not maximizers. (Although, it is debatable whether reliabilism truly is a version of consequentialism. See Goldman (2015) and Littlejohn (2012).) It would complicate the discussion considerably to discuss satisficing and maximizing views, so I thought it would be best to stick with a maximizing view and focus on objections that would apply with equal force to any satisficing view (provided that the suitable modifications are made). This is because the objections (suitably modified) apply to any view that takes permissibility to supervene upon outcomes and the maximizers and satisficers agree that permissibility supervenes upon the value realized by outcomes. The main difference between the maximizers and satisficers is that the maximizers think we are permitted only to bring about the best and the satisficers think that we are permitted to bring about anything that is good enough and allows that there can be things that are good enough that are suboptimal. Neither view has resources to explain why we should not bring about options that are better than a permitted option and some of the challenges discussed in this chapter have that shape.

It's easy to see how to rank options if Categorical Veritism is true. On this view we would say that the total value realized by your *epistemic state* in a world is identical to the total value realized by your *doxastic state* in that world. Your epistemic state is composed of your doxastic state (i.e., your full beliefs) and your credal state (i.e., your partial beliefs). We would assign some positive value to each true belief and then subtract out some negative value from each false belief.[11] Suppose you wonder whether this exit is the way to San Jose. You might believe that it is, believe that it is not, or suspend. It might be the way. It might not. If it is, believing that it is should count positively. If it is not, believing that it is should count negatively. If you suspend, the suspension should not count either way. To rank the options using an objective version of Categorical Veritism, we would have to compare the total epistemic value your doxastic state could realize if you believed that this was the way to San Jose to the total epistemic value your epistemic state could realize if you suspended or disbelieved. We would want to hold fixed the fact that this was (or was not) the way to San Jose. It might seem that believing that it is on the condition that it is will rank higher than suspending or disbelieving, but this overlooks some complications that we'll come back to later.

It's harder to see how to rank options if Gradational Veritism is true. The standard story goes something like this.[12] We begin by identifying the ideal state. This is the state in which you are maximally confident in all the truths (or all the truths you can grasp or all the truths you have attitudes concerning) and maximally unconfident in all the falsehoods (or all the falsehoods you can grasp or all the falsehoods you have attitudes concerning). This is the ideal because it's supposed to be ideally accurate. Whenever you are less than maximally confident in some truth, you deviate from the ideal. The less confident you are in a truth, the greater your deviation from the ideal. To determine how far off you are from the ideal, we sum up the deviation of each partial belief from the ideal.

The methods we are given for ranking options do not tell us how to answer two important questions about the value of credal states. We don't know what sort of value the ideal state realizes. We also don't know what sort of value the non-ideal state realizes. First, if all we know about states that include non-extremal credences is that they are at some distance from the ideal, it seems that we have a potentially powerful argument for skepticism. If we know a priori that *any* credal state that involves some non-extremal credence is worse than the ideal, it might be irrational to be in such

---

[11] In Littlejohn (2012) I argued that if we wanted to explain in consequentialist terms why it's wrong to believe *p* on the basis of weak evidence or unreliable methods we would have to say that the values of true and false belief differed in magnitude so that it's worse to believe one truth and one falsehood than to believe nothing at all. Dorst (forthcoming) calls this the *conservativeness constraint*. Using the lottery case, I argued that consequentialists will never get the threshold right, but that argument rested on two controversial assumptions. The first is that it's not rational to believe lottery propositions outright. The second is that it can be rational to believe things on the basis of testimony even when the probability of erring by so relying is greater than it would be if we were to believe that the tickets we hold for large lotteries will lose.

[12] See Joyce (1998) and Pettigrew (2013b).

a state. Suppose that it is possible to assign no credences whatever to the propositions we grasp. And suppose that the total value realized by the ideal state is also 0. If so, it would be irrational to have a credal state that involved any non-extremal credence.

Of course, a proponent of Gradational Veritism might say in response that some positive good *does* come of having the ideal credal state. This might help to mitigate part of the problem, but only if we have a further story about how defective states could nevertheless rank higher than states of universal suspension (or a state that assigns extremal credence to a handful of obvious logical truths). We need an argument that shows that you can be better off by being in a non-ideal state than you would be if you were to suspend across the board or suspend on all the non-tautologies.

At the root of these problems is this concern. If we wanted to model our value theory on, say, hedonism, and model our consequentialist view on utilitarianism, we need to see the states assessed for accuracy as value atoms that function like hedons and dolors. In the case of full belief, it is easy to see how this is supposed to go. Treat a true belief like a hedon, treat a false belief like a dolor, operate on the assumption that the best option maximizes these values, and work from there. In the case of partial belief, it is hard to see how this is supposed to work. Should we think of a partial belief that doesn't amount to full belief as more like a hedon if it's closer to the truth than not or should we see it as more like a dolor because it deviates from the ideal? We have decent enough formal tools for ranking options when limited to fixed sets of propositions, but I don't see how these materials could answer some basic questions about whether it's rational to get into the partial belief game if and when it can be avoided.

These worries extend to the hybrid views that tell us that both partial beliefs and full beliefs are potential bearers of epistemic goodness. The hybrid view faces a further worry, which is that it is difficult to say what sort of value we should attach to an element of the subject's epistemic state if it is both a partial belief and a full belief. Suppose you work with a kind of Lockean view according to which full belief just is a partial belief that is sufficiently confident.[13] Suppose that while I'm not maximally confident in *p*, I am sufficiently confident in *p* to count as having a full belief. By crossing the line, I would get some boost in total value (or decrease gradational inaccuracy) simply by increasing confidence in some truth. I would get a further boost in value by having a full belief in a true proposition. Is this double counting?

While I have some real concerns about the possibility of fleshing out the story to provide satisfactory answers to these questions, I want to move on. The real problem with combining veritism with epistemic consequentialism has little to do with the details and more to do with the operative assumptions about epistemic goodness (e.g., that the good of true belief calls for promotion and that such value is the fundamental epistemic good). The veritist works with a dubious value theory. The most fundamental problem with this project is the way that the veritist understands

---

[13] For sympathetic presentations of the Lockean view, see Dorst (forthcoming), Foley (2009), and Sturgeon (2008).

the value of accuracy. Work out your own way of filling out the missing details however you see fit. I don't think that on any admissible modification of the basic structure will we find a plausible view of epistemic norms.

1.3 The Value of Truth and the Varieties of Veritism

If you're looking for a careful defense of the idea that true belief is valuable, you will not find it in discussions of epistemic consequentialism. Veritism often acts as the unmotivated motivator. The most sophisticated discussion of the value of truth that I've found is in Lynch's work, so I want to see whether his arguments support the sort of veritist view that the consequentialists need.

Lynch makes an initial pitch for the value of truth in this passage:

> Nobody likes to be wrong. If anything is a truism, that is. And it reveals something else we believe about truth: that it is good. More precisely, it is good to believe what is true. (2004: 12)

Even if everyone had this preference, this observation doesn't provide much support for the idea that there's something good that attaches to each true belief. It only suggests that there's something bad about being mistaken. At best, this is a point in favor of the Necessity Thesis, one that tells us nothing about the Sufficiency Thesis. If people are risk averse and hate to make mistakes, what could entice them to take a risk?

Lynch provides a more promising line of argument in this passage:

> If truth was *not* a basic preference, then if I had two beliefs B1 and B2 with identical instrumental value, I should not prefer to believe B1 rather than B2. The considerations above already point to the fact that this isn't so, however. In particular, if we didn't have a basic preference for the truth, it would be hard to explain why we find the prospect of being undetectably wrong so disturbing. Think about a modification of the experience-machine scenario we began with. Some super neuroscientists give you the choice between continuing to live normally, or having your brain hooked up to a supercomputer that will make it seem as if you are continuing to live normally (even though you're really just floating in a vat somewhere). When in the vat, you will continue to have all the same experiences you would have in the real world. Because of this, you would believe that you are reading a book, that you are hungry, and so on. In short, your beliefs and experiences will be the same, but most of your beliefs will be false. (2004: 17)

He then offers these remarks about this thought experiment and experiments like it:

> If we didn't really prefer true beliefs to false ones, we would be simply ambivalent about this choice. Vat, no vat; who cares? But we don't say this. We don't want to live in the vat, even though doing so would make no difference to what we experience or believe. This suggests that we have a basic preference for truth. (2004: 17)

> Neither would I wish to live in the fool's paradise, where people just pretend to like and respect me. These examples, and others like them, show that we value something more than experience—even just pleasurable experience. We want certain realities behind those experiences, and thus we want certain propositions to be true. (2004: 138–9)

This suggests that something of value might be missing from our lives even if our lives were quite pleasant and that this value has to do with truth. He offers this by way of elaboration:

> In preferring not to live in either the vat or the Russell world, I do not simply prefer that the world be a certain way. My preference involves my beliefs and their proper functioning, so to speak. For not only do I not want to live in a world where I am a brain in a vat, I also don't want to live in a world where I am not so deceived, but believe that I am. That is, if such and such is the case, I want to believe that it is, and if I believe that it is, I want it to be the case. We can put this by saying that I want my beliefs and reality to be a certain way—I want my beliefs to track reality, to "accord with how the world actually is"—which is to say I want them to be true (2004: 18).

And this suggests that the reason that true belief matters is that it matters that we have a way to 'track reality'. The last line suggests that he thinks that some sort of veritist view does justice to intuitions about what's missing from life in Nozick's (1974) experience machine. I think there's something important and right here, but something that explains what's wrong with veritism.

1.3.1 Niggling doubts

I have concerns about most of the veritist assumptions about value. The Distinctiveness Thesis seems solid, though. Belief plays a distinctive role in our psychology and its value seems to be tied to the role it plays. It tracks reality by helping us to keep hold of the facts. If we drop the thesis, it's hard to see how the epistemic consequentialist arguments could work. If the Distinctiveness Thesis were false, we could get the goods that attach to accurate belief without belief. If the best options aren't best because they contain the best beliefs, it's hard to see how a norm that enjoins us to maximize some sort of epistemic value would require us to have the beliefs the consequentialist thinks we're required to have.

Armed with the Distinctiveness Thesis, we can cause trouble for the Sufficiency Thesis and Monism. It is easy to see why Sufficiency is important for the standard consequentialist arguments. If Sufficiency were false, it should be possible for two epistemic states to score equally well when scored by veritists and yet differ in terms of their epistemic value. Were we to allow that these states could differ in value, we couldn't rely on arguments that equate the epistemic ideal with perfect accuracy and treat the imperatives to maximize expected accuracy and expected epistemic value as extensionally equivalent.

There is a *prima facie* plausible argument against Sufficiency, one that uses part of the standard story about epistemic goodness. Consider Distinctiveness. According to Distinctiveness, belief is the distinctive bearer of epistemic goodness. On a natural reading of Sufficiency, such states are good (when they are) because they are accurate. On a standard story about belief and perception, both beliefs and perceptual experiences have accuracy conditions.[14] Indeed, it is typically part of the typical story about

---

[14] See McDowell (1998), Siegel (2010), and Schellenberg (2014) for discussion.

these experiences and beliefs that they share content and share accuracy conditions. If so, it would seem that Sufficiency would support a view on which both experience and belief share the very same good making features. So, they should both be good. So, it would seem that if experiences and beliefs can both be assessed for accuracy, we have to reject Sufficiency to account for the distinctive value of accurate belief.

In my view this argument rests on a mistaken assumption about experience.[15] I don't think experiences have representational content, so I don't think that they have the same good-making features that beliefs (allegedly) have. Experiences don't put us in touch with the facts in the same way that beliefs do. Most readers probably disagree with this point. If so, you have to answer a tricky question that I do not. How could belief be the distinctive bearer of epistemic goodness if it is not the distinctive bearer of the good-making features?

Because experience and belief are typically taken to be alike in possessing the properties that veritists identify as the good-making properties of belief, it might be worth asking veritists to explain why the putative good-making feature of good belief is a good-making feature. I know of only two answers to this question. Both answers start from some claims about the point, purpose, or aim of belief. The first says that the aim of belief is truth. The idea is that a belief will have the good-making features iff it fulfills its aim by being a true and accurate representation of reality. The problem with this line is that it doesn't seem to give us the resources we need to explain the Distinctiveness Thesis. On the standard line about experience, experiences can have contents that can be assessed for accuracy in the way that beliefs can, in which case the challenge to the Distinctiveness Thesis remains. The second answer says that the aim of belief is to provide us with reasons. Specifically, they should provide us with potential motivating reasons (i.e., things that could function as our reasons for believing, feeling, or doing things). If we're guided by these reasons, we're guided by reality because these reasons consist of facts or true propositions.

This second way of thinking about the aim of belief and its good-making features helps to save the Distinctiveness Thesis. I have identified a role that beliefs play that experiences do not. (It also fits nicely with the nice story that Lynch gives us about the value of truth, but we'll get back to that later.) Consider the experiences you had when you came to believe that your neighbor was stealing your Sunday paper. In the absence of the belief that your neighbor was the thief, you couldn't have been upset with the neighbor for taking your paper. These experiences couldn't render the belief that rationalizes the reactive attitudes otiose. If you had the experiences but didn't have the belief, your reason for being upset with him could not be that he took the paper. To you, the fact that he took the paper would not make your anger intelligible because for all you know this fact is not a fact. And if that wasn't your reason, it's quite possible

---

[15] See Brewer (2011) and Travis (2013) for critical discussion of the view that experiences have representational content. In Littlejohn (forthcoming), I argue that even if experiences had content, they wouldn't play the epistemological role that people often assume. Even if they had contents, our perceptual beliefs aren't cases in which we believe things for reasons. Thus, belief plays a distinctive epistemic role in that it has to be in place for us to be guided by reasons.

that any negative feelings you had toward him wouldn't be fitting. Your emotional responses are fitting only when an accurate belief is there to guide your emotional responses.

To my mind, this story about the role that belief plays in supplying potential motivating reasons is the best story about why belief aims at the truth and why beliefs have distinctive good-making features. It allows us to sidestep the tricky issues about the nature of perceptual experience because even if we think that perceptual experiences do have representational content, we tend not to think that experience involves the kind of commitment to the truth of this content that belief does. Unfortunately, I think that this story about the good-making features of belief causes serious trouble for all versions of veritism and for epistemic consequentialism. Upon this rock, I shall make my mess.

1.3.2 *Against gradational veritism and the hybrid view*

In defending the Distinctiveness Thesis, I said that belief plays a distinctive role in certain kinds of folk-psychological explanation. I should be clear that I think *full* belief plays this role. *Partial* belief does not play this role. If you are confident that *p* but you do not believe that *p*, you cannot believe things, feel things, or do things for the reason that *p*.

Adler draws our attention to the fact that certain reactive-attitudes do not, as he puts it, "admit of epistemic qualification":

Mild resentment is never resentment caused by what one judges to be a serious offense directed toward oneself tempered by one's degree of uncertainty in that judgment—for example, a student's mildly resenting her teacher's lowering her grade because she refused his persistent personal advances, although she is not sure that the grade wasn't deserved. For similar reasons, there is no actually engaged attitude corresponding to a conditional resentment (anger), whose condition can only later be known to be fulfilled. (2002: 217)

In the absence of the right kind of full belief, resentment isn't possible. As Gordon noted in his discussion of attributions of emotions, many attributions of these emotions require a corresponding attribution of full belief. You couldn't be angry about the fact that a grade was lowered unfairly unless (a) certain conditions obtained such that the belief that the grade was lowered unfairly would, when combined with these conditions, make you angry and (b) you did indeed believe your grade was lowered unfairly (1987: 48).

What is it about belief that equips it to play roles that experiences cannot? One answer is that only belief has propositional content, but this doesn't explain why *full* belief plays a distinctive role. A better answer is that belief is distinctive in being *committal*. Belief involves a kind of commitment to truth that other attitudes and mental states do not. If it seems to you that *p* because of how your experiences are but you don't believe it, you won't be mistaken about *p* or right about *p*. This feature of belief helps us understand why belief is a necessary condition on V-ing for the reason that *p*. To V for the reason that *p*, the (apparent) fact that *p* has to capture the light in which you took V-ing to be favorable, appropriate, right, etc. If you don't take it to be the case that *p*, the apparent fact that *p* wouldn't be an apparent fact. It thus couldn't be the light in which you took V-ing to be favorable, appropriate, right, etc.

We have seen that you can use this feature of full belief and the role that full belief plays in providing us with potential motivating reasons to argue for Distinctiveness. Beliefs are unique in bearing the fundamental epistemic good-making properties because the good-making properties have to do with 'tracking reality' so that we believe, feel, and do things for reasons that consist of facts. A nice feature of this account is that it helps to explain the Necessity Thesis. If a proposition you believe isn't true, it is not among the facts that would constitute reasons that could be our reasons for feeling, doing, or believing things. It would also explain why any false belief fails to do what beliefs are supposed to do. The false belief does not put us in touch with a fact that could rationally guide our actions, feelings, or thoughts. While this is a promising line of argument, it also gives us what we need to cause trouble for veritism.

Gradational veritism and the hybrid view both see credal states that don't constitute beliefs as states that can be epistemically good. On the account of epistemic good just sketched, some accurate states are good because they're states that can give us potential motivating reasons. Unfortunately, this is something that partial beliefs cannot do when they do not constitute full beliefs. Thus, they don't have the good-making feature that accounts for the value of the valuable full beliefs. Thus, *if* this is the sole fundamental epistemic good-making feature, gradational veritism and the hybrid views have to be mistaken. By failing to be full beliefs, these credal states cannot be good beliefs. The kind of accuracy they have isn't the kind of accuracy that accounts for the value realized by the full beliefs that are good beliefs.

1.3.3 *Against categorical veritism*

A crucial premise in the argument for Distinctiveness is the idea that the good-making properties are the properties in virtue of which beliefs 'track reality' and enable us to do, feel, or believe things for reasons that consist of facts. Since only true beliefs will have such properties, the premise supports Necessity. Since, however, some true beliefs will lack such properties, the premise also gives us the argument we need to reject Sufficiency. Just as Lynch appropriated Nozick's experience machine for his purposes, I shall appropriate it for mine. Lynch is right that there's something missing from the experience machine, but it would be a mistake to think that what's missing is *accuracy*. A subject's attitudes in the experience machine can be accurate even when that subject's attitudes do not 'track reality'. We can use Gettier cases to show that. Set the machine up to create a series of convincing appearances. As events outside the machine unfold, there might be the occasional 'match'. It might seem to the subject because of what's happening in the machine that something very nice is happening. It might also be that this nice thing *is* happening. Maybe you smile because you believe that your sister was just awarded her doctorate. Maybe you do this just as this occurs. It couldn't be that *your* reason for smiling is the fact that your sister has just been awarded the doctorate. That part of reality isn't a part of reality that you track. Your attitudes might happen to match events in the external world, but they don't thereby help these events or facts about them guide you in your thoughts, feelings, or deeds.

Two beliefs might score the same in terms of accuracy while differing in terms of whether they track reality. If the reason that some accurate beliefs are good is that these beliefs track reality, we have some reason to think that there's not much that's good about the accurate beliefs that fail to track reality. That is, we do if the point or purpose of belief is to put us in touch with the part of reality that consists of facts. Since I think that *is* what the point or purpose of belief is, I think that we can use the experience machine to undermine Sufficiency. This isn't the place to defend this, but I would suggest that only beliefs that constitute knowledge put you in a position to be guided by reasons that consist of facts.[16] If this is correct, only those true beliefs that constitute knowledge will have the good-making properties that are distinctive to belief. Since there can be differences between how accurate a subject's beliefs are and whether these beliefs constitute knowledge, I think that there's something seriously wrong with the way that Veritism in all its guises will rank options. In turn, I think that this should complicate the consequentialist arguments concerning putative epistemic norms.

1.4 Knowledge and the Good

Once we see that there are true beliefs that do not track reality (e.g., accidentally true beliefs formed in Gettier cases), we can see why Lynch's observations don't support veritism (i.e., because they don't support the Sufficiency Thesis) and why the Sufficiency Thesis is so dubious.[17] There's nothing good about the true beliefs that don't track reality, so there must be more to the fundamental epistemic good than mere accuracy. If, as I've suggested, only *knowledge* tracks the parts of reality that consist of facts, the intuitions that Lynch appeals to support an alternative to veritism and suggest that it's a mistake to rank options using the veritist value theory.

Even if I am right that the Sufficiency Thesis is mistaken, it might seem that this tells us little about epistemic consequentialism. The consequentialist is not committed to any particular account of epistemic goodness, so couldn't they adopt my preferred value theory?

---

[16] See Hyman (2015) for discussion and defense. Gordon (1987) and Unger (1975) defend similar views, as do Littlejohn (2012) and Williamson (2000).

[17] Opinion might divide over whether this holds true for all kinds of Gettier cases. Hughes (2014) and Locke (2015) think that fake barn cases are trouble for the idea that knowledge is necessary. In Littlejohn (2012) I relied on these objections to knowledge accounts of various kinds, but see Littlejohn (2014) for a response/retraction.

Gnosticism: Knowledge is the fundamental epistemic good, the fundamental epistemic disvalue is realized by belief that fails to constitute knowledge, and these are the only basic epistemic values and disvalues.[18]

A move from veritism to gnosticism is independently motivated. Many epistemologists seem to think that it is better to know than to simply have a true belief.[19] Gnosticism vindicates this intuition in a straightforward way. It also helps to solve (or dissolve) the swamping problem, a problem that seems to arise when we assign value to true belief and knowledge and then try to work out how knowledge could contain all the value contained in true belief along with some further value. If some true beliefs cannot do what beliefs are supposed to do (i.e., provide us with potential motivating reasons by putting us in touch with reality), we can see why the gnostic would think that the worries about swamping are misplaced. While there's much to be said for moving from veritism to gnosticism, this move only helps to highlight the problems with consequentialism.

There's some sense in which knowledge is good or it is good to know. In accepting this, what *precisely* have we accepted? Our talk of 'good', 'better', and 'best' is quite varied. Let's consider four ways of trying to understand the gnostic view:

Good Simpliciter: Knowledge is good simpliciter. The state of affairs of knowing a true proposition is among the states of affairs that are intrinsically good, states of affairs that have the goodness property, or states of affairs that are just plain good.

Good For: Knowledge is good for the knower. It is good for the knower to know things. Knowledge is thus among the value atoms that determines whether things go well or badly for the knower.

Good in a Way: Knowledge is good in a way. Just as a good toaster is good insofar as it can do what toasters are supposed to do, a belief that constitutes knowledge might be a good belief in a way that's similar.

Normatively Good: Knowledge is good in the sense that it is good that you believe only if you know. It is good because such beliefs conform to the norm that governs belief.

In which of these ways should the gnostic say that knowledge is good?[20]

---

[18] In Littlejohn (2015), this view was dubbed 'conscientiaism' but I think 'gnosticism' is a much better name for the view. For an application of gnosticism to puzzles in the philosophy of law, see Littlejohn (forthcoming). Thanks to Margot Strohminger for the name. (Matthew Benton suggested 'knosticism' but I think this took things too far!)

[19] See Kvanvig (2003).

[20] Even if the reader holds some remaining sympathy for veritism, it is clear that many of the critical remarks in this chapter about certain versions of gnosticism apply mutatis mutandis to veritism. If, say, knowledge is not good simpliciter or good for you, say, it is pretty clear that true belief isn't good simpliciter or good for you.

1.4.1 Good simpliciter and good for

Moore thought that 'good' (often?) functions as a predicative adjective. In saying that some conduct was good conduct, he thought we said that it was conduct and that it was good. On this use, 'good' functions to attribute the property of being good to something (e.g., persons, conduct, states of affairs). On this use, if we say that this was good conduct and that she was a good person, we would be saying that this conduct and this woman shared a property in common. They would share the goodness property. On this use if we said that Agnes was a good companion but not a good person, we would say, inter alia, that Agnes was good and that she was either not good or not a person.[21]

We also use 'good' to talk about things that are good for subjects. It might be thought that knowledge or true belief is good for the person, that her life is somehow improved just by the presence of knowledge or true belief. If the gnostic wanted, she could say that knowledge is good for people without any commitment to the idea that knowledge is good simpliciter. There is no obvious inconsistency in saying that something is good for some person and denying that this thing is just plain good. (Nor is there any obvious inconsistency in saying that something is good even if we deny that it is good for someone.)

If knowledge were good in one of these two ways, this might seem to be good news for consequentialists who accept the Totalizing and Promotion Theses. If some states of affairs are good simpliciter, it would be plausible that things are going better when these states of affairs are prevalent and it would, in turn, be plausible to suggest that the proper mode of responding to such values would be to promote them. If there are epistemic standings that would be good for us to stand in, this might suggest that the more often we stood in these standings the better things would go for us.

Is knowledge good in either of these ways? Some philosophers are skeptical of the idea that 'good' functions as a predicative adjective and skeptical of the idea that there are things that are just plain good.[22] Such skepticism, if not put to rest, spells trouble for any veritist or gnostic who wants to vindicate intuitions about value by saying that true beliefs or instances of knowledge are things that bear the goodness property. Why are philosophers skeptical of talk of the idea that some things might be good simpliciter? One worry is that it seems that we simply cannot use 'good' as a predicative adjective. If there is such a thing as the goodness property and it plays a useful role in our theory of epistemic norms, we should be able to grasp what it would be for

---

[21] If Agnes is my lovely pet dog, this makes perfectly good sense. If, however, Agnes was a wonderful companion who was, inter alia, a terrible person, it would be harder to see how I could say this consistently. If we used 'good' as a predicative adjective and said that Agnes was not a good person, we would say that she was either not a person or not good. Since she was a person, we should be able to conclude that she was not good, but this is inconsistent with saying that she is both good and a companion. In this context, it is clear that reading 'good' as a predicative adjective is completely unnatural.

[22] See Foot (1985) and Thomson (2008) for criticism of the Moorean view of 'good' and the goodness property. See Zimmerman (2001) for a response.

something to be good simpliciter and express this thought using terms like 'good'. But it seems that we cannot because when we use 'good' in sentences of the form 'a is a good F' it seems the *only* admissible reading of that sentence is one on which 'good' functions as an attributive adjective, not a predicative one.[23] If we thought that beliefs could be good simpliciter (if true or if they constituted knowledge) and thought that we could express this belief in language, we should be able to say that 'Such and such is a good belief' and get a reading according to which it entails both 'Such and such is a belief' and 'Such and such is good', but the way we read such sentences doesn't allow this. Consider, 'This is a good toaster' or 'Agnes is a good dog but a bad chef'.

Some people might think they grasp the truth of the view that some beliefs are good simpliciter but cannot express this in language or think that it can be expressed in language and deny the observation that 'good' functions exclusively as an attributive adjective in sentences of the form 'a is a good F'. Fair enough. We will see that there's a second objection to this proposal, but let's first consider a second way of understanding the gnostic view.

On the first use of 'good' it seems that if things are good, things are better for it even if things are not better for anyone at all. There is another use of 'good' according to which something is 'good' only if it is good for some subject. In this sense, the good has to do with the subject's interests. It's an interesting question how these two notions of good are related. I don't see any reason to think that if something has the property of being good that this involves something being good for some subject, and I see no reason to think that whenever something is indeed good for some subject there is something that has the property of being good. Moore, recall, thought that it was analytic that if some option is the best, it is the one to choose. I don't think he ever thought that it was analytic that if some option is best for some individual, some group, or the set of all possible individuals that this was the option to choose. If we want to connect the sense of 'good' that has to do with interests to the sense of 'good' that is used in trying to attribute the goodness property to some thing, we should demand an argument in support of any view that posits some entailment between claims about the goodness property and a subject's interests.[24]

One of the advantages of thinking of epistemic goodness in terms of things that are good for a subject is that we don't have to make sense of the idea that there are things that are good simpliciter. Another is that it might seem to handle some of our

---

[23] See Almotahari and Hosein (2015) for discussion.
[24] An anonymous referee pointed out that Goldman (1999: 88) might provide part of the argument requested in arguing that a subject's interests (e.g., in answering questions, satisfying curiosity) have significant implications when it comes to determining the total good realized by our epistemic state. (He suggests, for example, that a subject's failure to have answers to uninteresting questions might not matter for the score we assign to their belief states.) I fear that Goldman's arguments can only give us part of what we want. They don't speak to the problem that mere accuracy of a belief about something interesting or important might be insufficient for the realization of a value. They also don't speak to the problem that the inaccuracy of a state should be sufficient for the realization of disvalue quite apart from the interest we take in the relevant issues. For a helpful discussion of these issues, see Cote-Bouchard (2016).

intuitions about the importance of being able to track reality. We've already seen that these intuitions seem to cause trouble for veritism, so it would be good if we had a view that made some sense of them. In spite of this, we should reject both views.

It's important to the consequentialist project that rightness or rationality is determined by the interplay of some norm that tells us how value relates to rationality or rightness and how the options rank in terms of the total value they contain. The veritist ranks options in terms of the total amount of true beliefs. The gnostic ranks them in terms of total amount of knowledge. On the veritist view, the rational belief is the one that's part of the option that contains the greatest total amount of epistemic goodness (determined by adding up the values realized by the accurate states and subtracting out the disvalue realized by the inaccurate ones). On the gnostic view, the rational belief is the one that's part of the option that contains the greatest total amount of epistemic goodness (determined by adding up the values realized by the states that constitute knowledge and subtracting out the disvalue realized by the states that fail to constitute knowledge).

The trouble with this way of thinking about things is there is a potential gap between the probability that a particular state is accurate or constitutes knowledge and the probability that the good particular states will be part of the best option. Take a simple example. You might have thought that Trump would never be the GOP nominee *and* thought that you would never change your mind about this. As the evidence comes in, you might come to see that the first belief isn't quite as likely as you might have hoped. What about the second belief? If you manage to 'resist' modifying your first belief in light of the evidence, you just might be able to sustain this knowledge that you'll never change your mind. So, part of the cost of updating in light of the evidence is that you'd lose knowledge that you could have retained. Depending upon how the numbers work out, you can get cases where the kosher beliefs are too costly to keep or form and the bad beliefs are too costly not to form or too costly to drop.

We tend not to think that the way to show that a belief is rational is to show something about the *extrinsic* epistemic value associated with its formation, revision, or retention. A bad belief isn't rational by virtue of carrying with it good epistemic consequences that couldn't be acquired otherwise. This is the notorious problem of epistemic trade-offs.[25] The problem is actually somewhat worse on gnosticism than it is on veritism. There is no interesting relationship between the truth or falsity of a particular belief and its rational standing. There *is* an interesting relationship between the rational standing of a belief and its status as knowledge. It's plausible that if you know *p*, your belief about *p* is rational. The normative status that we're trying

---

[25] The problem first is discussed in Firth (1981). Jenkins (2007) presents a version of the worry in discussing epistemic entitlement. In Littlejohn (2012), I appealed to these intuitions about trade-offs to attack epistemic consequentialism. The same sort of objection to epistemic consequentialism is also found in Berker (2013) and Greaves (2014). See also Carr (2015).

to understand in terms of the interplay of ranked options and norms that use this ranking to determine a belief's status uses that status in the ranking. This is incoherent. It's equivalent to building rightness into the states of affairs we use in ranking options and then trying to use the ranking to determine which state of affairs we might rightly bring about. This is incoherent for two reasons. First, it is incoherent because it allows that there's something that's independent from the ranking that determines the status. (Otherwise, the status couldn't figure in the ranking.) Second, it is incoherent because it should allow that one of the things rightly brought about would be wrong to bring about because of where it stands in the ranking. (If we assume the Totalizing Thesis, it should be possible for a 'right' action to figure in options that rank very low simply because alternative options contain more 'right' actions.)

It looks as if there is a simple argument from gnosticism to the denial of epistemic consequentialism. Suppose it's rational to believe p if you know p. Whether you know p or not depends upon things like whether your belief about p is safe, not upon whether your belief about p is part of an option that contains the greatest amount of epistemic goodness. (The consequentialists *have* to concede this. They cannot say that a belief's status as knowledge is dependent upon the ranking because the ranking is given in terms of the amount of knowledge contained in the options.) Having conceded this, however, they cannot *then* say that rationality is determined by how the options are ranked. If an item of knowledge is included only in suboptimal options, it is nevertheless a rational belief.

Epistemic rationality does not permit or require trade-offs when it comes to knowledge. Because epistemic consequentialists have to allow for trade-offs, their view is at odds with gnosticism. Once we see that trade-offs are not allowed, we should see that it is implausible that knowledge is good simpliciter. If we thought that it was, we would think that trade-offs would be allowed if only there were no side-constraints that prohibited it. Even if we thought that such side-constraints existed, we would think that there was something regrettable about not being able to make the trade-off. We don't think that. We don't think that it's regrettable that someone knows p when that knowledge precludes knowing some other things. (For example, if you know that you are a star pupil, you know that you'll never know that you don't know much about history, that you'll never know that you don't know much about biology, that you'll never know that you don't know much about science books.)

1.4.2 *The remaining options*

There are other uses of 'good' to consider. We often treat 'good' as an attributive adjective. In saying that something is a good book, we don't seem to be saying that it has the property of being a book *and* the property of being good. In saying that something is a good book and that some second thing is a good toaster, we aren't saying that they share something in common. On this use, 'good' does *not* function to attribute the property of goodness to anything. When we say of some book that it is a good book, we are saying that it is good as a book or good for a book. There is some standard of evaluation that we use to evaluate books, and the good book comes up to snuff.

There is a final use of 'good' that is not evaluative at all. In saying that it would be 'good', 'better', or 'best' if something is done, we often mean to say that it is good because it should be done. Such things are good because required, not required because good. Consider this example.[26] Suppose one pile contains thousands of tickets for an upcoming lottery and another contains a handful. Suppose that nobody knows this yet, but the smaller pile contains the winning ticket. While the best outcome would be the one in which you pick the smaller pile, it would be best (and better and good) for you to pick the first. One seems evaluative and the other does not. If I say that it would be good to keep your lunch date or best to visit your sick relative, this might simply be my way of trying to get you to see that you have most reason to do these things and I might not base this judgment on any calculation of total value. Indeed, I might know full well that no calculation of total value would support such a claim. I might say, for example, that it would be best for you to do something even if I know full well that this wouldn't be what's best for the affected parties.

When it comes to the Promotion and Totalizing Theses, it is clear that these theses are plausible only for good simpliciter and good for.[27] If something is good only in the sense that it is a good instance of a kind, it does not make much sense to measure its goodness and then use this to rank options from better to worse. (If two toasters are good toasters and only one toaster is needed to toast things, the state of affairs that contains two does not seem better than the state of affairs that includes just one. If there is no need to toast anything at all, there is still a perfectly good distinction to drawn between good and bad toasters, but it also seems that there is no reason to think that the presence of absence of such toasters matters much to the ranking of options.) If something is good only in the sense that it is a good instance of a kind, it needn't call for promotion. The good-making features of a good book or toaster do not call for promotion. If something is good in the sense that it is normatively good (i.e., good because right or appropriate) and we can determine this without appeal to its role in determining rankings, this notion of good cannot be the one that's at play in the Totalizing Thesis. Even if it called for promotion, the fact that it called for promotion quite independently from considerations about the ranking of options is a fact that would cause trouble for the consequentialist. The stuff that we used to establish the propriety of the act or attitude renders the ranking otiose.

Once we see that the truth in gnosticism is captured by the idea that beliefs that constitute knowledge are good instances of a kind or good precisely in that they conform to the norms that govern belief, we can see that the truth in gnosticism

---

[26] Thanks to Julien Dutant for the example. For discussion, see Dutant (2013) and Piller (2009).
[27] See Baron (1995) for a helpful discussion of value and reasons to promote.

reveals the falsity of epistemic consequentialism. It doesn't make sense to rank options in terms of the amount of good they contain, and the idea that we should promote the relevant goods by choosing the option that contains the most of it conflicts with the apparent platitude that knowledge is all you need to rightly believe that something is so.

1.5 The Priority Thesis

Lynch captured something important about epistemic value. It's something that's easy to miss if we're fixated on questions about the value of truth and don't think about the possible differences between veritism and gnosticism. He's right that there is something good about beliefs that 'track reality', but mistaken if he thinks that all accurate beliefs track reality. We want accuracy, but we want more besides. The experience machine is all we need to demonstrate this. Someone can be in the experience machine and luck into the occasional true belief. In having such beliefs, however, they are not 'tracking' reality. If someone believes correctly that, say, her sister is being awarded her doctorate just when it happens to be that her sister is being awarded her doctorate, the subject isn't smiling for the reason that her sister is being awarded her doctorate. You can be totally out of touch with reality even when you have accurate beliefs.

Only beliefs that constitute knowledge track reality. There's no obvious value in having a true belief that doesn't track reality. The occasional accidentally accurate attitude formed in the experience machine does not track reality, put a subject in touch with reality, or enable her to believe things, feel things, or do things in light of how things are. Thus, it's hard to see that there's anything left of the idea that all true beliefs are intrinsically good or that any state of affairs in which someone believes a truth is one that is good. The very same examples that we can use to challenge the idea that all true beliefs are good can be used to challenge the idea that all true beliefs are good for us. Just as it's obvious that there are true beliefs that don't make you better off overall, the experience machine makes it obvious that there are some true beliefs that don't make you better off in any way. When you think about the cases where the relevant belief is true but does not track reality, it is hard to see how this kind of failure to track reality could be something that makes even a small contribution to your well-being.

Once we abandon these two ideas about the good of true belief, we should then ask whether there is any sense in which true beliefs are good simply by virtue of being true. It shouldn't come as a surprise that I think there is not. While I think there is something important about what Lynch says, the importance of it will be lost if we don't pursue this idea of his that the beliefs that have epistemic value are those that track reality. Three things are true about the good of true beliefs. First, the true beliefs that are good are those that constitute knowledge. Their status as knowledge is essential to understanding the sense in which they are good. Second, that the sense in which they are good is that such beliefs are good beliefs. Third, there is a further sense in which it is good to believe these beliefs, which is simply that such beliefs are the right ones to hold.

Let's consider the two ways in which it is plausible to say that knowledge is good:

Attributive Goodness: Knowledge is good in the sense that a belief that constitutes knowledge is a good belief (i.e., it is good precisely because it can do what beliefs are supposed to do much in the way that a good toaster is good precisely because it can do what toasters are supposed to do).

Normative Goodness: It is good to know in the sense that believing what you know ensures that you conform to the norm that governs belief (i.e., in this sense it is good because it conforms to the norm).

To understand the thesis about attributive goodness, it helps to understand why it matters that beliefs track reality. The best answer is that it matters whether we are guided by reasons and reasons are truths.[28] Reasons that consist of facts can only rationally guide us when we believe them to obtain *and* our beliefs track the part of reality that consists of the relevant facts. To be guided by a reason, the reason has to capture the light in which you took the relevant response to be appropriate. If your reason for driving to the store was that you were out of gin and bitters, it was the fact that you were out of the essentials that you took it that heading to the store was the thing to do. If you didn't take yourself to be out of gin or out of bitters, the mere fact that you were couldn't have convinced you that you should head to the store. Not only do you need belief to be guided by the fact if you didn't believe it to be a fact, you also need knowledge to be guided by it. This is what the experience machine shows. Only beliefs that enable you to be guided by such reasons are good beliefs. Putting you in touch with the facts so that they can guide your thoughts, feelings, and actions is a virtue of a belief just as the power to toast bread is a virtue of a toaster and being sharp is a virtue of a knife.

There is a further sense in which it is good to believe truths. It is normatively good to believe p when you know p. The idea here is that it is good to believe only when you know because it is only then that you conform to the norms governing belief.[29] The good comes from norm conformity, so it is not a kind of good that explains why some norm is in force. If knowledge is the fundamental standard that we use to evaluate beliefs, a belief is good because it meets this standard. It would be a mistake to say that beliefs that constitute knowledge do so because they are good in some further way where the goodness makes the belief meet the standard.[30]

---

[28] See Alvarez (2010), Hyman (2015), Littlejohn (2012), Unger (1975), and Williamson (2000) for defenses of this idea.

[29] See Williamson (2000) for a defense.

[30] It might seem that the proposal faces an obvious objection. If knowledge is attributively good and normatively good but not good in any further sense, it's hard to see how there could be any rational pressure to conform to the knowledge norm. The account seems to deny that there is some reason to promote the

As I said above, these claims about the value of knowledge pose a problem for consequentialism. Suppose knowledge suffices for rationality. Suppose further that the conditions that determine whether a belief constitutes knowledge can obtain independently from whether that belief is included in the best options. If so, it would be wrong to say, as consequentialists must say, that the status is determined by the ranking of options. What about the Priority Thesis? While I think we have to reject the Totalizing and Promotion Theses, the Priority Thesis might well be correct. Allow me to explain.

According to the Priority Thesis, the good is prior to the right. If rightness, rationality, or justification were an *ingredient* of knowledge, we would have a neat and tidy argument against the thesis. Unfortunately, I see no good reason to accept the idea that rightness, rationality, or justification is an ingredient of knowledge. For all that's been said, these might merely be necessary conditions on knowledge, and the claim that something is a necessary condition on knowledge implies nothing about priority. Indeed, for all that's been said, these might not even be necessary conditions on knowledge, in which case there wouldn't be any tension between gnosticism and the Priority Thesis at all.

In arguing against consequentialism, I did say that knowledge suffices for rationality, which is equivalent to saying that rationality is necessary for knowledge. Let me make one qualification that does not affect the previous argument. In arguing from gnosticism to the rejection of consequentialism, I did not need the strong premise that *every* case of knowledge is a case of rational belief, only the much weaker premise that there are *some* cases of knowledge that are cases of rational belief where the total amount of good realized by holding onto the rational belief is less than the total amount of epistemic good that could be realized in some alternative option that does not include this belief. There are plausible cases of knowledge without rational belief or justified belief. Some non-human animals know things. So do children.

---

good that comes from conforming to it. Here is one avenue of response. We could say that the knowledge norm is categorical in the sense that it applies to any subject that can be held responsible for her attitudes. On every occasion, the norm determines whether our beliefs are as they should be. On these occasions, though, there might be different reasons (e.g., non-epistemic reasons) that determine the importance of conforming to the norm. On this model, the standards that apply to belief apply categorically but the normative pressure to meet this standard varies from one occasion to another (e.g., on the basis of the importance of meeting or failing to meet the standard). A similar but different view might be that the normative pressure to conform to the norm applies equally across all the cases but is nevertheless a pressure that comes from outside of epistemology. Perhaps the practice of trying to meet epistemic standards and being held to such standards serves some non-epistemic purpose. The point is that the standard's content might be determined by one thing and the normative pressure for meeting this standard might derive from something else entirely. So, even if knowledge is not good simpliciter or good for you, there might be some further good that explains why you ought to revise your beliefs as if it did matter that you believed only what you know. We find suggestions for developing some of these ideas in recent work by Maguire and Woods (MS) and Owens (2012).

To my mind, it makes perfectly good sense to say that Agnes knows that I have come home from work even if Agnes is a dog.[31] If Agnes is the right kind of non-human animal (Dog? Hamster? Turtle? Spider? Fish? Flea?), it might make perfectly good sense to say that she knows things and yet be odd to say that her doubts, emotions, or beliefs are justified. A cow might perform an action that is optimific, but I don't think that they would act rightly, not even if the consequentialists are right about rightness. To know or perform an act that is optimific, one does not need the capacities required for accountability, but such capacities are required for being justified or rational.

This possibility is enough to show that a belief that is attributively good need not be normatively good. Once we have that, the gnostic can consistently say that they accept the claim about attributive goodness and say that a belief is an instance of a good belief iff it is knowledge. They can then say that in the special case where we are dealing with creatures that can be held accountable or responsible, attributive and normative goodness coincide. This position is consistent with the Priority Thesis. The reason that it is normatively good to believe only what you know is precisely that these are the beliefs that are attributively good. The view is *teleological* but not *consequentialist*.[32] It is teleological because the norm that governs belief tells us that the beliefs we ought to have are the beliefs we ought to have because they perform a function or serve some aim. The view is non-consequentialist because the good that such beliefs realize is not one that calls for promotion and doesn't determine what's right or rational by ranking options in terms of total value.

On the consequentialist view, we cannot determine whether something is right until we work out the total value of the various options and see whether it is contained in the options that rank highly enough. Satisficers and maximizers disagree about whether the right option has to be tied for first, but they both accept the Totalizing Thesis and Promotion Thesis. If you accept the Totalizing Thesis, you have to think that the normative status of an action or attitude isn't something we can discern just by thinking about its merit in isolation from the other actions or attitudes contained in the options that contain it. An act that brings about some positive outcome isn't justified by that fact. The justification of this act turns on whether there were feasible alternatives that would be overall better. If the epistemic consequentialists are consequentialists, they have to think that the same would hold for attitudes that

---

[31] Thanks to Maria Alvarez for pressing me on whether I thought that non-human animals had to have justified beliefs in order to have knowledge. It's possible that I did not quite capture the point she was making. If I haven't captured her point, I would happily claim credit for the point I thought she had made.

[32] Mehta (forthcoming) defends a view that is also teleological without being consequentialist. He thinks that knowledge is a standard of success and that it grounds further epistemic norms. I don't know if he would accept my explanation as to why knowledge is good (i.e., that the fundamental good that attaches to belief attaches to those beliefs that provide potential motivating reasons), but the view being proposed here is hardly the first attempt at stating a view that is both teleological and non-consequentialist. Indeed, my aim in Littlejohn (2012) was to show that the right way to derive a theory of epistemic norms was to identify the point or purpose of beliefs (i.e., which is to provide reasons) and work from there (e.g., explain why conforming to the norms of belief requires not just accuracy but non-accidental accuracy).

realize some good. An attitude that has no value might be justified because it is part of an option that ranks sufficiently high and an attitude that has value might not be justified because it is only included in options that do not rank highly enough.

Ross thought that when we think about situations in which we harm or help others, we can see that there is something wrong with the consequentialist attitude towards beneficence and maleficence. To determine whether we have violated a duty of beneficence or maleficence, Ross thought, we need to look to the results brought about (i.e., whether we harmed or helped), which is not the same as looking to these consequences along with those associated with all the feasible alternatives to see where the action ranked (i.e., to determine whether the harmful or helpful action was included in the option that maximized the good). If you injure someone, you have committed a wrong even if had you not acted someone would have brought about the very same injury. If you falsely describe someone in a less than flattering light, this is a wrong. It is a wrong even if that person would have been described in an even less flattering light by two more malicious slanderers had you remained silent. In the epistemic case, when we're evaluating our attitudes as we should, we focus on whether these attitudes are accurate or would constitute knowledge.

When we assess a belief, we do focus on the features that matter to veritists and gnostics (i.e., accuracy and the conditions required for knowledge), but we do not see the relevance of these features as the consequentialists do. We care about an aspect of the result of settling a question (i.e., whether the answer is one we know to be correct), not the way that all of our options were ranked in terms of the total value realized by our other attitudes in these possibilities. We do not think that the accuracy of some attitude matters only because of its effect on total accuracy, and we certainly think that it does matter even if this accurate attitude is one that is held only in suboptimal options.

References

Adler, Jonathan. 2002. *Belief's Own Ethics*. Cambridge, MA: MIT Press.
Ahlstrom-Vij, Kristoffer and Jeffrey Dunn. 2014. A Defence of Epistemic Consequentialism. *The Philosophical Quarterly* 64: 541–51.
Almotahari, Mahrad and Adam Hosein. 2015. Is Anything Just Plain Good? *Philosophical Studies* 172: 1485–508.
Alvarez, Maria. 2010. *Kinds of Reasons*. Oxford: Oxford University Press.
Baron, Marcia. 1995. *Kantian Ethics almost without Apology*. New York: Cornell University Press.
Berker, Selim. 2013. The Rejection of Epistemic Consequentialism. *Philosophical Issues* 23: 363–87.
Bradley, B. 2009. *Well-Being and Death*. Oxford: Oxford University Press.
Brewer, Bill. 2011. *Perception and its Objects*. Oxford: Oxford University Press.
Carlson, Eric. 1995. *Consequentialism Reconsidered*. Dordrecht: Kluwer.
Carr, Jennifer. 2015. Epistemic Expansions. *Res Philosophica* 92: 217–36.

Cote-Bouchard, Charles. 2016. Can the Aim of Belief Ground Epistemic Normativity? *Philosophical Studies* 173: 3181–98.
Dorst, Kevin. Forthcoming. Lockeans Maximize Expected Accuracy. *Mind*.
Dutant, Julien. 2013. In Defence of Swamping. *Thought* 2: 357–66.
Easwaran, Kenny and Branden Fitelson. 2012. An "Evidentialist" Worry about Joyce's Argument for Probabilism. *Dialectica* 66(3): 425–33.
Easwaran, Kenny and Branden Fitelson. 2015. Accuracy, Coherence, and Evidence. In Tamar Szabó Gendler and John Hawthorne (eds), *Oxford Studies in Epistemology*: Vol. 5. Oxford: Oxford University Press, 61–96.
Firth, Roderick. 1981. Epistemic Merit, Intrinsic and Instrumental. *Proceedings and Addresses of the American Philosophical Association* 55: 5–23.
Foley, Richard. 2009. Beliefs, Degrees of Belief, and the Lockean Thesis. In Franz Huber and Christoph Schmidt-Petri (eds), *Degrees of Belief*. Dordrecht: Springer, 37–47.
Foot, Philippa. 1985. Utilitarianism and the Virtues. *Mind* 94: 196–209.
Goldman, Alvin. 1986. *Epistemology and Cognition*. Cambridge, MA: Harvard University Press.
Goldman, Alvin. 1999. *Knowledge in a Social World*. Oxford: Oxford University Press.
Goldman, Alvin. 2015. Reliabilism, Veritism, and Epistemic Consequentialism. *Episteme* 12: 131–43.
Gordon, Robert. 1987. *The Structure of Emotion*. Cambridge: Cambridge University Press.
Greaves, Hilary. 2014. Epistemic Decision Theory. *Mind* 122(488): 915–52.
Hughes, Nick. 2014. Is Knowledge the Ability to φ for the Reason that *P*? *Episteme* 11: 457–62.
Hyman, John. 2015. *Action, Knowledge, and Will*. Oxford: Oxford University Press.
Jenkins, Carrie. 2007. Entitlement and Rationality. *Synthese* 157: 25–45.
Joyce, James. 1998. A Nonpragmatic Vindication of Probabilism. *Philosophy of Science* 65: 575–603.
Joyce, James. 2009. Accuracy and Coherence: Prospects for an Alethic Epistemology of Partial Belief. In F. Huber and C. Schmidt-Petri (eds), *Degrees of Belief*. Dordrecht: Springer, 263–97.
Joyce, James. MS. Why Evidentialists Need Not Worry about the Accuracy Argument for Probabilism.
Konek, Jason and Ben Levinstein. MS. The Foundations of Epistemic Decision Theory.
Kvanvig, Jonathan. 2003. *The Value of Knowledge and the Pursuit of Understanding*. Cambridge: Cambridge University Press.
Littlejohn, Clayton. 2012. *Justification and the Truth-Connection*. Cambridge: Cambridge University Press.
Littlejohn, Clayton. 2014. Fake Barns and False Dilemmas. *Episteme* 11: 369–89.
Littlejohn, Clayton. 2015. Who Cares What You Accurately Believe? *Philosophical Perspectives* 29: 217–48.
Littlejohn, Clayton. Forthcoming. Truth, Knowledge, and the Standard of Proof in Criminal Law. *Synthese*.
Locke, Dustin. 2015. Knowledge, Explanation, and Motivating Reasons. *American Philosophical Quarterly* 52: 215–32.
Lynch, Michael. 2004. *True to Life*. Cambridge, MA: MIT Press.
McDowell, John. 1998. *Meaning, Knowledge, and Reality*. Cambridge, MA: Harvard University Press.
Maguire, Barry and Jack Woods. MS. Explaining Epistemic Normativity.

Mehta, Neil. Forthcoming. Knowledge and Other Norms for Assertion, Action, and Belief: A Teleological Account. *Philosophy and Phenomenological Research.*
Moore, G. E. 1993. *Principia Ethica.* Revised edition. Cambridge: Cambridge University Press.
Nozick, Robert. 1974. *Anarchy, State, and Utopia.* Oxford: Blackwell.
Owens, David. 2012. *Shaping the Normative Landscape.* Oxford: Oxford University Press.
Pettigrew, Richard. 2013a. Accuracy and Evidence. *Dialectica* 67: 579–96.
Pettigrew, Richard. 2013b. Epistemic Utility and Norms for Credences. *Philosophy Compass* 8(10): 897–908.
Pettigrew, Richard. 2015. Accuracy and the Belief-Credence Connection. *Philosopher's Imprint* 15(16).
Pettigrew, Richard. 2016. Accuracy, Risk, and the Principle of Indifference. *Philosophy and Phenomenological Research* 92(1): 35–59.
Piller, Christian. 2009. Reliabilist Responses to the Value of Knowledge Problem. *Grazer Philosophische Studien* 79: 121–35.
Ross, W. D. 1930. *The Right and the Good.* Oxford: Oxford University Press.
Ryan, Sharon. 1996. The Epistemic Virtues of Consistency. *Synthese* 109: 121–41.
Schellenberg, S. 2014. The Relational and Representational Character of Perceptual Experience. In B. Brogaard (ed.), *Does Perception Have Content?* Oxford: Oxford University Press, 199–218.
Siegel, S. 2010. *The Contents of Visual Experience.* Oxford: Oxford University Press.
Sturgeon, Scott. 2008. Reason and the Grain of Belief. *Noûs* 42(1): 139–65.
Talbot, Brian. 2014. Truth-Promoting Non-Evidential Reasons for Belief. *Philosophical Studies* 168(3): 599–618.
Thomson, Judith Jarvis. 2008. *Normativity.* Chicago, IL: Open Court.
Travis, Charles. 2013. *Perception: Essays after Frege.* Oxford: Oxford University Press.
Unger, Peter. 1975. *Ignorance.* Oxford: Oxford University Press.
Vallentyne, Peter. 2006. Against Maximizing Act Consequentialism. In J. Dreier (ed.), *Contemporary Debates in Moral Theory.* Malden, MA: Wiley-Blackwell, 21–37.
Williamson, Timothy. 2000. *Knowledge and its Limits.* Oxford: Oxford University Press.
Zimmerman, Michael. 2001. *The Nature of Intrinsic Value.* Rowman and Littlefield.

2
Adaptive Misbeliefs, Value Trade-Offs, and Epistemic Responsibility

Nancy E. Snow

2.1 Introduction

In recent papers, Selim Berker (2013a, 2013b, 2015) challenges epistemic consequentialism, according to which the epistemic right is to be understood as that which conduces to the epistemic good. This schema offers an integrated picture of epistemic normativity by providing the outline of a unified theory, relating the good and the right, that tells us what we need to be good knowers. Epistemic consequentialism is thus a form of epistemic teleology in that it is a type of theory that takes epistemic value to be the end at which beliefs and/or belief-producing processes aim. According to Berker (2013a, 2013b), it parallels ethical consequentialism in structure.[1] Certain versions of epistemic consequentialism apparently condone epistemically irresponsible behavior, that is, holding false or ungrounded beliefs, when doing so leads to an overall increase in epistemic value. In this essay I examine a larger problem for epistemic consequentialists, namely, trade-offs between epistemic and pragmatic value. I argue that even when such trade-offs lead to an overall increase in value, holding false or ungrounded beliefs is still epistemically irresponsible.

This problem arises when we think about how epistemic and pragmatic value contribute to overall well-being. It seems that being a good knower in the sense of having true beliefs does not always enable us to be effective agents. There is a lively literature on what have been called "adaptive misbeliefs," that is, false beliefs, which, despite being false, help us to be effective agents and navigate the pitfalls of the world.[2] But being effective agents is essential for us to have overall well-being, which

[1] Paralleling act and rule consequentialism, different types of epistemic consequentialism can take beliefs or rules/processes as the units of epistemic evaluation (see Littlejohn 2010).

[2] Adaptive misbeliefs could have interesting implications for debates about self-knowledge, but they are not pursued here. For a fascinating discussion of self-enhancement biases, self-conceptions, and self-knowledge/self-ignorance, see Hazlett (2013), especially chapter 2.

includes, but is not limited to, having knowledge. So it seems that, in order to attain overall well-being, we need to admit that sometimes it is preferable to have adaptive misbeliefs instead of true beliefs. Adaptive misbeliefs, then, point to a possibly serious disconnect between being a good "knower" and being a good "doer," and threaten the assumption that knowledge and action can be seamlessly integrated into a single conception of overall human well-being.[3]

In section 2.2, I sketch in some detail what is perhaps the most thorough and persuasive argument for adaptive misbeliefs currently on offer, that provided by Ryan T. McKay and Daniel C. Dennett (2009a). In section 2.3, I relate a subset of adaptive misbeliefs to two examples given by Berker (2013b) in his critique of epistemic consequentialism. The examples Berker (2013b) gives are ones in which epistemic consequentialism prescribes knowers to make trade-offs in epistemic value—opting for less epistemic value in the present in order to achieve greater epistemic value in the future. Adaptive misbeliefs are structurally similar in that they typically trade off epistemic value for greater pragmatic value.[4] In section 2.3 I discuss a subset of adaptive misbeliefs—I call them "game-changing"—in which holding the misbelief contributes to a process whereby the belief is rendered true. In these cases, holding adaptive misbeliefs involves trade-offs in epistemic value of the kind Berker (2013b) illustrates using imaginative counterexamples. These cases of adaptive misbelief show that alleged problems for epistemic consequentialism are not confined to the realm of imagination, but are pervasive aspects of daily life. I say "alleged" problems for epistemic consequentialism because I don't think Berker's arguments succeed.[5] Real-life examples of adaptive misbeliefs that actually help people to function as agents and countenance trade-offs between epistemic and pragmatic value raise a different kind of problem for epistemic consequentialism, however. If adaptive misbeliefs threaten the notion that knowledge is seamlessly integrated with effective agency in a unified conception of well-being, how should conflicts between epistemic and pragmatic value be adjudicated? How should we judge the epistemic responsibility of knowers who hold adaptive misbeliefs and thereby sacrifice epistemic value for the sake of pragmatic value? I argue in section 2.4 that holders of adaptive misbeliefs who make such value trade-offs are epistemically irresponsible.

---

[3] Hazlett (2013), especially chapters 1–3, investigates in depth and detail a similar set of issues by drawing on psychological studies to challenge what he calls the "eudaimonic ideal of true belief." This is the thesis that "for any subject S and proposition that p, having a true belief about whether p is a more reliable bet, when it comes to wellbeing, than having a false belief about whether p" (Hazlett 2013: 29, 63).

[4] Some cases of adaptive misbeliefs allow not only for trade-offs of present epistemic value for the sake of greater future pragmatic value, but also trade-offs of present epistemic value for greater present pragmatic value. For example, my now holding the adaptive misbelief that I am a good speaker allows me the present pragmatic value of getting through my conference presentation now, so that pragmatic value is gained at the expense of epistemic value in the present moment, not just in the future.

[5] See, for example, the persuasive replies to Berker by Ahlstrom-Vij and Dunn (2014) and Goldman (2015).

2.2 A Primer on Adaptive Misbeliefs

In a nutshell, McKay and Dennett contend that adaptive misbeliefs are false beliefs that are produced by normal functioning systems, and that are (or were) evolutionarily adaptive in the biological sense of enhancing the fitness for survival and reproduction of their possessors.[6]

They begin their account by providing a working definition of belief they claim is broad enough to cover representational and dispositional accounts: "A belief is an endorsement of a particular state of affairs as actual" (McKay and Dennett 2009a, 493). They continue, "A misbelief, then, is a belief that to some degree departs from actuality—that is, it is a functional state endorsing a particular state of affairs that happens not to obtain" (493).

They go on to state and challenge an assumption of the orthodox view, namely, that "beliefs that maximise the survival of the believer will be those that best approximate reality" (493). On this account, beliefs about the world are tools designed to enable us to navigate the world. The authors continue: "to be reliable, such tools must be produced in us, it is assumed, by systems designed (by evolution) to be truth-aiming, and hence (barring miracles) these systems must be designed to generate *grounded* beliefs" (493–4; emphasis theirs). Grounded beliefs are appropriately based on evidence and other beliefs. In their search for adaptive misbeliefs, the authors are not concerned with systematically produced grounded beliefs that are true, nor with ungrounded beliefs that are true by accident. The quarry they seek is systematically produced, grounded false beliefs (see also 2009b, 546–7).

Adaptive misbeliefs must be produced by a normal functioning system, and not as a result of an abnormal or pathological system. McKay and Dennett (2009a) refer to normal functioning systems that produce adaptive misbeliefs as "forgivably" limited by evolutionary design and to abnormal or pathological systems as "culpably" limited by evolutionary design (see, e.g., 493). The authors go into considerable complexity on this issue, but two key ideas should be noted. The first is, as stated, that the class of misbeliefs they are after are not the products of pathology, such as delusions. This is connected with their point that adaptive beliefs must promote biological fitness. Delusions might be psychologically beneficial, but they are unlikely to be biologically adaptive. It might enhance my self-esteem and functioning in some contexts, for example, to be deluded about my physical strength and prowess as a warrior, but, given that I am actually small, clumsy, and weak, that delusion is unlikely to help me if I encounter a "fight or flight" situation in which my physical survival is at stake. Second, and less obvious but no less important than the point about pathological systems, is that adaptive misbeliefs are not mere flukes, malfunctions, or

---

[6] On "are (or were)": in their "Authors' Responses," McKay and Dennett (2009b: 550) admit to conflating "adaptive" with "adapted" or "evolved" in their target article, contending that misbeliefs that were adaptive in the evolutionary past but are not so today are of equal interest to them. In the rest of this chapter, I use the present tense.

by-products of a normal functioning system, but are the properly recurring outputs of that system, which functions as it was designed to do. Thus, the adaptive misbeliefs that interest the authors don't "reflect the wholesale failures of internal mechanisms to carry out their naturally selected functions,"[7] but are adaptive in their own right and not merely "carried along for the ride despite being useless or even harmless" (McKay and Dennett 2009b, 550).

McKay and Dennett (2009b, 550) nicely summarize these criteria for adaptive misbeliefs. An adaptive misbelief must be (1) a *bona fide* belief; (2) false, at least in part—as they say, it must at least exaggerate the truth; (3) adaptive or have been adaptive for its possessors; (4) biologically adaptive in the sense of enhancing the fitness for survival and reproduction of its possessor, and not only or necessarily psychologically beneficial; (5) produced by a normal functioning system; and (6) adaptive in a positively recurring way, not as a mere tolerable side-effect or by-product.

This is a rough and ready sketch of a much longer discussion. McKay and Dennett (2009a) discuss these criteria in some detail, then survey a series of candidates that might satisfy their criteria for adaptive misbeliefs, including, among others, beliefs in supernatural agency and self-deceptive beliefs. They settle on one class of misbeliefs, namely, positive illusions about oneself or loved ones. Here they draw, though not exclusively, on the work of psychologists Taylor and Brown (1988) and Taylor (1989). McKay and Dennett write:

A substantial body of research in recent decades . . . has challenged this view [that a cornerstone of mental health is close contact with reality], suggesting instead that optimal mental health is associated with *unrealistically positive* self-appraisals and beliefs. Taylor and colleagues (e.g., Taylor 1989; Taylor & Brown 1988) refer to such biased perceptions as "positive illusions," where an illusion is "a belief that departs from reality" (Taylor & Brown 1988, p. 194). Such illusions include unrealistically positive self-evaluations, exaggerated perceptions of personal control or mastery, and unrealistic optimism about the future.   (2009a: 505; emphasis theirs).[8]

---

[7] The authors qualify this point by noting that adaptive misbeliefs do not *directly* reflect the wholesale failures of internal mechanisms to carry out what they're designed to do, except for one interesting possibility (see 2009a: 501–2). They have in mind what they call "doxastic shear pins." Doxastic shear pins function analogously to shear pins in marine engines, which lock propellers to propeller shafts and are designed to break and release the propeller if it hits a hard object, thereby protecting more expensive equipment from being damaged. Shear pins function similarly to fuses, in that the latter are designed to break in order to prevent power surges from damaging the entire electrical system of a house. Doxastic shear pins, according to McKay and Dennett, are parts of belief evaluation machinery that are designed to "break" under psychological stress, thereby permitting the formation of comforting but false beliefs that an individual would otherwise not entertain, but embrace under stressful circumstances in order to control negative emotions, etc. For example, an individual's disposition to believe reliable testimony might "break" under the pressure of receiving news of the death of her child, thus allowing her to believe that he is alive, at least until she is able to get her emotions and coping abilities in order.

[8] McKay and Dennett are careful to distinguish the claim that optimal mental health is associated with unrealistically positive self-appraisals and beliefs from the more contested claim, also made by Taylor and Brown (1988), that "depressed individuals exhibit accurate perceptions and beliefs," and note that the latter phenomenon is known as depressive realism (2009b: 510, footnote 12).

Psychologists and philosophers have criticized Taylor and Brown's view. Psychologists Colvin and Block (1994) criticize Taylor and Brown (1988), concluding that the latter's thesis about positive illusions and mental health is borne out neither by their logic nor by their empirical evidence.[9] Philosophers, too, have entered the debate, criticizing Taylor and Brown (1988) on methodological as well as other grounds.[10] Thus, it bears noting that McKay and Dennett do not rely solely on Taylor and Brown's work, but buttress it with other studies that show (1) the pervasiveness of positive illusions; and (2) their adaptiveness in two respects: (a) as affecting deliberate actions; and (b) the direct effects they have on health.

Consider (1) pervasiveness. According to McKay and Dennett (2009a: 505), numerous studies reveal the "better-than-average effect"; that is, studies show that people believe they are better than average on a range of parameters, such as honesty, intelligence, and friendliness (see Alicke 1985). Most college students believe they'll have a longer than average lifespan, and most college professors believe they're better than average teachers (see Cross 1977). Most people, even those hospitalized for driving accidents, believe they're better than average drivers (see McKenna et al. 1991; Williams 2003). McKay and Dennett (2009a: 505) cite other studies, including several showing that most people see themselves as less liable to self-serving distortions than other people.

Now consider (2a), the effect of positive illusions on deliberate actions. In this regard, the authors make two points. First, they cite Taylor and Brown (1994), according to whom those with inflated perceptions of one's abilities are more likely to be successful than those with more modest self-perceptions (see McKay and Dennett 2009a, 505–6). Taylor and Brown (1994) quote, and presumably endorse, social-cognitivist Albert Bandura's view that the value of inflated perceptions of one's abilities lies in their motivational force. Those with inflated self-perceptions are more likely to undertake and, perhaps, succeed at tasks that challenge their actual abilities, whereas those with more realistic self-perceptions could lack the motivation to do so (see McKay and Dennett 2009a, 506). Haselton and Nettle (2006, 58), quoted in McKay and Dennett (2009a, 506), point out that if the evolutionary costs of trying and failing are low relative to the benefits of succeeding, then an illusional positive belief is better than either an illusional negative one or an unbiased belief. McKay and Dennett (2009a: 506) apply this logic to belief systems using the example of a fire alarm that is biased toward producing false alarms. A false alarm is better than the failure to detect a fire, but in and of itself, they say, it is no cause for celebration. They conclude, with one exception, that belief systems that generate misbeliefs about success produce them more as tolerable by-products than as adaptations. The exception is cases in which a misbelief about success motivates an individual to make greater gains than

---

[9] See Colvin and Block (1994), Taylor and Brown (1994)'s rejoinder, Block and Colvin (1994), and Colvin et al. (1995).
[10] See Badhwar (2008, 2014) and Flanagan (2007).

would have been possible without the misbelief—perhaps a person would not have won a bronze or silver medal, they argue, had he not falsely believed himself capable of getting the gold.

Interestingly, the best evidence the authors see for positive illusions directly affecting adaptive action occurs in cases of positive illusions about loved ones. The "better-than-average" effect shows up in people's beliefs about their partners. Among other studies, the authors report on Gagné and Lydon (2004), who found that 95 percent of participants rated their partners more positive than the average partner on intelligence, attractiveness, warmth, and sense of humor. Such biases, the authors note, can help to cement sexual relationships and provide a stable environment for the nurture of vulnerable infants. Biased appraisals of one's children, the authors observe, might facilitate parental care; they cite studies indicating systematic evidence of positive illusions in parenting. The "better-than-average" effect significantly predicted general parenting satisfaction (see McKay and Dennett 2009a, 506).

What about (2b), the direct effects that positive illusions have on health? McKay and Dennett (2009a, 506) cite studies by Taylor and others indicating that unrealistically positive illusions about one's medical condition and ability to influence it correlate with health and longevity. Taylor et al. (2000) speculated that positive illusions do this by reducing stress reactions; Taylor et al. (2003) found that "self-enhancing cognitions in healthy adults were associated with lower cardiovascular responses to stress, more rapid cardiovascular recovery, and lower baseline cortisol levels" (McKay and Dennett 2009a, 506).

I've belabored the overview of McKay and Dennett's view of adaptive misbeliefs in order to illustrate, if only briefly, the sophistication and complexity of their reasoning. I want to underscore two points in particular. First, though they rely on Taylor and Brown (1988) and Taylor (1989)'s work on adaptive misbeliefs, they bolster it with other studies. Second, they do not rush to embrace putative candidates for adaptive misbelief, but, instead, subject each case to thorough examination. The result, in my view, is a strong case for the likelihood that the adaptive misbeliefs that survive their critical scrutiny indeed satisfy their criteria.[11]

---

[11] Commentaries on McKay and Dennett's target article are divided. Some embrace and extend their view; for example, Sutton (2009: 535–7) and Boyer (2009: 513–14) argue that some false memories satisfy the criteria for adaptive misbeliefs; Sperber (2009: 534–5), that adaptive misbeliefs can be specific to cultures and culturally transmitted; and Brown (2009: 514–15), that social life fosters self-enhancing misbeliefs. Other commentators are more critical. For example, Dunning (2009: 517–18) argues that adaptive misbeliefs are often caused because environments fail to provide agents with the information needed to form accurate beliefs. Dweck (2009: 518–19), among other arguments, challenges the assumption that positive illusions are universal. She maintains that because different beliefs are adaptive in different cultures, evolution would have favored a readiness to believe, rather than specific classes of misbeliefs, as adaptive. Flanagan (2009: 519–20) argues that the class of alleged misbeliefs is a hodgepodge, such that many members of this class are not beliefs at all, but instead, "can-do" attitudes, hopes, etc. In like vein, Frankish (2009: 520–1) suggests that adaptive misbeliefs might not be beliefs, but pragmatic acceptances. To my mind, the arguments of neither Flanagan nor Frankish rule out the possibility that some members of the class of adaptive misbeliefs are genuine beliefs or have genuine belief-like components. Identifying

2.3 Epistemic Consequentialism and Adaptive Misbeliefs

How do adaptive misbeliefs bear on epistemic consequentialism? To answer this question, we need to go back to Berker. Berker (2013b) broadens construals of epistemic consequentialism to make them parallel more closely the structure of certain forms of ethical consequentialism, then raises problems for epistemic consequentialism by arguing from examples that are similar in some respects to certain cases of adaptive misbeliefs. Berker (2013b, 378) sees himself as offering a recipe for generating counterexamples to epistemic consequentialism that have a certain structure. The heart of these counterexamples is that they involve trade-offs among beliefs for the sake of aggregating epistemic value, such that a false belief can promote or conduce to many more true beliefs. Berker (2013b) argues that because of their countenancing trade-offs and aggregation, epistemic consequentialists are committed to maintaining that in such cases, holding a false belief can be justified, and can have epistemic value in virtue of conducing to greater epistemic good.

One of Berker's counterexamples resonates closely with a subset of adaptive misbeliefs—the case of Jane Doe—but to fully understand Jane's case, we need to examine the plight of her brother, John, also discussed by Berker. John Doe is a brilliant set theorist who is on the verge of proving the Continuum Hypothesis.[12] Sadly, John suffers from a disease that his doctors think will kill him in two months. John stubbornly clings to the belief that he will recover and live for the six months he needs to complete his work. This belief, Berker (2013b, 369) hypothesizes, causally contributes to John's staying alive and obtaining a large number of true beliefs about set theory. Consequently, he argues, the epistemic consequentialist is committed to saying that John's false belief is justified and has epistemic value.

Berker (2013b: 371–6) discusses and rejects several moves an epistemic consequentialist might make to avoid this conclusion, but the essential problem, he notes, is that epistemic consequentialism allows trade-offs across propositions in order to aggregate epistemic value. What this amounts to, he claims, is ignoring the separateness of propositions (see Berker 2013a). This is the epistemic analogue of ethical consequentialism's allowing trade-offs across persons, that is, countenancing situations in which some people are sacrificed or harmed for the sake of the greater good of the whole. Berker thinks that some epistemic consequentialists might modify their views to exclude trade-offs across propositions. Berker (2013b: 376–7) then gives us Jane Doe, John's sister, who is a brilliant chess master. Jane, too, has a disease that doctors think will kill her in two months and prevent her from playing in an important

---

the constitutive elements of adaptive misbeliefs, it seems to me, is an empirical matter, to be aided but not settled by philosophical arguments.

[12] See Berker (2013b: 369–72). He attributes the John Doe example to Roderick Firth (see Berker 2013b: 369).

chess tournament. Jane stubbornly believes she will recover in time to play, and this belief significantly raises the chances that she will recover. Jane's case does not allow a trade-off across propositions, but instead, "Jane's belief that she will recover promotes her being in a cognitive state which ... has the same propositional content as the state that promotes it" (Berker 2013b: 376). Berker (2013b: 376) argues that epistemic consequentialists must conclude that Jane's belief is epistemically justified, whereas he denies this.[13]

The problem that Jane's belief raises for epistemic consequentialism is not confined to an imaginative scenario, but is a pervasive fact of life. This is because Jane's belief is similar to a subset of adaptive misbeliefs that I call "game-changers." Suppose that misbeliefs about one's abilities (M) are the false and ungrounded products of the normal functioning of adaptive systems. M is game-changing if and only if M has either causal or constitutive roles in a process which is subsequent to the process by which M was originally generated. This subsequent process renders M true.

Like other adaptive misbeliefs, game-changing adaptive misbeliefs are produced by adaptive systems that generate them not as by-products, but as part of the normal operation of the systems. The beliefs are false and they are epistemically ungrounded. Candidates for game-changing adaptive misbeliefs include misbeliefs about oneself, e.g., about one's own abilities; misbeliefs about one's loved ones, e.g., that they are "better than average" in certain respects; and misbeliefs about one's health prospects. These three types of adaptive misbeliefs are "game-changing" in the sense that they can be parts of processes that result in true beliefs, specifically, processes that motivate the possessors of game-changing misbeliefs to transform facts about the world so as to render the misbeliefs true. The processes by means of which facts about the world are transformed are temporally subsequent to the processes that produce adaptive misbeliefs.

For example, suppose that I have a misbelief that I am a good swimmer, and this misbelief is part of a process that motivates me to go to a pool and jump in the water. As a result of going to a pool and jumping in the water, I learn that I am not a good swimmer, and am motivated to take swimming lessons and thereby learn to swim. Through these lessons, I become a good swimmer. The misbelief that I am a good swimmer is both causally and constitutively implicated in my coming to have the true belief that I am a good swimmer. It is causally implicated because it is part of a complex belief–desire set that motivates me to go to a pool and attempt to swim. It

---

[13] I have glossed over the specific arguments that Berker makes to justify his claims about trade-offs and aggregation for two reasons. The first is that I'm primarily interested in the larger issue of how epistemic value relates to other forms of value in the context of overall well-being—a point that Berker (2013b: 376) acknowledges but does not pursue when introducing Jane's case. Second, it seems to me that some epistemic consequentialists, most notably, Goldman, whose process reliabilism Berker (2013a, 2013b) targets, can argue that the processes by means of which the false beliefs are produced are unreliable (for example, wishful thinking), and thus not justification-conferring (see Goldman 2015). So not all epistemic consequentialists are forced to embrace the unpalatable conclusions that Berker seeks to foist upon them.

is constitutively implicated because its content is the same as or relevantly similar to that of the true belief that results from the process of my learning how to be a good swimmer. The process is a complex process by means of which the misbelief is part of a package that induces me to change a state of affairs in the world, namely, facts about my abilities as a swimmer. As a result of this process, the misbelief, in effect, becomes a true belief, in that it comes to correspond to a state of affairs in the world that I bring about.

We should note that the process by means of which I come to have the true belief that I am a good swimmer is not mere wishful thinking. Wishful thinking is just that—a cognitive state in which we wish that states of affairs obtain, but typically do nothing to bring those states of affairs about. In the case just described, my false belief that I am a good swimmer is part of a process in which I undertake a series of actions which eventually lead to the transformation of my abilities, and thus, to my belief's being true. I take it that at some point, when my belief about being a good swimmer actually tracks facts in the world, a prima facie case for its justification could be made according to some theory or other.

This does not imply that the initial misbelief is justified, even on the extreme versions of epistemic consequentialism that Berker (2013b: 375–7) considers in connection with Jane Doe's case. According to these extreme versions, "epistemic consequentialists should restrict the conducing relation in their theory of overall value so that an item in an evaluative focal point with a given propositional content only counts as conducing toward an epistemically valuable end if that epistemically valuable end *has the same propositional content*" (Berker 2013b: 375; emphasis his). His arguments, presumably, would apply to my swimmer case. Thus, even when an adaptive misbelief contributes to the process that renders it true, the trade-off in epistemic value doesn't justify the misbelief.

Is there a larger picture in terms of which a false and ungrounded belief, though epistemically unjustified, could be justified in terms of an increase in pragmatic value? To this question we now turn.

2.4 Trading Epistemic for Pragmatic Value: Implications for Epistemic Responsibility

The foregoing discussion about epistemic value is part of a larger story. We are agents as well as knowers. Our lives exhibit multiple kinds of value, which contribute to and partly constitute our overall well-being. In the cases of adaptive misbeliefs that we've encountered, a person might have pragmatic reasons for holding a false and ungrounded belief. That is, she might trade epistemic value for the sake of pragmatic value, and doing so might enhance her overall well-being by enabling her to be a more effective agent. In the discussion that follows, I am interested in how we might epistemically judge a person who does this. Can someone who holds an adaptive misbelief sacrifice epistemic for pragmatic value and still be considered epistemically responsible?

2.4.1 Caveats, framing principles, and epistemic responsibility

I make two caveats. First, McKay and Dennett (2009a, 2009b) argue that adaptive misbeliefs are "adaptive" in the sense of contributing to biological survival and reproduction. Typically, conceptions of human well-being go well beyond merely surviving and reproducing to include such desiderata as psychological well-being, life satisfaction, subjective well-being or feelings of contentment, objective achievements, fulfilling relationships, material well-being, and so on. What is interesting about adaptive misbeliefs is that they contribute not only to our biological fitness, but also to our psychological and agential fitness; that is, they can enable us to be more effective agents than we would be did we not hold the misbeliefs. In short, they can enable us to have greater functionality as agents in the world, even though epistemologists would, at least at first glance, say that having them detracts from our being responsible knowers, and thus should be avoided.

My second caveat follows from this last point. I do not prescribe the holding of adaptive misbeliefs, other things being equal. That is, I would not say that, other things being equal, if holding a misbelief M enables S to be an effective agent in the world, then S should hold M. S or any agent should seek to be an effective agent in the world on the basis of true and grounded beliefs. Thus, it is not the case that S's effectiveness as an agent should be purchased at the price of her status as a responsible knower. All things considered, conflicts between pragmatic and epistemic value should be avoided when possible. If McKay and Dennett (2009a, 2009b) are correct, however, and adaptive misbeliefs are pervasive, other things are not always equal and conflicts between pragmatic and epistemic value cannot always be avoided. It seems that, de facto, many of us already hold adaptive misbeliefs, and doing so can be pragmatically advantageous for us.

In what follows, then, I take the following as a normative framing principle, which tells us how we should think about value:

P1: Other things being equal, it is better for a person to have an overall conception of well-being in which different types of potentially competing values are well ordered and not conflicting. In other words, other things being equal, it is better for a person to have an overall conception of well-being in which values are seamlessly integrated.

I also endorse a practical corollary of P1, which specifies one way of attaining the seamless integration of values that P1 advises:

C1: Other things being equal, it is better if a person's effective agency is based on true beliefs that are grounded than on misbeliefs that are false and ungrounded.

How can we motivate P1 and C1; that is, what reasons do we have for accepting them as framing principles? P1 advises conflict avoidance among values. What's wrong with conflict? In its favor, we can say that conflict can sometimes be rewarding, forcing us to think through our commitments more deeply, putting us in cognitive/affective states of creative tension, and provoking us out of possible complacency about how we live our lives. On the other side, conflict can be annoying and costly. It can force us into states of uncomfortable cognitive dissonance, which in turn tempt us to indulge in sloppy thinking not for the sake of deeper understanding, but simply to relieve our discomfort. Conflict can also cause us to engage in ruminations about what we value and how highly we value it that are time-consuming and carry opportunity costs, that is, costs that are incurred by missing opportunities to engage in valuable activities that we might have pursued had we not been trying to resolve value conflicts. This is where the *ceteris paribus* clause does some work. If conflicts among values are beneficial, we might have good reason not to avoid them, at least, not at all costs. But when they are too costly or counterproductive, we have good reason to avoid them. In general, living a life free of serious conflicts among values is part of what it means to live a well-ordered life, and, other things being equal, a well-ordered life is conducive to effective functioning in the world.

Someone might point out that P1 gives us a reason to avoid conflict by holding false and ungrounded beliefs. In effect, the objection goes, we should achieve the seamless integration advised by P1 by sacrificing epistemic value. But C1 precludes this. C1 is a corollary of P1 because it stipulates that, when possible with respect to agency, pragmatic and epistemic value should be aligned. Our actions should be based on true beliefs about the world. Why? Kornblith (2002: chapter 5) provides an answer. In an interesting discussion of epistemic normativity, he makes a case for the distinctiveness and importance of epistemic evaluation among the many kinds of evaluations we make, and argues that truth must have a pre-eminent role in epistemic evaluations for pragmatic reasons. Because we care about achieving other values in our lives, such as happiness, we have pragmatic reasons for making accurate evaluations in those domains. Since truth is conducive to accuracy, "it is for pragmatic reasons that truth takes on the importance it does in epistemic evaluation" (Kornblith 2002, 161). Our interest in effective agency is an interest in accuracy with respect to our actions. We care about actually having values in our lives, and about actually attaining value-relevant goals, not just believing, perhaps falsely, that we have those values in our lives and attain value-relevant goals. Because of this, we have pragmatic reasons for wanting our actions to be effective in achieving our goals. Since true belief is accurate and false belief is not, we have an interest, *ceteris paribus*, in basing our actions on true belief. Here again, the *ceteris paribus* clause does some work, alerting us to possible situations in which we might have pragmatic reasons for basing our actions on false beliefs.

If we use P1 and C1 to frame our discussion, we need to investigate cases in which agents hold adaptive misbeliefs for pragmatic reasons; that is, cases in which agents countenance trade-offs between epistemic values, such as knowledge, truth, and accuracy, and pragmatic value for the sake of the pragmatic. An examination of cases of adaptive misbeliefs will allow us to make some generalizations concerning three kinds of case: (1) those in which holding an adaptive misbelief is epistemically irresponsible; (2) those in which a lack of cognitive competence with respect to a class of beliefs with a certain content renders a knower incapable of being held epistemically responsible or irresponsible for an adaptive misbelief with that content; and (3) those in which holding an adaptive misbelief is epistemically irresponsible, yet forgivable.

Before beginning our discussion, a brief word contrasting the characteristics of a responsible with those of an irresponsible knower is in order. First of all, cognitive competence is a necessary condition of a knower's being held epistemically responsible. I forgo pursuing the questions of whether it is the only necessary condition, or a necessary and sufficient condition. I do, however, find it plausible to think that circumstances can render a knower cognitively incompetent in some respects, but not in others. In other words, a knower can be locally, but not globally, cognitively incompetent, and this fact has implications for how we assess her epistemic responsibility for holding adaptive misbeliefs. I discuss an example of this in section 2.4.2.

Assuming that a knower is cognitively competent, what makes her responsible or irresponsible? The answer depends on the epistemological theory one holds. For example, epistemologists who are deontologically inclined would say that responsible knowers respect epistemic duties to hold true or justified beliefs—i.e., what is epistemically "right,"—and are irresponsible when they neglect or violate those duties.[14] Reliabilists don't seem to have a standard view about epistemic responsibility, though, in general, beliefs are justified so long as they're the products of a reliable process, whether the knower cares whether the process is reliable or not.[15] In responsibilist versions of virtue epistemology, responsible knowers are typically deemed to possess epistemic or intellectual virtues, such as humility, perseverance, curiosity, thoroughness, a desire for knowledge, and a high regard for truth.[16] Irresponsible knowers lack these virtues and perhaps even possess corresponding vices, such as intellectual arrogance or presumptuousness, a tendency to give up easily, intellectual laziness or torpor, a tendency to not be thorough and to settle for hasty generalizations, a proclivity for easy ignorance, and a disregard for truth.[17]

---

[14] Berker (2013a) makes a case for epistemic deontology.
[15] I am grateful to Jeffrey Dunn for making this point.
[16] See, for example, Code (1987), Zagzebski (1996), and Baehr (2011).
[17] Debates have occurred about whether epistemic virtues are enduring and global, that is, are deeply entrenched character traits that are regularly manifested in behavior across a wide variety of situation-types, or are local and situation-specific. See, e.g., Alfano (2012; 2013, chapter 5), King (2014), and Pritchard (2014). If epistemic virtues are global, then an intellectually humble person, for example, should display humility across a variety of situation-types—when investigating quantum physics as well as when checking train schedules. If they are local traits, then we should expect empirical evidence that people are intellectually humble only when studying quantum physics, but not in other contexts, such as when checking train schedules, remembering birthdays, etc. These debates parallel in some respects the situationist debate in ethics. On the situationist debate in ethics, see Snow (2010). There I argue for the globality of moral virtues, maintaining that we can, with effort, extend virtues that are initially local so they

As we'll see in a moment, breaches of epistemic duty, reliance on epistemically unreliable processes, and epistemic vices are implicated in some cases of adaptive misbeliefs. Moral vices or weaknesses could also be implicated, as when, for example, an insecure individual cannot face hard truths about her failings, and so opts for the easy course of ignoring or denying them. In such a case the epistemic vice of willful ignorance is rooted in deeper personality flaws. The person might not be able to believe certain propositions about herself for reasons that relate to her personality, upbringing, self-conception, abilities, and so on, and stubbornly clings to her misbelief despite being confronted with corrective evidence. Such cases of adaptive misbelief are prima facie evidence of a version of epistemic blind spots that parallels moral blind spots.[18]

2.4.2 Three cases of non-game-changing adaptive misbeliefs

Let us start with a case of non-game-changing adaptive misbelief that has a high pragmatic value relative to its epistemic value. Let's assume that Jack, who is cognitively competent, falsely believes that he is fit, strong, agile, etc., whereas in reality he is flabby, weak, and clumsy. This false belief gives Jack a certain confidence in his physical abilities that is epistemically unwarranted. His confidence proves pragmatically valuable, however, as it enables him to fend off a surprise attacker who otherwise would have killed him.

This example illustrates a general point: sometimes the pragmatic value of a misbelief is the *sine qua non* of its possessor's having any other kind of value, epistemic or otherwise, in her life.[19] Let us say that in this kind of case, the adaptive misbelief is the *sine qua non* of its possessor's having future global value, that is, value in any and all areas of his life, as opposed to having future local value, that is, value in some restricted area or domain. In effect, this argument turns Kornblith's (2002, chapter 5) point about the value of epistemic normativity on its head: though epistemic value is required for accuracy and, thus, success in achieving other values, there are occasions on which pragmatic value is necessary for the continued attainment of epistemic (or any other kind of) value.

The example is a case in which Jack's holding an adaptive misbelief affects his overall psychology in a way that enhances his physical survival. If we admit this case, we are on a spectrum (some might call it a slippery slope) of considering other cases

---

become globalized. I believe similar arguments extend to epistemic virtues, though I will not defend this claim here.

[18] An epistemic blind spot is "a consistent but inaccessible proposition" (Sorensen, 2014, accessed 7/4/15). Moral blind spots are cases in which an otherwise morally responsible person acts immorally or possesses immoral attitudes, yet is blind to these moral failings. For example, an otherwise moral man might be condescending toward women in his profession. He is unable to see them as professional equals and, blind to this failing, falsely believes that he is simply giving women their due. Even when his vice is pointed out to him, he stubbornly refuses to believe he is in the wrong.

[19] I take it this is obvious: if Jack is dead, he will be unable to have any value in his life.

in which the pragmatic value of holding an adaptive misbelief is the *sine qua non* for attaining other kinds of value. Consider Sue, whose son has been killed in a plane crash over the South China Sea. Upon hearing this news, Sue is crushed, and experiences disorientation, emotional trauma, and extreme distress. Despite the reliable testimony of experts, Sue refuses to believe her son is dead, and instead stubbornly clings to the false belief that he survived the crash. Sue's misbelief can be considered adaptive, since it provides her with the psychological wherewithal to survive an otherwise devastating emotional trauma. According to McKay and Dennett (2009a, 501–2), Sue's refusal to believe reliable testimony about her son's fate functions as a kind of "doxastic shear pin"; that is, her usual tendency to believe reliable testimony "breaks" under pressure in the circumstances in order to prevent her entire system from being severely damaged (see note 7). If so, the misbelief that her son is alive is part of a larger set of misbeliefs and refusals to believe that enable her to psychologically withstand the trauma, and is, consequently, a *sine qua non* of her continued ability to function psychologically and to have value in her life.

In both of these cases, adaptive misbeliefs function within the overall psychology of the agent to enhance his or her chances of survival and the continued attainment of global value. Yet our judgments of the epistemic responsibility of the knowers should diverge.

Jack's case illustrates (1), mentioned above: cases in which holding an adaptive misbelief is epistemically irresponsible. It is hard to see how Jack can be considered anything other than epistemically irresponsible for holding his misbelief, no matter the theory of epistemic responsibility one holds. (The possible exception for this case and for all of those we'll consider is epistemic consequentialism as Berker conceives of it, namely, as allowing for trade-offs among false and true beliefs when holding false beliefs leads to an overall gain in epistemic value.) It is also hard to see how one could judge Jack's misbelief to be forgivable. This is because his misbelief is formed independently of the specific circumstances under which it yields such high pragmatic value and under which it functions as a bridge to the continued attainment of other kinds of value. The fact that Jack's misbelief functions as it does is really just a fluke: Jack could not have known he would be attacked, and thus did not hold his misbelief as a precaution for that event. One might be tempted to claim that I am judging Jack's misbelief too harshly. Had he undertaken an exercise regimen, it might be argued, he would have been in much the same situation vis-à-vis the attack, in the sense that he would not likely have undertaken to become fit for the sake of fending off a possible attacker, yet his fitness would have helped him in the circumstances. Since we would have no reason to judge Jack's exercise routine negatively, why judge his misbelief so negatively? After all, the misbelief parallels the role of his fitness regimen in fending off a surprise attacker. Both rescue Jack in the circumstances and make future value possible for him.

The answer is that Jack's exercise regimen is not disvaluable in itself nor productive of disvalue, other than the pain that is unavoidably required, in the case of the flabby, for gain. By contrast, his adaptive misbelief is disvaluable in itself and causes a potential conflict between epistemic and pragmatic value that could have been avoided had Jack undertaken an exercise regimen. The important point about his misbelief is that it was not the only means that could have enabled Jack to acquire the abilities needed to fend off his attacker. He could have developed those abilities in ways not involving any false beliefs, namely, by embracing the facts about his lack of physical fitness and undertaking the exercise regimen needed to toughen up. Had Jack done so, he would not be in a situation of potential conflict among epistemic and pragmatic value. Since Jack had an alternative means of creating the conditions under which he could fend off attack that did not involve misbelief and the creation of potential conflict among values, his holding a misbelief violates P1 and C1, though holding it in fact allowed Jack to overcome his attacker and thus was a necessary condition of his attainment of future value in his life. Because, according to P1 and C1, "other things were not equal" in Jack's case, we cannot judge his holding his misbelief to be epistemically irresponsible but forgivable, notwithstanding the continued value that holding it allows him to attain.

Contrast Sue's case with Jack's. I take the example of Sue to illustrate (2), mentioned above: cases in which a lack of cognitive competence with respect to a class of beliefs with a certain content renders a knower incapable of being held epistemically responsible or irresponsible with respect to adaptive misbeliefs with that content. Sue, unlike Jack, cannot be held epistemically responsible for holding her misbelief, for her psychological condition at the time she forms the misbelief is one of disorientation and severe emotional trauma. In a very real sense, she is not herself, and is not, at the time she receives the news of the plane crash, cognitively fit to be able to form true or justified beliefs, at least not about her son, and thus cannot be held epistemically responsible for holding the beliefs she forms. If she does not satisfy the conditions for holding a knower epistemically responsible, she cannot be judged epistemically irresponsible for holding her adaptive misbelief about her son. Though I have not spelled out in detail the conditions under which a knower can be held epistemically responsible, it seems clear that she needs to be cognitively competent, that is, her relevant cognitive systems must be in good working order. As with moral responsibility, a person cannot be held epistemically responsible if she suffers from permanent or temporary cognitive impairment. Of course, the conditions causing the impairment make a difference for attributions of responsibility. If a person, while cognitively fit, knowingly ingests hallucinogenic drugs or becomes drunk and her cognitive abilities are thereby temporarily impaired, we hold her responsible for those choices as well as for her behavior and the beliefs she forms while in the impaired state. But this is not the case with Sue. Sue is dealt a powerful psychological blow, one that knocks her cognitive systems off track, so to speak.

If so, then an epistemic deontologist would not judge Sue irresponsible for failing to respect her epistemic duty of forming true and justified beliefs (at least in the case of her son), since the cognitive conditions needed for her to do that have, through no fault of her own, been impaired. Berker-type epistemic consequentialists (who countenance trade-offs between false and true beliefs for the sake of overall gains in epistemic value) could not fault her at all, since by holding her false belief she is able to carry on and continue to attain epistemic value.[20] In addition, she could not be accused of epistemic vice by virtue epistemologists. Process reliabilists would follow suit, saying that her otherwise reliable epistemic processes have been disrupted. If not all of her processes have been impaired, but only those relating to the fate of her son, the trauma has induced a region of epistemic blind spots. But she cannot be held responsible for these, and could be held responsible only if, after beginning to emerge from her emotional trauma, she stubbornly clung to her misbelief by willfully denying facts that she is increasingly competent to take in.

Can we generalize from the examples of Jack and Sue? Generalizing from Jack's case seems straightforward. If we can judge a cognitively competent agent epistemically irresponsible for holding an adaptive misbelief without which he would be unable to attain any other kind of value, it would seem that we should deem any other cognitively competent agent epistemically irresponsible for holding an adaptive misbelief that makes the less extensive, local attainment of value possible. So, for example, if I am cognitively competent yet have adaptive misbeliefs about my own abilities as a speaker, it seems that I am epistemically irresponsible for holding those adaptive misbeliefs, even if by holding them I make local gains in pragmatic value. This is because I have the ability and the option of holding justified true beliefs and working to improve my abilities, thereby gaining pragmatic value without sacrificing epistemic value in order to do so. In general, in cases of cognitively competent individuals, the *ceteris paribus* clauses of P1 and C1 aren't satisfied, so they cannot be excused of epistemic responsibility for holding an adaptive misbelief for pragmatic reasons.

Generalizing from Sue's case also seems straightforward. If a knower is innocently cognitively incompetent (cognitively incompetent through no fault of her own) with respect to a class of beliefs having a certain content, and an adaptive misbelief falls within this class, and the misbelief is such that, did she not hold it, she would be unable to attain any pragmatic or other kinds of value, it would seem that she does not meet the conditions for being held epistemically responsible or irresponsible with respect to that misbelief. In such cases, whether the value to be attained by holding the misbelief is extensive or global—affecting any value she might subsequently be able to attain—or less than global is beside the point. If cognitive competence is innocently lacking, a knower cannot be held responsible for holding a misbelief that enables her to attain either global or less than global value. Innocent cognitive incompetence, that is, cognitive incompetence brought about through no fault of the knower, with respect to a certain content-specific class of beliefs or misbeliefs is a condition that excuses one from being held epistemically responsible or irresponsible with respect to that class.

[20] Thanks to Jeffrey Dunn for making this point.

There is a third kind of case that we need to examine, one which parallels Sue's case in some respects, except that the knower who holds an adaptive misbelief that enables her to attain pragmatic or other kinds of value is cognitively competent. This case illustrates (3), mentioned above: cases in which holding an adaptive misbelief is epistemically irresponsible, yet forgivable. Consider Tanya. Tanya is a single mother who is struggling to raise three small children. Tanya learns that the eldest of her children, Thomas, is diagnosed with leukemia. On the basis of excellent medical evidence, the doctors give Thomas three months to live. Tanya stubbornly refuses to believe that he will die, and this adaptive misbelief that Thomas will recover gives her the strength to continue working, drawing a paycheck, caring for her other children, and caring for Thomas. Upon hearing the news of Thomas's prognosis, Tanya does not succumb to paralyzing emotional distress, as did Sue. Tanya does not consider herself to have the luxury of "shutting down" psychologically—she considers that she must carry on for the sake of her three children. Yet she can do so only by refusing to believe Thomas's bleak prognosis.

Tanya is cognitively capable of believing the bad news about Thomas, but "blocks it out" for the sake of maintaining emotional strength. Arguably, what Tanya is doing is epistemically irresponsible, for she is deliberately shutting down her cognitive capacities with respect to a certain class of beliefs—those pertaining to Thomas's chances for recovery—misbelieving, instead, that he will recover. Since she is cognitively competent, she can be held responsible for her misbelief and cannot be excused for holding it. She can, however, be forgiven. The reasons why her misbelief can be forgiven, I take it, need not be spelled out in great detail. Like the rest of us, Tanya is a finite human being. Her adaptive misbelief enables her to do the best she can in dire straits. It enables her to continue functioning as a responsible, loving mother. Unlike Jack's misbelief about his physical prowess, Tanya's misbelief was not formed in a frivolous way, but develops as an immediate response to a crisis in which Tanya must continue to be an effective agent. Tanya's misbelief is motivated by the need to carry on and care for her children, whereas Jack's misbelief, not formed in dire straits, luckily serves the purpose of enabling him to survive. If Tanya were psychologically stronger, she might not need to rely on her adaptive misbelief. But, being only human, the misbelief helps her to function in important ways that are life-sustaining for her and her children, and is thus pragmatically valuable. It helps her to block out information that would unsettle her, render her unable to cope with her plight, and leave her and her children materially and emotionally adrift.[21]

One might say that Tanya should seek medication that would strengthen her and allow her to function while holding the justified belief that Thomas is unlikely to survive. Doing this would bring her case closer to our analysis of Jack's as regards his exercise regimen, though there is an important difference. In Jack's case, exercise

---

[21] This analysis parallels to some extent Pettit (2004)'s analysis of substantive hope as giving its possessor cognitive resolve.

changes facts about the world to render his misbelief about his physical prowess true. In Tanya's case, taking medication would change facts about herself to enable her to take on board the hard truth about another. The fact that Tanya does not do this is yet another reason for judging her to be epistemically irresponsible. Can we forgive her for not doing this? Given her circumstances, I am inclined to say "yes." Perhaps she cannot afford a doctor or the prescription, the drug has unpalatable side effects, such as making her drowsy or foggy when she needs to be alert, she does not want to become addicted, and so on. The point in Tanya's case is that there are situations in which we can understand human frailties, and so can forgive people who are cognitively competent yet, motivated by the need to carry on, refuse to believe hard truths that would debilitate their agency. As with the cases of Jack and Sue, Tanya's case can be generalized, thereby delineating a third class of adaptive misbeliefs about which judgments of possessors' epistemic responsibility can be made.

2.4.3 Game-changing adaptive misbeliefs

Do game-changing adaptive misbeliefs change this evaluative landscape? It seems to me they do not. A slight change in Jack's case shows this. Suppose that, instead of holding general misbeliefs about his physical prowess, Jack holds the specific misbelief that he is fit enough to fend off a surprise attacker, that he is indeed attacked, and that this specific misbelief gives him the confidence to survive the attack. Jack's specific misbelief is game-changing in the sense that it contributes to a process by means of which Jack's actions change states of affairs to render the misbelief a true belief. The value of this true belief, and, presumably, the value-producing role of the corresponding misbelief in conducing to the changes that render it true, must be added into the sum total of the global value that will now accrue to Jack. But why should this accretion of value make a difference to our evaluation of Jack's misbelief? If Jack had the option at some earlier time of creating conditions under which he could survive a surprise attack without incurring the disvalue of holding false beliefs and thereby creating potential conflicts between epistemic and pragmatic value, P1 and C1 are violated. The gist of the argument for a positive evaluation of game-changing adaptive misbeliefs is that the end justifies the means; that is, the fact that they contribute to processes by which they're rendered true beliefs justifies the agent's holding the misbeliefs in the first place. However, if agents have the option of achieving the overall valued end, whatever it might be—fending off a surprise attack, becoming a good speaker, etc.—without holding a misbelief and thereby incurring disvalue and creating conflicts between values, they should, other things being equal, do so.

Our evaluation of Tanya's misbeliefs should not be altered if they become game-changers. Suppose that her misbeliefs about Thomas's recovery induce optimism, hope, and other positive attitudes on his part, help him to maintain a rigorous treatment regimen, and the disease goes into remission. Her misbeliefs thereby become part of a process by means of which Thomas's psychophysical state is strengthened and he recovers. This process renders Tanya's misbeliefs true. Whether or not one regards this as a plausible scenario, the point is that we would not evaluate Tanya's misbeliefs differently in the event that they were to become game-changing. Tanya is a cognitively competent agent who is responsible for her beliefs, she has the option to take medication that would allow her to function and to hold true beliefs about her son's chances of recovering but chooses not to, and she is under severe duress such that her holding adaptive misbeliefs pertaining to her son's recovery is forgivable. Should these misbeliefs become game-changing, P1 and C1 are nonetheless violated. Tanya's forgivable adaptive misbeliefs are not *ex post facto* rendered permissible, and her holding of them epistemically responsible, by their contributing to a process whereby they become true.

To see more clearly the thrust of my arguments with regard to Jack and Tanya, consider familiar parallels of action assessments. Suppose that Mark ardently wants his daughter to get into a good college. To attain that end, Mark bribes an admissions counselor. Few ethical theories (act utilitarianism is a possible exception) would evaluate this action as the morally permissible act of a responsible agent, especially if Mark has other means of procuring this end, such as encouraging his daughter to study, paying for tutoring lessons, and so on. Even rule consequentialists would judge this act as wrong, given that no general rule allowing such actions would maximize utility. In general, the end does not justify the means with respect to immoral actions or false beliefs, especially when moral or neutral actions or justified or true beliefs are options for the agent or knower.

Mark's case parallels Jack's. Ethical cases paralleling Tanya's are a bit trickier. If the only way that Janet, for example, can save a shipload of immigrants is by killing the despotic captain, consequentialists would judge this act as morally right. Deontologists and virtue ethicists would deem it wrong, but perhaps necessary. I opt for this latter route, and apply that evaluation to Tanya's adaptive misbeliefs. Why go this route instead of taking the consequentialist tack? It seems to me that what consequentialism misses is an acknowledgement of the gravity of situations in which agents are forced to kill or pressured into holding false beliefs for the sake of their own or others' survival. Graver cases are, for consequentialism, structurally and evaluatively similar to cases like Mark's, in which there is no urgency or pressure to perform an act which, on theories other than (act) consequentialism, is deemed morally wrong. In such cases, consequentialism either fails to acknowledge or, at best, inadequately registers the pressures that life can put on agents and their actions. Similarly, in cases of misbeliefs, consequentialist analyses fail to do justice to the pressures that can lead otherwise responsible agents to hold adaptive misbeliefs. But it seems to me that life circumstances play important roles in how we evaluate agents, their actions, and their beliefs, and theoretical approaches that can take account of such factors are preferable to those that ignore or gloss over them.

What about Sue's misbelief? Even if we were to change the original example and say, for the sake of argument, that Sue is cognitively competent when she holds her misbelief about her son, that misbelief cannot be game-changing. Suppose that Sue's misbelief inspires her to travel to the South China Sea and undertake a search for her son. She discovers him alive and marooned on a small island. Her misbelief contributes to a process whereby she discovers that it was, in fact, true all along. It does not change facts in a way that renders it true. So it is not a game-changing misbelief.

2.5 Conclusion

In this chapter, I've explored the implications of adaptive misbeliefs for debates about epistemic and pragmatic value. In section 2.2, I introduced readers to McKay and Dennett's (2009a, 2009b) account of adaptive misbeliefs, and in section 2.3 related a subset of adaptive misbeliefs, game-changing misbeliefs, to Berker's (2013a, 2013b) critique of epistemic consequentialism. In section 2.4, I broadened the outlook to encompass possible conflicts and trade-offs between epistemic and pragmatic value occasioned by adaptive misbeliefs and their implications for evaluations of epistemic responsibility. In a nutshell my conclusion about such trade-offs is this: the end of greater value does not justify the means of adaptive misbelief, even when adaptive misbeliefs are game-changing. This is true when the gains in value would be exclusively epistemic, as well as when the gains would be in pragmatic as opposed to epistemic value. That said, there are serious situations in which a person's holding an adaptive belief, though epistemically irresponsible, is forgivable.[22]

References

Ahlstrom-Vij, Kristoffer and Jeffrey Dunn. 2014. "A Defence of Epistemic Consequentialism." *Philosophical Quarterly* 64: 541–51.
Alfano, Mark. 2012. "Expanding the Situationist Challenge to Responsibilist Virtue Epistemology." *The Philosophical Quarterly* 62(147): 224–49.
Alfano, Mark. 2013. *Character as Moral Fiction*. Cambridge: Cambridge University Press.
Alicke, M. D. 1985. "Global Self-Evaluation as Determined by the Desirability and Controllability of Trait Adjectives." *Journal of Personality and Social Psychology* 49: 1621–30.
Badhwar, Neera K. 2008. "Is Realism Really Bad for You? A Realistic Response." *The Journal of Philosophy* 105(2): 85–107.
Badhwar, Neera K. 2014. *Well-Being: Happiness in a Worthwhile Life*. New York: Oxford University Press.
Baehr, Jason. 2011. *The Inquiring Mind: On Intellectual Virtues and Virtue Epistemology*. Oxford: Oxford University Press.
Berker, Selim. 2013a. "Epistemic Teleology and the Separateness of Propositions." *Philosophical Review* 122(3): 337–93.

---

[22] I am grateful to Jeffrey Dunn for invaluable comments on an earlier version of this chapter.

Berker, Selim. 2013b. "The Rejection of Epistemic Consequentialism." *Philosophical Issues* 23: 363–87.

Berker, Selim. 2015. "Reply to Goldman: Cutting up the One to Save the Five in Epistemology." *Episteme* 12(2): 145–53.

Block, Jack and C. Randall Colvin. 1994. "Positive Illusions and Well-Being Revisited: Separating Fiction from Fact." *Psychological Bulletin* 116(1): 21–7.

Boyer, Pascal. 2009. "Extending the Range of Adaptive Misbelief: Memory 'Distortions' as Functional Features." *Brain and Behavioral Sciences* 32: 513–14.

Brown, Jonathon D. 2009. "Positive Illusions and Positive Collusions: How Social Life Abets Self-Enhancing Beliefs." *Brain and Behavioral Sciences* 32: 514–15.

Code, Lorraine. 1987. *Epistemic Responsibility*. Hanover, NH and London: University Press of New England.

Colvin, C. Randall and Jack Block. 1994. "Do Positive Illusions Foster Mental Health? An Examination of the Taylor and Brown Formulation." *Psychological Bulletin* 116(1): 3–20.

Colvin, C. Randall, Jack Block, and David C. Funder. 1995. "Overly Positive Self-Evaluations and Personality: Negative Implications for Mental Health." *Journal of Personality and Social Psychology* 68(6): 1152–62.

Cross, P. 1977. "Not Can but Will College Teaching Be Improved?" *New Directions for Higher Education* 17: 1–15.

Dunning, David. 2009. "Misbelief and the Neglect of Environmental Context." *Brain and Behavioral Sciences* 32: 517–18.

Dweck, Carol. 2009. "Why We Don't Need Built-In Misbeliefs." *Brain and Behavioral Sciences* 32: 518–19.

Flanagan, Owen. 2007. *The Really Hard Problem: Meaning in a Material World*. Cambridge, MA: MIT Press.

Flanagan, Owen. 2009. "'Can Do' Attitudes: Some Positive Illusions Are Not Misbeliefs." *Brain and Behavioral Sciences* 32: 519–20.

Frankish, Keith. 2009. "Adaptive Misbelief or Judicious Pragmatic Acceptance?" *Brain and Behavioral Sciences* 32: 520–1.

Gagné, F. M. and J. E. Lydon. 2004. "Bias and Accuracy in Close Relationships: An Integrative Review." *Personality and Social Psychology Review* 8(4): 322–38.

Goldman, Alvin I. 2015. "Reliabilism, Veritism, and Epistemic Consequentialism." *Episteme* 12(2): 131–43.

Haselton, M. G. and D. Nettle. 2006. "The Paranoid Optimist: An Integrative Evolutionary Model of Cognitive Biases." *Personality and Social Psychology Review* 10(1): 47–66.

Hazlett, Allan. 2013. *A Luxury of the Understanding: On the Value of True Belief*. Oxford: Oxford University Press.

King, Nathan L. 2014. "Responsibilist Virtue Epistemology: A Reply to the Situationist Challenge." *The Philosophical Quarterly* 64(255): 243–53.

Kornblith, Hilary. 2002. *Knowledge and its Place in Nature*. Oxford: Clarendon Press.

Littlejohn, Clayton. 2010. "Epistemic Consequentialism (Tidied up just a Bit)." http://claytonlittlejohn.blogspot.com/2010/06/epistemic-consequentialism-tidied-up.html. Accessed February 16, 2015.

McKay, Ryan T. and Daniel C. Dennett. 2009a. "The Evolution of Misbelief." *Brain and Behavioral Sciences* 32: 493–510.

McKay, Ryan T. and Daniel C. Dennett. 2009b. "Authors' Responses." *Brain and Behavioral Sciences* 32: 541–61.

McKenna, F. P., R. A. Stanier, and C. Lewis. 1991. "Factors Underlying Illusory Self-Assessment of Driving Skill in Males and Females." *Accident Analysis and Prevention* 23(1): 45–52.

Pettit, Philip. 2004. "Hope and its Place in Mind." *Annals of the American Academy of Political and Social Science* 592: 152–65.

Pritchard, Duncan. 2014. "Re-evaluating the Situationist Challenge to Virtue Epistemology." In *Naturalizing Epistemic Virtue*, ed. Abrol Fairweather and Owen Flanagan, pp. 143–54. Cambridge: Cambridge University Press.

Snow, Nancy E. 2010. *Virtue as Social Intelligence: An Empirically Grounded Theory*. New York: Routledge.

Sorensen, Roy. 2014. "Epistemic Paradoxes." In *The Stanford Encyclopedia of Philosophy* (Spring 2014 Edition), ed. Edward N. Zalta. http://plato.stanford.edu/archives/spr2014/entries/epistemic-paradoxes/.

Sperber, Dan. 2009. "Culturally Transmitted Misbeliefs." *Brain and Behavioral Sciences* 32: 534–5.

Sutton, John. 2009. "Adaptive Misbeliefs and False Memories." *Brain and Behavioral Sciences* 32: 535–6.

Taylor, Shelley E. 1989. *Positive Illusions: Creative Self-Deception and the Healthy Mind*. New York: Basic Books.

Taylor, Shelley E. and Jonathan D. Brown. 1988. "Illusion and Well-Being: A Social Psychological Perspective on Mental Health." *Psychological Bulletin* 103(2): 193–210.

Taylor, Shelley E. and Jonathan D. Brown. 1994. "Positive Illusions and Well-Being Revisited: Separating Fact from Fiction." *Psychological Bulletin* 116(1): 21–7.

Taylor, Shelley E., M. E. Kemeny, G. M. Reed, J. E. Bower, and T. L. Gruenewald. 2000. "Psychological Resources, Positive Illusions, and Health." *American Psychologist* 55: 99–109.

Taylor, Shelley E., J. S. Lerner, D. K. Sherman, R. M. Sage, and N. K. McDowell. 2003. "Are Self-Enhancing Cognitions Associated with Healthy or Unhealthy Biological Profiles?" *Journal of Personality and Social Psychology* 85(4): 605–15.

Williams, A. F. 2003. "Views of US Drivers about Driving Safety." *Journal of Safety Research* 34 (5): 491–4.

Zagzebski, Linda Trinkaus. 1996. *Virtues of the Mind: An Inquiry into the Nature of Virtue and the Ethical Foundations of Knowledge*. Cambridge: Cambridge University Press.

3
The Naturalistic Origins of Epistemic Consequentialism

Hilary Kornblith

Reliabilism is a paradigm case of epistemic consequentialism. Just as the utilitarian begins with an account of the good (namely, pleasure), and then defines right action in terms of its relationship to the good, the reliabilist starts with an account of the epistemic good (namely, true belief) and defines right believing (or justification) in terms of its relationship to that good.[1] Within moral theory, we may ask not only about the details of one or another consequentialist theory, but why we should be consequentialists at all, rather than, say, deontologists or virtue theorists. Similar questions arise about epistemic consequentialism. In this chapter, I examine the motivations for one kind of epistemic consequentialism. That reliabilists have deep naturalistic commitments has been clear from the very beginning. In this chapter, I argue that these naturalistic commitments provide an important motivation for epistemic consequentialism.

3.1

When Alvin Goldman first presented his reliabilist account of epistemic justification in "What is Justified Belief?" (originally published in 1979), he began by introducing some constraints that his approach is meant to satisfy. As he remarked:

> I want a set of *substantive* conditions that specify when a belief is justified . . . I want a theory of justified belief to specify in non-epistemic terms when a belief is justified. This is not the only kind of theory of justification one might seek, but it is one important kind of theory and the kind sought here.   (Goldman 2012: 29–30)

Many might pass over these remarks today without any great notice, but this constraint is highly non-trivial, and it was even more controversial when Goldman wrote this paper than it is today.

---

[1] Indeed, this is the way in which Alvin Goldman introduces his reliabilist account of justification in the *locus classicus* of reliabilism, Goldman (2012: 29–30).

Thus, consider, for example, Roderick Chisholm's (1966, 1977, 1989) account of justification. Chisholm was, by far, the leading American epistemologist writing at the time, and his approach to epistemological issues was one that enjoyed very wide sympathy, as well as one that enjoyed universal recognition. Chisholm's epistemological theory presented a series of definitions of epistemic "terms of appraisal," but there was no attempt at all to satisfy Goldman's constraint that these should bottom out in any "substantive" conditions, characterizable in non-epistemic terms. Chisholm's account of epistemic terms of appraisal itself involved epistemic terminology from top to bottom. Goldman's approach was thus a very radical break with the Chisholmian tradition, a break embodied in this constraint presented on the very first page of "What Is Justified Belief?" before any of the details of his reliabilist account are articulated.

One might expect, therefore, that Goldman would offer an elaborate defense of this constraint, explaining why it is that an account of justification must ultimately be given in non-epistemic terms. But no such defense is offered. Goldman does comment:

The term "justified," I presume, is an evaluative term, a term of appraisal. Any correct definition or synonym of it would also feature evaluative terms. I assume that such definitions or synonyms might be given, but I am not interested in them.   (Goldman 2012: 29)

But this, of course, is no defense at all. Goldman merely announces that he wishes to develop an account of justification which will characterize it in wholly non-epistemic terms, and then he moves on to develop just such an account. For his readers, of course, this simply raises the question: Why should one feel the need for an account of justification in non-epistemic terms?

Goldman's allusion to synonyms for "justification," which would, as he remarks, inevitably themselves violate his constraint, suggests an answer. To say, for example, that a belief is justified just in case it is warranted, or reasonable, or some such thing, is wholly unilluminating. To the extent that these terms really are just synonyms for "justified," they offer no illumination of the phenomenon which a theory of justification seeks to understand. We need something more than just a synonym, or a set of synonyms, for "justification".

While these remarks are unexceptionable as far as they go, they certainly don't serve to motivate Goldman's constraint. Thus, for example, Chisholm did not simply offer a synonym for "justification," or a set of such synonyms. Rather, he sought to show how the notion of justification, and other epistemic terms, might be understood in terms of simpler epistemic notions. One might not be inspired by the Chisholmian project, but it is by no means trivial or unilluminating in the way that a list of synonyms is. So the fact that offering a list of synonyms for "justification" is philosophically unilluminating does not in any way suggest that we should abandon the Chisholmian project and look, instead, for an account of justification which honors the constraint which Goldman articulates.

What then is the motivation for Goldman's constraint? Although I cannot offer textual evidence for this, since Goldman himself says so little on its behalf, I do have a suggestion. Consider what Jerry Fodor has to say about the nature of intentionality:

> I suppose that sooner or later the physicists will complete the catalogue they've been compiling of the ultimate and irreducible properties of things. When they do, the likes of *spin*, *charm*, and *charge* will perhaps appear on their list. But *aboutness* surely won't; intentionality simply doesn't go that deep. It's hard to see, in face of this consideration, how one can be a Realist about intentionality without also being, to some extent or other, a Reductionist. If the semantic and the intentional are real properties of things, it must be in virtue of their identity with (or maybe their supervenience on?) properties that are themselves *neither* intentional *nor* semantic. If aboutness is real, it must be really something else. (Fodor 1987: 97)

One might, with equal justice, make the same remarks about the property of being justified. There is a real difference between beliefs which are justified and those which are not. A theory of justification should make sense of this difference. But just as we want to understand the place of intentionality in the physical world, since everything that exists is ultimately physically composed, we need to understand the place of justification in the physical world. Being justified is not one of the fundamental properties of things, in the way that, perhaps, spin, charge, and charm are. Nor are any of the other epistemic properties we might explain justification in terms of. What this means, however, is that any account of justification which locates it squarely within the natural world—that is, the only world there is—must explain justification in non-epistemic terms. To paraphrase Fodor: If epistemic properties are real, they must really be something else.

Fodor is appropriately cautious about the extent to which this idea commits him to reductionism. He says that one must, on this view, be, "to some extent or other," a reductionist. And he allows that an acceptable view need not identify intentional properties with physical properties; it may be that the intentional merely supervenes on the physical. Given Fodor's famous defense elsewhere (in Fodor 1981) of anti-reductionism, this is as it should be. To the extent that Goldman's view may be understood as motivated by similar concerns, then, it need not amount to a thoroughgoing reduction of epistemic notions to the non-epistemic, although that would certainly be acceptable. A proper account of justification, and other epistemic notions, however, must explain how they are rooted in the natural world.

Attributing such a motivation to Goldman certainly does not foist on him any kind of approach which is foreign to his deepest philosophical commitments. Goldman is rightly known, along with Quine,[2] as one of the foremost defenders of naturalistic epistemology. All I am suggesting here is that Goldman's insistence that an adequate theory of justification must be given in wholly non-epistemic terms flows directly from his naturalistic commitments.

---

[2] See especially Quine (1969).

3.2

There is one more constraint which Goldman insists on before getting down to the business of providing the substance of his account of justification: any acceptable account must be explanatory:

> Since I seek an explanatory theory, i.e., one that clarifies the underlying source of justificational status, it is not enough for a theory to state 'correct' necessary and sufficient conditions. Its conditions must also be appropriately deep or revelatory. (Goldman 2012: 30)

This insistence on an explanatory account is especially significant given the location of this work in the history of analytic epistemology. When Goldman began working in epistemology, the field was very much taken, as was Goldman himself, with developing a solution to the Gettier problem.[3] A good deal of the literature on the Gettier problem sought to develop necessary and sufficient conditions for knowledge which squared with our intuitions about hypothetical cases.[4] For much of this literature, it seemed that fitting our intuitions was, indeed, the only constraint on an account of knowledge. Many of the accounts offered were extraordinarily baroque, making the notion of knowledge look as if it had been cobbled together by a deeply divided committee, rather than being a theoretically unified phenomenon which might serve some genuinely explanatory purposes. Goldman's insistence that his account of justification and knowledge should be explanatory thus stood in sharp contrast to much of the other work going on in epistemology at the time.

There are a number of different ways in which one might develop this idea that an account of justification should be explanatory. Thus, consider Timothy Williamson's Knowledge First approach to epistemology, in which he attempts to show how it is that knowledge figures, quite centrally, in our everyday explanatory practices.[5] Although this is certainly not Williamson's idea, one might take a similar approach

---

[3] Goldman provides an interesting bit of philosophical history in his interview with Richard Marshall in Goldman (2015):

> Although *epistemology* proved to be my most enduring specialty, this hardly seemed inevitable at the start of my professional career. In fact, my doctoral dissertation (at Princeton) was on action theory, and I doubt that I even listed epistemology as a specialty when I entered the job market. However, as an assistant professor (at Michigan) I was called upon to teach epistemology, and inevitably (in that period) the course gave center stage to the Gettier problem. I formulated a novel approach to the subject during that course, and was then rapidly pulled into the field.

[4] For a useful review of this literature, see Shope (1983).

[5] See Williamson (2000). Of course, Williamson believes that the ways in which knowledge features in everyday explanations do not serve to give us an account of the necessary and sufficient conditions for knowledge. Indeed, Williamson believes that it is a mistake to look for such conditions. One might, however, endorse the idea that knowledge plays an important explanatory role, while also allowing that examining this role permits us to provide an account of the necessary and sufficient conditions for knowledge. I have defended exactly this approach in Kornblith (2002). For further discussion of the comparison between my approach and Williamson's, see Kornblith (2014a: 11).

to justification. In some ways, this would fit nicely with some of Goldman's concerns in "What Is Justified Belief?". As Goldman explains there:

> Unlike some traditional approaches, I do not try to prescribe standards for justification that differ from, or improve upon, our ordinary standards. I merely try to explicate the ordinary standards. (Goldman 2012: 29)

The appeal to everyday explanatory practices would certainly serve to advance our understanding of the ordinary standards Goldman alludes to. In later papers, Goldman would speak of this project as contributing to an understanding of our "epistemic folkways" (Goldman 1992).

There is another project which Goldman develops, however, beyond just explicating our epistemic folkways, which might be thought to fit better with a naturalistic approach to these issues. Thus, Goldman suggests that there is room for a "scientific epistemology," one which would provide a

> formulation of a more adequate, sound, or systematic set of epistemic norms, in some way(s) transcending our naïve epistemic repertoire. How and why these folkways might be transcended, or improved upon, remains to be specified... On my view, epistemic concepts like knowledge and justification crucially invoke psychological faculties or processes. Our folk understanding, however, has a limited and tenuous grasp of the processes available to the cognitive agent. Thus, one important respect in which epistemic folkways should be transcended is by incorporating a more detailed and empirically based depiction of psychological mechanisms.
> (Goldman 1992: 156)

A scientific epistemology might thus endorse epistemic practices which depart, in important ways, from the practices implicit in our everyday behavior.

Goldman's idea here seems to be that, given how little the folk know about the actual processes by which their beliefs are produced, and given the extent to which they are likely to have false beliefs about the reliability of various belief-producing processes, folk practice is likely to endorse as justification-conferring many belief-producing processes which are in fact unreliable. By drawing on work from the cognitive sciences, we may correct these misconceptions. A scientific epistemology would thus improve upon the standards implicit in our epistemic folkways.

While this conception of a scientific epistemology clearly identifies an interesting project, it is worth pointing out that there is one respect in which it simply takes on a certain part of our epistemic folkways. As Goldman conceives of it, an examination of our epistemic folkways reveals that our ordinary concept of justified belief turns out to be nothing more nor less than reliably produced belief. So the project of scientific epistemology, as Goldman seems to conceive of it, does not alter, or even reexamine, the folk concept of justification. What it does, instead, is correct certain misapplications of that concept by the folk. There is nothing especially scientific about the notion of justification which a scientific epistemology appeals to, on this view. Science enters in only to help us wield the folk concept more accurately.

I want to suggest another way of developing the idea of a scientific epistemology, however, one which takes seriously the idea that an account of justification should be explanatory, and which embeds it more fully in scientific epistemic practice. At this point, I will no longer be giving an account of anything Goldman is committed to, although I will argue that it fits well not only with Goldman's naturalistic orientation, but also with his reliabilist account of justified belief. And here, I want to draw on some ideas suggested by Stephen Stich (1993).

If you want to know what makes for a good basketball player, it makes sense to study the behavior of obviously good basketball players. If you want to know what makes for good chess play, it makes sense to study the behavior of obviously good chess players. And if you want to know what makes for good belief acquisition, it makes sense to study obviously good believers. In each of these cases, one will not go into one's investigation with no idea whatsoever about what makes for the good exemplars. In the case of basketball, one will surely recognize, in advance of any serious study, that good offense is relevant, and that involves scoring points, and good defense is relevant as well, and that involves preventing others from scoring points. And it is similar for these other activities. But the crude ideas one may have about what constitutes good examples of each kind, sufficient as they are for getting one's investigation started, are likely to be modified over the course of one's study.[6] Winning is obviously quite central to being a good chess player, but much as counting wins and losses is enough to provide a sample of excellent chess players for study, it wouldn't be surprising if, in the end, simple win/loss records did not suffice for determining chess playing ability. So one will start these investigations with a passable recognitional capacity for good exemplars, and some rough ideas about what makes for a good exemplar, but a full understanding of what constitutes good basketball play, or good chess playing, or good belief acquisition, will be the result of one's investigation, not something one has fully in hand before the investigation even starts.

If one wants to study good exemplars of belief acquisition, an obvious suggestion is that one should look to the ways in which scientific investigations are carried out. By studying the actual conduct of successful scientists—and here "conduct" includes the kinds of psychological processes which go on in the course of scientific theorizing and testing—one may well discover features of good epistemic practice which could not have been discovered from the armchair. In particular, one may well discover not only that there are ways of arriving at one's beliefs which actually meet one's pretheoretical

---

[6] I was reminded by an anonymous referee of the famous case of the Oakland Athletics, documented in Lewis (2003). Billy Beane, manager of the Athletics, discovered a number of different properties of baseball players that proved far more predictive of their value to a team than the ones which were traditionally examined. Those who follow sports carefully, and have a mind for statistics, have been much concerned with finding those properties of athletes that are both highly projectable and deeply revelatory of their value to their teams. The result has often been that statistical categories which seem at first blush to be highly gerrymandered turn out, instead, to be among the most projectable and revealing. The moral here, of course, is not one about sports in particular, but rather about inquiry in general.

conception of good belief acquisition, but which one had mistakenly thought did not answer to the conception; one may also find that one's pretheoretical conception of good belief acquisition ought to be modified in important ways. Our recognitional capacities for good exemplars, and our pretheoretical views about what make for good exemplars, allow us, after careful investigation, to develop more subtle and nuanced views about the nature of good examples of the kind.

At the same time, it is important to recognize that there are some limitations to just how transformative such an investigation is likely to be. Our conception of a good basketball player is, I believe, likely to undergo some real revision if we carefully study good examples of the kind, but we should not think that it is really very likely that scoring lots of points, and preventing one's opponent from scoring lots of points, is just irrelevant here. And the same is true, I believe, in investigating what makes for good belief acquisition.

This idea that we should study good exemplars, and that these exemplars should come from successful scientific practitioners, is just what Stich has suggested. But I want to part company with Stich when he suggests that true belief has very little to do with good belief acquisition.[7] This is not the place for a detailed response to Stich,[8] so let me just say here that my ideas on this issue are far closer to Goldman's. Just as scoring points is surely quite central to good basketball play, and winning games is surely quite central to good chess play, I do believe, with Goldman, that the acquisition of true belief, and thus having beliefs produced by way of reliable processes, is quite central to good belief acquisition. The dispute between Goldman and Stich about the importance of true belief need not occupy us here, however, since this is an in-house dispute between epistemic consequentialists, rather than a dispute about whether epistemic consequentialism is the right approach to understanding justified belief.

One of the virtues of this approach to providing an account of justification is that it lends real substance to disagreements about the goals of cognitive activity. At times, disagreements about these goals can seem like mere table thumping, with some insisting that, of course, truth is the central cognitive goal, while others insist, equally vehemently, that it is not. Similarly, some wish to see the goal of cognition as limited to a single target—usually true belief—while others wish to insist that there are a number of such goals. If the way to moving forward in understanding justification is by examining scientific practice as a paradigm of good belief acquisition, then there is an empirical question about what the goals implicit in this practice are. This is a tractable question, and one deserving of serious investigation.[9]

---

[7] Stich develops this idea much further in Stich (1990).

[8] I have responded in some detail in Kornblith (2014c).

[9] One might reasonably wonder, as an anonymous referee did, how one distinguishes those goals which are definitive of cognitive activity from those which are not. Why should one think, for example, that the pursuit of truth is at least one of the goals of cognitive activity, and the pursuit of fame or adulation is not? Here too I would want to insist that one does not begin an inquiry into these goals from a wholly neutral starting place. One must begin somewhere, and our pretheoretical ideas will inevitably provide a starting

Of course, the idea that good belief acquisition, as illustrated by way of scientific practice, is not only a goal-directed activity, but is one which is best understood in terms of its success in achieving those goals is nothing more nor less than epistemic consequentialism. We will thus need to look more closely at the move from examining obviously good cases of belief acquisition to the understanding of belief acquisition in terms of its success in achieving certain goals.

3.3

One further distinctive feature of Goldman's approach to giving an account of justified belief has to do with the distinction between propositional justification and doxastic justification.[10] While almost all accounts of justified belief at the time Goldman introduced his reliabilist view took propositional justification to be the more fundamental notion,[11] Goldman's approach reversed the traditional order of explanation. This is a highly non-trivial difference.

Richard Feldman and Earl Conee's evidentialism nicely illustrates the traditional approach. In offering an account of justified belief, they begin with an articulation and defense of the following claim:

EJ Doxastic attitude D toward proposition p is epistemically justified for s at t if and only if having D toward p fits the evidence S has at t.   (Conee and Feldman 2004: 83)

This account of epistemic justification, of course, is an account of *propositional* justification. A proposition may be justified for a person at a time, on this account, even if that person doesn't believe that proposition, so long as the proposition fits the evidence the person has. By the same token, a person may believe a proposition for reasons that have nothing to do with his or her evidence, but this has no bearing on whether the proposition is epistemically justified for the person. Arguably, any account of justified belief should give an account of propositional justification.

With this notion of propositional justification in hand, Feldman and Conee go on to define doxastic justification in terms of it. Roughly, a belief is doxastically justified for a person at a time if and only if it is propositionally justified, and the belief is based on the evidence which provides its propositional justification. This is Feldman and

---

point for any such inquiry, even if that starting point is subject to revision as inquiry proceeds. But the idea that one may have an empirical study of the goals implicit in a social practice is one which is at the heart of much social scientific research. It is the success of these sorts of inquiries—along the usual dimensions of prediction and explanation—that encourages me in thinking that an empirical approach to the goals of cognition may prove equally fruitful and illuminating.

[10] Goldman uses different terminology here, referring to *ex ante* and *ex post* justification. See Goldman (2012: 47–8). I follow what has become the more standard terminology.

[11] Indeed, this understates things. Doxastic justification, when it was considered at all, was regarded as the derivative notion, and propositional justification was seen as more fundamental. But it was quite common to give an account of propositional justification without even so much as mentioning doxastic justification.

Conee's well-foundedness condition (Conee and Feldman 2004: 93). A proposition which is not believed is not, of course, doxastically justified, nor is a belief doxastically justified when it is based on evidence which fails to provide the proposition believed with propositional justification, even if the agent is in possession of evidence which does provide propositional justification for the proposition believed.

This is, it must be admitted, an utterly natural approach. Questions about whether an agent is doxastically justified in holding a particular belief seem to involve two quite different issues: one has to do with a certain psychological question, namely what the agent's belief is actually based on; the other has to do with a question about whether that psychological basis legitimizes belief in the proposition the agent in fact believes. The psychological question is one which philosophers have no special expertise in addressing. The question about the standards which must be met in order for belief to be legitimated, on the other hand, fits squarely within the province of philosophy. More than this, the question about legitimation seems, on its face, to have nothing to do with questions of psychology.[12] The real philosophical work, on traditional views, thus falls entirely on the side of giving an account of propositional justification.

It is thus no surprise that traditional accounts of propositional justification drew either entirely, or almost entirely,[13] on logical and probabilistic relations among propositions. Goldman's way of viewing things, however, reversed the order of explanation here, by viewing doxastic justification as the more fundamental notion. Explaining propositional justification in terms of doxastic justification turned attention away from logical and probabilistic relations, and transformed the understanding of propositional justification in ways that required a frank appeal to psychological notions. This difference can be illustrated by seeing how these two different ways of viewing justification apply to the epistemology of logic.

Consider some complicated tautology, t. On traditional approaches, what kind of evidence does one need in order to believe propositions such as t? Empirical claims, of course, require evidence if they are to be epistemically justified. A theory of propositional justification will make clear what the relationship must be between the evidence for an empirical claim and the claim itself if that claim is to be justified. If one has evidence which entails the empirical claim, then, to be sure, the claim is propositionally justified. Exactly what logical or probabilistic relations might hold between one's evidence and an empirical claim that will confer propositional justification when one's evidence is non-entailing is, of course, controversial. But in both the case of entailing evidence, and the case of non-entailing evidence, the relationship between one's evidence and the proposition justified may be illustrated by way of

---

[12] I have discussed the importance of this apsychological feature of traditional approaches to epistemological questions in Kornblith (2014b) and in Kornblith (1982).

[13] On some accounts of propositional justification, sensory states may serve as justifiers, so the propositions which they justify will not stand in logical or probabilistic relations to the things which justify them, at least if sensory states are not regarded as having propositional content.

an argument, with one's evidence serving as premises and the proposition justified serving as conclusion.[14]

The case of tautologies such as t, on the other hand, are interestingly different. As in the case of empirical claims, we can show the justificatory status of t by way of an argument, but tautologies, of course, can be proven by way of arguments from no premises. What this shows is that one needs no evidence at all in order to be propositionally justified in believing a tautology. All tautologies are propositionally justified for every agent at all times precisely because no evidence is needed in order to justify them.

This does not mean, of course, that all agents at all times are doxastically justified in believing every tautology. For one thing, one must believe a proposition in order to be doxastically justified in believing it, and no one, it is safe to say, believes every tautology. More than this, in order to be doxastically justified in believing a claim, one's belief must be well founded: it must be based on one's evidence in the right sort of way.[15] So the mere fact that one believes a tautology, even though that guarantees on traditional views that one's belief is propositionally justified, does not assure that one's belief is doxastically justified. One might believe t for bad reasons. Someone who believes t because they like the sound of a sentence expressing it, or because it reminds them of some pleasant experience, is not doxastically justified in believing t. On the other hand, someone who believes t as a result of having proved it from no premises has a belief which is not only propositionally justified, but one which is well founded. Such a belief is thus doxastically justified. This is, to be sure, one natural account of the epistemology of logic.

Goldman's approach, on the other hand, begins with doxastic justification. A belief is doxastically justified, according to Goldman, if and only if it is reliably produced. Empirical beliefs, such as my belief that there is a computer in front of me now, are the product of psychological processes whose reliability may be investigated empirically. But the agent who holds an empirical belief need not have investigated the reliability of the process by which such a belief was produced in order to be justified; indeed, such an agent need have no beliefs at all about the process by which such beliefs are produced. So long as the belief producing process was reliable, the resulting belief, according to Goldman, is doxastically justified.

---

[14] As noted above, things are somewhat more complicated on views which allow mental states which lack propositional content to count as evidence.

[15] This requirement, that one's belief must not only be based on the evidence which propositionally justifies one's belief, but it must be based on that evidence *in the right sort of way*, is ineliminable. Thus, suppose I come to believe $p \vee q$ on the basis of my belief that p. I thus have entailing evidence that $p \vee q$. But one might reasonably wonder whether that belief is inferentially justified if I also draw the conclusion that $p \mathrel{\&} q$, and the conclusion that $p \rightarrow q$, and, indeed, every conclusion of the form $p * q$ for every connective '$*$' that I can think of. In such a case, it surely seems that my belief that $p \vee q$, though based on evidence which propositionally justifies it, is not based on that evidence in the right sort of way. Michael Bishop makes a similar point in Bishop (2010), as does John Turri—who makes use of an example very much like this one—in Turri (2010).

The same approach applies to beliefs about logic, such as Mary's belief that *t*. If Mary's belief that *t* was reliably produced, then Mary is doxastically justified in believing *t*. Her belief was the product of some psychological process, and the nature of that process, and the reliability of that process, may be empirically investigated. But Mary need not know anything about the process by which her belief was produced, or believe anything about that process, in order to be doxastically justified in her belief.

Having provided the reliabilist account of doxastic justification, Goldman then defines propositional justification in terms of it:

Person S is [propositionally] justified in believing *p* at *t* if and only if there is a reliable belief-forming operation available to S which is such that if S applied that operation to his total cognitive state at *t*, S would believe *p* at *t*-plus-delta (for a suitably small delta) and that belief would be [doxastically] justified. (Goldman 2012: 48)[16]

Whether an agent is propositionally justified in believing a particular proposition thus depends, on this account, on the availability to the agent of belief-forming operations which would reliably produce the belief. Thus, if Jane is a particularly astute logician and she can "just see," as she would put it, that a particular proposition is a tautology, then, assuming that the psychological process which would produce that belief in her under the right conditions is in fact reliable, then Jane is propositionally justified in believing that proposition. Jane is propositionally justified in believing this claim even if she has never thought about the proposition. On the other hand, if Goofus is hopelessly confused about logic, and rarely answers even the most basic logic problems correctly, then, on this account, he is not propositionally justified in believing the very same tautology. The fact that there is a proof of the tautology from no premises is just irrelevant to its justificatory status for Goofus, on Goldman's account, because Goofus, unlike Jane, is not in possession of reliable psychological processes which would produce belief in the tautology under appropriate conditions.

The traditional account of propositional justification is thus not only importantly different in intention from Goldman's account. The two accounts also pick out different classes of beliefs as propositionally justified. My point here, however, is not to argue that one of these accounts gets the extension of "propositionally justified belief" correct while the other errs. Instead, what I want to focus on is the way in which Goldman's account offers a psychologized view of even propositional justification, in contrast to the more traditional apsychological accounts of justification which Goldman was responding to.

On Goldman's view, a belief is doxastically justified if it is produced by the right sort of process; a proposition is propositionally justified for an agent if that agent has available the right sort of process for producing belief in that proposition. The focus of Goldman's account, then, may turn to the question of what makes a

---

[16] I have replaced Goldman's terminology of *ex ante* and *ex post* justification with the more widely used *propositional* and *doxastic* justification.

belief-producing process the right sort of process. What kinds of processes, that is, are justification-conferring?

Goldman's answer, of course, is that the feature of a process which makes it justification-conferring is just reliability. But the focus on psychological processes is compatible with other views about the justification-conferring feature. One could, for example, agree with Goldman that the proper way to view justification is in terms of the justification-conferring feature of processes, but provide an account of what that feature might be which views reliability as neither necessary nor sufficient for justification. One might argue that processes which reflect the agent's most deeply held epistemic standards are, in virtue of that feature, justification-conferring. Or one might hold that processes which reflect epistemic standards which can survive suitably idealized reflective scrutiny are justification-conferring. Or one might hold that the transitions which justification-conferring processes license must conform to certain a priori specifiable standards. A process-oriented account of justification does not, by itself, demand a reliabilist account of the justification-conferring feature of psychological processes, nor does it require a commitment to any sort of epistemic consequentialism. What then is Goldman's reason for filling in the process-oriented account in consequentialist terms?

Here, we must return to the two constraints noted earlier which Goldman places on a successful account of justification: justification must be explicated in nonepistemic terms, and the account of justification must, in some suitable sense, be explanatory. Each of these constraints plays a role in Goldman's decision to provide a consequentialist account of the justification-conferring feature of psychological processes.

Thus, consider the requirement that justification be explicated in non-epistemic terms. Deontological approaches to justification, such as Chisholm's, could be set in a process-oriented format. Justification-conferring processes would be those which conform to an agent's epistemic duties. The notion of an epistemic duty, however, straightforwardly violates Goldman's requirement that justification be explicated in non-epistemic terms, and the Chisholmian program, as noted above, made no attempt to give an account of such duties in the kind of substantive, naturalistic vocabulary which Goldman insisted upon.

Psychologizing logical or probabilistic accounts of propositional justification presents a different problem. One might suggest, for example, that a process is justification-conferring just in case its algorithmic representation is nothing more nor less than conditionalization on evidential input. The appeal to evidence here would still be an epistemic notion which would need to be discharged in favor of more naturalistically acceptable notions, but I will assume that this problem can be taken care of. The suggestion, however, that human inferential processes must track Bayesian conditionalization or other probabilistic or logical accounts of justification sets a standard for doxastic justification which human beings are very unlikely to meet. The kinds of inferential heuristics which our psychological processes realize simply do not meet such a standard.[17] The result of this way of viewing things would thus be an implausible and far-reaching skepticism.

This dovetails nicely with Goldman's requirement that an account of justification should be explanatory. Our use of epistemic terminology—talk of beliefs being justified or not; talk of knowledge—serves important explanatory purposes. As has now frequently been noted, we need to be able to identify inquirers whose beliefs constitute knowledge if we are to take on their beliefs as our own, and to pass them on to others by way of testimony.[18] We routinely distinguish between justified and unjustified beliefs, and between beliefs which are or are not knowledge. The ways in which we mark these distinctions serve to guide our inquiries. More than this, the conduct of our inquiries is not just some elaborate and idiosyncratic social ritual in which the practice itself is all that is important, rather than its outcome. If we are to understand the practice of inquiry at all, it seems, we must see it as a kind of goal-directed behavior. Inquiries are judged as successful or not by the extent to which they reach their goals, and our epistemic terminology serves to distinguish between various features of successful and unsuccessful epistemic practice.[19] The problem with skeptical accounts of justification and knowledge is thus not that they fail to fit with our intuitions, but rather that they fail to explain the ways in which our ability to wield these distinctions—between justified and unjustified belief, and between beliefs which are and are not knowledge—serves not only to guide our inquiries, but is instrumental in explaining their successes.

But this kind of explanatory inquiry, one which sees the attempt to explain what justification is as one which investigates features of many of the psychological processes which we actually make use of in arriving at our beliefs,[20] and which explains why

---

[17] Indeed, for this reason, Nisbett and Borgida concluded early on that work on human inference had "bleak implications for human rationality." See Nisbett and Borgida (1975). Subsequent work in this area has, for the most part, drawn back from such dire conclusions, and recognized the reliability of many of these heuristics when placed in the environments in which they are used. For a sample of this literature, see Nisbett and Ross (1980); Kahneman, Slovic, and Tversky (1982); Gilovich, Griffin, and Kahneman (2002); Adler and Rips (2008); Kahneman (2011). I have discussed the ways in which many of these processes are far more reliable than they first appear in Kornblith (1993). This has also been a focus of much of Gerd Gigerenzer's work. See, for example, Gigerenzer, Todd, and the ABC Research Group (1999).

[18] This point is the centerpiece of Craig (1990), and it is now a staple of the literature on testimony.

[19] This is, as I have been urging, an empirical claim about the nature of inquiry, and hence as one which is subject to revision or refutation in the light of future research. Thus, as one referee suggested, one might think that there are important non-consequentialist dimensions of evaluation of inquiry, either in addition to the consequentialist sorts of evaluation, or instead of them: our practices of praising and blaming inquirers might be thought of in non-consequentialist terms, as well as our assessment of their motivations and character traits. Whether these sorts of evaluations are best understood in non-consequentialist terms is worthy of extended attention. That there are consequentialist ways of understanding these evaluations, however, and that such a consequentialist account would have a straightforward explanation of how these evaluations contribute to the success of inquiry, seems undeniable.

[20] I don't mean to suggest here that this approach will inevitably endorse every psychological process as justification-conferring. There is certainly room for allowing, what is clearly true, that many beliefs are produced in ways that do not result in justified beliefs. As pointed out above, however, this way of thinking

it is that these processes tend to be instrumental in the success of our inquiries and of our non-epistemic behaviors, will inevitably give rise to a consequentialist account of the right-making feature of epistemic processes. Surely the most salient feature of these processes, and the one which explains why they play the role they do, not only in advancing inquiry, but in the success of our non-epistemic ventures as well, is their tendency to produce true (or approximately true) beliefs. And this just is, of course, a consequentialist account of justification. It is the tendency of these processes to produce true beliefs which shows that justified beliefs form a unified, explanatory kind, rather than a mere heterogenous class. And this is what a naturalistic approach to justification demands.

3.4

If we think about justification from a naturalistic perspective, we are thus led to accept epistemic consequentialism. The insistence that epistemic terminology be explained in non-epistemic terms; the commitment to a unified and explanatory account of key epistemic terms; and the explanation of propositional justification in terms of doxastic justification, rather than the other way around, all work together to motivate epistemic consequentialism. Those unsympathetic to naturalism, of course, will not see this as a reason to adopt epistemic consequentialism, but it is important, nonetheless, to see how it is that these views form a coherent package.

References

Adler, Jonathan, and Rips, Lance, eds. (2008) *Reasoning: Studies in Human Inference and its Foundations*, Cambridge: Cambridge University Press.
Bishop, Michael (2010) "Why the Generality Problem Is Everybody's Problem," *Philosophical Studies*, 151, 285–98.
Chisholm, Roderick (1966) *Theory of Knowledge*, 1st edition, Upper Saddle River, NJ: Prentice-Hall.
Chisholm, Roderick (1977) *Theory of Knowledge*, 2nd edition, Upper Saddle River, NJ: Prentice-Hall.
Chisholm, Roderick (1989) *Theory of Knowledge*, 3rd edition, Upper Saddle River, NJ: Prentice-Hall.
Conee, Earl, and Feldman, Richard (2004) *Evidentialism: Essays in Epistemology*, Oxford: Oxford University Press.
Craig, Edward (1990) *Knowledge and the State of Nature: An Essay in Conceptual Synthesis*, Oxford: Oxford University Press.
Fodor, Jerry (1981) "Special Sciences," in *RePresentations: Philosophical Essays on the Foundations of Cognitive Science*, Cambridge, MA: MIT Press, 127–45.

---

about justified belief largely takes skepticism off the table before the project of investigating justified belief is even begun. I don't see this as a disadvantage of this way of thinking.

Fodor, Jerry (1987) *Psychosemantics: The Problem of Meaning in the Philosophy of Mind*, Cambridge, MA: MIT Press.
Gigerenzer, Gerd, Todd, Peter, and the ABC Research Group (1999) *Simple Heuristics that Make Us Smart*, Oxford: Oxford University Press.
Gilovich, Thomas, Griffin, Dale, and Kahneman, Daniel, eds. (2002) *Heuristics and Biases: The Psychology of Intuitive Judgment*, Cambridge: Cambridge University Press.
Goldman, Alvin (1992) "Epistemic Folkways and Scientific Epistemology," in *Liaisons: Philosophy Meets the Cognitive and Social Sciences*, Cambridge, MA: MIT Press, 155–75.
Goldman, Alvin (2012) "What Is Justified Belief?" in *Reliabilism and Contemporary Epistemology*, Oxford: Oxford University Press, 29–49.
Goldman, Alvin (2015) "Interview with Richard Marshall: Thinking about Mindreading, Mirroring and Embedded Cognition et al." http://www.3ammagazine.com/3am/thinking-about-mindreading-mirroring-and-embedded-cognition/.
Kahneman, Daniel (2011) *Thinking, Fast and Slow*, New York: Farrar, Straus and Giroux.
Kahneman, Daniel, Slovic, Paul, and Tversky, Amos, eds. (1982) *Judgment under Uncertainty: Heuristics and Biases*, Cambridge: Cambridge University Press.
Kornblith, Hilary (1982) "The Psychological Turn," *Australasian Journal of Philosophy*, 60, 238–53.
Kornblith, Hilary (1993) *Inductive Inference and its Natural Ground*, Cambridge, MA: MIT Press.
Kornblith, Hilary (2002) *Knowledge and its Place in Nature*, Oxford: Oxford University Press.
Kornblith, Hilary (2014a) *A Naturalistic Epistemology: Selected Papers*, Oxford: Oxford University Press.
Kornblith, Hilary (2014b) "Beyond Foundationalism and the Coherence Theory," in Kornblith (2014a: 17–31).
Kornblith, Hilary (2014c) "Epistemic Normativity," in Kornblith (2014a: 71–87).
Lewis, Michael (2003) *Moneyball: The Art of Winning an Unfair Game*, New York: W. W. Norton and Company.
Nisbett, Richard, and Borgida, Eugene (1975) "Attribution and the Psychology of Prediction," *Journal of Personality and Social Psychology*, 32, 932–43.
Nisbett, Richard, and Ross, Lee (1980) *Human Inference: Strategies and Shortcomings of Social Judgment*, Upper Saddle River, NJ: Prentice-Hall.
Quine, W. V. O. (1969) "Epistemology Naturalized," in *Ontological Relativity and Other Essays*, New York: Columbia University Press, 69–90.
Shope, Robert (1983) *The Analysis of Knowing: A Decade of Research*, Princeton, NJ: Princeton University Press.
Stich, Stephen (1990) *The Fragmentation of Reason: Preface to a Pragmatic Theory of Cognitive Evaluation*, Cambridge, MA: MIT Press.
Stich, Stephen (1993) "Naturalizing Epistemology: Quine, Simon and the Prospects for Pragmatism," in C. Hookway and D. Peterson, eds. *Philosophy and Cognitive Science*, Cambridge: Cambridge University Press, 1–17.
Turri, John (2010) "On the Relationship between Propositional and Doxastic Justification," *Philosophy and Phenomenological Research*, LXXX, 312–26.
Williamson, Timothy (2000) *Knowledge and its Limits*, Oxford: Oxford University Press.

4
Epistemic Teleology
Synchronic and Diachronic

Ralph Wedgwood

According to a widely held view of the matter, whenever we assess beliefs as 'rational' or 'justified', we are making *normative* judgements about those beliefs. In this discussion, I shall simply assume, for the sake of argument, that this view is correct. My goal here is to explore a particular approach to understanding the basic principles that explain which of these normative judgements are true. Specifically, this approach is based on the assumption that all such normative principles are grounded in facts about *values*, and the normative principles that apply to beliefs in particular are grounded in facts about *alethic* value—a kind of value that is exemplified by believing what is true and not believing what is false. In this chapter, I shall explain what I regard as the best way of interpreting this approach. In doing so, I shall also show how this interpretation can solve some problems that have recently been raised for approaches of this kind by Selim Berker, Jennifer Carr, Michael Caie, and Hilary Greaves.

4.1 The Value-based Conception of Normativity

In this discussion I shall explore what I call the 'value-based conception of normativity'. According to this conception, *orderings* or *rankings* of *states of affairs*—rankings of the sort that could be expressed in English by means of comparative evaluative terms like 'better' and 'worse'—lie at the heart of normativity.

According to this conception, all of the key terms used to assess beliefs—such as 'rational' and 'justified' and the like—can be used to express *evaluative* concepts. When the terms are used in this way, for a belief to be 'rational' or 'justified' is for it to be a belief that is *good* in a certain way, while for a belief to be 'irrational' or 'unjustified' is for it to be a belief that is in a certain corresponding way *bad*.[1] (In this

---

[1] It is important here to realize quite how many ways of being good—that is, how many different values—there are. Most philosophers working in ethical theory have dramatically underestimated both how many such ways of being good there are, and the extent to which terms like 'good' are context-sensitive. Even

discussion, I shall assume that, even if the terms 'rational' and 'justified' differ in their connotations or pragmatic features, in the contexts that are pertinent to our purposes they express the same concept.)

Like every other kind of goodness, rationality and justifiedness come in *degrees*: one belief can be more irrational, or more unjustified, than another; and for one belief to be 'more irrational' than a second belief is for the first belief to be in a certain way *worse* than the second. This relation of *being more irrational than*, like the relation of being *worse than*, is irreflexive, asymmetric, and transitive. In this way, the relation of *being at least as irrational as*, just like the relation of being *at least as bad as*, provides at least a *partial ordering* of the items that it relates.

Our focus here is on the use of terms like 'rational' and 'justified' to assess beliefs. More precisely, when we say that 'a belief' is rational, we are really predicating rationality of the relevant thinker's *having* the relevant belief at the time in question—that is, in effect, of the *state of affairs* that consists in the thinker's having that belief at that time. In this way, interpreting 'rational' as expressing an evaluative concept is consistent with the assumption that the basic function of evaluative concepts is to evaluate and rank alternative states of affairs. To simplify our discussion, I shall just speak of the rationality of beliefs and the like. But what really counts as 'rational' or as 'irrational' is the thinker's having the belief at the time in question.

In addition to being used to assess beliefs, terms like 'rational' and 'justified' can also be used to assess other items besides beliefs:

a. They can be used to assess whole *systems* of mental states, such as belief-systems, or collections of plans and intentions.
b. They can be used to assess not only mental states, but also *mental events*—and especially mental events in which the thinker *forms* a new mental state of some kind, or *revises* (or *reaffirms*) some of her old mental states. These mental events include *judgements*—events in which we form a new belief or reaffirm an old belief—and also *choices* or *decisions*—events in which we form, revise, or reaffirm our plans and intentions.

This distinction, between assessing the rationality of static mental states like beliefs and intentions, on the one hand, and assessing the rationality of mental events in which we change or revise our mental states, on the other, is one way of understanding the distinction between *synchronic* and *diachronic* rationality. As we shall see later on, however, there is another deeper and more important way of understanding this distinction as well.

Although I shall assume that the evaluative concepts expressed by terms like 'rational' and 'justified' rank states of affairs of all these kinds, I shall not assume that the states of affairs ranked by these evaluative concepts include states of affairs

---

Thomson (2008), who rightly emphasizes the many ways in which the term 'good' is used, in the end gives what seems to me an unduly limited catalogue of all the different concepts that the word can express.

that consist in the thinker's simply *lacking* any doxastic attitude (even suspension of judgement) towards a certain proposition. Perhaps such states of affairs—consisting, not in doxastic attitudes, but in the *absence* of such attitudes—are not evaluated by these concepts at all.[2] I shall also assume that this limitation on the domain of states of affairs that are evaluated by these concepts is non-trivial, since thinkers may be totally *attitudeless* towards certain propositions (even if these propositions are logically complex propositions built up out of atomic propositions towards which the thinkers *do* have attitudes).

Besides this way of using terms like 'rational' and 'justified' as evaluative terms that apply to mental states and mental events, there is also another way of using these terms. When using the terms in this other way, we speak of the '*requirements* of rationality' and of what is 'rationally *required*' of a thinker at a particular time; and we can also speak of what is 'rationally *permissible*'—that is, consistent with all rational requirements—for a thinker at a time.

The connection between these two ways of using terms like 'rational' or 'justified' is, I propose, quite simple. The terms 'required' and 'requirement' mean just what they sound like: they mean what is *needed* or *necessary*. To say that something is necessary, as the modal logicians taught us many years ago, is equivalent to universally quantifying over possibilities: something is necessary if and only if it is the case in *all* the possibilities in the relevant domain.

As virtually all philosophers of language and semanticists agree, the domain of possibilities that we are quantifying over is determined by the *context* in which terms like 'necessary' and 'required' are used. I shall follow tradition in representing these possibilities by talking about *possible worlds*. So, whenever we speak of what is 'necessary' or 'required', something in the context of our conversation determines a domain of possible worlds. To simplify matters, let us assume that this is simply the domain of worlds that we are *thinking of* in the context. For example, we may be thinking of the possible worlds that are in some way *available* to you at the present time, through the way in which you avail yourself of the opportunities that you have for exercising your cognitive capacities at this time. Moreover, in each context where we speak of the 'requirements of rationality', there will be some items—call them the 'relevant items'—that we are interested in assessing for rationality in that context. For example, we may often be we are interested in assessing the possible total belief-systems that you might have right now. Then the relevant item in each world will be the total belief-system that you have now in that world.

So, suppose that the context has determined a domain of worlds, and a relevant item that is up for assessment in each of these worlds. Then it may be that within

---

[2] In fact, towards the end of this section, I shall argue, against Carr (2015), that there may be no way of comparing the degree of irrationality of one belief-system that is defined over one set of propositions with the degree of irrationality of a second belief-system that is defined over a second *distinct* set of propositions. See note 6, this chapter.

this domain of worlds, there are some worlds where the relevant item is *maximally rational*—that is, *no less rational* than the corresponding relevant item in any other world. Just to have a label, let us call these the 'rationally favoured' worlds. Then, in general, something is rationally required if and only if it is the case at all the rationally favoured worlds. For example, suppose that we are thinking of the possible worlds that are available to you now, and we are interested in assessing the possible total belief-systems that you might have now. Then what is rationally required of you now is everything that is the case at all the worlds that both (a) are available to you now, and (b) are worlds where the total belief-system that you have now is no less rational than the total belief-system that you have at any other available world.

So long as there are always worlds within the relevant domain where the relevant item is maximally rational, this account guarantees that the operator 'It is rationally required that...' obeys all the principles that apply to deontic modals like 'ought' or 'should' according to standard deontic logic—that is, the modal system KD. This makes it plausible, it seems to me, that the notion of a 'rational requirement' can be expressed by speaking, in a certain way, of how we 'should' or 'ought to' think.[3]

However, in addition to assessing beliefs as 'rational' or 'justified', we also assess beliefs as 'right' or 'wrong', 'correct' or 'incorrect'; and these terms typically seem to express different concepts from those that are most commonly expressed by 'rational' or 'justified'.

It is not standard in ordinary English to speak of one belief's being 'less correct' than another. But it still seems possible to make sense of the idea of degrees of incorrectness or wrongness. At least, we can qualify terms like 'wrong' and 'incorrect' by a range of modifiers: one thing might be 'utterly wrong' (or 'deeply wrong' or 'egregiously wrong'), while another thing might only be 'slightly wrong' (or 'not [too] far wrong'). So these terms seem capable of functioning as evaluative terms: a correct belief is in a way a *good* belief, while an incorrect belief is in a corresponding way a *bad* belief; and it seems that this value of correctness and incorrectness, like all other values, comes in degrees.

There may be many different concepts that terms like 'correct' can express. But in this discussion, I shall explore the idea that these terms can express a kind of *alethic value* that beliefs can possess. Consider a belief—that is, a state of affairs consisting in a certain thinker's believing a certain proposition A at a certain time. If 'correct' expresses this kind of alethic value, then this belief is correct just in case A—the proposition that is believed—is *true*; and it is incorrect just in case A is not true. Moreover, with this kind of alethic value, we can understand the idea of degrees of incorrectness in the following way: if A is *true*, then the greater the degree of confidence with which the thinker believes A, the *less* incorrect the belief is; if A is

---

[3] Compare the semantics of deontic modals that was originally developed by the deontic logicians of the 1960s and 1970s—such as David Lewis (1973), usefully summarized by Lennart Åqvist (1984)—and later applied to the empirical data of language use by linguists such as Angelika Kratzer (2012). For more on this conception of rational requirements, see Wedgwood (2017: 148–52).

not true, then the greater the degree of confidence with which the thinker believes *A*, the *more* incorrect the belief is.[4]

This, then, is one thing that it could mean to say that one belief-state towards a proposition *A* is 'more incorrect' than another such belief-state. When the term is used in this way, it also seems to make sense to say that while one belief-state b_1 is *slightly* more incorrect than another such belief-state b_2, the belief-state b_3 is *much* more incorrect than another belief-state b_4. That is, we can compare the *differences* in degrees of incorrectness between *pairs* of such belief-states.[5] This suggests that it may in principle be possible to *measure* a belief-state's degree of incorrectness, by means of an appropriate *scoring rule*. We shall return to the question of what this scoring rule might be like in section 4.5.

In addition to assessing individual beliefs as correct or incorrect, we can also assess whole belief-systems. If there is indeed a scoring rule that measures the degree of incorrectness of each individual belief-state, then it is tempting to think that the way to assess whole belief-systems is by some kind of *weighted sum* of the degrees of incorrectness of the individual belief-states that make up this belief-system.

The reason for thinking that the way to assess a whole belief-system is by means of a *weighted* sum of the individual belief-states' degrees of incorrectness is just that some of the propositions that are the objects of these individual belief-states may be *more important* than others. We should allow that these weights are determined holistically by the whole set of propositions in which the thinker has belief-like or doxastic attitudes of any kind. In that case, these weights would only be defined for each set of propositions; and there may not be any way of comparing the incorrectness of one belief-system, which consists of attitudes towards *one* set of propositions, with another belief-system, which consists of attitudes towards *another* set of propositions. However, we may not need to make such comparisons anyway: it may be enough if the relevant kind of alethic value yields only a *partial* ordering of the items to which it applies.[6]

This, then, is the approach that I shall explore in this discussion. This approach is based on the assumption that all normative terms that we use to assess beliefs express

---

[4] For the seminal discussion of this way of evaluating beliefs, see Joyce (1998).

[5] In other words, these degrees of incorrectness form a *difference structure*. For an explanation of why this supports the idea of cardinal measurement, see Krantz et al. (1971: 150–2 and 157–8).

[6] Whether one should 'expand' one's belief-system by forming a new doxastic attitude towards a proposition that one previously had no attitudes towards is not in my view a question about *epistemic* rationality at all. Typically, exogenous mental events that are outside one's control simply *compel* one to start having attitudes towards a proposition. (For example, one might have a *sensory experience* that compels one to start having an attitude towards a proposition that forms part of the content of the experience; or a new proposition might simply *occur* to one, as a hypothesis, which in effect would also compel one to start having some attitude towards the proposition.) Even suspending judgement about a proposition, or wondering whether it is true, is a kind of broadly doxastic attitude towards the proposition; and such an attitude may well be less rational than having a more definite level of confidence in the proposition. For this reason, then, I disagree with the arguments of Carr (2015) that an account of epistemic rationality needs to include a story about when such 'epistemic expansions' are rational.

either (a) evaluative concepts—which stand for values that come in degrees, and yield an at least partial ranking of the items to which they apply—or else (b) concepts of the 'requirements' of such values, of the kind that I have explained, which can be expressed by deontic modals like 'should' and 'ought'. Two sets of such evaluative concepts stand out as particularly central—namely, the concepts that can be expressed by terms like 'rational' or 'justified', and the concepts that can be expressed by terms like 'right' or 'correct'. We shall explore the approach that is based on the assumption that one fundamental kind of assessment of beliefs, which can be expressed by terms like 'right' and 'correct', is in terms of this kind of *alethic* value.

4.2 'Consequentialism', 'Utility', 'Decision Theory', 'Teleology'

Different philosophers have deployed different terminology to refer to this value-based approach to epistemology. Unfortunately, much of this terminology is at least potentially misleading.

Thus, some philosophers, such as Selim Berker (2013), speak of 'epistemic consequentialism'. But consequentialism is best understood as the doctrine that the value or normative status of the relevant states of affairs (whether these states of affairs be *acts*, or *beliefs*, or anything else) is derivative from the value of these states of affairs' *total consequences*.

There are various ways of thinking of 'the total consequences' of a state of affairs. One way, for example, is in terms of *counterfactual* or *subjunctive* conditionals: the total consequence of a state of affairs consists of the conjunction of everything that would be the case if the state of affairs in question obtained. Alternatively, one might think that the total consequence of a state of affairs is nothing short of a whole possible world. Then we might propose that the way in which the value of states of affairs is derivative from the value of possible worlds is to be explained in terms of *conditional objective chances*: the value of a state of affairs is the weighted sum of the values of all possible worlds that are compatible with that state of affairs, weighting the value of each world by the conditional objective chance of the world, conditional on that state of affairs.

At all events, the value-based approach that I have sketched does not assume that the value of beliefs, or belief-systems, or events of belief-revision, is in any way derivative from the value of their total consequences. On the contrary, each of these items can instantiate the value of correctness, or the value of rationality, *in its own right*: its value is not derivative from the value of 'consequences' in any interesting sense. To put what is essentially the same point in other words, according to this approach what are relevant are not the values that these items (such as beliefs or belief-systems or belief-revisions) *promote*, but the values that these items themselves *instantiate*.[7]

---

[7] For a discussion of the importance of this distinction between what *promotes* values and what *instantiates* these values, see Pettit (1991: 231).

Some other philosophers, such as Richard Pettigrew (2013), refer to this value-based approach as 'epistemic utility theory'. But this too is misleading, because 'utility' strictly speaking is a measure of *subjective preference*.[8] Fundamentally, the value-based approach to normativity is quite general: it could invoke values of any kind—not just this one very specific kind of value, 'utility'. Specifically, I am focusing on the two crucial values that I have called *rationality* and *correctness*. It is doubtful whether it would be plausible to identify either of these values with utility. At all events, this is certainly not something that we should assume at the outset. So it is important not to be misled by the terminology of 'epistemic utility'.

Other philosophers, such as Hilary Greaves (2013), have spoken of 'epistemic decision theory'. This description is also potentially misleading. Although the term can be used more broadly, in the strict sense, decision theory, or rational choice theory, as its name suggests, is concerned with *decisions* or *choices*. As I use the term, a choice or decision is a mental event in which an agent forms, revises, or reaffirms her *plans* or *intentions* about how to act. In this sense, a belief is not a decision—nor is there any reason to think that our beliefs are typically, or indeed ever, chosen by us, in the way in which our intentional actions are chosen. Decision theory is concerned with rational choices or decisions; we are concerned here with a different topic—namely, rational belief and rational belief revision. So the term 'decision theory' also seems best avoided here.

A slightly better term to use in this context is 'teleology'. Even this term is potentially misleading too, because it suggests an *aim* or *telos*—and many philosophers seem to think that every aim (or *telos*) must be either intended by an agent or else an evolutionary proper function of some kind. I shall not argue here that beliefs have an 'aim' of either of these kinds. We can, however, interpret this talk of an 'aim' more metaphorically, so that it refers only to a fundamental value. This is how John Rawls (1971: 21) understood 'teleology', as referring to the view that 'the good is prior to the right'. Taken in this sense, the terminology of 'epistemic teleology' seems acceptable.

4.3 Trade-Offs

I have proposed that the degree of incorrectness of a whole belief-system is some kind of weighted sum of the degrees of incorrectness of the individual belief-states that make up this belief-system. This proposal about the relation between the value of individual beliefs and the value of whole belief-systems obviously allows for a kind of trade-off. One belief-system b_1 can be, overall, better than another such system b_2, even though there is some particular proposition A such that the attitude towards A involved in b_1 is worse than the attitude towards A involved in b_2.

Selim Berker (2013) has objected to such trade-offs, building on some objections to reliabilism that were originally made by Roderick Firth (1981). In objecting to these trade-offs, Berker correctly notes that the idea that such trade-offs are possible

---

[8] For this point, see especially Broome (1991).

is structurally analogous to a famous feature of classical utilitarianism. According to utilitarianism, the goodness of a possible world is measured by the total sum of welfare that it contains. So a world in which there are ten individuals, each of whom has a welfare level of 90, is less good than a world in which there are just these ten individuals, and nine of them have a welfare level of 100, and one of them has a welfare level of 10. This implication of utilitarianism is troubling enough, but given utilitarianism's commitment to act-consequentialism, it also follows that an *act* whose consequence is the first world is less good than an act whose consequence is the second world, and if no other acts are available, the agent *ought* to perform the second act rather than the first.

Philosophers who (like me) reject utilitarianism offer different diagnoses of the fundamental flaw in utilitarianism that is revealed by this troubling implication. According to one diagnosis, the fundamental flaw lies in utilitarianism's conception of how the goodness of a whole world is related to the welfare-levels of the individuals that it contains—a conception that wrongly attaches no importance to *equality* between different individuals' welfare levels. A second much more radical diagnosis is that ethical theory should not countenance such trade-offs between the interests of distinct individuals at all.

The second diagnosis seems, at least in my judgement, far too extreme. There are plenty of cases in which we must countenance such trade-offs. A world w_1 where there is one fabulously well-off individual x_1 and nine wretchedly badly-off individuals $x_2 \ldots x_{10}$ is clearly inferior to a world w_2 where x_1 is slightly less well off than in w_1 and $x_2 \ldots x_{10}$ are dramatically better off than in w_1. But this comparison between the worlds w_1 and w_2 involves a trade-off between the loss to the fabulously well-off individual x_1 and the gains to the wretchedly badly-off individuals $x_2 \ldots x_{10}$. Whatever insight there may be in Rawls's (1971: 27) famous remark 'Utilitarianism does not take seriously the distinction between persons', it should not be interpreted as equivalent to this extreme second diagnosis, which crazily rejects all trade-offs whatsoever.

So, it seems to be the first diagnosis of this fundamental flaw in classical utilitarianism, and not the second diagnosis, that is correct here. In general, whenever a value is exemplified both by a complex state of affairs, and also by some of the simpler states of affairs that are the constituents of that complex state of affairs, some trade-offs seem unavoidable. The only question is: which trade-offs? The thesis that there are no trade-offs at all is simply incredible.

In section 4.1, I proposed that the degree of incorrectness of a whole belief-system is simply a weighted sum of the degrees of incorrectness of the individual belief-states that constitute that system. I also proposed that these weights are determined by the set of propositions that are the objects of the belief-states in question—and that in consequence there may be no way of comparing the degree of incorrectness of a belief-system that is defined over one set of propositions with the degree of incorrectness of a second belief-system that is defined over a different set of propositions.

It follows from these proposals that one belief-system b_1 can, overall, have a better degree of incorrectness than another belief-system b_2, even though there is some particular proposition A_1 such that the attitude towards A_1 involved in b_1 has a worse degree of incorrectness than the attitude towards A_1 involved in b_2. For example, perhaps b_1 involves an incorrect attitude towards A_1, but correct attitudes towards a large number of other propositions $A_2, \ldots A_n$, while b_2 involves a correct attitude towards A_1, and incorrect attitudes towards $A_2, \ldots A_n$. (This could be the case, for instance, because A_1 is false and $A_2, \ldots A_n$ are true, and b_1 involves total disbelief in all these propositions—including the false proposition A_1, and also all the true propositions $A_2, \ldots A_n$—while b_2 involves confident belief in all these propositions.)

In this case, however, surely b_1 *is* better, in terms of its overall degree of incorrectness, than b_2. This trade-off seems positively plausible, at least to me. Still, someone who—like Berker—wishes to press this objection might insist that it is implausible to say that the thinker *should* have b_1 rather than b_2: surely, the thinker should not believe a false proposition like A_1 just to gain true beliefs in $A_2, \ldots A_n$?

I concede that it does sound strange to say that the thinker should *revise* her beliefs by shifting from b_2 to b_1. But I suggest that there are two reasons for why it sounds strange, which are both quite compatible with the proposals that I have made. First, in any normal case, when a thinker is in the belief-system b_2 and is considering the propositions $A_1, \ldots A_n$, there will be other options available besides just sticking with b_2 or shifting to b_1. For example, the option b_3 of *disbelieving* the false proposition A_1, and confidently believing all the true propositions $A_2, \ldots A_n$, is also available, and that option is clearly preferable to both b_1 and b_2. If an option like b_3 is available, then plainly the thinker should not shift to b_1.

Secondly, the question about whether we should *revise* our beliefs in a certain way is in principle different from the question of whether we should *hold* a certain system of beliefs. In fact, it seems to me that—when it comes to degrees of incorrectness (as opposed to degrees of irrationality)—the correctness of a belief-revision is simply identical to the degree of incorrectness of the belief-system that results from the belief-revision. However, it seems hard to hear the question of whether we '*should*' revise our beliefs in a certain way as a question about the requirements of *correctness*—as opposed to as a question about the requirements of *rationality*. As I shall explain later on, just because b_1 has a better degree of incorrectness than b_2, it certainly does not follow that the transition from b_2 to b_1 is rational; indeed, this transition may well be grossly irrational.

In these ways, then, I can explain why it sounds bizarre to say that the agent should shift from b_2 to b_1 in this case. Since it is hard to see any other reason for doubting that b_1 has a better degree of incorrectness than b_2, I conclude that the proposals that I have made in section 4.1 are immune to the objections that have been raised by Berker.

4.4 The Probabilistic Connection between Correctness and Rationality

So far, I have discussed these two key evaluative concepts—rationality and correctness—quite separately, without exploring any of the relations between them. I have also not said anything about how to measure the *degree of irrationality* that is exemplified by a belief (or system of beliefs) or by a mental event in which we revise (or form or reaffirm) our beliefs. One of the most promising ideas explored in recent epistemology—especially in a series of seminal works by James M. Joyce (1998 and 2009)—focuses on the possibility of a fundamental connection between rationality and the kind of alethic value that I am referring to here with the term 'correctness'.

Suppose that there is some crucial notion of what is *epistemically possible* for a thinker at a given time—a kind of possibility that, at least ideally, rationally should be guiding the thinker at that time. There are several features that this notion of epistemic possibility may be presumed to have. For example, if A is a logical truth, then no proposition incompatible with A is epistemically possible—in that sense, all logical truths are epistemically necessary. It may also be that all conceptual or analytic truths are epistemically necessary in the same way (even if, like 'If B, then Actually B', they are not metaphysically necessary).

This kind of epistemic possibility can be used to define some useful further notions. Consider two belief-systems, b_1 and b_2. Suppose that it is epistemically *impossible* for b_1 to have a better degree of incorrectness than b_2, but epistemically *possible* for b_2 to have a better degree of incorrectness than b_1. Then we can say that b_2 at least *weakly dominates* b_1. If in addition it is epistemically *necessary* that b_2 must have a better degree of incorrectness than b_1, we can say that b_2 *strongly dominates* b_1.

Suppose that a belief-system b_1 is strongly dominated by some available alternative belief-system b_2; and suppose that b_2 is not even weakly dominated by any other available belief-system in this way. In this case, it seems that b_1 cannot be maximally rational. There will be some other belief-system distinct from b_1—perhaps b_2, or perhaps some third available belief-system b_3—that is maximally rational.

As Joyce (1998) has shown, this dominance principle has several important implications. Given certain assumptions about how these degrees of incorrectness are to be measured, and about the relevant notion of epistemic possibility, this principle entails that, so long as enough belief-systems are available, no probabilistically incoherent belief-systems can be maximally rational. In this way, the dominance principle may explain why rationality requires having a probabilistically coherent belief-system.

I shall not dispute the dominance principle here. It is, however, a very *weak* principle: it only applies in a very narrow range of cases—namely, in cases in which a belief-system is strongly dominated by some available alternative. There seem to be forms of irrationality that cannot be captured in this way. (For example, belief-systems that make it impossible to learn anything from experience, or from induction, seem to be irrational; but it is doubtful whether they are strongly dominated by any available alternative.) We need to find a more general principle—presumably, a principle that entails the dominance principle as a special case.

A more general principle will not be hard to find if we may suppose that the relevant kind of epistemic possibility comes in *degrees*: that is, some propositions are *more possible* than others. In picturesque terms, we might suppose that the epistemically possible worlds form a *space*, and some sets of possible worlds take up larger proportions of the space than others. These proportions between subsets—or in more picturesque terms, sub-regions—of the whole space of epistemically possible worlds could then be measured by means of a *probability function*.

If the space of epistemically possible worlds does indeed have this structure, then the idea implicit in the dominance principle—that for every rational thinker and every time, there is a kind of epistemic possibility that rationally should be guiding the thinker at that time—can be developed into the more specific idea that for every rational thinker and every time, there is a *probability function* that should be guiding the thinker at that time. Just to give it a label, let us call this probability function the *rational* probability function for this thinker at this time.

Several further refinements could be introduced into this proposal. For example, perhaps there is not always a *unique* probability function that rationally should guide each thinker at each time; perhaps, sometimes, it is only a big *set* of such probability functions that rationally should be guiding the thinker at the time. However, I shall ignore these complications here: to fix ideas, I shall assume that there is always a unique rational probability function for each thinker and time.

Suppose that it is indeed the case that for every thinker and time, there is a rational probability function of this kind; and suppose also, as I suggested in section 4.1, that the degrees of incorrectness discussed above can be *measured* on an interval scale, by means of an appropriate scoring rule.[9] Then we can make sense of a belief-system's *expected* degree of incorrectness—where a belief-system's expected degree of incorrectness is the weighted sum of its epistemically possible degrees of correctness, weighting each of these degrees of incorrectness by the appropriate 'rational probability' of the belief-system's having that degree of incorrectness.

My proposal is that each belief-system's degree of irrationality is determined by how its expected degree of incorrectness compares with that of the available alternatives. According to this rational probability function, there will be at least one belief-system that optimizes—that is, minimizes—expected incorrectness (that is, no available alternatives to this belief-system have a lower expected degree of incorrectness); this belief-system's expected degree of incorrectness is the optimal available expected degree of incorrectness. The *greater* the extent to which, according to this rational

---

[9] I shall assume that there is a unique correct way of measuring these degrees of incorrectness—although beyond making a few remarks about this measure in section 4.5, I shall not be able to give a complete account of this measure here.

probability function, a belief-system's expected degree of incorrectness *falls short* of this optimal available expected degree of incorrectness, the *more irrational* the belief-system is. In general, the degree of irrationality of every available belief-system is measured by the *difference* between its expected degree of incorrectness and the optimal available expected degree of incorrectness.[10]

As I shall explain in section 4.5, for every thinker and every time t, there is always at least one belief-system b_t, which is available (at least in principle) to the thinker at t, such that b_t minimizes expected incorrectness according to the probability function that rationally should be guiding the thinker at t if she has this belief-system b_t at t. These belief-systems are the ones that it is maximally rational for the thinker to have at that time. In short, maximally rational belief minimizes expected incorrectness.

This general account of rational belief will entail Joyce's dominance principle as a special case. If a belief-system b_1 is strongly dominated by an alternative b_2, that alternative b_2 will have a better—that is, lower—expected degree of incorrectness. So, the belief-system b_1 cannot minimize expected incorrectness. Since maximally rational belief-systems must minimize expected incorrectness, this strongly dominated belief-system b_1 cannot be maximally rational. In this way, the dominance principle can be explained on the basis of the more general and more fundamental principle that every maximally rational belief-system must minimize expected incorrectness.

4.5 The Structure of Incorrectness

In section 4.4, I proposed that a belief-system's degree of irrationality is determined by how its expected degree of incorrectness compares with that of the available alternatives. To develop this proposal, we will need to explore the nature of both (a) these degrees of incorrectness and (b) this rational probability function—since these are the two elements in terms of which each belief-system's expected degree of incorrectness is defined.

As I have already implied, if the idea of a belief-system's expected degree of incorrectness even makes sense, then these degrees of incorrectness must be measurable on at least an interval scale. This measure can be represented by a scoring rule that assigns each belief-system an 'incorrectness score'—which can be represented by means of a real number. The structure of these degrees of incorrectness can be studied by exploring the features of this scoring rule.

I shall assume here that belief-systems can be modelled by credence functions—where each credence function assigns a real number between 0 and 1 to each of the propositions that the thinker has a doxastic attitude towards. The credence functions of some actual thinkers may be probabilistically incoherent (for example, a thinker

---

[10] For a related approach, which measures a credence function's 'degree of incoherence' by its overall distance from the closest coherent function, see de Bona and Staffel (2017).

may assign different credences to two propositions A and B, even though in fact A and B are logically equivalent), so not all of these credence functions will be probability functions.

In addition, I shall also assume that thinkers may be completely *attitudeless* towards certain propositions—indeed, they may even be attitudeless towards logically complex propositions like '$A \vee B$' even if they have attitudes towards the atomic propositions A and B out of which those complex propositions are composed. To capture this possibility, we must allow that these credence functions may be only partially defined: the set of propositions for which such a function is defined need not be a complete propositional algebra (that is, a field of propositions that is closed under operations like negation, disjunction, and the like). Probability functions, unlike credence functions, cannot be partially defined in this way: every probability function assigns a probability to every proposition in a complete algebra. Still, we may say that a credence function 'coincides' with a probability function if and only if it is possible to *extend* the credence function into that probability function.[11]

Strictly speaking, to capture the ways in which actual thinkers' attitudes may be indeterminate, we should also allow that some belief-systems cannot be represented by a unique real-valued credence function, but only by a set of such functions. However, to keep things simple, I shall ignore this complication, and I shall pretend that every belief-system can be modelled by a unique (though perhaps only partially defined) real-valued credence function.

The proposals that I have made so far already entail that this scoring rule must have certain features. First, it must have the feature that Joyce (2009: 279) calls 'truth-directedness'. Suppose that the truth values, true and false, are identified with 1 and 0 respectively. Then the incorrectness score that a belief-system gets for each proposition A is determined purely by the *distance* between A's truth value and the credence that the function that models the belief-system assigns to A; the smaller this distance, the better the score—and the best possible score is achieved when there is no distance at all between the credence and the truth value.

I have also proposed that the incorrectness score for a whole belief-system is just a weighted sum of the incorrectness scores that the belief-system gets for all the individual propositions that the thinker has doxastic attitudes towards. This implies that the scoring rule must have the feature that Joyce (2009: 271f.) calls 'separability': the scoring rule has an additive structure of this kind.

There seem to be other features that it is intuitively plausible to ascribe to this scoring rule, such as 'continuity' and 'convexity', among others. But the most important feature for our purposes is what is known among statisticians as 'propriety'.[12]

---

[11] For the idea of extending a partially defined preference ranking into a complete ranking, see Joyce (1999: 103–6). The idea that I am invoking here is the analogue of that idea for belief-systems.
[12] For discussions of the idea of a 'proper' scoring rule, see for example Joyce (2009: 276) and Greaves and Wallace (2006).

That is, the scoring rule must ensure that if each belief-system's expected incorrectness score is calculated according to a given probability function P, then any belief-system that can be modelled by a credence function that coincides with P itself will always have an *optimal* expected incorrectness score. If the scoring rule is not just 'proper' but 'strictly proper', then when calculated according to P, the belief-systems that can be modelled by credence functions that coincide with P will have the *uniquely best* expected incorrectness score of all possible belief-systems.

For the rest of this discussion, I shall assume that this scoring rule is not just proper, but *strictly* proper.[13] Thus, when judged from the standpoint of a probability function P, the *only* belief-systems that have an optimal expected incorrectness score are those that can be modelled by credence functions that coincide exactly with P itself. In section 4.4, I proposed that every belief-system's degree of irrationality is measured by the difference between its expected degree of incorrectness and the optimal available expected degree of incorrectness according to the appropriate 'rational probability' for the thinker at the time. This proposal, together with the strict propriety of the incorrectness scoring rule, implies that, for every thinker and every time, the maximally rational belief-systems for the thinker to have at that time will *always* be ones that can be modelled by credence functions that *coincide* with the appropriate 'rational probability' function for that thinker at that time. It follows of course that every maximally rational belief-system must be probabilistically coherent: it must match the particular probability function that counts as the rational probability for the thinker at the relevant time.

This assumption does not make the appeal to belief-systems' expected degree of incorrectness redundant. The notion of expected incorrectness is still necessary for explaining the degree of irrationality of rationally *sub-optimal* belief-systems. However, on these assumptions, the rationally optimal belief-systems will be those that match the relevant rational probability function. So, on these assumptions, it is of great importance to understand exactly which probability function—out of all the infinitely many probability functions that exist—counts as the appropriate rational probability function of this kind. I shall consider this question in section 4.6.

4.6 The Character of Rational Probability

Given that this rational probability function is a measure on the space of epistemically possible worlds that I described above, I have in effect already identified several features that this probability function must have. Specifically, this function must assign probability 1 to every logical and conceptual truth—including conceptual truths that (like 'If B, then Actually B') are not metaphysically necessary. Since metaphysical possibility and epistemic possibility come apart in this way, we should presumably

---

[13] For some reasons in favour this assumption, see Wedgwood (2013a).

also allow that truths that are metaphysically but not epistemically necessary (like 'Hesperus = Phosphorus') may have probabilities that are less than 1.

Why should this rational probability function have these features? The reason seems to be this. These logical and conceptual truths are in some way guaranteed to hold by the essential nature of our concepts, which are among the essential constituents of the mental states that we have—while truths that are metaphysically but not epistemically necessary may be guaranteed to hold by the essential nature of the relevant objects, properties, and relations, but are not in the same way guaranteed to hold by the essential nature of our mental states or their constituents.

This suggests a general way to understand this rational probability function: it must capture everything that the essential nature of the thinker's mental states either guarantees, or at least makes likely, to be true. This understanding of this probability function fits naturally with an 'internalist' view of rationality—that is, with the view that the attitudes that it is rational for a thinker to have at a given time are determined purely by the mental states and events that are present in the thinker's mind at that time, and not by any facts about the external world that could vary while these mental states and events remained unchanged.[14] At the same time, this understanding seems to address the main complaint that externalists have raised against internalism—namely, that if it is to be a genuine value, rationality must have a real (and not merely presumed) connection of some kind with the truth.[15]

One picturesque way of conceiving of this rational probability function is to imagine an *angel* perched inside the thinker's head—where the angel's advice to the thinker takes the form of this rational probability function. Unfortunately, this angel is uncertain about many empirical propositions about the world. However, the angel knows all relevant truths about the mental states and events that are present in the thinker's mind at the time; and she can assign probabilities to these empirical propositions by relying on what she knows about these mental states and events, together with everything that the essential nature of these mental states and events either guarantees or makes likely to be true. (Thus, for example, the angel knows all logical and conceptual truths involving concepts that the thinker possesses, among other things.)

As I explained in section 4.5, the proposals that I have made so far imply that at every time, every thinker rationally should have a system of beliefs that matches the probability function that count as the rational probability function for that thinker at that time (given that she has this system of beliefs). What this means, in effect, is that many of the great questions of epistemology become in effect questions about these rational probability functions.

---

[14] This is not the 'accessibilist' version of internalism, but the 'mentalist' version instead. I have discussed this kind of internalism elsewhere; see for example Wedgwood (2002).

[15] For such externalist criticisms of internalism, see for example Goldman (1999).

Some features of the probability function that count as the rational probability for a particular thinker at a particular time will vary between different thinkers and different times—even if these thinkers possess exactly the same concepts at these times. These features of these probability functions are in a sense *empirical*: they depend on contingent features of these thinkers' mental lives at these times, and not merely on the concepts that they possess or the capacities that are required for them to count as rational thinkers at all. Other features will be found in *every* probability function that counts as the rational probability of any thinker who possesses these concepts. These features are broadly a priori: they depend only on the concepts that these thinkers possess and the capacities that are presupposed by their being rational thinkers in the first place.

The fact that all logical and conceptual truths have probability 1 is presumably an a priori feature of these rational probability functions. But there may also be other such a priori features as well. For example, perhaps every one of these rational probability functions must obey the 'Principal Principle'—so that, for example, if one of these probability functions assigns probability 1 to the proposition that a coin that is about to be tossed has a 0.5 chance of landing heads (and none of the other propositions that have probability 1 directly concern the outcome of the toss in an 'inadmissible' way), then this function must also assign probability 0.5 to the proposition that the coin will land heads.[16]

There may also be certain universal principles governing the *empirical* features of these rational probability functions. Let us return to the image of this rational probability function as an angel perched inside your head, giving you advice on the basis of what she can work out from what she knows about the mental states and events inside your mind. This image suggests that one of the things that the angel will tell you about (even if you may often fail to take in the angel's advice) is everything that she knows about what is going on inside your mind. In other words, the rational probability function will incorporate a kind of *positive introspection principle*: if *A* is one of the relevant truths about the mental states that are currently present in your mind, then the rational probability function for you at this time must assign probability 1 to *A*.[17]

We can illustrate this introspection principle by considering the phenomenon of *self-undermining beliefs*. For example, consider Moore's paradox, which concerns the first-person present-tensed propositions that one could express by saying something

---

[16] For an illuminating discussion of the Principal Principle, see Meacham (2010).

[17] If this strong 'positive introspection' principle is acceptable, then arguably a corresponding 'negative introspection' principle would also be acceptable: that is, if *B* is one of the relevant *false* propositions about what mental states you have at time *t*, then the rational probability function for you at *t* will assign probability 0 to *B*. These introspection principles may seem implausible, but they are not theses about what credence you will actually have—or even about the credences that you are realistically in a position to have. In the jargon of epistemologists (see Turri 2010), they are theses about *propositional*, not *doxastic*, justification—that is, about the attitudes that it is (ideally) rational for you to have, not about the attitudes that you will actually rationally have.

of the form 'A and I do not believe that A'. Clearly, such a proposition may be true. Moreover, nothing prevents this proposition from having high probability conditional on one's evidence. (Just suppose that you simultaneously receive messages from two fabulously reliable oracles—one testifying that you will never believe A, and the other testifying that A is true.) Still, it surely cannot be rational for you to believe this paradoxical proposition, even for an instant, because it should be obvious to you that if you believe this proposition, it is false.

Here is an explanation of why a perfectly rational thinker will never have such self-undermining beliefs, even for an instant. According to the introspection principle, for every thinker x and every time t, if x has a belief-system b_i at t, then the rational probability function for x at t must assign probability 1 to the proposition *that she has this belief-system b_i at t*. Clearly, no probability function can assign a high probability to 'A and I don't believe that A' at the same time as assigning probability 1 to the proposition 'I believe that: A and I don't believe that A', at least not if it is effectively a conceptual truth that belief distributes over conjunction. (In that case, the probability function would also have to assign probability 1 to 'I believe that A' at the same time as assigning high probability to that proposition's negation 'I don't believe that A'.) According to my proposals, it is perfectly rational to have a certain credence in a proposition only if that credence coincides with the relevant rational probability of the proposition. Thus, it cannot be perfectly rational to have high credence in this Moore-paradoxical proposition.

This approach can also explain not just self-undermining beliefs, but also *self-supporting* beliefs—such as the belief that one could express by saying 'I have at least one belief about my beliefs'. One might have no independent evidence supporting this belief, but it is obvious that if one believes this proposition, it will be true. So it seems that it is always rational to believe it. This can be explained on the basis of the fact that any probability function that assigns probability 1 to 'I believe that: I have at least one belief about my beliefs' must also assign probability 1 to 'I have at least one belief about my beliefs', given that it is a conceptual truth that the latter proposition is about one's beliefs, and so believing this proposition entails having at least one belief about one's beliefs.

In this way, the rational probability function that should be used to calculate each belief-system's expected degree of incorrectness (and so also, according to my proposals, each belief-system's degree of irrationality) depends in part on which belief-system the thinker actually has. If the belief-system that the thinker has at t is b_i, then the probability function that determines the available belief-systems' expected degrees of incorrectness (which in turn determines b_i's degree of irrationality) must be a probability function that assigns probability 1 to the proposition that the thinker has this belief-system b_i at t.[18] It does not follow that this belief-system b_i

---

[18] This feature of rational belief is in my view exactly parallelled by a corresponding feature of rational choice; for a discussion of this feature of rational choice, see Wedgwood (2013b).

is maximally rational—since even if this probability function assigns probability 1 to the proposition that the thinker has b_i, some other belief-system b_j might have a much better expected degree of incorrectness according to this probability function. (This will clearly be the case, for example, if b_i is probabilistically incoherent.)

In effect, the truth about what is present in the thinker's mind at the time can be thought of as at least part of the 'evidence' that the thinker has at this time. Indeed, we can simply *identify* the 'evidence' that the thinker has at this time with those propositions that (a) are assigned probability 1 by the rational probability function for that thinker at that time, but (b) unlike a priori truths are not assigned probability 1 by *all* rational probability functions for all thinkers and all times. On this conception of evidence, we may imagine that at each time the rational angel knows all the truths that constitute the thinker's evidence at the time—including all the truths about the beliefs and other mental states and events that are present in the thinker's mind at that time—and so the angel's advice is a probability function that gives all these evidence propositions probability 1. What perfect rationality requires of each thinker at each time is that she should have some belief-system that matches the probability function that would constitute the rational angel's advice given that she has that belief-system.

This idea could be developed in a number of ways. For example, some philosophers might suppose—perhaps along the lines that have been proposed by Timothy Williamson (2000: ch. 8)—that there is a special privileged a priori Ur-prior probability function, which *all* thinkers should start out from before any particular evidence is acquired. Given this supposition, it would be plausible to identify the rational probability function, for a given thinker at a given time, with the result of *conditionalizing* this a priori Ur-prior on the thinker's total evidence (including the truth about the mental states and events that are present in the thinker's mind at that time). In the picturesque terms that I have suggested, on this view, at every time the angel simply conditionalizes this a priori Ur-prior on the total evidence that the thinker has at that time.

However, many philosophers are sceptical about the idea of the special privileged Ur-prior probability function. Some of these philosophers might propose that so long as a belief-system meets certain basic constraints of synchronic coherence, 'anything goes': every such synchronically coherent belief-system is perfectly rational. This is a kind of radical subjectivism about rational belief.[19] My idea could be developed so that it conforms to this subjectivist proposal—so long as it is one of these basic constraints of synchronic coherence that it is incoherent to have incorrect beliefs about the mental states and events that are currently present in one's mind. On this subjectivist proposal, the rational probability function for a thinker at a given time will always be a probability function that is as close as possible to the belief-system that the thinker actually has at that time. On this approach, the rational angel's advice

---

[19] For example, van Fraassen (1984) might be taken as one proponent of such a radical subjectivist view.

at each time takes the form of a probability function that (a) meets all constraints of rational coherence, (b) assigns probability 1 to the evidence (including the truth about the mental states and events that are present in the thinker's mind at that time), and (c) is otherwise as close as possible to the thinker's actual belief-system at that time.

There is a third view that is intermediate between these two extremes—between the extreme rigorism of the a priori Ur-prior and the extreme permissivism of the radical subjectivist approach. This intermediate view proposes that the thinker is rationally required to be guided by her *actual past* beliefs; but unlike with the theory of the special a priori Ur-prior, there is no reason to suppose that all rational thinkers must start out with the *same* set of ultimate priors. On this approach, the rational angel's advice at each time takes the form of a probability function that (a) meets all constraints of rational coherence, (b) assigns probability 1 to the evidence (including the truth about what is present in the thinker's mind at that time), and (c) is otherwise as close as possible to the belief-system that the thinker actually had *immediately before* that time.

In section 4.7, I shall explore this third proposal about the rational probability function in more detail. As I shall explain, this proposal introduces a new and deeper understanding of the notion of 'diachronic rationality'.

4.7 Diachronic Rationality

I suggested in section 4.1 that one way to think of the distinction between synchronic and diachronic rationality is simply as marking a difference in the items whose rationality is being assessed—specifically, the difference between (a) statically enduring mental states (like belief-states) and (b) mental events (such as events in which we form or revise our beliefs).

There is, intuitively, a connection between these two kinds of rationality. Although one might form a belief in a proposition *A* and then immediately forget all about *A* in the next instant, the normal effect of forming a belief in *A* is precisely that one thereby acquires an enduring state of believing *A*. In general, the normal effect of each of these mental events is to have a certain constellation of static states, which we can view as the *output* of the mental event. The mental event itself occurs against the background of some *prior* mental states; we can view this background as the mental event's *input*. Thus, the mental event can be understood as a *transition* from this input to the relevant output.

An intuitively appealing account of the rationality of mental events of this kind is that such transitions are rational to the extent that they guarantee that their output will be no less rational than their input.[20] So, in particular, a perfectly rational mental

---

[20] This does not yet amount to a precise general account of how to *measure* 'the extent to which a transition guarantees that the output will be no less rational than the input'. For cases where the thinker's evidence remains the same, one such measure is proposed by Staffel (2017); but it remains an open question

event will always map a perfectly rational input onto a perfectly rational output. This account effectively defines the rationality of mental events in terms of the rationality of mental states.

There is also, however, a deeper question that is raised by the contemporary debates about diachronic rationality. This is the question of whether what I have called the 'rational probability function', for a thinker at a given time, is determined purely by what is true of the thinker at that time, or whether it is also determined, at least in part, by something about the thinker's *past*.[21]

In section 4.6, I considered the radical subjectivist approach to rational belief. For these subjectivists, rationality is simply a matter of coherence between the attitudes that the thinker has at a single time. On this view, even if one's beliefs arbitrarily undergo a sudden radical revolution—as in the Biblical story of Paul's conversion on the road to Damascus (Acts 9: 3–9)—this need not be irrational in any way. However, just as we can make sense of coherence among the mental states that a thinker has at a time, we can also make sense of *coherence over time*—that is, coherence between the beliefs that a thinker has at one time and the beliefs that the thinker has at an immediately preceding time. Coherence over time is in effect a kind of *conservatism*: it involves minimizing the changes that one makes to one's belief-system in adjusting to new evidence over time. If rationality requires this sort of conservatism, this requirement would be diachronic in a deeper way.

One way to understand diachronic requirements of this deeper kind would be on the basis of the principle that I briefly sketched at the end of section 4.6. This was the principle that if the thinker has a particular belief-system b_1 at a time t_1, then b_1's degree of irrationality is determined by how it compares with the available alternatives in terms of their expected degrees of incorrectness according to a probability function P_1 that (a) meets all constraints of rational coherence, (b) assigns probability 1 to the evidence that the thinker has at that time (including the truth about the mental states, like the belief-system b_1, in the thinker's mind at t_1), and (c) is otherwise as close as possible to the belief-system b_0 that the thinker had at the *immediately preceding* time t_0.

How should we understand this idea of a probability function P_1's being 'otherwise as close as possible' to the thinker's prior belief-system b_0? Consider the special case where the thinker's prior belief-system b_0 was perfectly probabilistically coherent, and so coincides with a probability function P_0. In this special case, the probability function that assigns probability 1 to the new evidence (including the truth about what is in the thinker's mind at t_1) but is otherwise 'as close as possible' to the old belief-system b_0 *may* just be the result of *conditionalizing* P_0 on the evidence that

---

how to develop such a measure for cases involving the acquisition (or loss) of evidence, where the input state is less than perfectly rational.

[21] This is the issue that is raised by the debate between synchronists like Hedden (2015) and their opponents like Podgorski (2016).

the thinker has at t_1. However, as I shall explain in section 4.8, it need not *always* be the case that the rational probability function results from the thinker's prior belief-system by conditionalization in this way. If so, then conditionalization is at best an *approximation* to the truth about diachronic rationality. Unfortunately, however, I shall not be able to explore the conditions under which diachronic rationality does conform to conditionalization: that task will have to await another occasion.[22]

At all events, any version of this kind of conservatism about rational belief implies that every thinker is rationally required to have a certain kind of trust in her past beliefs. It is a good question why the thinker should trust her past beliefs in this way. Broadly speaking, it is analogous to other famous epistemological questions, such as why the thinker should trust her experiences or her episodic memories. Within our framework, these questions in effect become questions about the relevant 'rational probability function'. But the fundamental import of the questions remains the same.

I cannot attempt a full exploration of these questions here. But to fix ideas, I shall offer a conjecture about how they might be answered. According to this conjecture, the answer to this question involves three elements. The first element is the thesis that a tendency to maintain and continue relying on some of one's past beliefs is partially constitutive of being a thinker at all. The second element is the thesis that it is essential to all beliefs that they have some tendency to be rational, and, as I have suggested, it is an essential and necessary feature of rationality that it has at least a certain weak connection to the truth. Finally, the third element is the point that both of the two extreme views of rational belief that were considered at the end of section 4.6 are implausible. Contrary to the radical subjectivist view, our thinking would be objectionably arbitrary if there were nothing that guided us in responding to new evidence and new experiences. Contrary to the view that posits an a priori Ur-prior, there does not seem to be a special privileged Ur-prior that all thinkers should start out from. So there is nothing else in our minds that can reliably guide us in this way that has a stronger essential connection to the truth than our past beliefs.

Together, these three points may provide an explanation of why we should trust our past beliefs in this way—specifically, an explanation that respects both the internalist insight that rationality supervenes purely on the mental states and events in the thinker's mind, and also the point (which externalists rightly insist on) that rationality must have some real and not merely imagined connection to the truth. In this way, the proposals that I have suggested so far can provide a sketch of how the

---

[22] This is one of several ways in which this conception of diachronic rationality differs from the familiar subjective Bayesian approach of the sort that was advocated by Jeffrey (2003). Besides not being committed to conditionalization's being the only rational method of belief revision, it is not restricted to cases where the thinker's prior beliefs are probabilistically coherent; it can allow for beliefs' being forgotten and evidence's being lost over time; and it may allow for further constraints of rational coherence (like the Principal Principle), in addition to probabilism itself.

alethic-value-based conception of epistemology might account for diachronic requirements of rationality.[23]

4.8 Self-Supporting and Self-Undermining Beliefs

In this final section, I shall explain how the picture that I have sketched above can deal with *self-supporting* and *self-undermining* beliefs, which some philosophers have taken to provide challenging problems for this approach. My solution to these problems will rely heavily on the idea that the rational probability function satisfies the positive introspection principle that I described in section 4.6 above.

My proposals imply that a perfectly rational belief-system can always be modelled by a credence function that coincides with the relevant rational probability function. As I understand this, a credence function can 'coincide' with a probability function even if the credence function is only partially defined. For the rest of this discussion, however, I shall ignore this complication. I shall assume that the thinker does have attitudes towards all the propositions that feature in the cases that we shall consider. This means that for our purposes, we need not worry about the distinction between a credence function (which may be only partially defined) and a probability function (which is defined for every proposition in the relevant algebra). In effect, we will work with the simplifying assumption that every rational belief-system can be modelled by a credence function that is identical to a probability function.

My proposals about the rational probability function, as I have explained, incorporate a positive introspection principle, according to which the rational probability function must assign probability 1 to the truth about the relevant mental states and events that are present in the thinker's mind at the relevant time. Taken together, these proposals imply that, at least in the relevant cases, there are some significant limits on what it is rational to believe. In particular, as has been shown by Andy Egan and Adam Elga (2005), if the thinker correctly introspects her level of credence in a proposition A, it cannot be rational for her to have too high a level of confidence in the biconditional proposition that she could express by saying 'A is true if and only if it is not the case that my credence in $A \geq 0.5$'. As Egan and Elga put it, you cannot rationally believe that you are an 'anti-expert' about A.

Suppose that the thinker has credence 1 in the biconditional that she could express by saying 'A is true if and only if it is not the case that my credence in $A \geq 0.5$'. Now, either her credence in $A \geq 0.5$ or it is not. Suppose that her credence in $A \geq 0.5$. Then she will have a maximally confident introspective belief that her credence in $A \geq 0.5$; and given her belief in the biconditional, this introspective belief will commit her

---

[23] This sketch of an explanation of why it is rational for us to be guided by our past beliefs is modelled on the account of why it is rational for us to trust our sensory experiences that I gave elsewhere (Wedgwood 2011).

to having a credence of 0 in A. Alternatively, suppose that it is not the case that her credence in $A \geq 0.5$. Then the thinker will introspect that fact about her beliefs, and together with the biconditional, she will be committed to having a credence of 1 in A. So, either way, if she has too much confidence in this biconditional, introspection guarantees probabilistic incoherence.

Some philosophers have tried to exploit this point to raise objections to probabilism, or to the idea that a perfectly rational belief-system must minimize expected incorrectness. Thus, for example, Carr (2017) imagines that a 'perfectly reliable... teacher' might tell you that A is true if and only if it is not the case that your credence in $A \geq 0.5$. But even if a perfectly reliable teacher tells you this, according to my proposals, it cannot be rational for you to believe what this teacher says. In effect, if your teacher tells you this, your only rational option is to doubt your teacher's reliability.

We need not deny that you might learn that you are *going to be* an anti-expert about some proposition in the *future*. You might rationally come to believe at t_0 that A is true if and only if it is not the case that the credence in A that you will have at a later time $t_1 \geq 0.5$. But when t_1 comes, you cannot rationally retain this belief by believing the proposition that you could express by uttering the biconditional 'A is true if and only if it is not the case that the credence that I *now* have in $A \geq 0.5$'. Admittedly, there may be no way of explaining how you rationally lose your confidence in this biconditional at t_1 by appeal to anything like conditionalization. If so, however, what this would show is that conditionalization is only an approximation to the full story about diachronic rationality—an approximation that gets it right in a wide range of cases, perhaps, but not in tricky cases of this sort.[24]

Michael Caie (2013) has focused on cases of self-referential propositions—like the propositions that you might express by saying something like 'I do not believe *this very proposition*'. More precisely, he focuses on propositions that you might express by saying, 'It is not the case that my confidence in the truth of *this very proposition* ≥ 0.5'. Caie assumes that as a matter of logic or analytic truth, this proposition is true if and only if it is not the case that your confidence in this proposition ≥ 0.5.

However, I do not see why we should accept that this is a matter of logic or analytic truth. Every proposition that you are capable of even considering or having any attitudes towards, I propose, is such that there is some doxastic attitude that it is perfectly rational for you to have towards it.[25] Given the conception of rational belief that I am sketching here, there could not be any perfectly rational attitude for you to have towards a proposition A for which it was an analytic truth that A is true if

---

[24] For a compelling argument for the conclusion that conditionalization is only an approximation to the full story about diachronic rationality, see Arntzenius (2003).

[25] The underlying idea is that propositions of the relevant kind are Fregean *Gedanken*, which, as I have argued elsewhere (Wedgwood 2007: ch. 7), are essentially individuated by the conditions under which it is rational to take doxastic attitudes towards them.

and only if it is not the case that your confidence in $A \geq 0.5$. So I must conclude that it is not possible for you even to consider or to have any attitudes towards any such proposition. Whatever the sentence 'I do not believe this very proposition' expresses, as uttered on your lips, it cannot be a proposition of this sort.[26]

I shall close by considering a number of cases that have been explored by Hilary Greaves (2013), which she takes to constitute problems for the general idea of an alethic-value-based epistemology of the sort that we have been discussing here. Officially, every one of these cases concerns *synchronic* rationality, since these cases are stipulated to be cases in which the thinker acquires no new evidence. Greaves is interested in exploring a version of this value-based approach that she takes to be analogous to 'practical decision theory'—that is, to the theory of rational choice. According to this version of the approach, having a certain belief-system is construed as an 'epistemic act', where the rationality of such acts is explained by the kind of practical decision theory that she has in mind. According to this kind of decision theory, the rationality of an act is explained by a set of credences as well as by an appropriate value. So, Greaves specifies each of the cases that she considers by means of what she calls an 'initial' set of credences. In each case, certain belief-systems or sets of credences turn out to maximize some kind of expected value according to those initial credences; she labels each set of credences that maximizes this kind of expected value the thinker's 'final' credences.

This interpretation of the value-based framework has a number of features that seem somewhat strange, at least to me. First, it is odd to compare the statically enduring state of having a certain belief-system to an *act*: acts are naturally thought of as events, rather than statically enduring states; further, acts typically involve part of what occurs in the agent's environment, as well as what occurs in the agent's mind. On the practical side, the item that seems most analogous to a belief-system is not an act or even a decision but rather a collection of *plans* or *intentions*, which like a belief-system is a statically enduring state. (In formal presentations of decision theory, the item whose rationality is being explained is typically identified with a *system of preferences*, but if we stick more closely to ordinary folk-psychological thought, it seems that the practical mental state whose rationality is in question is typically a collection of plans and intentions.) This interpretation of practical decision theory as fundamentally concerned with the rationality of collections of intentions also suits the fact that, strictly speaking, decision theory is a purely *synchronic* theory, specifying the relations of coherence that rationality requires between the preferences, credences, and intentions that the agent has at any given time; as a synchronic theory, it is more easily understood as primarily concerned with statically enduring mental states than with mental events or transitions.

Secondly, it is hard to understand exactly what role the 'initial credences' are supposed to play in the cases that Greaves describes. Since the thinker acquires no

---

[26] This approach to these self-referential cases is due to Prior (1961). I am indebted here to conversation with my colleague Andrew Bacon.

new evidence, surely the thinker should just persist with the initial credences that she already has. (Even if we understand these 'initial credences' as corresponding to what I have called the relevant 'rational probability' function, it seems that the thinker should just have a set of credences that matches this probability function.) What Greaves (2013: 936) herself says is the following: 'In other words, the agent's awareness of certain facts—the facts given in the case-specification—gives rise to rationality constraints on her credences; the 'initial' credence function is one respecting these rationality constraints.' But if (because of the thinker's 'awareness of certain facts') the thinker really is rationally required to have a credence function that respects certain constraints, then it cannot be true that she is rationally permitted at the same time to have a 'final' credence function that does not respect these constraints. So the role of these 'initial' credences remains obscure.

Still, Greaves's description of the cases seems intuitively to make sense. It seems to me that when we have an impression that these cases make sense, we are tacitly forgetting the stipulation that these cases do not involve the acquisition of evidence. We are supposing instead that the thinker *learns* that the case that she is in has the specified features, and we then inquire into how it is rational for the thinker to *respond* to acquiring this information. For example, consider what Greaves (2013: 916) calls the 'Leap' case:

Bob stands on the brink of a chasm, summoning up the courage to try and leap across it. Confidence helps him in such situations: specifically, for any value of x between 0 and 1, if Bob attempted to leap across the chasm while having degree of belief x that he would succeed, his chance of success would then be x. What credence in success is it epistemically rational for Bob to have?

Intuitively, this case makes perfect sense. But this, I suggest, is because we interpret it as a case in which Bob *learns* that his chance of success in leaping across the chasm corresponds exactly to his degree of belief in the proposition that if he tried to leap across, he would succeed. The question that we want to answer about this case is: how (if at all) should Bob revise his degree of belief in this proposition in response to learning this?

On this interpretation of this case, it is clear what the theory that I have proposed will say. It will say that *whatever* credence Bob might have in this proposition, that credence will be perfectly rational. This is because every such credence x forms part of a belief-system b_x such that x is the probability that is assigned to the proposition in question by the probability function that meets all constraints of rational coherence (including the Principal Principle), assigns probability 1 to all of Bob's evidence (including the proposition that Bob has this belief-system b_x), and is otherwise as close as possible to Bob's prior belief-system.

Admittedly, it is tempting to say that in this case, Bob should have a more extreme credence, such as either 0 or 1. However, this inclination is probably explained by the difficulty in separating an austerely epistemic use of 'should' from a more *practical* use. In a more practical sense, these extreme credences have something to be said for them that the more intermediate credences lack: these extreme credences will lead to definite safe decisions, either to leap across the chasm, or to step back and find another route forward, while the more intermediate credences will lead to a more difficult and alarming decision. However, if we set these practical considerations aside, there seems to me nothing strictly epistemic to be said in favour of any of these credences over any of the others. (Imagine that Bob is not trying to leap across the chasm, but is just inquiring in a spirit of purely idle curiosity about whether he would succeed if he tried. Then it does not seem obvious that it is less rational for him to have an intermediate credence like 0.5 in this proposition rather than an extreme credence like 0 or 1.)

With all of Greaves's other examples, the theory that I have proposed will straightforwardly agree with the verdicts that she regards as intuitively plausible. For example, consider Greaves's (2013: 915f.) 'Promotion' case:

Alice is up for promotion. Her boss, however, is a deeply insecure type: he is more likely to promote Alice if she comes across as lacking in confidence. Furthermore, Alice is useless at play-acting, so she will come across that way iff she really does have a low degree of belief that she's going to get the promotion. Specifically, the chance of her getting the promotion will be $(1 - x)$, where x is whatever degree of belief she chooses to have in the proposition P that she will be promoted.

Here, there is a uniquely rational credence for Alice to have: 0.5. This is the only available credence that matches the rational probability function that should be guiding her given that she has all this evidence (including the fact that she has this very credence).

In all these cases, however, it is not really the value-based framework itself that explains why my approach yields the intuitively correct verdicts. What explains this is the character of the rational probability function. Specifically, it is explained by the following two features of this probability function:

i. First, for every thinker x, time t, and belief-system b_t, it is perfectly rational for x to have b_t at t if and only if b_t matches the probability function that counts as the rational probability for x at t, given that the thinker x has this belief-system b_t at t.
ii. Secondly, whenever the thinker's evidence changes, this probability function also changes to the probability function that (a) conforms to all constraints of rational coherence, (b) assigns probability 1 to all the thinker's evidence (including the truth about the new belief-system that the thinker now has), and (c) is otherwise as close as possible to the belief-system that the thinker had at the immediately preceding time.

As condition (b) of this point (ii) makes clear, these features of the rational probability function include the positive introspection principle that I have described. In general, the explanation of these features of the rational probability function relies on the internalist-but-still-truth-connected conception of rationality that I alluded to in the previous section; it does not directly rely on the idea that rational belief-systems must minimize expected incorrectness.

In this way, my proposed interpretation of the connection between epistemic rationality and minimizing expected incorrectness (or optimizing expected alethic value) is not, as Greaves (2013: 926) puts it, 'ambitious'. That is, it does not attempt to derive *all* of the distinctive features of rational belief from this idea of the connection between rationality and alethic value. But I suggest that the goal of finding such an ambitious interpretation is chimerical. Once we abandon the attempt to give such an ambitious interpretation, we can understand how rationality is connected to correctness—that is, to alethic value—without sacrificing the plausibility of our account of rationality.[27]

References

Åqvist, Lennart (1984). 'Deontic Logic', in Dov Gabbay, ed., *Handbook of Philosophical Logic* (Dordrecht: Reidel), 605–714.
Arntzenius, Frank (2003). 'Some Problems for Conditionalization and Reflection', *Journal of Philosophy* 100(7): 356–70.
Berker, Selim (2013). 'The Rejection of Epistemic Consequentialism', *Philosophical Issues* 23: 363–87.
Broome, John (1991). ' "Utility" ', *Economics and Philosophy* 7(1): 1–12.
Caie, Michael (2013). 'Rational Probabilistic Incoherence', *Philosophical Review* 122(4): 527–75.
Carr, Jennifer (2015). 'Epistemic Expansions', *Res Philosophica* 92(2): 217–36.
Carr, Jennifer (2017). 'Epistemic Utility Theory and the Aim of Belief', *Philosophy and Phenomenological Research* 95(3): 511–34.
de Bona, Glauber, and Staffel, Julia (2017). 'Graded Incoherence for Accuracy-Firsters', *Philosophy of Science* 84(2): 189–213.
Egan, Andy, and Elga, Adam (2005). 'I Can't Believe I'm Stupid', *Philosophical Perspectives* 19(1): 77–93.
Firth, Roderick (1981). 'Epistemic Merit, Intrinsic and Instrumental', *Proceedings and Addresses of the American Philosophical Association* 55: 5–23.
Goldman, Alvin (1999). 'Internalism Exposed', *Journal of Philosophy* 96 (6): 271–93.
Greaves, Hilary (2013). 'Epistemic Decision Theory', *Mind* 122(488): 915–52.
Greaves, Hilary, and Wallace, David (2006). 'Justifying Conditionalization: Conditionalization Maximizes Expected Epistemic Utility', *Mind* 115(459): 607–32.

---

[27] Earlier versions of this chapter were presented at the University of Kent, the University of Konstanz, and the University of Michigan. I am grateful to the members of those audiences—and especially to my commentator in Kent, Richard Pettigrew, and my commentator in Michigan, Daniel Drucker—and also to Jeffrey Dunn, one of the editors of this volume, for helpful comments. Finally, I am also indebted to Catrin Campbell-Moore, Jason Konek, Ben Levinstein, and Julia Staffel, who had an online discussion of this chapter—and especially to Julia Staffel, who gave me an extremely useful summary of the group's comments.

Hedden, Brian (2015). 'Time-Slice Rationality', *Mind* 124(494): 449–91.
Jeffrey, Richard C. (2003). *Subjective Probability: The Real Thing* (Cambridge: Cambridge University Press).
Joyce, James M. (1998). 'A Nonpragmatic Vindication of Probabilism', *Philosophy of Science* 65(4): 575–603.
Joyce, James M. (1999). *Foundations of Causal Decision Theory* (Cambridge: Cambridge University Press).
Joyce, James M. (2009). 'Accuracy and Coherence: Prospects for an Alethic Epistemology of Partial Belief', in Franz Huber and Christoph Schmidt-Petri, ed., *Degrees of Belief*, Synthese Library Vol. 342 (Berlin: Springer): 263–97.
Krantz, David H., Luce, R. Duncan, Suppes, Patrick, and Tversky, Amos (1971). *Foundations of Measurement I: Additive and Polynomial Representations* (London: Academic Press).
Kratzer, Angelika (2012). *Modals and Conditionals: New and Revised Perspectives* (Oxford: Oxford University Press).
Lewis, David (1973). *Counterfactuals* (Oxford: Blackwell).
Meacham, C. J. G. (2010). 'Two Mistakes Regarding the Principal Principle', *British Journal for the Philosophy of Science* 61(2): 407–31.
Pettigrew, Richard (2013). 'Introducing . . . Epistemic Utility Theory', *The Reasoner* 7(1): 10–11.
Pettit, Philip (1991). 'Consequentialism', in Peter Singer, ed., *A Companion to Ethics* (Oxford: Blackwell): 230–40.
Podgorski, Abelard (2016). 'A Reply to the Synchronist', *Mind* 125(499): 859–71.
Prior, A. N. (1961). 'On a Family of Paradoxes', *Notre Dame Journal of Formal Logic* 2(1): 16–32.
Rawls, John (1971). *A Theory of Justice* (Cambridge, MA: Harvard University Press).
Staffel, Julia (2017). 'Should I Pretend I'm Perfect?' *Res Philosophica* 94(2): 301–24.
Thomson, Judith (2008). *Normativity* (Chicago, IL: Open Court).
Turri, John (2010). 'On the Relationship between Propositional and Doxastic Justification', *Philosophy and Phenomenological Research* 80(2): 312–26.
van Fraassen, Bas (1984). 'Belief and the Will', *Journal of Philosophy* 81(5): 235–56.
Wedgwood, Ralph (2002). 'Internalism Explained', *Philosophy and Phenomenological Research* 65(2): 349–69.
Wedgwood, Ralph (2007). *The Nature of Normativity* (Oxford: Clarendon Press).
Wedgwood, Ralph (2011). 'Primitively Rational Belief-Forming Processes', in Andrew Reisner and Asbjørn Steglich-Petersen, ed., *Reasons for Belief* (Cambridge: Cambridge University Press): 180–200.
Wedgwood, Ralph (2013a). 'Doxastic Correctness', *Proceedings of the Aristotelian Society*, Supp. Vol. 87: 38–54.
Wedgwood, Ralph (2013b). 'Gandalf's Solution to the Newcomb Problem', *Synthese* 190(14): 2643–75.
Wedgwood, Ralph (2017). *The Value of Rationality* (Oxford: Oxford University Press).
Williamson, Timothy (2000). *Knowledge and its Limits* (Oxford: Clarendon Press).

5

The "Consequentialism" in "Epistemic Consequentialism"

Julia Driver

A good deal has recently been written on epistemic consequentialism. It is a literature that draws on an analogy between consequentialism in ethics (C) and approaches to understanding epistemic success in terms of promotion of the epistemic good (EC). It is quite natural to view beliefs as aiming at the epistemic good.[1] This is one core tenet of the epistemic consequentialist, but it is quite intuitive and shared by a wide range of people. It is not yet epistemic consequentialism. But we can get there, they argue, by considering an analogy with ethical consequentialism: one might hold that action aims at the good—and one can fill in, here, one's favorite account of value. Just as an example, hedonists will view the intrinsic good as pleasure. Everything we think of as good is good because of the pleasure generated or instantiated. Combine this with consequentialism's commitment to promotion or maximization of the good, and we get a rough idea of what epistemic consequentialism is about. On this view, the epistemically responsible agent is one who is in the business of promoting true or correct belief. Something like this was expressed by William Alston:

> Epistemic evaluation is undertaken from what we might call the "epistemic point of view." That point of view is defined by the aim at maximizing truth and minimizing falsity in a large body of beliefs.   (Alston 1989: 83)

But this very general characterization leaves several issues unaddressed, for example, "aim at" is ambiguous. Does the epistemically responsible agent need to *try* to arrive at the truth in order for the belief to be correct or justified? That seems very implausible, since many of my justified true beliefs are those that really just happen, for example, as the result of a well-functioning perceptual system, as when I walk outside and come to believe that the sky is blue. The more natural view is to hold that truth is a criterion or standard of correctness, in which case it is not necessary for the epistemically

---

[1] Just for convenience I will view the epistemic good as true belief, but I am non-committal on this issue. Fill in whatever view of epistemic good one finds plausible: significant true belief, accurate belief, etc.

responsible agent to always be seeking to acquire a true belief. This is an important distinction returned to later in the chapter

Another very general characterization of epistemic consequentialism is offered by Kristoffer Ahlstrom-Vij and Jeffrey Dunn:

(EC) Epistemic consequentialism is the idea that the epistemically *right* (e.g. the justified) is to be understood in terms of conduciveness to the epistemic *good* (e.g. true belief).

(Ahlstrom-Vij and Dunn 2014: 541)

One very prominent version of the (EC) approach is process-reliabilism, which Selim Berker characterizes this way:

What makes a belief epistemically justified is its connection to a process (or indicator, or method, or . . .) that conduces towards the promotion of true belief and the avoidance of false belief. (Berker 2013a: 363)

An example of a reliable process would be perception under the right circumstances, as in the earlier example, when I am justified in believing that the sky is blue when I perceive it as blue, because, very roughly, perception is a reliable way to acquire true belief, and so provides justification. Process-reliabilism is analogous to rule-consequentialism, in which an action's rightness is determined via the utility of the *rule* or *system of rules* the action conforms to.[2]

While process-reliabilism has been the dominant form, other forms of epistemic consequentialism can be spelled out, and may offer some ways around some of the problems, though certainly not all, that have been raised for process-reliabilism. My aim is to develop an approach to epistemic consequentialism by analogy with sophisticated objective consequentialism in ethics. I believe that this approach can provide responses to criticisms of process-reliabilism presented by Selim Berker (2013a: 363). However, I also think that there are shortcomings for the epistemic version of the theory that may be exposed by the analogy. Thus, I am not endorsing this approach in epistemology. However, I also believe that developing the epistemic consequentialism approach in a different way can be illuminating for those who do endorse the analogy.

5.1 Epistemic Consequentialism

Is epistemic consequentialism really consequentialism? Perhaps what is meant by "epistemic consequentialism" is a form of teleology, in which the *right* is understood in terms of the *good*. So, for example, the right belief is just the true one (or the accurate one, etc.), and is thus simply an *instantiation* of the good. Other writers have pointed out possible problems with this, if we were to understand "right" as "justified." So, let's consider how a genuine form of epistemic consequentialism might

---

[2] A well-known version of this view is presented in Hooker (2000).

work: the sophisticated epistemic consequentialist by analogy with the sophisticated ethical consequentialist.

Peter Railton (1984) made a case for *sophisticated consequentialism* by noting that consequentialists could avoid the problem posed by special relationships if they made the distinction between subjective and objective consequentialism.[3] Subjective consequentialism, as Railton uses the term, is the view that what one ought to do is *think* in terms of promoting, or maximizing the good. Objective consequentialism, on the other hand:

> Is the view that the criterion of the rightness of an act or course of action is whether it in fact would most promote the good of those acts available to the agent ... Let us reserve the expression *objectively consequentialist act (or life)* for those acts (or that life) of those available to the agent that would bring about the best outcomes ... let us say that a *sophisticated consequentialist* is someone who has a standing commitment to leading an objectively consequentialist life, but who need not set special stock in any particular form of decision making.
> (Railton 1984: 152–3).

The idea is that trying to achieve the good can be self-undermining, and the best approach might be to avoid *trying* to promote the good as a matter of course and instead cultivate dispositions and emotions that tend to promote the good. If the objective standard is a kind of regulative ideal, then one can set one's mind to living a life more likely to actually promote the good, and adjust one's behavior accordingly. But one can also be an objective consequentialist and hold that whether the standard offers up a regulative ideal or not is purely empirical. The *standard* set by objective consequentialism in epistemology would be something along these lines:

(OEC) The right belief is the belief that promotes the epistemic good.

One question that immediately arises is what does this mean in terms of how we should act or deliberate. *Ought* one try to promote true belief? Is the right belief the belief that the epistemic agent acquires through *trying* to promote true belief? This would be a form of *subjective* epistemic consequentialism, and, as noted earlier, seems wildly implausible, partly for reasons Railton discusses for subjective ethical consequentialism. It seems self-undermining—there are efficiency costs to the trying, if nothing else. Here epistemic success is understood as trying to promote true belief rather than actually *achieving* that goal.

Again on the objective view, whether one ought to *try* to promote the epistemic good is an empirical issue. The best way to promote the epistemic good depends upon what sorts of procedures are more likely to actually succeed. Perhaps we can cultivate certain intellectual and perceptual practices and dispositions, however, that are truth-conducive. This is not the same as process-reliabilism, since the beliefs are still evaluated according to their own promotion of the good, and not via the process.

---

[3] For the exposition of subjective objective consequentialism I draw on my work in Driver (2001).

The processes themselves are also subject to a consequentialist evaluation. This last claim is part of process-reliabilism, the preceding claim is not.

Recall how Railton makes the original distinction between objective and subjective consequentialism: one is an objective consequentialist if one holds that what is being evaluated is right, virtuous, etc. on the basis of its consequences—so it provides a standard of evaluation. Subjective consequentialism, in Railton's view, holds the view that the agent ought to be trying to achieve the good. This seems extraordinarily odd in cases where trying to achieve the good is counterproductive. But most subjective consequentialists hold something a bit less demanding: an action is right to the extent that recognition that it promotes the good is recoverable from the agent's psychology; for example, it must be a function of the agent's beliefs and desires, even if the agent is not actively trying to "promote the good" under that description. Otherwise, the theory would not be plausible.

We could view the objective/subjective distinction as offering competing standards of right. This is generally how subjective consequentialists have viewed the distinction, while also holding that the primary sense of "right" is subjective. This view can take many forms. One might hold that the right action is the one that maximizes expected utility on the basis of the agent's actual beliefs and actual desires. This has the advantage of tying rightness to the agent's actual psychology, and thus the action can be fully attributed to the agent's "true self." The agent is then thought to fully own the action. However, most reject this standard of right because it would lead to highly counterintuitive judgments of rightness. It is too subjective, since it would commit one to holding that truly terrible actions were right as long as the agent believed that in so acting they were maximizing the good. So, usually, some sort of constraint is added. For example, one might hold that the right action is the action that the *reasonable* agent expects to maximize the good. Or, one might hold that the right action is the action that maximizes the good relative to what the morally good and reasonably well-informed agent believes and desires. Or, one might hold that the right action is the action that maximizes foreseeable good, where foreseeable may mean "foreseeable by the reasonable agent" or "foreseeable in virtue of the evidence that exists, even if the agent is not herself aware of this evidence." There are many other possibilities. Frank Jackson (1991) provides a decision-theoretic standard, which maintains that what an agent ought to do is recoverable from that agent's probability function, that is, what the agent believes, "combined with what the agent ought to desire" (468). Jackson, and many other writers, note that "right" has an objective sense as well as subjective senses, so the real questions in the debate have to do with which sense, if any, is the primary sense; and, if one is an objective consequentialist, what is the real function of the subjective senses? Advantages of viewing the subjective standards as the most important have to do with worries about (1) moral luck problems and (2) agent-ownership.

As far as moral luck goes, it seems unfair to view someone as having done the wrong thing when their actions go awry for no fault of their own. This is one reason why subjective standards are so appealing—we have much better control over our own psychology than we do over events in the world. So, the argument goes, that should be what we care about in attributing rightness to an action that is produced by those mental states. But objective consequentialists will argue that their view of rightness is simply a standard, and one that holds that the specific content of the agent's psychology provides a different sort of standard, one for praise and blame. And we evaluate those praise and blame standards, as well as any associated decision procedures, in terms of how well they do, in fact, produce good *systematically*.

As far as agent-ownership goes, the idea that Jackson and others appeal to in defending their respective subjective views has to do with holding that the most important thing we are concerned with in making judgments of rightness has to do with what comes immediately before the agent's actions. Jackson (1991) writes that consequentialism "must... tell a story from the inside about how to recover what an agent ought to do from consequentialism's value function, a story in terms of what is in the agent's mind at the time of action" (468). A right action is the action of the agent acting rightly, and an agent acting rightly acts on what she believes to be the case, and what she ought to desire. If we cannot connect the action to the agent's actual psychology, then it is wrong to view the action as really the action *of the agent*, as opposed to something that just happened as a result of something else the agent did. I believe that there is a powerful intuition at work here, but I think also that the objective consequentialist can say all of this, but within a different theoretical framework. Again, right is a standard, and from this standard we can, along with facts about the world, extract certain decision-procedures, and other sorts of standards that address the agent's inner states. Objective consequentialism can tell this story. Further, the standard suggested by Jackson does not itself fully answer to the agent-ownership issue, since it appeals to what the agent ought to desire, and not to what the agent in fact desires. One could still act rightly even if one had the wrong desires, as long as what results is what would have resulted had the agent possessed the correct desires.

Note that there are *three* different types of subjective standard in this list: psychology-sensitive standards, evidence-sensitive standards, and a standard that is psychology-sensitive on belief, but not on desire. The latter is Jackson's standard, which, I have argued, doesn't solve the action-ownership problem much better than the objective consequentialist. Psychology-sensitive standards do, though to be plausible they tend to get closer and closer to an objective standard. So, for example, if I go from holding that the right action is the action the agent foresees will have the best effects to holding that the right action is the action that foreseeably has the best effects, I have, really, shifted from a psychology-sensitive standard to either an evidence-sensitive standard or the objective view. Thus, we are left with evidence-sensitive standards, and the ones that do not overlap with psychology-sensitive ones are not appealing to what is recoverable from the agent's psychology. "The right action is the action that maximized expected utility relative to the evidence available at the time" for example. This does not solve either the moral luck problem or the agent-ownership problem. It solves one other problem: the worry that rightness is unknowable on the objective view, but that problem is one most objective consequentialists are willing to bite the bullet on, or to deal with by putting, perhaps, time-sensitive constraints on "actual" consequences.

Thus, the sophisticated consequentialist argues that standards for praise and blame, and the standard for right and wrong, come apart. And there is certainly evidence for this in our actual critical practices, "She did the wrong thing, but I don't blame her given what she knew at the time" for example.

The *global* sophisticated consequentialist will also maintain that consequentialist evaluative standards will apply not just to actions but to intentions, motives, virtues—or any other thing related to human agency. This helps explain the normative ambivalence we sometimes feel in practical deliberation: when the right action associated with a character trait is vicious rather than virtuous, for example. It may be true that causing harm to another is the right thing to do in the circumstances, even though this goes against virtuous dispositions such as the tendency to avoid causing harm. A person in this sort of situation will properly feel conflicted. Analogous cases in epistemology seem to be well accepted. A certain belief could promote the truth, while arising from processes that, generally speaking, are not truth-conducive. Michael's wishful thinking might lead him to believe that he is an especially good student in political science—which in turn accounts for the extra effort he puts into his political science class, which in turn accounts for his acquisition of more true beliefs. We can be happy that he is more knowledgeable than he would have been without the wishful thinking, in this instance, and still be worried about his wishful thinking.

One important thing to note is that while the sophisticated consequentialist view is *indirect*, it is not indirect in the same way that theories like rule-consequentialism are. Process-reliabilism is like rule-consequentialism in that it understands the rightness of a belief in terms of the consequences produced by something else associated with the belief—in this case, the process producing the belief. The rightness of the belief is not a matter of the effects of that belief. Sophisticated consequentialism holds that the right belief promotes the good, but one likely ought not aim at promoting the good in acquiring the belief. Good is achieved indirectly in another way, by indirection through practical deliberation.

5.2 Problems

The problems discussed thus far are internecine between the subjective and objective consequentialists. There are other problems that arise for an objective form of epistemic consequentialism that can be pushed *externally* by those who are critical of consequentialism itself. The first two of these problems are trade-off problems.

First, consider cases of selfless trade-offs, trade-offs between the believer's own beliefs and those of other believers. This sort of tradeoff does not seem epistemic in the right way. Consider a modified version of the John Doe case discussed by Selim

Berker (2013a) (which is, in turn, modified from a case presented by Roderick Firth). Suppose that John Doe needs to deceive himself about his health—he needs to form the belief that he will, in fact, live another six months in order to solve some problems for set theory. Once those problems are solved, then of course he will have more true beliefs, but others will as well. We can modify the case so that John Doe *still* needs to deceive himself about his health, in order to be able to program a computer that will solve the problems. Unfortunately, he will die before the problems are solved. The trade-off here is that he is making himself believe falsely in order that others will have more true beliefs. Is this *epistemically* right or *epistemically* justified? This would lead to an even more severe version of the separateness of propositions problem that Berker discusses in relation to process-reliabilism. Just intuitively, making an epistemic sacrifice so that others may be epistemically enriched seems like a *morally* good action rather than an epistemically good one, though, of course, it could be both. Indeed, on some version of pluralistic consequentialism, where epistemic goods are counted as intrinsic goods—such as Ideal Utilitarianism—it is morally good to do things that promote knowledge, impartially considered.[4] Even on the relatively simpler hedonism, knowledge will have a great deal of instrumental value, given some very plausible empirical assumptions.

Or, consider the following case:

Conrad is the sort of person who consistently offers very bad arguments for his beliefs. Almost all of his beliefs are false, and yet he manages, amazingly, to survive. His arguments are so bad, in fact, that whenever someone talks to Conrad they end up, for very good reason, believing the opposite of Conrad's conclusions. Since Conrad's conclusions are invariably false, his interlocutors always come away with true beliefs.

Conrad is like an anti-expert. One is better off epistemically, if one deviates from Conrad's set of beliefs. It would be very odd, then, to view Conrad as a good epistemic agent in virtue of the fact that wherever he goes true beliefs are produced.

Thus, understandably, if the consequentialism analogy is to be taken seriously, epistemic *egoism* seems to be the form of the theory that is most widely adopted by epistemologists. Egoism is distinguished from standard forms of consequentialism by adding "extent" in measuring pleasure. It isn't just my pleasure that counts, but the pleasure of all sentient creatures. But this doesn't seem like what the epistemic consequentialist really wants: extent should be measured relative to the individual believer's set of beliefs, not the set of beliefs of all sentient creatures. So, an agent's beliefs are right if those beliefs maximize true belief *for that agent*. Egoism is not taken very seriously as an *ethical* theory. For one thing, it lacks impartiality. If I recognize

---

[4] This was the view held by G. E. Moore who was a pluralist about intrinsic value, holding that, among other things, knowledge had intrinsic value—though his views on how much value it had seemed to change between *Principia Ethica* (Moore 1988/1902) and his *Ethics* (Moore 1965/1912). In *Principia* he viewed it as necessary to the genuine appreciation of beauty, though with little value of its own, whereas in *Ethics* he would explicitly cite knowledge as one of the intrinsic goods to be added to the list.

true belief as a good for me, then I must also recognize it as a good for other epistemic agents. This puts pressure on expanding the scope of the good consequences, but that seems absurd in the epistemic cases. Thus, the analogy might be best thought of as one between epistemology and *prudence*, rather than epistemology and ethics. The epistemic consequentialist does not believe that responsible epistemic agents aim at achieving the epistemic good *impartially* considered. Another consideration to favor the prudence analogy is that we do not tend to think we have special *epistemic* obligations in the sense that for me to be a responsible epistemic agent, it is not required that I try to generate true beliefs in my children, other family members, or friends. Of course, I may morally have such an obligation, but I myself can be a perfectly good epistemic agent without generating true beliefs in others, even close family members.

Second, consider selfish or self-interested trade-offs: this involves a trade-off between the agent's own beliefs for achieving a greater epistemic good. Here is a case discussed by Berker in his criticism of Goldman:

I am a scientist seeking to get a grant from a religious organization. Suppose, also, that I am an atheist: I have thought long and hard about whether God exists and have eventually come to the conclusion that he does not. However, I realize that my only chance of receiving funding from the organization is to believe in the existence of God: they only give grants to believers, and I know I am such a bad liar that I won't be able to convince the organization's review board that I believe God exists unless I genuinely do. Finally, I know that, were I to receive the grant, I would use it to further my research, which would allow me to form a large number of new true beliefs and to revise a large number of previously held false beliefs about a variety of matters of great intellectual significance. (Berker 2013b: 364)

The right belief is not necessarily the belief that is an instantiation of the epistemic good, i.e. that is itself a true belief; it is the belief the believer has, true or false, that generates the greatest number of significant true beliefs in the believer. Berker views this as violating the "separateness of propositions" norm: the quality of a belief is to be considered on its own, it has its own standing, so to speak, its own value that doesn't vary on the basis of other propositions that are caused by it. But on the sophisticated view, we can hold that this belief is right, while still holding that there is something epistemically wrong with the agent. For example, if the agent is prone to false beliefs, the agent's epistemic good might be undermined in other ways, and the agent has a bad epistemic character. So, perhaps the agent is deserving of epistemic blame even having formed the epistemically bad belief. On the other hand, if the agent, as in the case described by Berker, intentionally seeks to cultivate a false belief for the sake of more significant true beliefs, then I don't think that we would want to say that such a belief was wrong exactly, though I see Berker's point about viewing it as epistemically good or desirable as being odd. Shouldn't I evaluate the belief on its own terms, by considering *its* truth or falsity? How this might be dealt with in the moral case may be instructive if we view the beliefs as analogous to actions rather than persons. In the moral case, we tend to speak of actions as being *pro tanto* wrong. So, for example, lying is *pro tanto* wrong. If I need to tell a lie, in order to achieve a much more significant good, such as saving an innocent person's life, then the action, though *pro tanto* wrong, is all things considered right. By analogy, then, epistemically, that a belief is false is a *pro tanto* reason against it, but it could be outweighed by other considerations, such as the fact that it generates more significant true beliefs. Then the belief, though *pro tanto* epistemically wrong, is all things considered epistemically right.

The third worry is a kind of conflation problem: epistemic consequentialism conflates truth and justification. This worry was nicely articulated by Steven Maitzen:

> If the nominal aim is the reason for having, or pursuing, justification, then it ought to follow that beliefs are justified insofar as they serve the nominal aim and unjustified insofar as they do not. But this consequence gives rise to an obvious problem. If justification is essentially a matter of serving the nominal aim, then it seems we would evaluate no true belief as unjustified and no false belief as justified, no matter how the beliefs were formed or sustained.
>
> (Maitzen 1995: 870)

This is not a proper worry if the right belief *promotes* true belief. This is because the right belief could be a false belief. Also, the praiseworthy and the right might come apart. My false belief may not itself be evidentially justified, but it is still the right one. I may also possess an evidentially justified true belief that is the wrong belief, because it fails to promote the good. For an example of the former consider William James' views on why it is epistemically permissible to believe something without sufficient evidence, that might well be false, in order to leave oneself open to future knowledge:

> *Do you like me or not?* ... Whether you do or not depends, in countless instances, on whether I meet you half-way, am willing to assume that you must like me, and show you trust and expectation. The previous faith on my part in your liking's existence is in such cases what makes your liking come. But if I stand aloof, and refuse to budge an inch until I have objective evidence, until you shall have done something apt ... ten to one your liking never comes ... The desire for a certain kind of truth here brings about that special truth's existence; and so it is in innumerable cases of other sorts ... There are, then, cases where a fact cannot come at all unless a preliminary faith exists in its own coming. And where faith in fact can help create that fact, that would be an insane logic which should say that faith running ahead of scientific evidence is the "lowest kind of immorality" into which a thinking being can fall. (James 1963: 209)

It looks like William James might be at least sympathetic to some consequentialist considerations. One doesn't ignore the evidence, of course, but it is rational to believe without sufficient evidence in situations where the question at hand is important enough and has not, in one's own mind, been ruled out. This leaves us open to taking on many false beliefs, but we need to be willing to do this in the interests of gaining more, and significant, true beliefs. This may be because the false belief itself leads to more truths, though I believe he has in mind that it is the openness to the truth, that may also require one to risk false belief, that allows one to acquire more true beliefs.

5.3 Conclusion

In this chapter I have tried to discuss a version of epistemic consequentialism that is not process-reliabilism, and that offers a way to understand this approach in epistemology on analogy with sophisticated consequentialism. This form of consequentialism holds that there is an objective standard of right, but it isn't necessarily the case that agents should be trying to actually maximize the good. It distinguishes between the standard of right and standards of praise and blame. I have discussed how this approach might deal with some popular criticisms of the process-reliabilist view, and also expressed an opinion that what most writers on epistemic consequentialism rely on is not so much an analogy between ethics and epistemology but, rather, an analogy between prudence and epistemology.[5]

References

Ahlstrom-Vij, K. and Dunn, J. (2014), "A Defense of Epistemic Consequentialism," *The Philosophical Quarterly* 64(257): 541–51.

Alston, W. (1989), "Concepts of Epistemic Justification," in his *Epistemic Justification*, New York: Cornell University Press.

Berker, S. (2013a), "The Rejection of Epistemic Consequentialism," *Philosophical Issues* 23(1): 363–87.

Berker, S. (2013b), "Epistemic Teleology and the Separateness of Propositions," *Philosophical Review* 122: 337–93.

Driver, J. (2001), *Uneasy Virtue*, Cambridge: Cambridge University Press.

Hooker, B. (2000), *Ideal Code, Real World*, Oxford: Oxford University Press.

Jackson, F. (1991), "Decision-Theoretic Consequentialism and the Nearest and Dearest Objection", *Ethics* 101(3): 461–82.

James, W. (1963), "The Will to Believe," in *William James: Pragmatism and other Essays*, New York: Washington Square Press.

Maitzen, S. (1995), "Our Errant Epistemic Aim," *Philosophy and Phenomenological Research* 55(4): 869–76.

Moore, G. E. (1965/1912), *Ethics*, New York: Oxford University Press.

Moore, G. E. (1988/1902), *Principia Ethica*, Amherst, NY: Prometheus Press

Railton, P. (1984), "Alienation, Consequentialism, and the Demands of Morality," *Philosophy & Public Affairs* 13(2): 134–71.

---

[5] An earlier version of this chapter was presented at a workshop on Epistemic Consequentialism held at the University of Kent, at the Saint Louis Ethics Workshop, and at PerFECt2, The Penn Reasons and the Foundations of Epistemology Conference 2, November 12, 2016. I would like to thank the audiences and participants of those meetings for the valuable feedback I received. In particular, I would like to thank Kristoffer Ahlstrom-Vij, Daniel Singer, and Brian Talbot, for their thoughtful and very helpful comments.

6

Good Questions

Alejandro Pérez Carballo

We care about the truth. We want to believe what is true, and avoid believing what is false. But not all truths are created equal. Having a true botanical theory is more valuable than having true beliefs about the number of plants in North Dakota. To some extent this is fixed by our practical interests. We may want to keep our plants looking healthy, and doing botany is more likely to help us do that than counting blades of grass. But setting our practical interests aside, there is something more valuable, *epistemically*, about our botanical beliefs than about those we get out of counting blades of grass.

That, at least, is the intuition driving this chapter. I think it is a powerful intuition, but it remains to be cashed out. The central task of the chapter will be to do just that. More specifically, I want to offer a way of evaluating different courses of inquiry—different research agendas, as it were—from a purely epistemic perspective.

I will situate myself within a broadly Bayesian picture of our cognitive economy. On this picture, a cognitive agent can be represented by a probability function—the agent's *credence* function. I will also think of epistemic rationality in broadly decision-theoretic terms: epistemic rationality is a matter of maximizing expected *epistemic value*, where the notion of epistemic value will be modeled using an *epistemic utility function*—an assignment of numerical values to credence functions relative to a given state of the world. An agent's epistemic value function can be seen as incorporating information about which lines of inquiry are more epistemically valuable for an agent. Judgments about the value of questions, I will suggest, can be used to motivate incorporating considerations other than accuracy into our account of epistemic value. In particular, I will argue that we should incorporate explanatory considerations into the epistemic decision-theoretic framework, and offer a proof of concept: a way of doing so that is friendly to the overall consequentialist picture.

6.1 Evaluating Questions Relative to a Decision Problem

Think of a course of inquiry as a collection of questions. We can identify any such collection with a single question: what is the answer to each of the questions in the collection? Any way of evaluating questions will thus correspond to a way of evaluating courses of inquiry.

We can devise a framework for evaluating questions using familiar decision-theoretic tools.[1] We need only assume that we can identify the value of a question with the expected value of *learning* the (true) answer to that question. For whenever you are facing a choice among a set of options, you can evaluate questions according to how likely, and to what extent, learning its true answer will help you make the right choice.

An example might help illustrate this in more detail. Two coins will be tossed. You are told that the first coin is fair. The second one is biased: there is a 70 percent chance it will land heads. Consequently, you assign credence .5 to the first coin landing heads, and .7 to the second one landing heads. You are then asked to predict a particular outcome: you will be rewarded only if you predict the actual outcome. The reward will depend on what the prediction is, according to this table (where, e.g. 'HT' stands for the act of predicting that the first coin lands heads and the second coin lands tails):

	HH	HT	TH	TT
Reward if correct (in $)	0	5	10	15

After computing the expected utility of each possible action, you realize that TH is the action that maximizes expected utility.[2]

Before you state your choice, however, you are told that an Oracle you take to be fully reliable will answer for you only one of these two questions:

(?H1) Did the first coin land heads?

(?H2) Did the second coin land heads?

If you have nothing to lose, you should ask one of these questions.[3] But which one?

To answer this, we need to consider two different issues. First, all things being equal, we prefer to ask a question Q over another Q' if we are less opinionated about the

---

[1] As will become clear later in this chapter, I will rely on the working hypothesis—widely accepted in the linguistics literature and in work in the erotetic logic tradition (e.g. Belnap 1963; Groenendijk and Stokhof 1984; Hamblin 1958, 1973; Karttunen 1977)—that we can identify a question with the collection of its possible answers. But with some of the questions most central to inquiry—why-questions in particular—it is sometimes far from trivial to figure out what the possible answers are—a point famously emphasized in Bromberger 1962. (See also Friedman 2013 for recent, relevant discussion.) Exactly how to extend the framework I introduce below so as to evaluate such questions is a task for another day.

[2] Your credence assignment is as follows: $C(HH) = C(TH) = .35$, $C(HT) = C(TT) = .15$. Thus, the expected utility of TH is $3.5, that of TT is $2.25. The expected utility of HH is $0, and that of HT is $.75. (I'm being sloppy in using e.g. 'HH' to stand both for the proposition that both coins land heads and for the action of predicting that both coins land heads. But context should have resolved the ambiguity.)

[3] We know from a result by I. J. Good that for any Q (and any decision problem) the value of asking Q is never negative, so long as asking Q is cost-free. See Good 1967. Good attributes the result to Raiffa and Schlaifer 1961. For a general discussion of Good's theorem, see Skyrms 1990.

answer to Q than about the answer to Q'. If we have good evidence that the answer to Q is p, but no evidence pointing to what the right answer to Q' is, we have a *pro tanto* reason for asking Q' rather than Q. At the same time, if we expect that having an answer to one question will have little impact on our choice—perhaps we would choose the same action no matter what the answer to that question is—we may have reason to ask a different question instead. We need a way of arbitrating between these potentially conflicting considerations.

Following I. J. Good (1967), let us set the value of a question as the weighted average of the value of (learning) its answers. The value of each answer p is obtained as follows.[4] First, let a be the alternative that maximizes expected value relative to your current credence function. Now let a' be the alternative that maximizes expected value relative to the result of updating your credence function with the proposition p. The value of (learning) p is the difference in the *posterior* expected value (i.e. the expected value calculated using the result of updating your credence function with p) between a' and a.[5]

Return to the coin example. Relative to your prior credence function, TH was the action that maximized expected utility. But if you learned that the first coin landed heads (henceforth, 'H1') you would no longer pick TH. For assuming you update your credence function by conditionalizing on your evidence, that would be a sure loss. The sensible thing to do if you learned H1 would be to pick HT, since the expected utility (relative to your new credence function) of each other option is $0. Now, the expected value of HT relative to the result of updating your credence function with the information at hand is $1.5. Since upon learning H1 the expected value of TH would be $0, the net gain in utility from learning H1 is $1.5, so that $V(\text{H1}) = \$1.5$.

Similarly, we can compute the expected gain in utility from learning that the first coin landed tails (i.e. T1): it is the expected value of whichever action maximizes your posterior expected utility minus the expected value of TH, both calculated using the posterior. Since T1 would not affect your choice, we have that $V(\text{T1}) = 0$.

We can then set the value of ?H1 to the weighted average of the values of its answers, so that $V(?\text{H1}) = \$.75$.[6] And in the same way, we can assign a value to ?H2—it is easy to verify that $V(\text{H2}) = \$0$, and $V(\text{T2}) = \$7.5$, so that the weighted average of the value of H2 and T2, i.e. $V(?\text{H2})$, equals $2.25.[7] The upshot is that the value of ?H2 is higher than that of ?H1, so that Good's strategy recommends you ask ?H2, as we would expect.

---

[4] Throughout, I will use lowercase italics as variables ranging over propositions—including 'act' propositions in the sense of Jeffrey 1983. I will reserve lowercase small caps for names of specific propositions (e.g. 'H1', etc.).
[5] As it turns out, one could also assign value to a proposition p by looking at the difference between the *prior* expected values of the action that maximizes expected value relative to the result of conditionalizing on p and the action that maximizes expected value relative to your prior. The value of p will of course be different if we do things this way, but the resulting V(Q) will be the same. See Rooy 2004, p. 397.
[6] Since $C(\text{H1}) \times V(\text{H1}) + C(\text{T1}) \times V(\text{T1}) = .5 \times \$1.5 + .5 \times \$0$.
[7] Since $C(\text{H2}) \times V(\text{H2}) + C(\text{T2}) \times V(\text{T2}) = .7 \times \$0 + .3 \times \$7.5$.

126 GOOD QUESTIONS

I want to use this strategy to spell out a way of evaluating questions from a purely epistemic perspective. But first we need to find the right decision problem.

6.2 Epistemic Decision Problems

Suppose you could will to believe. That is, suppose you could control what credence function you have. Then you could be seen as facing a decision problem: that of deciding, among different possible credence functions, which one to adopt. Like any other decision situation, this one would take place against the backdrop of a given utility function: an assignment of numerical values to each possible option—in this case, to each credence function—relative to a given state of the world.

To take a simple example, suppose you have a newly minted coin which will be tossed once (tomorrow) and then destroyed. Suppose you assign .2 credence to H and .8 credence to T (never mind why). You are now faced with the following decision situation. If the coin lands heads, you will get x dollars, where x is the credence you assign to H. If the coin lands tails, you will get y dollars, where $y = (1 - x)$ is the credence you assign to T. If all you care about is money, and you are able to control what credence function to have, you should adopt the credence function that assigns zero to H. This is because the expected utility of adopting credence x in T is given by:

$$0.2 \times x + 0.8 \times (1 - x),$$

which is maximized at $x = 0$.

A *cognitive decision problem*, as I will understand it, is a decision problem where the options are the agent's possible credence functions. An *epistemic decision problem* is a cognitive decision problem where the utility function captures one (or more) epistemic dimension(s) of evaluation. In the example above, the utility function in question was defined as follows:

$$u(C, s_H) = \$1 \times C(H)$$
$$u(C, s_T) = \$1 \times C(T),$$

where s_H is the state of the world in which the coin lands heads and s_T the one in which the coin lands tails. Note that, relative to this function, the utility of C at s_H (resp. s_T) is higher the closer $C(H)$ (resp. $C(T)$) is to the truth value of s_H (resp. s_T). Arguably, then, such a utility function captures a concern for the truth, and the corresponding decision problem thus counts as an epistemic decision problem.[8]

Whether you think that a particular cognitive decision problem counts as an epistemic decision problem will then depend on whether you think the relevant utility function counts as an *epistemic* utility function. But suppose we can agree that a

---

[8] Cf. Horwich 1982 p. 127ff, as well as Maher 1993 p. 177ff. As is well known, this epistemic utility function is not *proper*, in that the expected epistemic utility of a credence function C relative to C itself may sometimes be something other than C.

particular decision problem is an epistemic decision problem. Then we can use Good's strategy in order to evaluate questions relative to that decision problem. This, I submit, would count as an *epistemic* way of evaluating questions.

Granted, the discussion above was framed under the supposition that we can believe at will. And while some still try to maintain that some form of doxastic voluntarism is right, it would be a pity if the applicability of my proposal depended on their success.[9]

Fortunately, I think we can ultimately discharge this assumption in one of at least two ways. In order to use expected utility theory we need not assume that among the options ranked in terms of expected utility, it is 'up to the agent' which one to take. Furthermore, we would learn something about epistemic agents like ourselves if we looked at what epistemic changes are rational for agents who can form beliefs at will.

On the first point: whenever we have a range of options and an assignment of utility to each option relative to each possible state of the world, we can apply expected utility theory to evaluate each of the relevant options. Nothing in the apparatus requires assuming that it is 'up to the agent' which option to take. If we think of all possible epistemic states of an agent as options, and we have a utility function defined for each such option (relative to a state of the world), we can then use expected utility theory to evaluate each of those options. The value of a question can then be understood along the following lines: the better position the question puts you in with respect to evaluating your epistemic options, the better the question.

On the second point: we talk, sometimes, of beliefs 'aiming at the truth'. But this, one might object, borders on incoherence unless beliefs can be formed at will. Talk of the aim of belief, one might continue, suggests that beliefs are the result of a voluntary choice.[10] The response, of course, is to insist that talk of beliefs 'aiming at the truth' is metaphorical. Still, the complaint should put some pressure on us to spell out the metaphor a bit more clearly.

One way of doing so—not the only one[11]—is due to Allan Gibbard. The suggestion, as I understand it, is to suppose that while *we* cannot form beliefs at will, there could be agents that can. Thinking about such agents can shed light on questions about what we should believe:

If a person is epistemically rational, we can then hypothesize, then it is *as if* she chose her beliefs with the aim of believing truths and shunning falsehoods. She doesn't literally set out to believe truths, the way she might set out to get a high score on a test by intentionally putting down the right answers. But it is as if she did: it is as if she aimed at truth and away from falsehood in her beliefs in the same way one aims at any other goal.[12]

---

[9] I'm treating doxastic voluntarism as entailing that one can decide what to believe. But this is something that proponents of doxastic voluntarism will plausibly want to deny—for discussion, see e.g. Shah 2002. All that matters for my purposes, however, is that the decision-theoretic framework can be profitably deployed in epistemology without presupposing any form of doxastic voluntarism.

[10] Cf. Shah and Velleman 2005, p. 498f.   [11] See e.g. Velleman 2000, p. 244ff.

[12] Gibbard 2008, p. 144f.

128 GOOD QUESTIONS

From this, Gibbard claims, we can extract a constraint on epistemic rationality:

> A way of forming beliefs should at least satisfy this condition: if one forms beliefs that way, it will be as if one were, by one's own lights, forming beliefs voluntarily with the aim of believing truths and not falsehoods.[13]

Assuming this is a good strategy, the following should seem quite plausible. A way of evaluating questions should at least satisfy this condition: it will be as if one were evaluating questions with an eye towards solving an epistemic decision problem.

6.3 Evaluating Questions with Accuracy Measures

Consider another example. Again, fix a coin and suppose it will be tossed exactly three times. You have a choice among all credence functions defined over the smallest collection of propositions closed by conjunction and negation that includes each of the following:

- The first toss of the coin will land heads. (H1)
- The second toss of the coin will land heads. (H2)
- The third toss of the coin will land heads. (H3)
- The coin is 80 percent biased towards tails. (B)
- The coin is fair. (F)

To keep things simple, let's restrict our attention to credence functions such that

$$C(\text{B}) = C(\neg \text{F}),$$

so that, for all x,

$$C(x) = C(\text{B}) \times P_{.2}(x) + C(\neg \text{B}) \times P_{.5}(x),$$

where P_n is a probability distribution that treats the three tosses as independent random variables with $P_n(\text{H1}) = P_n(\text{H2}) = P_n(\text{H3}) = n$, $P_n(\text{B}) = 0$ if $n = .5$, and $P_n(\text{B}) = 1$ otherwise. In short, we are restricting our attention to the class $\mathcal{C}$ of *mixtures* of two fixed probability functions, $P_{.5}$ and $P_{.2}$, which correspond to the two different possible biases of the coin.[14]

You are then facing a cognitive decision problem—that of selecting one credence function among those in $\mathcal{C}$. Given an epistemic utility function, you can evaluate different questions from an epistemic perspective, for example:

(?B)   Is the coin biased?

(?H1)   Will the first toss land heads?

---

[13] Gibbard 2008, p. 146.
[14] The inclusion of B in the domain of $P_{.5}$ and $P_{.2}$ allows us to keep things cleaner.

The choice is not straightforward, in part because learning the answer to each of the questions will give you information about the answer to the other one. Learning about the bias of the coin will change your credence in H1. And learning H1 will change your credence about the bias of the coin.

6.3.1 Comparing questions from an epistemic perspective

To fix ideas, let's stipulate that we are dealing with a set W of sixteen possible worlds: eight on which the coin is fair—one for each possible outcome of the three tosses—and eight on which the coin is biased.

Let us also stipulate that our utility function is given by the well-known *Brier score*:[15]

$$\beta(C, x) = - \sum_{w \in W} (C(w) - \mathbb{1}_{x=w})^2,$$

where $\mathbb{1}_{x=w}$ equals 1 if $x = w$ and 0 otherwise. Given that accuracy is a plausible dimension of epistemic evaluation and that the Brier score is a reasonable measure of accuracy, I will assume that the resulting decision problem is an epistemic decision problem.

We can use this decision problem to compare ?B and ?H1 as before. First, identify ?B with the set $\{B, \neg B\}$ and identify ?H1 with the set $\{H1, \neg H1\}$. To determine the value of each question, recall, we first need to figure out the value of the choice that maximizes expected (epistemic) utility relative to your prior credence function C_0.

It is well-known that β is *strictly proper*, in the sense that for all credence functions C, the expected β-value relative to C is maximized at C. Thus, we know that the choice that maximizes expected utility (relative to your prior) is C_0 itself. For the same reason, we know that the choice that would maximize expected utility if you were to learn B (resp. $\neg$B), and you conditionalized on that evidence, would be your posterior credence function $C_0(\cdot \mid B)$ (resp. $C_0(\cdot \mid \neg B)$).

To compute the value of ?B, we then need to determine (a) the difference in expected value, relative to $C_0(\cdot \mid B)$, between $C_0(\cdot \mid B)$ and C_0, and (b) the difference in expected value, relative to $C_0(\cdot \mid \neg B)$, between $C_0(\cdot \mid \neg B)$ and C_0. By parity of reasoning, in order to compute the value of ?H1, we need to determine (c) the difference in expected value, relative to $C_0(\cdot \mid H1)$, between $C_0(\cdot \mid H1)$ and C_0, and (d) the difference in expected value, relative to $C_0(\cdot \mid \neg H1)$, between $C_0(\cdot \mid \neg H1)$ and C_0. We can then think of the value of each question as a function of your credence in B,[16] whose values can be read off Table 6.1.[17]

From an epistemic perspective, then, as long as your credence in B is between 0.3 and 0.6, you should prefer learning the answer to ?B over learning the answer to ?H1.

---

[15] To avoid unnecessary clutter, I write $C(w)$ instead of $C(\{w\})$ when w is a possible world.
[16] Recall that your credence in B determines your credence in H1.
[17] A *Mathematica* notebook with the relevant computations can be viewed at (or downloaded from) http://perezcarballo.org/files/gq.nb.pdf.

Table 6.1. The values assigned to each of ?B and ?H1 as a function of the prior credence in B, using the Brier score as the relevant epistemic utility function.

	0.1	0.2	0.3	0.4	0.5	0.6	0.7	0.8	0.9
V(?B)	0.04	0.07	0.092	0.105	0.11	0.105	0.092	0.07	0.04
V(?H1)	0.105	0.093	0.086	0.084	0.086	0.09	0.097	0.108	0.124

Table 6.2. The values assigned to each of ?B and ?H1 as a function of the prior credence in B, using the log score as the relevant epistemic utility function.

	0.1	0.2	0.3	0.4	0.5	0.6	0.7	0.8	0.9
V(?B)	0.325	0.5	0.611	0.673	0.693	0.673	0.611	0.5	0.325
V(?H1)	0.691	0.686	0.677	0.664	0.647	0.627	0.602	0.573	0.539

We obtain similar results if, instead of the Brier score, we use a different epistemic utility function, such as the *logarithmic score*:[18]

$$\lambda(C, w) = \log C(w).$$

The values of $V(?B)$ and $V(?H1)$ can also be seen as a function of your credence in B (see Table 6.2).

There is no one General Lesson to be drawn here. The point is simply to illustrate how this framework allows for a principled way of ranking questions from an epistemic perspective, assuming that accuracy is the only dimension of epistemic value. For any two questions, you can compare the expected value of learning their true answers. This is given by the weighted average of the value of each of the questions' answers, where this equals the difference in expected value, relative to the result of updating on that answer, between your posterior and your prior.

6.3.2 Limitations of an 'accuracy-only' account of epistemic value

Appealing to accuracy measures will not always allow us to distinguish among different questions. Suppose you only assign non-trivial credence to four atomic propositions, $p \land q$, $p \land \neg q$, $\neg p \land q$, and $\neg p \land \neg q$, and suppose you take p and q to be independent of one another. If $C(p) = C(q)$, then the expected gain in accuracy from learning the answer to the question whether p will equal that of learning the answer to the question whether q.

---

[18] This not a quirk of the particular choice of numbers. Indeed, in the majority of cases, the two utility functions will agree on which question to ask. For example, for all but 10 out of 45 combinations of multiples i and j of 0.1 between 0.1 and 0.9, if the possible bias of the coin is i and you assign credence j to the proposition that the coin is biased, both utility functions will agree on which question to ask.

For example, suppose the coin from above is going to be tossed exactly twice. Further suppose that you are certain that the coin is fair, so that $C(B) = 0$, and $C(H1) = C(H2) = 0.5$. If we use the Brier score as our epistemic utility function, we have:

$$V(?H1) = C(H1) \cdot V(H1) + C(\neg H1) \cdot V(\neg H1),$$
$$V(?H2) = C(H2) \cdot V(H2) + C(\neg H2) \cdot V(\neg H2),$$

where

$$V(H1) = -\sum_w C(w \mid H1) \cdot (\beta(C(\cdot \mid H1), w) - \beta(C, w)),$$
$$V(\neg H1) = -\sum_w C(w \mid \neg H1) \cdot (\beta(C(\cdot \mid \neg H1), w) - \beta(C, w)),$$
$$V(H2) = -\sum_w C(w \mid H2) \cdot \beta(C(\cdot \mid H2), w) - \beta(C, w)),$$
$$V(\neg H2) = -\sum_w C(w \mid \neg H2) \cdot (\beta(C(\cdot \mid \neg H2), w) - \beta(C, w)).$$

Given the symmetry of the situation, however, we can find a permutation σ of the set of worlds such that, for each w:[19]

$$C(w \mid H1) = C(\sigma(w) \mid H2)$$
$$C(w \mid \neg H1) = C(\sigma(w) \mid \neg H2)$$
$$\beta(C, w) = \beta(C, \sigma(w))$$
$$\beta(C(\cdot \mid H1), w) = \beta(C(\cdot \mid H2), \sigma(w))$$
$$\beta(C(\cdot \mid \neg H1), w) = \beta(C(\cdot \mid \neg H2), \sigma(w)),$$

and this is enough to show that $V(H1) = V(H2)$ and $V(\neg H1) = V(\neg H2)$, so that $V(?H1) = V(?H2)$.

This may not come as a surprise. After all, it doesn't seem as if, from an epistemic perspective, there are reasons for preferring the question whether the first toss landed heads over the question whether the second toss landed heads. There are cases, however, where things are not as clear. These are cases in which, although accuracy considerations cannot distinguish between two questions, there are seemingly epistemic considerations that favor one of the two questions.

Suppose our coin from above is going to be tossed five times in a row. As before, your credence function is defined over an algebra that contains the proposition that the coin is 80 percent biased towards tails (B) as well as propositions that allow

---

[19] Since you are certain that the coin is fair, we are essentially dealing with four possible worlds, determined by the four possible sequences of outcomes. Let $\sigma(w)$ be the world that reverses the outcome of the two coin tosses in w, so that (e.g.) if in w the first toss lands heads and the second toss lands tails, then in $\sigma(w)$ the first toss lands tails and the second one heads.

you to specify each of the possible outcomes of the ten coin tosses—conjunctions, disjunctions, and negations of H1, ..., H5. Now consider the following case:

KNOWN OUTCOME: This time, the domain of your credence function includes the proposition (call it M) that the coin was minted five days ago. We assume, again, that your credence in F (the proposition that the coin is fair) equals your credence in ¬B. Suppose now that four of the five coin tosses land heads, and that you update by conditionalizing on your evidence. Your resulting credence function will then be $C' = C(\cdot \mid \#H = 4)$. As it turns out, $C(M) = C'(B)$.

It follows from Bayes' theorem that your posterior credence in B will be approximately 0.7, assuming you update by conditionalization.[20] And since the outcome of the coin tosses is probabilistically independent of M, this will also be your posterior credence in M. Since M and B are also probabilistically independent of one another, it follows that the value of the question whether M and the value of the question whether B will be the same—assuming, that is, that we are dealing with an accuracy measure.[21]

If we think there are no epistemic considerations other than accuracy that matter for evaluating credence functions relative to a given state of the world, we will think any comparisons we are inclined to make in cases like KNOWN OUTCOME reflect non-epistemic considerations. But we needn't think this. We *could* think there are epistemic considerations other than accuracy, and that our judgments in cases like KNOWN OUTCOME reflect such considerations. On this view, there is something more valuable, epistemically and in light of your other beliefs, about knowing the answer to whether B as opposed to knowing the answer to whether M.

Indeed, cases like KNOWN OUTCOME lend support to the view that epistemic considerations other than accuracy are reflected in our judgments about the value of questions. Knowing whether the coin is heavily biased towards heads will be crucial for determining whether you have a good explanation of the outcome of the four coin tosses. In contrast, knowing whether the coin was minted five days ago would have

---

[20] From Bayes' theorem we know that

$$C(B \mid \#H = 4) = \frac{C(B)C(\#H = 4 \mid B)}{C(\#H = 4)}.$$

By construction, it thus follows that

$$C(B \mid \#H = 4) = \frac{0.5 \times 5 \times 0.8^4 \times 0.2}{0.5 \times (5 \times 0.5^5 + 5 \times 0.8^4 \times 0.2)} = \frac{0.8^4 \times 0.2}{0.5^5 + 0.8^4 \times 0.2}.$$

A bit of algebra finally gives us that

$$C(B \mid \#H = 4) = (1 + 0.5^4 \times 0.8^{-4} \times 0.2-1)^{-1} \approx \frac{81}{113} \approx 0.7.$$

[21] If we measure accuracy with the Brier score, we can use the same reasoning from above, involving H1 and H2, to show that the value of ?B and the value of ?M will be the same (relative to C'.) But the same will be true on any measure of accuracy that satisfies EXTENSIONALITY, in the terminology of Joyce 2009, p. 273f.

no effect, beyond the increase in expected accuracy, on the epistemic standing of your credence function.

Note that I am *assuming* that facts about the bias of the coin can explain facts about the distribution of heads in a sequence of coin tosses. On some interpretations of probability, no such explanatory relations could hold.[22] But the point I am making is a structural one. All we need is a credence function defined over an algebra of propositions such that:

- only four atomic propositions get assigned non-trivial probability;
- two logically independent propositions, among those obtained by disjunction of two of those atomic propositions, are assigned the same non-trivial probability;
- one of those two propositions, but not the other, contributes to explaining some propositions in the algebra that get assigned credence one.

As long as you think such examples can be constructed, you should agree with this: there are situations where explanatory considerations point towards one of two questions which cannot be distinguished in terms of their expected contribution to the overall accuracy of your body of beliefs.

6.4 Beyond Accuracy

If we are to rely on epistemic decision problems to compare questions in cases like KNOWN OUTCOME, we need to find epistemic utility functions that take into account considerations other than accuracy. Unfortunately, most work on epistemic utility theory has only looked at measures of accuracy as a source of epistemic utility functions.[23] As a result, there is a paucity of examples for us to choose from. If we want to extend our framework so as to account for cases like KNOWN OUTCOME, we will have to go beyond examples of epistemic utility functions that are found in the literature.

6.4.1 Weighted accuracy

The reason the question whether B is better than the question whether M, I've been saying, is this: the value of learning B outstrips the corresponding gain in accuracy. If you were to learn that B, you would be in possession of a (reasonably) good explanation of something you believe to be true. Relative to a world in which both B and M are true, it would be better to have an accurate degree of belief in B than to have an equally accurate degree of belief in M. Our epistemic utility function, if it is to accommodate our judgment in KNOWN OUTCOME, needs to be sensitive to this difference.

---

[22] This is particularly clear on the most straightforward version of finite frequentism.
[23] As we will see below, however, Joyce himself has described the form that an epistemic utility function could take if it is to incorporate considerations other than accuracy. See the discussion of 'additive scoring rules' in Joyce 2009, p. 272.

Here is one way of doing so. Suppose we can measure the relative explanatory strength of each proposition p and suppose we can define a function λ that assigns a *weight* $\lambda(p)$ to each proposition p that is inversely proportional to its explanatory strength.[24] We can then define an epistemic utility function that treats accuracy with respect to p in a way that is proportional to $\lambda(p)$: for any credence function C and world w, the smaller $\lambda(p)$, the more the difference between $C(p)$ and p's truth-value in w matters for the epistemic standing of C at w. One such utility function is a simple modification of the Brier score, which we get to in two steps. First, let's define the *full Brier score* of C at $x \in \mathcal{W}$ as follows:

$$\beta_F(C, x) = -\sum_{p \subseteq \mathcal{W}} (C(p) - \mathbb{1}_{x \in p})^2,$$

where $\mathbb{1}_{x \in p}$ equals 1 if $x \in p$ and 0 otherwise. The full Brier score is a strictly proper epistemic utility function, much like the Brier score β. Now, define the full λ-Brier score of C at $x \in \mathcal{W}$ as follows:

$$\beta_F^\lambda(C, x) = -\sum_{p \subseteq \mathcal{W}} \lambda(p) \cdot (C(p) - \mathbb{1}_{x \in p})^2.$$

It is easy to see that, as long as $\lambda(p) > 0$ for all p, β_F^λ is a strictly proper epistemic utility function.[25] For example, turn back to KNOWN OUTCOME, let $\mathcal{W}_0$ denote the

---

[24] I speak of 'explanatory strength' *simpliciter*, but only to keep things simple. Nothing prevents us from building into our function λ a particular class of explananda—say, true propositions that are in need of explanation. If we think there is an objective fact of the matter as to what are the facts in need of explanation, then we can fix λ accordingly. If instead we think that what facts are in need of explanation depends in part on a particular agent, we will have to let λ vary from agent to agent, so that $\lambda(p)$ measures the extent to which p explains what the agent takes to be in need of explanation—where this may well be a function of the agent's credence in p, among other things. All that matters for our purposes is that λ be held fixed for a given decision problem. I return to these issues in section 6.5.

[25] *Proof*: The expected β_F^λ-score of Q relative to P is:

$$\sum_w P(w) \cdot -\sum_{p \subseteq \mathcal{W}} \lambda(p) \cdot (Q(p) - \mathbb{1}_{x \in p})^2.$$

Fix an enumeration x_i of the members of $\mathcal{W}$ and an enumeration p_j of the subsets of $\mathcal{W}$. We can now think of this sum as an $n \times 2^n$ matrix, with $n = |\mathcal{W}|$, where the cell i, j is of the form $P(w_i) \times -\lambda(p_j) \cdot (Q(p_j) - 1)^2$ if $x_i \in p_j$ and of the form $P(w_i) \times -\lambda(p_j) \cdot Q(p_j)^2$ otherwise. For a fixed j, we can write the sum the j-th row as

$$-\lambda(p_j) \cdot \left(\sum_{x_i \in p_j} P(x_i) \times (Q(p_j) - 1)^2 + \sum_{x_i \notin p_j} P(x_i) \times Q(p_j)^2 \right),$$

or, equivalently,

$$-\lambda(p_j) \cdot \left(P(p_j) \cdot (1 - Q(p_j))^2 + (1 - P(p_j)) \cdot Q(p_j)^2 \right).$$

Thus, the expected β_F^λ-score of Q relative to P can be written as:

$$-\sum_{p \subseteq \mathcal{W}} \lambda(p) \left(P(p) \times (1 - Q(p))^2 + (1 - P(p))Q(p)^2 \right).$$

Now, note that the function

$$a \cdot (1 - x)^2 + (1 - a) \cdot x^2$$

relevant set of possible worlds, and let $\mathcal{F}_0$ denote the collection of subsets of $\mathcal{W}_0$. For any proposition p in the domain of your credence function *other* than B, let $\lambda_0(p) = 1$, and set $\lambda_0(\text{B}) = 1/2$. This is an assignment of weights to the relevant propositions that gives B special status. Intuitively, since we are supposing that B has more explanatory strength than any other proposition, we want to give more importance to accuracy with respect to B than to accuracy with respect to any other proposition. Since the full λ-Brier score of P at w is defined as *minus* the weighted average of the distance between $P(p)$ and p's truth-value at w, in order to give more weight to the distance between $P(\text{B})$ and B's truth-value we need to multiply the term of the sum corresponding to the distance between $P(\text{B})$ and B's truth-value by a *smaller* factor.

It is worth taking a moment to check that the full λ_0-Brier score is an epistemic utility function that treats distance from the truth with respect to B differently from distance from the truth with respect to any other proposition. To fix ideas, let $w_0 \in \text{B}$ and suppose P and Q are probability functions defined over $\mathcal{F}_0$ with $\beta(P, w_0) = \beta(Q, w_0)$. Since $\beta(P, w_0) = \beta(Q, w_0)$, we know that $\beta_F(P, w_0) = \beta_F(Q, w_0)$. Now,

$$\beta_F^{\lambda_0}(P, w_0) = -\left(1/2(P(\text{B}) - 1)^2 + \sum_{p \neq \text{B}}(P(p) - \mathbb{1}_{w_0 \in p})^2\right).$$

Thus:

$$\beta_F^{\lambda_0}(P, w_0) = \beta_F(P, w_0) + 1/2(P(\text{B}) - 1)^2 = \beta_F(Q, w_0) + 1/2(P(\text{B}) - 1)^2,$$

and

$$\beta_F^{\lambda_0}(Q, w_0) = \beta_F(Q, w_0) + 1/2(Q(\text{B}) - 1)^2$$

so that $\beta_F^{\lambda_0}(P, w_0) < \beta_F^{\lambda_0}(Q, w_0)$ iff $(P(\text{B}) - 1)^2 < (Q(\text{B}) - 1)^2$ iff $P(\text{B}) > Q(\text{B})$. Thus, the epistemic utility of P at w_0, relative to $\beta_F^{\lambda_0}$, will be less than that of Q at w_0, again relative to $\beta_F^{\lambda_0}$, iff $P(\text{B}) < Q(\text{B})$. In other words, if two credence functions are equally accurate with respect to w_0, where B is true in w_0, $\beta_F^{\lambda_0}$ will favor P over Q iff P assigns higher credence to B than Q does.

6.4.2 Justifying a weight function

Admittedly, the particular choice of our weight function λ_0 can seem somewhat *ad hoc*.[26] Even if it made sense to assign more importance to accuracy with respect

---

takes its minimum at $x = a$. Thus, for each p, P and Q,

$$\lambda(p) \cdot (P(p) \cdot (1 - Q(p))^2 + (1 - P(p)) \cdot Q(p)^2) > \lambda(p) \cdot (P(p) \cdot (1 - P(p))^2 + (1 - P(p)) \cdot P(p)^2),$$

since $\lambda(p) > 0$. As a result, if $P \neq Q$, the expected β_F^λ-score of Q relative to P is strictly smaller than that of P relative to P.

[26] I am setting aside the question of how to justify specific numerical assignments. After all, all that mattered to our reasoning above was that the weight assigned to B was strictly smaller than the one assigned to every other proposition.

to B than to accuracy with respect to any other proposition, this was only because of the details of the case at hand. Relative to the limited range of propositions we were considering, B, unlike M, has the benefit of providing a potential explanation for some of the propositions you take to be true. But things would have been different if we had been considering a different range of propositions, some of which might have been very well explained by the truth of M.

One response to this worry would be to relativize the choice of epistemic utility function to the particular collection of propositions over which the agent's credence is defined. If we are working with credence functions defined over an algebra that contains propositions that are well explained by B, but no proposition that is explained by M, then we should adopt an epistemic utility function that gives greater weight to accuracy with respect to B than to accuracy with respect to M.

Still, this will tell us nothing about what to do if our algebra contains the proposition that the coin is very shiny—which could be well explained by M—as well as the proposition that four out of the first five tosses of the coin landed heads—which could be well explained by B.

Granted, we could always *count* the number of propositions that could be well explained by one vs the other. But even if that strategy is on the right track (I doubt that it is), it won't be fine-grained enough for many purposes. The explanation in terms of M of the proposition that the coin is very shiny may not be as good as the explanation in terms of B of a proposition about the distribution of heads in a given sequence of tosses. So the relative epistemic merit of accuracy with respect to a given proposition p cannot be a function simply of the number of propositions in a given algebra that admit of an explanation in terms of p.

Better then to define epistemic utility relative to specific explanatory goals. Given a specific explanandum e, say that an epistemic utility function is *e-centered* iff it assigns greater weight to accuracy with respect to p the more p would contribute to the best explanation of e.[27] Given an e-centered epistemic utility function, we can use it to compare credence functions relative to any given world. This, in turn, would allow us to compare questions with respect to the goal of giving an explanation of e.

Now, justifying any *particular* e-centered epistemic utility function would require having something close to a full theory of explanation: we would need a way of determining what the best explanation of e (at a given world) is and a way of comparing propositions in terms of how much they contribute to that explanation. Alas, I do not have a full theory of explanation to offer. In section 6.5, I aim to give something like a proof of concept: a way of incorporating explanatory considerations in a specific way in order to define what is, arguably, an e-centered epistemic utility function.

---

[27] This is not, of course, the only option. One might want the function that determines how much weight to give to accuracy with respect to p to be sensitive not only to how much it contributes to the *best* explanation of e, but also to how much it contributes to non-optimal explanations that meet some adequacy conditions.

6.5 Explanation & Stability

Let us start by taking on a few non-trivial theoretical commitments. A diagnosis for a good explanation of *e*, let us say, is that it makes *e* very *stable*: given the putative explanation, *e* couldn't have easily failed to be the case.[28] This is no doubt an overly simplistic theory of explanation,[29] but it does capture a strand of many independently attractive accounts of explanation.

6.5.1 The stability of being well explained

Start by thinking of laws of nature. Laws of nature have a high degree of stability.[30] They are also some of the best candidates for explanatory bedrock. We all know the explanatory buck has to stop somewhere. We all agree that stopping at the laws of nature is as good a place as any. I say it is no coincidence that their high stability goes hand in hand with their not being in need of an explanation. It is because laws of nature are so stable—because they would have obtained (almost) no matter what—that they do not cry out for explanation.[31]

Jim Woodward, for example, has argued that a good explanation is one that subsumes the explanandum under an *invariant* generalization, where *invariance* is essentially a form of stability across a specific range of cases.[32] If an explanandum is subsumed under a stable generalization, the explanandum itself will also be stable. (Note that, on this view, what makes for a good explanation of *e* is not that the explanation makes *e* stable, but rather that the explanation itself is stable. Still, we can use the extent to which an explanation makes *e* stable as a diagnosis of how good an explanation it is.)

Finally, on Michael Strevens' *kairetic* account of explanation, a sure sign of a good explanation is that it makes the explanandum stable: for, according to Strevens, a good explanation of *e* is (roughly) one that isolates the facts that 'make a difference'

---

[28] This characterization of stability is taken, almost verbatim, from White 2005. White argues that stability, thus understood, is a virtue of explanations—at least of those explanations whose explananda cry out for explanation. His goal is to appeal to explanatory considerations in order to solve Goodman's 'new riddle' of induction.

[29] Among other things, it will not do when it comes to explanations of very low probability events. But these are vexed issues beyond the scope of the chapter. See Woodward 2010 for discussion and references.

[30] Indeed, some would go so far as to use stability in order to *characterize* what laws of nature are. See, e.g. Lange 2005, 2009. For a different take on the relationship between stability and law-likeness, see Mitchell 1997 and Skyrms 1977, 1980.

[31] This is not to say that we cannot explain a given law of nature. There may be other explanatory virtues that are not captured by the notion of stability. For my purposes, however, all I need is that there be an important dimension of explanatory value that is captured by the notion of stability (the same applies to the worries about low probability events mentioned in footnote 29).

[32] Woodward 2005. The details of Woodward's account need not concern us here, but see Woodward 2001.

to the causal path that ends with e.[33] And what distinguishes difference-makers (you guessed) is that they are as stable as possible.[34]

Let us tentatively accept, then, that whether e is sufficiently stable according to p is a reasonable proxy for whether p contributes to a good explanation of e, so that the more stable e is, according to p, the more p contributes to an explanation of e. This allows us to specify a strategy for determining how much a particular proposition would affect the explanatory status of e:[35]

> EXPLANATION PROVIDES RESILIENCE (EPR): The contribution of p to explaining e is proportional to the stability of e according to p.

What is it for e to be stable *according to p*? Intuitively, a particular proposition p *makes e stable* if p entails that e couldn't have easily failed to obtain. More precisely, p makes e (where e is a true proposition) stable iff for a 'wide range' of background conditions b, p entails that, had b not obtained, e still would have obtained. Whether p makes e stable will thus depend on what counts as a 'wide range' of background conditions. For our purposes, we can assume that this is settled by context. Indeed, for our purposes we can assume that for any context there is a range of background conditions B such that whether e is stable depends on the proportion of $b \in B$ such that e would have obtained even if b had been false.

6.5.2 Explanation sensitivity in epistemic utility functions

We can now formulate a constraint on epistemic utility functions along the following lines:[36]

> EXPLANATION SENSITIVITY: Relative to the goal of explaining e, accuracy with respect to p matters, epistemically, to the extent that p would contribute to an explanation of e.

Now, given EPR, EXPLANATION SENSITIVITY entails the following condition:

---

[33] Strevens 2008.

[34] This isn't quite right. What distinguishes difference-makers from other causal factors that played a role in e's occurrence is that they are the result of abstracting away, from a given 'causal model' of e, all the details that aren't necessary to secure the entailment of e. Still, the resulting difference-makers will turn out to be those features of the causal history of e that suffice to guarantee the occurrence of e while being as stable as possible.

[35] Note that saying that p contributes a lot to a good explanation of e does not amount to saying that p alone is a good explanation of e. It could be that p does more than what is necessary to make e stable. For our purposes, however, we need not concern ourselves with the question what is *the* explanation of e.

[36] We may want to qualify this further. We may, for example, restrict this to explananda that 'cry out for explanation'. Or we may want to make this a condition only on the epistemic utility of a credence function at worlds in which the explanandum is true. For present purposes, however, I suggest we stick to the simplest formulation, especially since the examples we will consider involve explananda that *do* cry out for explanation, and of whose truth the relevant agent is certain.

STABILITY BIAS: Relative to the goal of explaining e, accuracy with respect to p matters, epistemically, to the extent that p makes e stable.

Thus, we can get some traction out of EXPLANATION SENSITIVITY if we find a way of comparing the stability of an explanandum according to different propositions.

There are no doubt many ways of doing so. For concreteness, let us pick a relatively simple measure of stability. Assume first that we have a fixed set B of background conditions for a given explanandum e. The stability of e according to a proposition p, which we denote by $s(e, p)$, is the proportion of $b \in B$ such that p entails $\neg b \,\square\!\!\rightarrow e$. We can now define an e-centered epistemic utility function as follows. For each p, let

$$\lambda_s(p) = \frac{1}{1 + s(e, p)}.$$

For a given p, then, $\lambda_s(p)$ will be a number between 1 and ½ that is inversely proportional to the extent to which e is stable according to p. Thus, the full λ_s-Brier score

$$\beta_F^{\lambda_s}(C, x) = -\sum_{p \subseteq \mathcal{W}} \lambda_s(p) \cdot (C(p) - \chi_p(x))^2$$

is an e-centered epistemic utility function, for accuracy with respect to p will be assigned a weight proportional to how much p contributes to an explanation of e.

Turn back, once again, to KNOWN OUTCOME. Assume, as seems plausible, that M—the proposition that the coin was minted two days ago—contributes nothing to the stability of #H = 4—the proposition that four of the five tosses landed heads. In contrast, B—the proposition that the coin was 80 percent biased towards heads, does increase the stability of #H = 4. After all, given the truth of B, #H = 4 would have obtained even if the initial conditions of the coin tosses had been slightly different.[37]

We can illustrate this further by means of a different example. On your desk in your office sits a paper by a colleague. You owe her comments but haven't had a chance to look at the paper. Unfortunately, student papers are just in, and you need to attend to those before your friend's. You print all of your student papers and, without looking at them, put them on a pile on your desk as you rush out. The next day, you arrive in your office and notice something strange. At the top of the pile sits your colleague's paper. And as you look through the pile, you notice that it consists entirely of copies of your colleague's paper.

---

[37] OK, this isn't quite right, for at least two reasons. For one, the bias of a coin has little to no effect on the outcome of the coin flips we are familiar with—see Jaynes 2003, ch. 10 for the surprising details. But even if we ignore that complication, the number of tosses we're dealing with is small enough that it simply isn't reasonable to suppose that the bias of the coin can have such a big effect on the sequence of outcomes. Better then to think of the case as one involving a large number of tosses, with 80% of them landing heads. Then we can appeal to the Law of Large Numbers to ensure that B really does have an effect on the stability of the claim that the proportion of heads in the sequence is 80%. But I will stick to the simpler formulation, at the cost of having to lie a little (as Paul Halmos would put it), for ease of exposition.

Let R be the proposition that every paper on your desk is a copy of your colleague's paper. You consider two possible explanations of R. One, which we'll call G, tells the following story: your colleague gave her paper to each of the other members of your department; all of them printed a copy at the same time; the pile of papers came out right before your students' papers were printed; since you were in a rush you didn't notice that the papers you picked up from the printer weren't those you had printed. The other, which we'll call F, tells a simpler story: your colleague, who really wanted you to look at her paper, got the custodian to let her into your office; she replaced the pile of your student papers with copies of her own papers, hoping you would just take the hint and read her paper already.

Now, as things stand you think G and F are equally likely given R. And you think R is equally likely given G as it is given F. Nonetheless, your (high) credence in R given F is more stable than is your credence in R given G. This is because, conditional on G, your ending up with a bunch of copies of your colleague's paper on your desk was just a fluke: had one of your other collegues printed her copy a few seconds later, your print job would have taken precedence and the pile would have contained a bunch of your students' papers; had you gone to the printer a few seconds later you would have noticed a print job in progress and would have checked to make sure the pile on the printer corresponded to your print job; had you hit print on your machine a few seconds earlier, you would have arrived at the printer before any of your other colleagues' print jobs came out. In contrast, conditional on F, G was pretty much bound to happen.

If having a good explanation of R is among our epistemic goals, I have been claiming, accuracy with respect to a proposition should matter more to the extent that it contributes to an explanation of R. So, from that perspective, accuracy with respect to F should matter more than accuracy with respect to G, at least if we suppose (as I will) that F is a better explanation of R than G is.[38]

Note that I'm *assuming* that my judgments about the stability of the explanandum given each of G and F are correct. That is, I'm assuming that, according to G, R could have easily failed to obtain; and I'm assuming that, according to F, R couldn't have easily failed to obtain. Thus, whatever the set of background conditions, B is fixed by the context so that we are allowed to vary those conditions while still remaining within the sphere of worlds that could have easily obtained, the proportion of those $b \in B$ such that F entails $\neg b \mathbin{\Box\!\!\rightarrow}$ R is *much* bigger than the proportion of those $b \in B$ such that G entails $\neg b \mathbin{\Box\!\!\rightarrow}$ R. As a result, $s(R, F) \gg s(R, G)$, which entails that $\lambda_s^R(F) \ll \lambda_s^R(G)$. Hence, the full λ_s-Brier score will assign greater weight to accuracy with respect to F than to accuracy with respect to G.[39]

---

[38] I am assuming that F and G are, and that you take them to be, logically independent. As a result, accuracy with respect to one of the two propositions is perfectly compatible (even by your own lights) with inaccuracy with respect to the other.

[39] Note that nothing in what I've said so far requires taking a stand on the debate between those who think that Inference to the Best Explanation is compatible with (subjective) Bayesianism (e.g. Lipton 2004)

6.5.3 Methodological aside

On the proposal currently on the table, epistemic utility functions can be used to incorporate considerations other than accuracy into an evaluation of epistemic states. In particular, we can use them to take explanatory considerations into account for the purposes of comparing different epistemic states at different states of the worlds. More specifically, I've suggested we use e-centered epistemic utility functions in order to compare epistemic states in terms of how well they are doing relative to the goals of accuracy and of having a good explanation of e.

Now, there is one way of thinking about the epistemic utility framework on which it essentially provides us with a way of assessing an agent's 'epistemic decisions' by *her own* epistemic lights. On this way of interpreting the framework, the epistemic standing of an agent's epistemic state relative to a given world is relative to *that agent's* epistemic utility function. So if we think, as seems plausible, that this can only get off the ground if an agent can have reasonable access to what her own epistemic utility function is, then we will find no use for e-centered epistemic utility functions. After all, an e-centered epistemic utility function is in part determined by what *in fact* counts as a good explanation of e. And if an agent is mistaken about what counts as a good explanation of e—or if she simply lacks a view as to what a good explanation of e is— her own way of epistemically evaluating an epistemic state may not correspond to an e-centered epistemic utility function.

To be sure, this interpretation of the epistemic utility framework is optional. We could say that an agent is epistemically rational just in case she forms her beliefs as if she were aiming to maximize the expected epistemic utility of her epistemic state— where it is up to *us*, as theorists, to determine what the epistemic utility of an epistemic state at a world is. (The contrasting claim would be: an agent is rational just in case she forms her beliefs as if she were aiming to maximize the expected epistemic utility of her epistemic state—where what epistemic utility an epistemic state has, at a given world, is determined by the agent's own views.)

Still, it would be surprising if in order to take into account considerations other than accuracy we are forced to choose a particular way of interpreting the epistemic utility framework.

Fortunately, we can recast most of what I've said so far so that it is compatible with an 'internalist' interpretation of the framework. Recall the suggestion: an e-centered epistemic utility function is one that gives more weight to accuracy with respect to p the more p contributes to explaining e—where we measured p's contribution to

---

and those who think it is not (e.g. van Fraassen 1989). In particular, nothing in what I've said so far requires endorsing a form of 'explanationism' that goes beyond subjective Bayesianism (cf. Weisberg 2009 for discussion). All I've claimed is that, relative to the goal of explaining e, accuracy with respect to propositions that contribute to such an explanation should matter more than accuracy with respect to propositions that do not. But this is compatible with the claim that such explanatory considerations have no additional evidential import.

142 GOOD QUESTIONS

explaining e in terms of how much the truth of p would increase the counterfactual stability of e. We could have instead made the alternative suggestion: an e-centered epistemic utility function *for an agent* is one that gives more weight to accuracy with respect to p the more the agent takes p to contribute to explaining e—where we measure the agent's estimation of p's contribution to explaining e in terms of how much the truth of p would increase the counterfactual stability of e *according to the agent's beliefs*. More specifically, for a fixed set of background conditions B, say that the stability of e according to a proposition p *and a credence function* C, which we denote by $s_C(e, p)$, is the proportion of $b \in B$ such that $C(\neg b \mathbin{\Box}\!\!\to e \mid p)$ is sufficiently high.[40] We can now define an e-centered epistemic utility function *for an agent with credence function C* as follows. For each p, let

$$\lambda_{s_C}(p) = \frac{1}{1 + s_C(e, p)}.$$

For a given p, then, $\lambda_{s_C}(p)$ will be a number between 1 and ½ that is inversely proportional to the extent to which e is stable according to p and C.

Of course, in order for this to work, we'll need to assume that the agent's credence function is defined over a much richer algebra—in particular, one that includes all the relevant counterfactuals. But this is to be expected if we are going to rely on an agent's own judgment about the explanatory worth of a proposition to be what determines her epistemic utility function.

6.6 Closing

The epistemic utility framework yields a natural way of evaluating questions from an epistemic perspective. And the richer our notion of epistemic utility—the more it departs from an accuracy-only perspective—the more fine-grained our comparison of questions will be. Of course, any move away from a pure accuracy-centered perspective needs to be justified on epistemic grounds. I've offered one possible way of doing so: allowing explanatory considerations to play a role in determining the epistemic merits of a credence function at a world. In doing so, I relied on a somewhat narrow account of what it takes for a proposition to contribute to an explanation, but one that I hope can give a sense of how the full story could eventually be told.

A few issues are left outstanding. First, can we avoid having to relativize epistemic utility to individual explanatory goals? One possibility worth exploring involves identifying a feature of an agent's credence in e that reflects whether the agent takes

---

[40] If we assume, as we have so far, that $C(e) = 1$, then $s_C(e, p)$ will be proportional to the following measure:

$$\rho_C(e, p) = \frac{1}{|B|} \cdot \sum_{b \in B} \mid C(e \mid p) - C(\neg b \mathbin{\Box}\!\!\to e \mid p) \mid,$$

which is essentially a counterfactual version of Skyrms's measure of *resilience*—see e.g. Skyrms 1977, 1980.

e to be in need of explanation.[41] This would allow us to incorporate the value of 'explanatory closure' *simpliciter* into epistemic utility functions.

A second issue is whether stability is the best tool for measuring the explanatory worth of a proposition. While the particular examples I've considered in this chapter do presuppose that the extent to which p increases the stability e is a reasonable proxy for whether p contributes to explaining e, the overall structure of the proposal could be preserved even if we ended up favoring a different measure of explanatory worth. As long as we can assign a numerical value to a given proposition p that measures the contribution of p to explaining e, we can use those numbers to generate weighted accuracy measures which, if I am right, will result in e-centered epistemic utility functions.

Finally, there is the question whether considerations other than explanatory power and accuracy ought to be incorporated into an epistemic utility function. If so, we will need to understand whether all such considerations can be agglomerated into an over-all, 'all epistemic things considered' notion of epistemic utility. That would give rise to a very powerful apparatus, one that could allow us to better understand the role of good questioning in inquiry.[42]

References

Belnap, Nuel D. Jr. (1963). *An Analysis of Questions: Preliminary Report*. Technical Memorandum 1287. Santa Monica, CA: System Development Corporation.

Bromberger, Sylvain (1962). "An Approach to Explanation". In: *Analytical Philosophy*. Ed. by R. J. Butler. Vol. 2. Oxford: Oxford University Press, pp. 72–105. Reprinted in Bromberger 1992, pp. 18–51.

Bromberger, Sylvain (1992). *On What We Know We Don't Know*. Chicago, IL and Stanford, CA: The University of Chicago Press and CSLI.

Friedman, Jane (2013). "Question-directed Attitudes". *Philosophical Perspectives* 27.1, pp. 145–74.

Gibbard, Allan (2008). "Rational Credence and the Value of Truth". In: *Oxford Studies in Epistemology*. Ed. by Tamar Szabó Gendler and John Hawthorne. Vol. 2. Oxford: Oxford University Press, pp. 143–64.

---

[41] For a proposal amenable to the present framework, see the discussion of the 'Salience Condition' in White 2005, p. 3ff.

[42] A much earlier version of this chapter—a descendant of chapter 3 of Pérez Carballo 2011—has been circulating for a little while. (That version contains a discussion of how to adapt the epistemic utility framework to compare credence functions that have different domains, which is now part of Pérez Carballo 2016.) Thanks to Rachael Briggs, Fabrizio Cariani, David Christensen, Paolo Santorio, Mark Schroeder, James Shaw, Katia Vavova, Roger White, members of the Coalition of Los Angeles Philosophers, participants in my Fall 2013 graduate seminar (joint with Chris Meacham) on Epistemic Value at UMass Amherst, as well as audiences at the Australian National University, the University of Sydney, and the University of Southern California for helpful comments and advice at different stages of this project. Thanks also to Jeff Dunn, Kristoffer Ahlstrom-Vij, and an anonymous referee for Oxford University Press for helpful comments on a previous draft of this chapter. For extensive and invaluable feedback, special thanks to Sylvain Bromberger, Chris Meacham, Agustín Rayo, Bob Stalnaker, and Steve Yablo.

Good, Irving J. (1967). "On the Principle of Total Evidence". *The British Journal for the Philosophy of Science* 17.4, pp. 319–21.

Groenendijk, Jeroen and Martin Stokhof (1984). "Studies in the Semantics of Questions and the Pragmatics of Answers". PhD thesis. University of Amsterdam.

Hamblin, Charles L. (1958). "Questions". *Australasian Journal of Philosophy* 36.3, pp. 159–68.

Hamblin, Charles L. (1973). "Questions in Montague English". *Foundations of Language* 10.1, pp. 41–53.

Horwich, Paul (1982). *Probability and Evidence*. Cambridge: Cambridge University Press.

Jaynes, Edwin T. (2003). *Probability Theory: The Logic of Science*. Cambridge: Cambridge University Pres.

Jeffrey, Richard C. (1983). *The Logic of Decision*. Chicago, IL: University of Chicago Press.

Joyce, James M. (2009). "Accuracy and Coherence: Prospects for an Alethic Epistemology of Partial Belief. In: *Degrees of Belief*. Ed. by Franz Huber and Christoph Schmidt-Petri. Vol. 342. Synthese Library. Dordrecht: Springer Netherlands, pp. 263–97.

Karttunen, Lauri (1977). "Syntax and Semantics of Questions". *Linguistics and Philosophy* 1.1, pp. 3–44.

Lange, Marc (2005). "Laws and their Stability". *Synthese* 144.3, pp. 415–32.

Lange, Marc (2009). *Laws and Lawmakers*. New York: Oxford University Press.

Lipton, Peter (2004). *Inference to the Best Explanation*. Second edition. London: Routledge.

Maher, Patrick (1993). *Betting on Theories*. Cambridge Studies in Probability, Induction, and Decision Theory. Cambridge: Cambridge University Press.

Mitchell, Sandra D. (1997). "Pragmatic Laws". *Philosophy of Science* 64, S468–S479.

Pérez Carballo, Alejandro (2011). "Rationality without Representation". PhD thesis. Massachusetts Institute of Technology.

Pérez Carballo, Alejandro (2016). "New Boundary Lines". Unpublished manuscript, University of Massachusetts, Amherst, NY.

Raiffa, Howard and Robert Schlaifer (1961). *Applied Statistical Decision Theory*. Boston, MA: Harvard University Press.

Rooy, Robert van (2004). "Utility, Informativity and Protocols". *Journal of Philosophical Logic* 33.4, pp. 389–419.

Shah, Nishi (2002). "Clearing Space for Doxastic Voluntarism". *The Monist* 85.3, pp. 436–45.

Shah, Nishi and J. David Velleman (2005). "Doxastic Deliberation". *The Philosophical Review* 114.4, pp. 497–534.

Skyrms, Brian (1977). "Resiliency, Propensities, and Causal Necessity". *Journal of Philosophy* 74.11, pp. 704–13.

Skyrms, Brian (1980). *Causal Necessity*. New Haven, CT: Yale University Press.

Skyrms, Brian (1990). *The Dynamics of Rational Deliberation*. Cambridge, MA: Harvard University Press.

Strevens, Michael (2008). *Depth: An Account of Scientific Explanation*. Cambridge, MA: Harvard University Press.

van Fraassen, Bas C. (1989). *Laws and Symmetry*. Oxford: Oxford University Press.

Velleman, J. David (2000). "On the Aim of Belief". In: *The Possibility of Practical Reason*. Oxford: Oxford University Press, pp. 244–81.

Weisberg, Jonathan (2009). "Locating IBE in the Bayesian framework". *Synthese* 167, pp. 125–43.

White, Roger (2005). "Explanation as a Guide to Induction". *Philosopher's Imprint* 5.2, pp. 1–29.

Woodward, James (2001). "Law and Explanation in Biology: Invariance Is the Kind of Stability That Matters". *Philosophy of Science* 68.1, pp. 1–20.

Woodward, James (2005). *Making Things Happen: A Theory of Causal Explanation*. Oxford: Oxford University Press.

Woodward, James (2010). "Scientific Explanation". In: *The Stanford Encyclopedia of Philosophy*. Ed. by Edward N. Zalta. https://plato.stanford.edu/entries/scientific-explanation/. Accessed Spring 2010.

PART II

Accuracy-First Epistemology: For and Against

7

Can All-Accuracy Accounts Justify Evidential Norms?

Christopher J. G. Meacham

7.1 Introduction

Some of the most interesting recent work in formal epistemology has focused on the project of developing scoring rule arguments for Bayesian norms.[1] These scoring rule arguments apply the apparatus of decision theory to the epistemic realm, appealing to epistemic analogs of decision-theoretic principles in order to show that we should satisfy these norms.

One reason this project is interesting is that it provides a justification for Bayesian norms which avoids many of the problems facing older attempts, such as Dutch book arguments and representation theorem arguments. A second reason this project is interesting is that it has been seen as providing a way of justifying Bayesian norms that's compatible with *Veritism*—the view that the only epistemic goal is to have beliefs that are as accurate as possible, and that every epistemic norm must ultimately boil down to and be justified in terms of this goal.[2] The thought is that if we can plug in some measure of accuracy into our decision-theoretic principles, and then show how it follows from this that we should satisfy various Bayesian norms, then we'll be able to provide a *purely alethic justification* for Bayesian norms—a justification that doesn't appeal to anything besides the goal of having accurate beliefs. And if we can provide purely alethic justifications for all of the main Bayesian norms, then we have a way of justifying the Bayesian framework that is congruous with Veritism.

---

[1] The term "Bayesian" is often applied to views that endorse both Probabilism (the claim that a subject's credences should be probabilistic) and Conditionalization (the claim that a subject's new credences, upon receiving evidence, should be equal to her prior credences conditional on her evidence). Here I use the term "Bayesian norm" broadly, to include any norm that imposes a constraint on a subject's credences or degrees of belief. Thus Probabilism and Conditionalization are examples of what I'll call "Bayesian norms", as are norms like Lewis's (1980) Principal Principle, van Fraassen's (1995) Reflection Principle, Indifference Principles, and the like.

[2] For a defense of this view, see Goldman (2002).

Reconciling Bayesianism and Veritism would be a remarkable achievement. For a number of the central Bayesian norms are *evidential norms*, norms whose prescriptions depend on what one's evidence is. And, as Easwaran and Fitelson (2012) note, Veritism seems to be in tension with the existence of evidential norms. According to Veritism, the only thing we should care about (epistemically speaking) is having accurate beliefs. But the existence of evidential norms suggests that we should also care about having beliefs that line up with our evidence. And it seems like these two desiderata can come apart: a subject can have beliefs that line up with the evidence but are nonetheless false. So if accuracy is the only thing we should care about, then it looks like we should give up on norms which care about other things as well, like evidential norms.

In response to these kinds of worries, Pettigrew (2013b) and Joyce (MS) have argued that scoring rule arguments can provide us with an array of purely alethic justifications for the main Bayesian norms, including evidential norms. And they've maintained, at least implicitly, that these justifications are compatible with one another. Indeed, Pettigrew (2013b) has argued that not only can scoring rule arguments provide us with such justifications, existing scoring rule arguments *do* provide us with such justifications. I'll call this stance on the justificatory status of the main Bayesian norms the "All-Accuracy Account":

> *The All-Accuracy Account* There are scoring rule arguments that provide us with compatible purely alethic justifications for the main Bayesian norms, including evidential norms like the Principal Principle, the Indifference Principle, and Conditionalization.

In this chapter I'll raise several worries for the All-Accuracy Account. I'll raise some worries about whether the existing scoring rule arguments provide justifications for these norms that are compatible and purely alethic. And I'll raise some concerns regarding whether it's even possible to provide purely alethic justifications for evidential Bayesian norms.

Despite the critical nature of this chapter, it should not be seen as an attempt to bury scoring rule arguments. Like many others, I think that the investigation of scoring rule arguments is one of the most important recent developments in formal epistemology, and that the work done by Joyce, Pettigrew, and others in exploring this framework is invaluable. Rather, this chapter should be understood as an attempt to get clear on what these arguments actually establish, one which suggests an appropriately modest stance regarding these accomplishments. Or, if one prefers, this chapter can be understood as an attempt to provide a helpful "to do" list of challenges for proponents of views like the All-Accuracy Account to address.

The rest of this chapter will proceed as follows. In section 7.2 I'll provide some background on scoring rule arguments, and the dominance principles that these arguments employ to derive various Bayesian norms. In section 7.3 I'll assess the claim that the scoring rule arguments that have been offered for these different Bayesian norms are compatible. I'll argue that many of the standard scoring rule arguments rely on implausible dominance principles, and that when these principles are fixed up, many of these arguments are no longer compatible. In section 7.4 I'll assess the claim that the scoring rule arguments that have been offered for these different Bayesian norms provide purely alethic justifications. I'll argue that the most explicit argument that's been offered for this conclusion is unsound. In section 7.5 I'll consider whether purely alethic justifications for evidential norms are possible. I'll suggest that such justifications are not possible unless one adopts contentious versions of these norms which many would reject. In section 7.6 I'll suggest that even if one adopts a contentious version of a norm like the Principal Principle, it's not possible to provide a purely alethic justification for such a norm. In section 7.7 I'll conclude by sketching some big-picture morals.

7.2 Background

In this section, I'll lay out some background regarding scoring rule arguments. There are a number of ways to develop such arguments. My presentation here will largely follow Pettigrew's, as he's presented perhaps the most detailed attempt to provide a unified set of scoring rule arguments for the Bayesian norms.[3] In what follows I'll lay out some preliminary terminology, briefly discuss the epistemic utility functions these arguments employ, and sketch the decision-theoretic principles these arguments employ in order to obtain the various Bayesian norms.

7.2.1 Preliminaries

Let F be the *doxastic propositions* of a subject; that is, the set of propositions about which a subject has beliefs. Let W be the set of consistent truth assignments to these propositions. I'll call the elements of W the *worlds* of a subject.[4] I'll assume that F is closed under the usual logical operations (conjunction, disjunction, negation, etc). Following Pettigrew (2013b), I'll assume that F and W are finite.

Let a subject's *credence function* be a function cr which takes propositions as arguments, and yields real numbers in the [0,1] interval that represent the subject's confidence in that proposition, with higher numbers representing greater degrees of confidence.

7.2.2 Epistemic utility

Let an *epistemic utility function* be a function U which takes a credence function and a world as arguments, and yields a real number representing the epistemic utility of holding that credence function at that world.

---

[3] See Leitgeb and Pettigrew (2010a, 2010b), Pettigrew (2012, 2013a, 2013b, 2014).
[4] These "worlds" will not, of course, be as fine-grained as possible worlds, which correspond to consistent assignments of truth values to *every* proposition (regardless of whether anyone has beliefs about them or not).

Proponents of Veritism, such as Pettigrew (2013b) and Joyce (MS), maintain that satisfactory epistemic utility functions must be "alethic," and must assign quantities that value accuracy and nothing else. As such, they require satisfactory epistemic utility functions to satisfy certain constraints. For example, since they want accuracy to be an overriding factor, they require epistemic utility functions to satisfy:[5]

Truth-Directedness: If for all propositions A, $cr(A) \geq cr^*(A)$ if A is true at w and $cr(A) \leq cr^*(A)$ if A is false at w, and for some A, A is true at w and $cr(A) > cr^*(A)$, or A is false at w and $cr(A) < cr^*(A)$, then $U(cr, w) > U(cr^*, w)$.

Likewise, since they want accuracy to be the *only* relevant factor—and thus want factors such as the content of propositions to be irrelevant—they require epistemic utility functions to satisfy:[6]

Extensionality: Let $f_{w,w^*} : F \to F$ be a bijection between true and false propositions at w with true and false propositions at w^*; i.e. if $f_{w,w^*}(A) = B$, then either A is true at w and B is true at w^*, or A is false at w and B is false at w^*. If cr and cr^* are such that, for all A, $cr(A) = cr^*(f_{w,w^*}(A))$, then $U(cr, w) = U(cr^*, w^*)$.

These are the two most prominent constraints on alethic utility functions. Some proponents of Veritism have suggested that alethic utility functions should satisfy some other constraints as well, though there is disagreement regarding what exactly these further constraints should be.

Fortunately, we needn't hash out the details of this debate here. For there is one epistemic utility function which is widely agreed to be adequate, namely, the epistemic utility function associated with the Brier score.[7] Let the *indicator function* be a function I which takes a world w and a proposition A as arguments and yields either 0 (if A is false at w) or 1 (if A is true at w). Then the epistemic utility function associated with the Brier score is:[8]

$$U(cr, w) = -\sum_{A \in F} (I(w, A) - cr(A))^2. \tag{1}$$

For the purposes of this chapter, I'll follow Pettigrew (2013b) in assuming that this is the correct epistemic utility function.[9]

---

[5] See Joyce (2009). [6] See Joyce (2009).
[7] Though see Levinstein (2012) for a reason to be wary of the Brier score.
[8] The Brier score itself is what you get if you remove the minus sign out front: it's a measure of *inaccuracy*, such that the higher the values it yields, the less accurate the credence function.
[9] Some, like Joyce (MS), hold that there is no unique correct epistemic utility function. Instead, there's a small group of "kosher" utility functions, any one of which is good enough. But proponents of such views still hold that the utility function associated with the Brier score is one of the functions that's good enough; and that's sufficient for our purposes.

7.2.3 Dominance norms and Bayesian norms

Scoring rule arguments have been offered for a number of different Bayesian norms.[10] I'll largely focus here on the arguments offered by Pettigrew. These arguments generally appeal to a dominance norm of some sort, and proceed by using this dominance norm and an epistemic utility function to derive the relevant Bayesian norm.

Let's see how these arguments go. In what follows, let F be the set of doxastic propositions of the subject; W the worlds associated with F; cr, cr^*, and cr^{**} credence functions defined over F; and U the correct epistemic utility function.

One of the core Bayesian norms is *Probabilism*:

Probabilism: A subject's credences should be probabilistic.

The scoring rule arguments for Probabilism employ something like *Strict Dominance* as a dominance norm:

Definition: A function cr is *strictly dominated* by cr^* for a subject *iff*, for all $w \in W$, $U(cr, w) < U(cr^*, w)$.

Strict Dominance: If a subject is such that (i) cr is strictly dominated by cr^*, and (ii) cr^* is not strictly dominated by any cr^{**}, then it is impermissible for that subject to adopt cr.

There's some variation in the literature regarding the exact form of the dominance norm employed in the argument for Probabilism. Some employ a slightly weaker notion of dominance, some omit the second clause, and some employ one notion of dominance in the first clause and a slightly different notion of dominance in the second.[11] But for our purposes, these differences won't matter.

Another core Bayesian norm is *Conditionalization*:[12,13]

Conditionalization: If a subject with probabilistic credences cr receives evidence E, her new credences cr_E should be:

---

[10] For example, see Joyce (1998), Greaves and Wallace (2006), Joyce (2009), Leitgeb and Pettigrew (2010a, 2010b), Pettigrew (2012), Easwaran (2013), Pettigrew (2013a, 2013b, 2014).

[11] For example, see Joyce (2009) for instances of the first and second variations, and Pettigrew (2013b) for an instance of the third. I present Strict Dominance in the text (as opposed to one of these variants) in order to keep the form of the different dominance norms I present in this section as similar as possible.

[12] The formulation of Conditionalization given here is a standard one. Pettigrew (2013b) applies the label "Conditionalization" to a different kind of norm—a synchronic norm regarding what plans one should make, not a diachronic norm about what credences one should have. One might motivate moving from a diachronic norm to a synchronic norm in various ways (e.g., see Meacham (2010), Hedden (2015), and Moss (forthcoming)), but since the synchronic rule described in Pettigrew (2013b) diverges quite a bit from the diachronic rule Bayesians generally endorse (and the rule discussed in other places, such as Leitgeb and Pettigrew (2010b)), I've stuck with the standard formulation here.

[13] Like most formulations of Conditionalization, this formulation leaves open a number of questions regarding how exactly the norm should be understood (see Schoenfield (forthcoming) and Meacham (2016) for discussions of some of these issues). For example, should we understand cr as the subject's credences after she's received all of her evidence except E, the most recent piece of evidence she's received, or should we understand cr as a credence function at some arbitrary time, and E as the cumulative evidence the subject's received since then? That said, the ambiguities of this formulation are largely orthogonal to the issues I'll be raising in this chapter, so I'll put these complications aside.

$$cr_E(A) = cr(A \mid E), \text{ if defined.} \tag{2}$$

The scoring rule arguments for Conditionalization need to employ something like what I'll call *Credal Expected E-Dominance*:[14]

Definition: Let the subject's credences be cr_0. Assume cr_0 is probabilistic, and let cr and cr^* be probability functions. Then cr is *credal expected E-dominated by* cr^* for that subject *iff*:

$$\sum_{w \in E} cr_0(w) \cdot U(cr, w) < \sum_{w \in E} cr_0(w) \cdot U(cr^*, w). \tag{3}$$

Credal Expected E-Dominance: If a subject is such that the next piece of evidence she'll receive is E at t', and is such that (i) cr is credal expected E-dominated by cr^*, and (ii) cr^* is not credal expected E-dominated by any cr^{**}, then it is impermissible for that subject to adopt cr at t'.

Some formulations of the decision-theoretic norms this argument requires obscure the diachronic nature of these norms, and the norm's appeal to the subject's evidence.[15] But these features of the norm are crucial to getting the derivation to go through. As one might expect, you can't get diachronic results about what credences a subject should have given certain evidence without building diachronic features and appeals to evidence into one's decision-theoretic norm.

In addition to Probabilism and Conditionalization, most Bayesians accept a chance-credence principle of some kind. There is some disagreement about how to best formulate this principle, but one popular formulation, borrowing from Lewis (1980), is:[16]

Principal Principle: Let ch_G be the chance function picked out by G. The credences of a subject with total evidence G, cr_G, should be such that:

$$cr_G(A) = ch_G(A), \text{ if defined.} \tag{4}$$

Pettigrew's (2013a) scoring rule argument for the Principal Principle employs what I'll call *Chancy Expected Dominance*:

---

[14] This is, roughly, a dominance-style formulation of the decision-theoretic norm employed by Leitgeb and Pettigrew (2010b) in their scoring rule argument for Conditionalization. But there are a number of other ways to formulate and divide up the norms the argument requires; see, for example, Easwaran (2013). (There are also a number of other interesting issues regarding these arguments that I lack the space to discuss; see Schoenfield (forthcoming).)

[15] e.g., see Pettigrew (2013b) and the formulation of Maximize Subjective Expected Utility.

[16] This formulation follows from the conjunction of Lewis's formulation and Conditionalization. Lewis's initial formulation only makes appeal to a subject's initial credences, prior to the receipt of evidence.

Definition: Let C be the set of possible chance functions. Let E be the total evidence of the subject. A function cr is *chancy expected dominated* by cr^* for that subject *iff*, for all $ch \in C$:

$$\sum_{w \in W} ch(w \mid E) \cdot U(cr, w) < \sum_{w \in W} ch(w \mid E) \cdot U(cr^*, w). \tag{5}$$

Chancy Expected Dominance: If a subject is such that (i) cr is chancy expected dominated by cr^*, and (ii) cr^* is not chancy expected dominated by any cr^{**}, then it is impermissible for that subject to adopt cr.

It's worth noting that Chancy Expected Dominance's appeal to the subject's evidence is crucial to the success of the argument. After all, we want the permissible credences regarding chance events to *vary* depending on what a subject's evidence is. (For example, if a subject has no evidence other than that the chance of heads is 1/2, their credence in heads should be 1/2. But if the subject has no evidence other than that (i) the chance of heads is 1/2 *and* (ii) the coin landed heads, their credence in heads should be 1.) And one can't derive a norm whose prescriptions are evidence-dependent, like the Principal Principle, without employing a decision-theoretic norm that appeals to evidence.[17]

Finally, some Bayesians endorse a fourth norm, an Indifference Principle of some kind. There are a number of different kinds of Indifference Principle, but one popular version of this principle, considered by Pettigrew (2014), is:[18]

Indifference Principle: The credences of a subject with total evidence E, cr_E, should be such that:

$$\forall w_i, w_j \in E,\ cr_E(w_i) = cr_E(w_j). \tag{6}$$

Pettigrew's (2014) scoring rule argument for this Indifference Principle employs *Worst-Case Dominance*:

Definition: Let E be the total evidence of a subject. A function cr is *worst-case dominated* by cr^* for that subject *iff* there is some $w \in E$ such that, for all $w^* \in E$, $U(cr, w) < U(cr^*, w^*)$.

Worst-Case Dominance: If a subject is such that (i) cr is worst-case dominated by cr^*, and (ii) cr^* is not worst-case dominated by any cr^{**}, then it is impermissible for that subject to adopt cr.

---

[17] At first glance the version of the dominance norm used to derive the Principal Principle given in Pettigrew (2013b) doesn't seem to make any claims about evidence. But it needs to be understood as implicitly making claims of this kind (as the version presented in Pettigrew (2013a) does) in order for the argument to go through.

[18] This is the principle that Pettigrew (2014) calls "PoI+", but the same general points apply with respect to what Pettigrew calls "PoI." In both cases, the principle's prescriptions are sensitive to what the subject's evidence is (in the latter case, requiring the subject to not have any evidence), and in both cases the derivation of the principle won't follow unless we employ a norm in which the subject's evidence plays a role.

Again, some presentations of the scoring rule argument for the Indifference Principle employ formulations of these decision-theoretic norms that obscure their appeal to the subject's total evidence.[19] But these appeals to the subject's total evidence are a vital part of these norms. For without such appeals, the derivation of the Indifference Principle won't go through.

7.3 Compatibility

Proponents of the All-Accuracy Account maintain that scoring rule arguments provide us with compatible and purely alethic justifications for the main Bayesian norms. One worry for this claim, which we'll focus on in this section, has to do with whether the scoring rule arguments for these different norms are compatible.

Pettigrew is the most prolific producer of scoring rule arguments for Bayesian norms, as well as one of the most careful, so I'll focus on his arguments here. The scoring rule arguments for Bayesian norms generally take the following form: first they argue that we should adopt a certain kind of epistemic utility function, then they argue that we should adopt a certain decision-theoretic norm, and then they show how to use this utility function and decision-theoretic norm to derive the relevant Bayesian norm. As we saw in section 7.2.3, the decision-theoretic principles Pettigrew employs are generally dominance principles of the following form:[20]

> X-*Dominance:* If a subject is such that (i) cr is X-dominated by cr^*, and (ii) cr^* is not X-dominated by any cr^{**}, then it is impermissible for that subject to adopt cr.

By plugging in different notions of dominance into this schema, we get different decision-theoretic principles. And we can use these different principles to derive the different Bayesian norms.

I'll argue that this method of deriving Bayesian norms is problematic. First, I'll suggest that these kinds of dominance principles are only plausible in isolation. When considered jointly, these principles become implausible. Second, I'll note that even though we can get around this worry by modifying the dominance principles these derivations employ, doing so requires us to reassess these derivations. In particular, I'll show that once we've chosen which forms of dominance we want to be epistemically relevant, we can formulate principles tracking these notions of dominance that *are* jointly plausible. But once we adopt these modified principles, we need to reassess

---

[19] e.g., the version of the dominance norm used to derive the Indifference Principle given in Pettigrew (2013b) doesn't seem to make any claims about evidence. But it needs to be understood as implicitly making claims of this kind (as the version endorsed in Pettigrew (2014) does—see sections 4 and 6 for the key caveats and revisions) in order for the argument to go through.

[20] Though the form is a bit different in the case of diachronic dominance principles (such as Credal Expected E-Dominance).

these derivations of Bayesian norms. For in many cases these derivations will no longer be compatible.

To get a feel for how this problem arises, let's start by considering why Pettigrew formulates these dominance principles using the above schema. It's clear why the schema includes the first clause—the thought that there's something *prima facie* wrong with dominated options is a key part of the intuition underwriting these dominance norms. But why does this schema include the second clause? At first glance, anyway, it's tempting to simply drop the second clause and adopt a schema like this:

X-Dominance (v0):   If a subject is such that cr is X-dominated by cr^*, then it is impermissible for that subject to adopt cr.

Pettigrew's (2013b) reason for rejecting the Dominance (v0) schema is that it leads to absurd results in cases in which there are no undominated credences. If every credence function is dominated by another credence function, then Dominance (v0) will entail that every credence function is impermissible. If we take epistemic dilemmas—situations in which every epistemic option is impermissible—to be impossible, then this is a *reductio* of Dominance (v0).[21]

One way to avoid this problem is to modify the Dominance (v0) schema so that being dominated only rules out a credence function if there are undominated credence functions to be had. This yields the following schema:

X-Dominance (v1):   If a subject is such that (i) cr is X-dominated by cr^*, and (ii) there are undominated credence functions, then it is impermissible for that subject to adopt cr.

But, as Pettigrew (2013b) notes, this revised schema is still problematic. For both Dominance (v0) and (v1) yield the wrong results in certain cases. Here is a slight variant of a case Pettigrew (2013b) considers. Suppose a subject can adopt any one of a countably infinite sequence of credence functions defined over two worlds, w_1 and w_2. And suppose the epistemic utilities of adopting each of these credence functions at each world are given by the following table:

---

[21] This is a bit quick, for one can avoid a *reductio* by rejecting any of the premises that led to the contradiction, and there are other premises one could reject other than Dominance (v0). In particular, one could reject the premise that there are any normatively relevant notions of dominance such that there will be no undominated options in some cases. But this is an unattractive option: since these schemas are supposed to spell out the general relationship between normatively relevant notions of dominance and what we ought to believe, one would like to avoid having to make substantive assumptions about what dominance relations can hold.

In a similar fashion, one can respond to the counterexample to Dominance (v0) and Dominance (v21) given as we shall see by maintaining that there aren't any normatively relevant notions of dominance that will yield to the pattern of dominance relations the case describes. But again this is an unattractive option, given that these schemas are supposed to spell out the general relationship between normatively relevant notions of dominance and what we ought to believe.

158 CAN ALL-ACCURACY ACCOUNTS JUSTIFY EVIDENTIAL NORMS?

	cr_0	cr_1	cr_2	...	cr_n	...
w_1	2	1	2	...	n	...
w_2	2	$2-\frac{1}{2}$	$2-\frac{1}{4}$	...	$2-\frac{1}{2^n}$	...

Given a dominance relation that tracks these epistemic utilities, cr_0 will be the only undominated credence function. The function cr_0 will not be dominated, since it yields a higher epistemic utility at w_2 than any other credence function. But for every $i > 0$, cr_i will be dominated by cr_{i+1}. And since i is unbounded, it follows that every $cr_{i>0}$ will be dominated.

Given Dominance (v0) or (v1), it follows that cr_0 will be the only permissible credence function. But this doesn't seem right. For example, every probability function that assigns a non-zero value to w_1 will assign some $cr_{i>0}$ a higher expected utility than cr_0. Thus it seems like at least some $cr_{i>0}$s should be permissible.

The moral, Pettigrew notes, is that being dominated isn't in itself a bad thing. Whether being dominated is a bad thing depends on the status of what's doing the dominating. If an option is dominated by something which has a mark against it, then this doesn't suffice to rule out the dominated option. Being dominated only rules out an option if it's dominated by something which is itself unimpeachable. Thus, in the example above, the fact that every $cr_{i>0}$ is dominated doesn't rule them out, as every credence function that dominates them is itself dominated by something else.

Call an option *unimpeachable iff* no normatively relevant factor tells against it. If we restrict our attention to cases in which the only normatively relevant factor is X-dominance, then an option will be unimpeachable *iff* it's not X-dominated. Given Pettigrew's moral—that being dominated only tells against an option if the dominating option is unimpeachable—this suggests the following schema:

X-Dominance (v2):   If a subject is such that (i) cr is X-dominated by cr^*, and (ii) cr^* is not X-dominated by any cr^{**}, then it is impermissible for that subject to adopt cr.

This is, of course, precisely the schema Pettigrew employs.

Dominance (v2) works well if we assume that X-dominance is the only normatively relevant factor. But suppose that's not the case, and that there are two normatively relevant factors. Perhaps, in addition to X-dominance, there is also a "side constraint" that directly states that certain options are impermissible.[22] Or perhaps there are two normatively relevant notions of dominance, X-dominance and Y-dominance. How should we proceed, in order to determine what options are permissible?

One approach is to apply each of these constraints sequentially. So, for example, one might first apply a side constraint to narrow down the set of permissible options, and then appeal to X-Dominance (v2) to narrow down the set of permissible options some more. Or one might appeal to X-Dominance (v2) to narrow down the set of permissible options, and then appeal to Y-Dominance (v2) to further narrow down

---

[22] I borrow this "side constraints" terminology from Pettigrew (2013b), who himself borrows it from Nozick (1974).

the set of permissible options. The problem with this approach, as Easwaran and Fitelson (2012) show, is that the final result can be order-dependent.[23] That is, the set of permissible options one is left with after applying both constraints can depend on the order in which we apply these constraints. This leaves us in the uncomfortable position of having to decide between different orderings, and of having to provide some rationale for why this is the right ordering to choose.

A second approach is to apply both of these constraints to the entire set of options, and to then take the intersection of the options that remain to be the permissible options. So, for example, one might take the intersection of the options not ruled out by a side constraint, and the options not ruled out by X-Dominance (v2). Or one might take the intersection of the options not ruled out by X-Dominance (v2), and the options not ruled out by Y-Dominance (v2). This approach avoids the ordering problems that afflicted the first approach, since there is no order in which the constraints are applied—they're each applied independently.

But this approach is problematic for the same reasons that Dominance (v0) was problematic. For if, say, X-Dominance (v2) and Y-Dominance (v2) jointly rule out every option, then this approach will entail that every option is impermissible. Assuming that epistemic dilemmas are impossible, this is a *reductio* of this approach.[24]

A third approach avoids this problem by modifying the schema so that being dominated only rules out a credence function if there are unimpeachable credence functions to be had—credence functions that are undominated with respect to every normatively relevant notion of dominance, compatible with any side-constraints, and so on:

X-*Dominance (v3):*   If a subject is such that (i) cr is X-dominated by cr^*, and (ii) there are unimpeachable credence functions, then it is impermissible for that subject to adopt cr.

Then, as before, one applies constraints to the entire set of options, and takes the intersection of what remains to yield the permissible options.

But both the second and third approaches yield the wrong results in some cases. Suppose there are exactly two normatively relevant factors, X-dominance and

---

[23] Though see Pettigrew's (2014) for an instance of someone willing to bite the bullet here. (In order to resolve the tension between the Principal Principle and the Indifference Principle, Pettigrew suggests that we apply the norms that yield the Principal Principle before we apply those yielding the Indifference Principle.)

[24] Again, as mentioned in footnote 21, this is a bit quick, for one can avoid this *reductio* in other ways, such as by rejecting the assumption that there are two normatively relevant notions of dominance that will rule out every option in this way. Again, however, this is an unattractive option: since these schemas are supposed to spell out the general relationship between normatively relevant notions of dominance and what we ought to believe, one would like to avoid having to make substantive assumptions about what dominance relations can hold.

In a similar fashion, one can respond to the counterexample given below to both the second and third approaches by maintaining that there are not any normatively relevant notions of dominance that will yield to the pattern of dominance relations the case describes. But again, this is an unattractive option given that these schemas are supposed to spell out the general relationship between normatively relevant notions of dominance and what we ought to believe.

160 CAN ALL-ACCURACY ACCOUNTS JUSTIFY EVIDENTIAL NORMS?

Y-dominance, where X-dominance tracks X-utility, and Y-dominance tracks Y-utility. And consider three credence functions defined over a pair of worlds w_1 and w_2, whose utilities at each world are:

		cr_1	cr_2	cr_3
X-utility:	w_1	99	100	101
	w_2	99	100	0
Y-utility:	w_1	100	99	0
	w_2	100	99	101

Evaluating this case using the second approach, we find that cr_3 is not ruled out as it's neither X- nor Y-dominated by anything. But cr_1 is impermissible because it's X-dominated by cr_2, and cr_2 is X-undominated. And cr_2 is impermissible because it's Y-dominated by cr_1, and cr_1 is Y-undominated.

Evaluating this case using the third approach, we find that cr_3 is again not ruled out because it's neither X- nor Y-dominated by anything. (Indeed, since we've stipulated that X- and Y-dominance are the only normatively relevant factors, cr_3 is unimpeachable.) But cr_1 is impermissible because it's X-dominated by cr_2, and there exist unimpeachable credence functions (i.e., cr_3). And cr_2 is impermissible because it's Y-dominated by cr_1, and there exist unimpeachable credence functions.

So both the second and third approaches entail that cr_3 is the only permissible credence function. But these verdicts don't seem right. For example, *every* probability function will take cr_1 to have either a higher expected X-utility or a higher expected Y-utility than cr_3. And every probability function which assigns a credence greater than ≈ 0.02 to each world will take cr_1 to have *both* a higher expected X-utility and a higher expected Y-utility than cr_3.

In light of this, let's consider a fourth approach. Recall Pettigrew's moral: whether being dominated is a bad thing depends on the status of what's doing the dominating. In particular, being dominated only rules out an option if the dominating option is unimpeachable.

This suggests the following schema:

X-Dominance (v4): If a subject is such that (i) cr is X-dominated by cr^*, and (ii) cr^* is unimpeachable, then it is impermissible for that subject to adopt cr.

And, as before, one applies constraints to the entire set of options, and takes the intersection of what remains to yield the permissible options.[25]

If we adopt this fourth approach, then in the example above cr_1, cr_2, and cr_3 will all come out permissible. The function cr_1 won't be ruled out, for while cr_1 is

---

[25] In some places, at least, it seems Pettigrew would endorse this fourth approach (e.g., see his argument in favor of "Dominance-" in section 3 of Pettigrew (2013b), and compare Dominance- to Dominance (v4)). In other places, however, Pettigrew seems to prefer the first approach (see footnote 23).

X-dominated by cr_2, cr_2 isn't unimpeachable, as it's Y-dominated by cr_1. Likewise, cr_2 won't be ruled out, for while cr_2 is Y-dominated by cr_1, cr_1 isn't unimpeachable, as it's X-dominated by cr_2.

I suggest that this fourth approach is the one we should adopt. And Dominance (v4) is the schema we should employ to formulate dominance principles.

The dominance-style derivations of Bayesian norms provided in the literature tend to use Dominance (v0) or (v2)-style principles, not Dominance (v4)-style principles.[26] The appeal to Dominance (v2)-style principles is unproblematic if we assume that the notion of dominance being employed is the only normatively relevant factor, as in that case Dominance (v2) and Dominance (v4) are equivalent. But the appeal to Dominance (v2)-style principles *is* problematic if we assume that there are multiple normatively relevant factors—something we're committed to if we want to endorse more than one of these arguments. For if there are multiple normatively relevant factors, it's Dominance (v4), not Dominance (v2), that correctly describes how dominance facts bear on what it's permissible to believe. And once we adopt these Dominance (v4)-style principles, these derivations of the Bayesian norms may no longer go through.

7.3.1 Two examples

The dominance principle derivations of Bayesian norms given in the literature tend to use Dominance (v0) and (v2)-style principles. I've argued that we should replace them with Dominance (v4)-style principles. But once we make these replacements, and take all of the normatively relevant factors into account, these derivations of Bayesian norms may no longer go through. To get a feel for how this goes, let's work through two simple examples.

For the first example, suppose there to be exactly two normatively relevant factors, strict dominance and chancy expected dominance. To simplify the discussion, let's assume we're restricting our attention to subjects with no evidence.

Now consider the argument that employs strict dominance to establish Probabilism. It's been shown in the literature that every non-probabilistic credence function is strictly dominated by a credence function which is itself not strictly dominated by anything.[27] Given Strict Dominance (v2), this entails that non-probabilistic credence functions are impermissible. But given Strict Dominance (v4), this entailment doesn't follow—to show that every non-probabilistic credence function is impermissible, it needs to be shown that every non-probabilistic credence function is strictly dominated by a credence function which is itself neither strictly dominated *nor* chancy expected dominated. And this is not true. For there are cases in which some non-probabilistic credence functions are only strictly dominated by credence functions

---

[26] e.g., see Joyce (2009) for versions of Dominance (v0)-style principles, and Pettigrew (2014) and Pettigrew (2013a) for versions of Dominance (v2)-style principles.
[27] e.g., see Pettigrew (2013c) and the references therein.

which are themselves chancy expected dominated.[28] Thus, given these assumptions about what's normatively relevant, Strict Dominance (v4) won't entail that all non-probabilistic credence functions are impermissible. And the attempt to establish Probabilism by appealing to strict dominance won't work.

That said, given this particular stance regarding what factors are normatively relevant, the failure of this argument doesn't really matter. For while the argument from strict dominance to Probabilism fails, the argument from chancy expected dominance to the Principal Principle succeeds, and the Principal Principle entails Probabilism. Thus we can replace the argument from strict dominance to Probabilism with an argument from chancy expected dominance to Probabilism.

Let's see how the dominance argument for the Principal Principle goes. Given Chancy Expected Dominance (v4), showing that every Principal Principle-violating (or "PP-violating") credence function is impermissible requires showing that every PP-violating credence function is chancy expected dominated by a credence function which is itself neither chancy expected dominated nor strictly dominated. Pettigrew (2013a) shows that every PP-violating credence function will be chancy expected dominated by a PP-satisfying credence function which is not chancy expected dominated. Furthermore, every PP-satisfying credence function is probabilistic, and no probabilistic credence function is strictly dominated.[29] Thus every PP-violating credence function is chancy expected dominated by a credence function which is itself neither chancy expected dominated nor strictly dominated. And so, given these assumptions about what factors are normatively relevant, Chancy Expected Dominance (v4) will entail that all PP-violating credence functions are impermissible. And thus the attempt to establish the Principal Principle by appealing to chancy expected dominance succeeds.

Let's turn to the second example. As before, suppose that there are exactly two normatively relevant factors, but this time let these factors be chancy expected dominance and worst-case dominance. To simplify things, let's again assume that we're restricting our attention to subjects with no evidence.

Let's start by assessing the prospects for a dominance argument for the Indifference Principle. Pettigrew (2014) shows that every Indifference Principle-violating (or "IP-violating") credence function is worst-case dominated by the IP-satisfying credence function which is itself not worst-case dominated. And given Worst Case Dominance (v2), this would entail that violating the Indifference Principle is impermissible. But given Worst Case Dominance (v4), more needs to be shown: it needs

---

[28] The existence of such cases was shown by Easwaran and Fitelson (2012). Here is a simplified version of such a case, offered by Pettigrew (2013b). Consider a subject with a credence of 3/5 in both A and $\neg A$, who knows that the chance of A is 3/5, and knows nothing else about the chances (such as the chance of $\neg A$). As Pettigrew (2013b) shows, the subject's non-probabilistic credences will be strictly dominated by a narrow band of probabilistic credence functions which assign values of around 1/2 to A and $\neg A$. But since none of these probabilistic credence functions assign 3/5 to A, all of them are chancy expected dominated.

[29] e.g., see Joyce (1998).

to be shown that every IP-violating credence function is worst-case dominated by a credence function which is itself not worst-case dominated *and* not chancy expected dominated. And, given some mild assumptions about chance assignments, this won't be true.[30] The only function which isn't worst-case dominated—the IP-satisfying credence function—will be chancy expected dominated by other credence functions.[31] Thus, given these assumptions about what's normatively relevant, Worst Case Dominance (v4) won't entail that violating the Indifference Principle is impermissible. And thus the dominance argument for the Indifference Principle fails.

Likewise, the dominance argument for the Principal Principle fails. To show that violating the Principal Principle is impermissible given Chancy Expected Dominance (v4), it needs to be shown that every PP-violating credence function is chancy expected dominated by a credence function which is itself neither chancy expected dominated nor worst-case dominated. But given the same mild assumptions as before, there won't be any such function—the only functions which aren't chancy expected dominated will be worst-case dominated. So, given these assumptions about what's normatively relevant, Chancy Expected Dominance (v4) won't entail that violating the Principal Principle is impermissible. And thus the argument from chancy expected dominance to the Principal Principle fails. So, given these assumptions about what's normatively relevant, Chancy Expected Dominance (v4) won't entail that violating the Principal Principle is impermissible, and the dominance argument for the Principal Principle will fail.[32]

---

[30] For example, the following assumptions suffice: (1) some ur-chance function (i.e., possible initial chance function) assigns a different non-zero value to some pair of worlds, and (2) the assignments of ur-chance functions don't overlap; i.e., they assign non-zero values to disjoint sets of worlds. (This second assumption will be disputed by some proponents of Humean accounts of chance. But this argument for the Principal Principle is supposed to be independent of whether one is a Humean.)

[31] One can see this intuitively as follows. Pettigrew's derivation shows that credence functions conditional on E that aren't mixtures of the possible chance functions which assign 1 to E will be chancy expected dominated. For subjects with no evidence, it follows that credence functions that aren't mixtures of the possible chance functions will be chancy expected dominated. Now, suppose that (1) some ur-chance function ch assigns a different non-zero value to some pair of worlds, call them w_1 and w_2, and (2) ur-chance functions don't overlap; i.e., they assign non-zero values to disjoint sets of worlds. Given (1) and (2), the IP-satisfying credence function can't be a mixture of ur-chance functions, for the IP-satisfying credence function will assign the same non-zero value to w_1 and w_2, while any mixture of ur-chance functions satisfying (1) and (2) must assign w_1 and w_2 either 0 (if ch gets zero weight in the mixture) or distinct non-zero values (if ch gets non-zero weight in the mixture). And since the IP-satisfying credence function can't be a mixture of ur-chance functions, it will be chancy expected dominated.

[32] In this case these failures are predictable, since (given the kinds of mild assumptions described in footnote 30) the Principal Principle and Pettigrew's Indifference Principle will yield inconsistent prescriptions. Thus, if one has set up one's framework correctly, it *shouldn't* follow that subjects are obligated to satisfy both the Principal Principle and the Indifference Principle. (The fact that the Dominance (v4) schema yields this result is a mark in favor of it over (say) the Dominance (v0) and (v2) schemas, which will inconsistently require subjects to satisfy both.) But even in cases in which these failures are not predictable, the same general points hold. We need to be careful to track all of the normatively relevant factors in play, and see whether the argument goes through given those factors. For the fact that these arguments work in the special case in which there's only one normatively relevant factor is no indication that they'll continue to work once other normatively relevant factors are added into the mix.

These are two simple examples of how scoring rule arguments for Bayesian norms can break down once we move to Dominance (v4)-style principles, as I've argued we should. In both of these examples there are only two epistemically relevant factors in play. More plausible stances will take there to be more than two epistemically relevant factors.[33] But the general moral is the same for both simple stances and more complicated ones. In order to assess whether an argument for a Bayesian norm goes through, we need to be aware of, and take into consideration, *all* of the normatively relevant factors. And the fact that an argument goes through in the special case in which there's only one normatively relevant factor is no indication that it'll still go through after we introduce other normatively relevant factors.

7.3.2 Summing up

Let's take stock. I've argued that the dominance arguments for Bayesian norms should adopt Dominance (v4)-style principles. If this is right, then the dominance arguments for Bayesian norms which appeal to Dominance (v0)- or (v2)-style principles are no good. And while arguments employing Dominance (v2)-style principles suffice in cases in which the notion of dominance being employed is the only relevant factor (since in these cases the Dominance (v2) and (v4) schemas are equivalent), these arguments aren't compelling when there are multiple normatively relevant factors in play, as we're required to think if we want to endorse more than one of these arguments at the same time.

Once we realize that we need to adopt Dominance (v4)-style principles, our assessments of the arguments for Bayesian norms becomes a more holistic process. For what a Dominance (v4)-style principle takes to be impermissible will depend on what credence functions are unimpeachable, and thus on what exactly the normatively relevant considerations are. And this makes establishing that (say) it's impermissible to violate the Principal Principle a much trickier task. For this isn't something one can establish on its own, once and for all. Rather, one can only show that, *given that such and such are all of the normatively relevant factors*, it's impermissible to violate the Principal Principle. And any time one wants to take a different stance with respect to what the normatively relevant factors are, the argument needs to be revisited.[34]

---

[33] Of course, there's a sense in which proponents of Veritism will ultimately want the only epistemically relevant factor to be accuracy. But they can still maintain that there are several different kinds of dominance that are all grounded by this concern, and which should all be taken into account when evaluating whether a credence function is permissible. In any case, the main thrust of this section—that the standard scoring rule arguments that have been provided for these Bayesian norms aren't compelling if we take there to be multiple normatively relevant factors in play, and that if we want to endorse more than one of these arguments, we need to show that we can construct analogs of these arguments that take all of the epistemically relevant factors into account—is independent of the question of Veritism.

[34] Although this discussion has followed Pettigrew in focusing on dominance-style decision-theoretic principles, I take the general moral to apply regardless of what kinds of decision-theoretic principles are in play. Namely: if there are multiple normatively relevant factors to take into consideration, then a plausible account of what's permissible will be holistic. One can model this holism by appealing to a set of rules that cross-reference each other (as in the text), or by adopting a single decision-theoretic principle which takes

7.4 Purely Alethic Justification

Advocates of the All-Accuracy Approach take existing scoring rule arguments to provide compatible purely alethic justifications for many Bayesian norms, including evidential Bayesian norms. In the last section we considered whether these arguments provide compatible justifications. In this section, we'll turn to consider whether these arguments provide purely alethic justifications; i.e., justifications that don't appeal to any epistemic value other than that of having accurate beliefs.

Why think that the scoring rule arguments that have been given for these norms yield purely alethic justifications? The most explicit argument for this claim comes from Pettigrew (2013b). Pettigrew replies to Easwaran and Fitelson's (2012) worries regarding the compatibility of Joyce's Vertism and evidential norms as follows:

> Joyce's argument assumes that the only goal of a credal state is accuracy... That is, Joyce's argument assumes a version of credal virtue monism... I wish to defend the monism required for Joyce's argument... The major stumbling block for this version of credal value monism is that there seem to be evidential norms; and their force seems to stem from the evidential goals at which they demand that we aim.... we agree that the evidential norms hold, but we show that they follow from the goal of accuracy alone, not from a distinct evidential goal....
>
> My strategy is this: Recall the form of Joyce's argument for Probabilism as I presented it above. It has two components: the first is the claim that the measure of accuracy—namely, the negative Brier score—measures cognitive value; the second is a decision-theoretic norm, namely, [Strict] Dominance. From these, via a mathematical theorem, Joyce derives Probabilism. I claim that any evidential norm can be derived in the same manner. We retain the first component, namely, the identification of cognitive value with accuracy—this is the core of veritism. But we change the decision-theoretic norm. Different decision-theoretic norms give rise to different credal norms, some of which are the evidential norms we wish to recover.[35]

More concisely, Pettigrew's case for maintaining that there are scoring rule arguments that provide purely alethic justifications for the main Bayesian norms goes as follows. First, Pettigrew makes the following claim:

> *Claim.* If one can derive a norm using a purely alethic epistemic utility function (a function that takes only considerations regarding accuracy into account) and a decision-theoretic rule that employs this utility function, then one has provided a purely alethic justification for that norm.

Second, Pettigrew holds that the utility function associated with the Brier score is purely alethic. Third, Pettigrew notes that there are scoring rule arguments which show how one can derive the main Bayesian norms by plugging this utility function into various decision-theoretic dominance rules. Together, these three claims entail

---

all of these factors into account. But either way, one will need to settle on what the normatively relevant factors are before one can demonstrate whether a given option is permissible or impermissible.

[35] Pettigrew (2013b), pp. 591–2.

that there are scoring rule arguments which provide purely alethic justifications for these Bayesian norms.

But this argument is unsound. It's unsound because Claim is false. Deriving a norm using an alethic utility function and a decision rule doesn't show that we have a purely alethic justification for that norm. For while the utility function may be alethic, the decision rule need not be. And if we employ a decision rule that takes factors other than accuracy into account, then our justification of the norm won't be purely alethic.

Let's look at a couple of examples. Consider a decision rule that takes a utility function, ignores it, and then declares every option permissible. One could use the Brier-based utility function and this decision rule to derive:

Permission: Every credence function is permissible.

Given Claim, it follows that we've provided a purely alethic justification for this norm. But, of course, we've done nothing of the kind—the derivation of this norm has nothing to do with accuracy.

For another example, consider a decision rule that takes a utility function, evaluates the expected utility of each credence function (relative to the credences of the subject whose epistemic obligations we're assessing), and takes a credence function to be permissible *iff* it minimizes expected utility. One could use the Brier utility function and this decision rule to derive the negation of Probabilism. Given Claim, it follows that we have a purely alethic justification for rejecting Probabilism. Again, this is clearly incorrect—for while this decision rule and utility function combination does take accuracy into account, it's aiming away from the truth, not toward it.

Here's a third example. Let G be the proposition that God exists. And let's say that cr is G *dominated* by cr^* for the subject *iff* $cr(G) < cr^*(G)$. Now suppose someone adopted, as decision rules, both Straight Dominance and:

G Dominance: If a subject is such that (i) cr is G dominated by cr^*, and (ii) cr^* is not G dominated by any cr^{**}, then it is impermissible for her to adopt cr.[36]

Using the Brier-based utility function score and these decision rules, one can derive:

Theism: It's impermissible to adopt any credence function for which $cr(G) < 1$.[37]

---

[36] For the reasons discussed in section 7.3, the second clause of both Straight Dominance and G Dominance should be "(ii) cr^* is unimpeachable," or (if straight dominance and G dominance are the only normatively relevant factors) "(ii) cr^* is neither straight dominated nor G dominated by any cr^{**}." But since I'm bracketing these issues for the purposes of this section, I've just followed Pettigrew in formulating these principles using the Dominance (v2) schema.

[37] There are, of course, plenty of historical examples of people arguing that we're rationally committed to a norm like this. But regardless of what one thinks of the merits of those arguments, no one would take *this* argument to provide a purely alethic justification for Theism. (Among other things, one can swap G with any proposition one likes—say, the proposition that goblins exist—and get an argument of exactly the same form.)

Given Claim, it follows that we have a purely alethic justification for Theism. But this is wrong. For even though these decision rules do take accuracy into account, and are to some extent aiming toward the truth, accuracy isn't the only thing they're taking into account. Thus this derivation hasn't provided us with a purely alethic justification for Theism.

So Pettigrew's case for why these scoring rule arguments provide purely alethic justifications for evidential Bayesian norms is unconvincing. For his case hangs crucially on the truth of Claim—that being able to derive a norm from a purely alethic utility function and a decision-theoretic rule provides a purely alethic justification for that norm. But, as we've seen, Claim is false. For one can't determine whether we have a purely alethic justification just by ensuring that the utility function one employs is alethic. One also has to ensure that the decision-theoretic rule being employed is alethic, and that the combination of the utility function and the decision-theoretic rule remain alethic.

Let's take a step back from the particular details of Pettigrew's argument. One can see more generally that the scoring rule arguments that have been offered are, by themselves, of little use in addressing the initial worry regarding whether one can provide purely alethic justifications for evidential norms.

Recall the initial worry sketched in section 7.1. Purely alethic justifications can only appeal to the goal of accuracy, but evidential norms also seem to aim at the goal of having beliefs that line up with the evidence. And the goals of accuracy and lining up with the evidence can, it seems, come apart. So it's not clear how one could provide purely alethic justifications for evidential norms.

Now, the scoring rule arguments for evidential norms that have been offered all employ decision-theoretic rules in which evidence plays a key normative role. The use of these decision-theoretic rules suggests that these derivations are taking potentially non-alethic factors—evidence—into account. And we haven't been given any story for how these appeals to evidence follow from purely alethic goals. So these scoring rule arguments for evidential norms don't ultimately do anything to address the initial worry we started with. They simply shift the burden from that of showing how to provide purely alethic justifications for evidential norms to that of showing how to provide purely alethic justifications for evidence-employing decision-theoretic principles. And this burden is no easier to meet.[38]

---

[38] This is not, of course, to say that this burden can't be met. (For example, one can see some of the work done by Easwaran (2014) as an attempt to discharge part of this burden.) But by and large, little has been done to try to provide purely alethic justifications for the decision-theoretic principles that the arguments sketched in section 7.2.3 employ.

7.5 On the Possibility of Purely Alethic Justification

In section 7.4 we considered whether the scoring rule arguments that have been offered for evidential Bayesian norms yield purely alethic justifications for those norms. I argued that in order to show that these arguments provide purely alethic justifications, one would need to show that the decision-theoretic principles these arguments employ are themselves purely alethic. And this has yet to be done. But this discussion leaves open the possibility that someone could provide such a justification. Let's now turn to consider whether providing such a justification is possible. That is, let's consider the question of whether providing a purely alethic justification for evidential norms is possible.

In order to provide a purely alethic justification for a norm, the norm itself needs to be purely alethic; that is, the norm itself needs to make prescriptions which depend only on "truth-seeking" or alethically acceptable factors.[39] If changes to alethically unacceptable factors change the norm's prescriptions, then it won't be possible to provide a purely alethic justification for the norm—for the norm takes factors other than alethic factors into account. So if we want to determine whether it's possible to provide a purely alethic justification for a given norm, the first thing to do is to assess whether the norm's prescriptions take only alethically acceptable factors into consideration.

Of course, determining whether a factor is alethically acceptable can be tricky. For whether a factor is alethically acceptable depends on what kind of normative evaluation we're performing.

To see why, let's first consider a similar issue in ethics. Suppose you're a consequentialist. Then you'll hold that the correct moral norms will make prescriptions which only depend on "best-outcome-seeking" or "consequentially acceptable" factors. But what factors count as consequentially acceptable will depend on the kind of normative evaluations you're concerned with. For example, you might be concerned with:

---

[39] The claim that one can only provide purely alethic justifications for purely alethic norms is, strictly speaking, only true for what one might call "epistemic ur-norms": conjunctions of every epistemic norm, which yield all of the facts regarding what's epistemically permissible (with respect to a certain mode of evaluation). To see why, suppose one provided a purely alethic justification for some principle X. One could decompose X into two principles, $X1$ and $X2$, where $X1$ imposes all and only the normative constraints that X imposes in cases involving something purple, and $X2$ imposes all and only the normative constraints that X imposes in cases not involving something purple. Then we'd have a purely alethic justification for $X1$ (since we have a purely alethic justification for X, and X entails $X1$), even though $X1$ is not purely alethic (because it's prescriptions partially depend on non-alethic factors; e.g., whether purple things are involved).

That said, except for special cases in which the individual norms are gruesome decompositions of purely alethic norms (as in the case described above), the claim will also hold for individual norms. That is, unless it's part of a gruesome decomposition, an individual norm will be susceptible to purely alethic justification *iff* it's purely alethic. And since the kinds of individual norms discussed in the literature are not gruesome decompositions of this kind, we can generally proceed as if this claim holds for individual norms without worry.

objective evaluations: what a subject should do given what will bring about the best results,

subjective evaluations: what a subject should do given what she believes will bring about the best results, or

prospective evaluations: what a subject should do given what she should believe will bring about the best results.

Consider your beliefs about the outcomes of acts. Whether these beliefs are a consequentially acceptable factor will depend on which of these kinds of evaluations you're performing. If you're performing an objective evaluation, then your beliefs about the outcomes of acts are independent of what you should do, and (thus) such beliefs are not a consequentially acceptable factor. If, on the other hand, you're performing a subjective evaluation, then your beliefs about the outcomes of acts are essential to determining what you should do, and thus are a consequentially acceptable factor.

If you're a Veritist, then you'll hold that the correct epistemic norms will make prescriptions which only depend on "truth-seeking" or "alethically acceptable" factors. But what factors count as alethically acceptable will depend on the kind of normative evaluations you're concerned with, e.g.:

objective evaluations: what a subject should believe given what is true,

subjective evaluations: what a subject should believe given what she believes to be true, or

prospective evaluations: what a subject should believe given what she should believe to be true.

So consider what factors should play into one's verdicts if one is concerned with purely alethic justifications. If one is performing an objective evaluation, then the only factors relevant to the verdict should be the cr being evaluated, and the truth values of the propositions cr assigns values to (yielding a verdict which is relative to the world w at which we're evaluating cr). If one is performing a subjective evaluation, then the only factors relevant to the verdict should be the cr being evaluated, and the subject's credences (cr_s) in the propositions cr assigns values to (yielding a verdict which is relative to the subject for which we're evaluating cr). And if one is performing a prospective evaluation, then the only factors relevant to the verdict should be the cr being evaluated, and the credences the subject should have (cr_{sp}) in the propositions cr assigns values to (yielding a verdict which is relative to the subject for which we're evaluating cr).

What kind of evaluation are we concerned with here? At first glance, it doesn't seem like we're concerned with objective evaluations of what a subject should believe. For what a subject objectively ought to believe, it seems, is just whatever's true, and that yields a distinctly uninteresting batch of prescriptions. Likewise, at first glance, it doesn't seem like we're concerned with proscriptive evaluations of what a subject should believe. For on this approach one would be required to plug in what a subject should believe in order to figure out what a subject should believe, which threatens to be circular. This suggests that it's something like subjective evaluation that we're concerned with. Moreover, a perusal of the literature on scoring rule arguments makes it clear that it's subjective evaluation that this literature is concerned with. (For example, consider the focus on the *expected* epistemic utility of adopting a credence function, the appeal to constraints like Propriety which presuppose the relevance of maximizing expected utility, and so on.) So in what follows, let's narrow our focus to the following question: is providing a purely alethic *subjective* justification for evidential norms possible?

In order to provide a purely alethic justification for a norm, the norm must make prescriptions which depend only on alethically acceptable factors. Given a subjective mode of evaluation, the only alethically acceptable factors are the cr being evaluated and the subject's credences cr_s. So the following is a necessary condition on being able to provide a purely alethic subjective justification for a norm:

> *Supervenience:* One can't alter the verdicts of the norm without altering either the credence function cr being evaluated or the credences of the subject cr_s with respect to which the evaluation is being performed.

At first glance, none of the evidential Bayesian norms we considered in section 7.2.3 appear to satisfy this condition (though, as we'll see in a moment, this depends on the notion of evidence we employ). In all three cases, it seems, one can flip a verdict from permissible to impermissible by tweaking the subject's evidence, while leaving cr and cr_s unchanged.

Consider Conditionalization. Suppose a subject has a credence of 1/2 in A ($cr_s(A) = 1/2$), receives E as evidence, and we're evaluating whether it's permissible for her to adopt a credence function that assigns a credence of 1 to A ($cr(A) = 1$). If E = A, then according to Conditionalization adopting cr could be permissible. But if E = ⊤ (the tautology), then according to Conditionalization adopting cr would be impermissible. Thus we have a case where Conditionalization flips its verdicts, even though cr and cr_s remain unchanged.

Or consider the Principal Principle. Suppose a subject has credences cr_s, total evidence E, and we're evaluating whether a credence function that assigns a credence of 1/2 to $A(cr(A) = 1/2)$ is permissible. If E = the proposition that the chance of A is 1/2, then according to the Principal Principle holding cr could be permissible. But if E = the proposition that the chance of A is 1, then according to the Principal Principle holding cr is impermissible.

Or consider the Indifference Principle. Suppose a subject has credences cr_s, total evidence E, and the credence function cr being evaluated is such that $cr(w_1) \neq cr(w_2)$. If E = w_1, then according to the Indifference Principle holding cr could be permissible. But if E = ⊤, then according to the Indifference Principle holding cr is impermissible.

So, it seems, none of the evidential Bayesian norms we've considered satisfy Supervenience. More generally, since all we need to construct a counterexample to the condition is for the norm's verdicts to take the subject's evidence into account, it seems that no evidential norm could satisfy this condition. Thus, it seems, it's not possible to provide a purely alethic subjective justification for evidential norms.

There is, however, a way to avoid this conclusion. Howson and Urbach (1993) have suggested a picture of evidence on which a subject's evidence is just whatever the subject has a credence of 1 in. If we adopt this picture of evidence, then one can't change a subject's evidence without also changing her credences. Thus on this picture of evidence all of the counterexamples to Supervenience considered above, which involve changing the subject's evidence while leaving her credences the same, are impossible. So if we adopt something like Howson and Urbach's picture of evidence, we can maintain that evidential norms *can* satisfy Supervenience.[40]

But defending the possibility of purely alethic justifications for evidential norms this way has some big drawbacks. Many people (like me) don't like Howson and Urbach's thin picture of evidence, and would prefer to endorse a more substantive picture of evidence.[41] And this way of defending the possibility of purely alethic justifications for evidential norms is of little help to such people.

Moreover, proponents of substantive evidence will be actively hostile to the prospect of justifying versions of these evidential norms that employ Howson and Urbach's notion of evidence. This is because they'll take the Howson and Urbach versions of these norms to be false, and thus impossible to successfully justify.

---

[40] Note that to get the evidential norms to satisfy Supervenience, it's crucial that one's account of evidence be such that one has E as evidence *iff* one has a credence of 1 in E, as per Howson and Urbach's account. Merely having the entailment go one way or the other won't suffice.

To see this, first consider accounts on which having E as evidence entails having a credence of 1 in E, but not vice versa. For example, consider something like Williamson's (2000) account, on which one has evidence E *iff* one knows E. Suppose a subject comes to have a credence of 1 in E by coming to know E. Then, given this account of evidence, Conditionalization will prescribe conditionalizing on E. On the other hand, suppose a subject comes to have a credence of 1 in E but doesn't know E. Then Conditionalization won't prescribe conditionalizing on E. So given this account of evidence, subjects with the same credences can be given different prescriptions by evidential norms. So evidential norms will fail to satisfy Supervenience.

Second, consider accounts on which having having a credence of 1 in E entails that E is evidence, but not vice versa. For example, consider an account on which one has evidence E *iff* one has a credence of 1 in E or one has been told E by an authoritative source. Suppose a subject has a credence of 1/2 in E and has been told E by an authoritative source. Then, given this account of evidence, Conditionalization will prescribe conditionalizing on E. On the other hand, suppose a subject has a credence of 1/2 in E and hasn't been told E by an authoritative source. Then Conditionalization won't prescribe conditionalizing on E. So given this account of evidence, subjects with the same credences can be given different prescriptions by evidential norms. So again, evidential norms will fail to satisfy Supervenience.

[41] I take Howson and Urbach's picture of evidence to be "thin" in the sense that it provides a reductive analysis of evidence in terms of other components of the Bayesian apparatus (i.e., credence). Proponents of more substantive pictures of evidence, which can't be reduced in this way, include Lewis (1996), Williamson (2000), Neta (2008), and Dunn (2010).

Consider Conditionalization. Suppose a subject is hit on the head with a rock, and as a result of this mental trauma, comes to have a credence of 1 that unicorns exist.[42] The version of Conditionalization that employs Howson and Urbach's notion of evidence will take this to be a case of receiving evidence, and will maintain that the subject should adopt the credences they'd get by conditionalizing on the proposition that unicorns exist. Pretty much every version of Conditionalization that employs a more substantive notion of evidence, on the other hand, will not take this to be a case of receiving evidence, and will maintain that the subject's credences should remain the same. So these two different understandings of Conditionalization will yield conflicting prescriptions. And thus proponents of the substantive evidence version of Conditionalization will take the Howson and Urbach version to be false, and hence something which can't be successfully justified.

The same is true for other evidential norms, like the Principal Principle and the Indifference Principle. The Howson and Urbach versions of these norms will yield prescriptions that conflict with those of the substantive evidence versions of these principles. And thus proponents of the substantive evidence versions of these principles will take the Howson and Urbach versions of these principles to be false, and any purported justifications of them erroneous.

So proponents of substantive evidence will not just fail to be mollified by the possibility of providing a purely alethic justification for the Howson and Urbach versions of these norms. They'll be actively hostile to the idea of there being successful justifications for these norms (whether purely alethic or not), because they'll take these norms to be false.

So is it possible to provide purely alethic (subjective) justifications for evidential norms? Unless one adopts something like Howson and Urbach's picture of evidence, and the corresponding understanding of these norms, the answer is "no." And, as proponents of substantive evidence have argued, there are a number of reasons to dislike Howson and Urbach's picture of evidence.[43,44]

---

[42] For a lengthier discussion of this kind of case, and of different ways of thinking about evidence, see Dunn (2010).

[43] For an in-depth discussion of these issues, and further references, see Dunn (2010).

[44] It's natural to wonder here whether the assumption that evidence is veridical could provide one with a way to construct purely alethic justifications for evidential norms. If we were concerned with objective justification, and were assessing what a subject should believe given what's true, then the assumption that any proposition one receives as evidence is true might help. But if we're concerned with subjective justification, and assessing what a subject should believe given what she believes to be true, then it's whether the subject *believes* her evidence is true, not whether it's actually true, that will matter. Thus while this veridicality assumption might help with providing purely alethic objective justifications for evidential norms, it won't help to provide purely alethic subjective justifications for evidential norms. And it's subjective justifications that the scoring rule literature we're discussing is concerned with.

(Note that Howson and Urbach's account of evidence entails that subjects always believe their evidence is true. So insofar as the thought was to improve our odds of being able to provide purely alethic justifications for evidential norms by adopting an account of evidence on which evidence is veridical, or has whatever analog of veridicality that's relevant to the mode of evaluation we're concerned with, then Howson and Urbach's account already has the desired features in the context of subjective evaluations.)

7.6 Purely Alethic Justification and Content-Sensitive Norms

In section 7.5, we considered whether it's possible to provide purely alethic (subjective) justifications for evidential norms. I argued that it's not, unless you buy something like the contentious picture of evidence proposed by Howson and Urbach, and the corresponding contentious understanding of these evidential norms. In this section let's consider how things go if we do grant something like Howson and Urbach's picture of evidence. In particular, let's consider whether, even given this picture of evidence, it's possible to provide purely alethic justifications for evidential norms whose prescriptions concern particular kinds of propositions, like the Principal Principle.

Here is a *prima facie* reason to worry about the possibility of such justifications. One can only provide a purely alethic justification for a norm that's purely alethic—a norm that cares only about accuracy, and directs subjects to adopt the most accurate beliefs they can.[45] In the case of purely alethic subjective justification, this will be accuracy as assessed by the evaluating credence function. Every other factor about a subject's doxastic state should be irrelevant. For example, the *content* of the beliefs we're evaluating shouldn't matter, just whether they're accurate. Now, it seems like norms whose prescriptions concern particular kinds of propositions will necessarily take the content of the propositions we're evaluating into account. For example, the Principal Principle will treat some kinds of propositions—propositions about chances—differently from other propositions. But if this is right, then it seems norms whose prescriptions concern particular kinds of propositions, like the Principal Principle, can't be given purely alethic justifications.

Let's see how one might make this worry more precise. As we saw in section 7.5, one can't provide a purely alethic justification for a norm if its prescriptions depend on alethically unacceptable factors. Given a subjective mode of evaluation, this yields Supervenience as a necessary condition on being able to provide a purely alethic justification for a norm. But this isn't the only constraint that a norm must satisfy in order to be susceptible to purely alethic justification. For a norm could make prescriptions that depend only on alethically acceptable factors (and thus satisfy Supervenience) and yet use these factors to direct subjects away from the truth, or in directions orthogonal to the truth.

Some further constraints on such norms are suggested by the discussion of alethic utility functions in section 7.2.2. We saw it suggested there that alethic utility functions should satisfy constraints like Truth-Directedness and Extensionality. One natural

---

[45] In the case of purely alethic *subjective* justification, this will be accuracy assessed with respect to the evaluating credence function. Again, strictly speaking, this is only true for the epistemic "ur-norm", not individual norms; see footnote 39. But, again, given the kinds of individual norms we're concerned with, we can put this caveat aside.

thought is to try to transform these constraints on utility functions into constraints on norms. Let's see how one might do that. In particular, given the *prima facie* worry sketched above, let's see how one might transform the Extensionality constraint on utility functions into an analogous constraint on norms.[46]

Recall the form of the Extensionality constraint on utility functions:

Extensionality: Let $f_{w,w^*} : F \to F$ be a bijection between true and false propositions at w with true and false propositions at w^*; i.e. if $f_{w,w^*}(A) = B$, then either A is true at w and B is true at w^*, or A is false at w and B is false at w^*. If cr and cr^* are such that, for all A, $cr(A) = cr^*(f_{w,w^*}(A))$, then $U(cr, w) = U(cr^*, w^*)$.

This condition requires utility functions to not care about the content of propositions. It says that if you have a mapping f from propositions at w to propositions at w^* that preserves truth value, and if the values cr assigns to these propositions are the same as the values cr^* assigns to what f maps them to, then the epistemic utility of holding cr at w is the same as the epistemic utility of holding cr^* at w^*. Why? Because (the proponent of Extensionality says) all that matters to the epistemic utility of a credal state is how close or far its beliefs are from what's true. Thus permuting *which* beliefs are close or far from the truth shouldn't make a difference to the utility of holding those beliefs.

How should we formulate an analogous constraint on norms, given that we're interested in assessing credal states using a subjective mode of evaluation? To get such a constraint, we need to change a couple things. First, since we're performing a subjective evaluation, we want a constraint which employs what the evaluating subject *believes* to be true or false in place of what's actually true or false. So we'll want to replace appeals to w/w^* with appeals to evaluating credence functions cr_s/cr_s^*. And we'll want to replace appeals to the truth values of propositions at w/w^* with appeals to the credence assigned to those propositions by cr_s/cr_s^*. Second, since we want a constraint on prescriptions instead of utility assignments, we want a constraint which bears on the permissibility of credal states instead of the utility assignments to credal states. So we'll want to replace the requirement that $U(cr, w) = U(cr^*, w^*)$ with the requirement that cr have the same deontic status with respect to cr_s as cr^* has with respect to cr_s^*.

Making these substitutions gives us:

Extensional Prescriptions: Let $f_{cr_s, cr_s^*} : F \to F$ be a bijection that pairs propositions assigned a given value by cr_s with propositions assigned the same value by cr_s^*; i.e., if $f_{cr_s, cr_s^*}(A) = B$, then $cr_s(A) = cr_s^*(B)$. If cr and cr^* are such that, for all A, $cr(A) = cr^*(f_{cr_s, cr_s^*}(A))$, then cr has the same deontic status with respect to cr_s as cr^* has with respect to cr_s^*.

---

[46] To be clear, I won't be providing anything like a theorem linking the adoption of Extensionality to the adoption of an analogous constraint on norms (which I call Extensional Prescriptions). Rather, I'll be arguing that (i) Extensional Prescriptions is the analog of Extensionality in the case of norms, and (ii) the same thoughts that motivate Extensionality also motivate Extensional Prescriptions.

This condition requires *norms* to not care about the content of propositions. It says that if you have a mapping f from propositions to propositions such that the values cr_s assigns to these propositions are the same as the values cr_s^* assigns to what f maps them to, and if the values cr assigns to these propositions are the same as the values cr^* assigns to what f maps them to, then the deontic status of holding cr (assessed with respect to cr_s) is the same as the deontic status of holding cr^* (assessed with respect to cr_s^*). Why? Because (the proponent of Extensional Prescriptions says) given a subjective mode of evaluation, all that matters to the deontic status of a credal state is how close or far it is from what the evaluating credal state believes to be true. Thus permuting *which* beliefs are close or far from what the evaluating credal state believes to be true shouldn't make a difference to the deontic status of the credal state.[47]

Compatibility with Extensional Prescriptions, like compatibility with Supervenience, is a plausible necessary condition on being able to provide a purely alethic subjective justification for a norm. Thus if content-sensitive norms like the Principal Principle are incompatible with Extensional Prescriptions, then it seems that such norms can't be given purely alethic subjective justifications. And given some widely held assumptions, content-sensitive norms like the Principal Principle *will* conflict with Extensional Prescriptions. Let's see why this is so in the case of the Principal Principle, by working through an example.

Let cr_s be a probabilistic credence function such that:

$cr_s(\langle ch(F) = 1/4 \rangle) = 2/3 \quad cr_s(F) = 1/3$
$cr_s(\langle ch(F) = 1/2 \rangle) = 1/3 \quad cr_s(G) = 1/2$

Note that these assignments are compatible with the Principal Principle.[48] Let's stipulate that all of cr_s's other assignments are compatible with the Principal Principle as well. Let's further stipulate that cr_s's assignments are compatible with every other constraint on credences that one wants as long as these constraints are compatible with the Principal Principle.[49]

---

[47] In the text I grant Extensionality, and then proceed, via the most straightforward way of transforming Extensionality into a constraint on norms, to obtain Extensional Prescriptions. But I think Extensional Prescriptions is not the most plausible constraint on norms of its kind. A more plausible principle would further restrict the bijections it appeals to, in order to avoid potential worries regarding the equivalence of probability-satisfying and probability-violating credence assignments. Such a principle, call it Extensional Prescriptions*, would add the following requirement to the bijection f: it must map worlds to worlds, and map propositions corresponding to each set of worlds (e.g., $\{w_1, w_2, ...\}$) to propositions corresponding to the set of worlds those worlds are mapped to (i.e., $\{f(w_1), f(w_2), ...\}$).

Working backwards, one could appeal to Extensional Prescriptions* to argue that we should adopt "Extensionality*" (a principle like Extensionality, but with the further constraint on the bijections f) instead of Extensionality. For Extensionality* is the most straightforward transformation of Extensional Prescriptions* into a constraint on utility functions.

That said, these issues have little bearing on the topic of this section. For content-sensitive norms like the Principal Principle will be incompatible with both Extensional Prescriptions and Extensional Prescriptions*, so it won't matter which principle we adopt. For this reason, I'll put these complications aside, and proceed in the text as if Extensional Prescriptions was unproblematic.

[48] Since $cr_s(F) = \sum_{x \in [0,1]} cr_s(\langle ch(F) = x \rangle) \cdot x$, as the Principal Principle requires (see Lewis (1980)).

[49] Thus these constraints can't include the Indifference Principle described in section 7.2.3, since this principle conflicts with the Principal Principle (cf. footnote 32).

Even though cr_s satisfies all these constraints, one might still hold that cr_s is impermissible if evaluated with respect to a credence function that assigns very different values than cr_s. For such a credence function will take cr_s's assignments to be far from the truth. But these worries won't arise if we're evaluating cr_s with respect to a credence function that assigns the same values as cr_s. And we have no other reason to worry about cr_s's permissibility, since we've granted that cr_s is compatible with every other constraint one might want. Thus everyone in this debate will grant that cr_s is permissible with respect to itself.

Premise 1. cr_s is permissible with respect to cr_s.

Let cr_s^* be a credence function which flips cr_s's assignments to F and G, and assigns the same values as cr_s to every other proposition. Thus:

$cr_s^*(\langle ch(F) = 1/4\rangle) = 2/3 \quad cr_s^*(F) = 1/2$
$cr_s^*(\langle ch(F) = 1/2\rangle) = 1/3 \quad cr_s^*(G) = 1/3$

Note that these assignments are incompatible with the Principal Principle.[50] So, given the Principal Principle, it will always be impermissible to adopt cr_s^*, even when evaluated with respect to itself.

Premise 2. cr_s^* is impermissible with respect to cr_s^*.

Now consider a bijection f that maps F to G, G to F, and every other proposition to itself.[51] This bijection will be such that, for all A, $cr_s(A) = cr_s^*(f(A))$. Thus Extensional Prescriptions will require that if cr_s is permissible with respect to cr_s, then cr_s^* is permissible with respect to cr_s^*.

Premise 3. cr_s is permissible with respect to cr_s iff cr_s^* is permissible with respect to cr_s^*.

Thus given the Principal Principle and Extensional Prescriptions we get a contradiction: cr_s is permissible (with respect to itself), cr_s^* is impermissible (with respect to itself), but both must have the same deontic status (with respect to themselves). So if we adopt the Principal Principle, we must reject Extensional Prescriptions. And if we reject Extensional Prescriptions, we have to give up on the thought that we can provide purely alethic justifications for every prescription. Thus one can't both adopt the Principal Principle and hold that we can provide purely alethic justifications for every prescription.

More generally, we can see that principles which make prescriptions regarding particular kinds of propositions (like propositions about chances) will conflict with Extensional Prescriptions. For Extensional Prescriptions says that if a credal state is

---

[50] Since $1/2 = cr_s^*(F) \neq \sum_{x \in [0,1]} cr_s^*(\langle ch(F) = x\rangle) \cdot x = 1/3$.
[51] If we adopt Extensional Prescriptions* instead of Extensional Prescriptions, as I suggest in footnote 47, then we'll generally need to spell out a more extensive bijection. But this is relatively straightforward to do.

permissible, then any permutation of its credences that keeps their distance from the evaluating credence function the same should also be permissible. But, for principles which are content-sensitive, such permutations can move us from credal states that satisfy the principle to credal states that violate it. So content-sensitive principles aren't susceptible to purely alethic justification.

Let's conclude by considering a reply to this worry, suggested by some remarks by Pettigrew (2013b) and Joyce (MS). To provide a purely alethic justification for a norm, one needs to provide a justification that doesn't appeal to anything besides the goal of having accurate beliefs. But one might try to escape the worries sketched above by understanding "accuracy" in a looser way than I've been understanding it here. Pettigrew (2013b) suggests a notion of accuracy according to which a credal state is perfectly accurate when it lines up with the chances, not when it lines up with the truth. And Joyce (MS) endorses a similar move, arguing that the Principal Principle is compatible with Veritism by maintaining that "proponents of accuracy-centered approaches will see [lining up one's credences with the chances] as comprising an essential part of the duty to rationally pursue accuracy."[52] Given one of these modified notions of accuracy, one can construct an accuracy-based argument for the Principal Principle. And while these accuracy-based justifications for the Principal Principle will yield a norm that conflicts with Extensional Prescriptions, one might argue that this only goes to show that Extensional Prescriptions is too stringent a constraint, given this more relaxed understanding of accuracy.

The trouble with this move is that it's a bait and switch. Recall what we were initially concerned with: we were concerned with the notion of accuracy (and the corresponding notion of purely alethic justification) relevant to Veritism. And the notion of accuracy relevant to Veritism was closeness to the truth. Now, one can modify one's notion of accuracy so that it tracks something other than closeness to the truth. But one can't, at the same time, claim that this is the notion of accuracy relevant to Veritism.[53]

Here's another way to put the point. Call this modified notion of accuracy "accuracy*," call a justification which doesn't appeal to anything other than the goal of having accurate* beliefs "purely alethic justification*," and call the thesis that all epistemic norms can be given purely alethic justifications* "Veritism*." In response to the worries sketched above, this reply notes that one can provide purely alethic justifications* for evidential norms like the Principal Principle, and thus can reconcile evidential norms with Veritism*. But this reply doesn't address these worries, it just changes the topic. For these worries concerned whether one could reconcile evidential norms with Veritism, not whether one could reconcile evidential norms with Veritism*.

---

[52] See Joyce (MS), p. 16.
[53] To press the point further, recall that the intuitive motivation for Veritism was precisely that one shouldn't take any factors other than closeness to the truth into account. Yet these modified notions of accuracy do just that.

Another worry for this move is that it seems one could make the same kind of maneuver to reconcile Veritism with virtually any norm. In the maneuver suggested by Pettigrew and Joyce, one modifies the notion of accuracy so that it assesses closeness to the chances instead of closeness to the truth, in order to provide a purely alethic justification for the Principal Principle. But one could equally well modify the notion of accuracy so that it assesses closeness to Donald Trump's credal state instead of closeness to the truth, in order to provide a purely alethic justification for Trumpism, the claim that one should line up one's beliefs with Trump's.[54] Or one could modify the notion of accuracy so that it assesses closeness to one's current credal state instead of closeness to the truth, in order to provide a purely alethic justification for Calcification, the claim that one should never change one's beliefs.[55]

Now, perhaps the thought is that this chance-tracking notion of accuracy is tenable, while these other modified notions of accuracy are not, because the chances (unlike Trump's credal state) are closely tied to the truth. First, if this is the thought, then it's something that needs to be demonstrated, not assumed. And demonstrating how the chances are tied to the truth in the right way is precisely what we needed to do, in order to provide a purely alethic justification for the Principal Principle, when we employed our *original* notion of accuracy. So, at best, this version of the maneuver just brings us back to where we started.

Second, if the literature on these issues is any guide, then providing a non-question-begging argument for why lining up one's beliefs with the chances is a good way to get true beliefs is a project with poor prospects. (For example, see Strevens (1999) for an extended criticism of such arguments.) And even if we put that literature aside, we've just seen a positive reason for doubting that providing a rationale for the Principal Principle along these lines is possible. For if it were possible, then one should be able to provide a purely alethic justification for the Principal Principle in a way that's compatible with constraints like Extensional Prescriptions. And as we've seen, this can't be done.

In section 7.5 we saw that it's not possible to provide a purely alethic justification for evidential norms unless one adopts something like Howson and Urbach's versions of these norms. In this section we saw that even if we do adopt the Howson and Urbach's versions of these norms, then, if we understand "purely alethic justification" in the way that's relevant to the issues at hand, there will be evidential norms for which it's not possible to provide purely alethic justifications. For norms which are susceptible to purely alethic justification should be compatible with constraints like Extensional Prescriptions. And evidential norms which are content-sensitive, like the Principal Principle, are not.

---

[54] Or should line up with what one believes Trump's beliefs to be (if we want to precisely mirror the form of the Principal Principle).

[55] Or should line up with what one believes one's beliefs to be (if we want to precisely mirror the form of the Principal Principle). The name "Calcification" comes from Christensen (1991).

7.7 Conclusion

For most of this chapter I've been taking Joyce and Pettigrew to be advocating the All-Accuracy Account. But some passages, such as this passage from Joyce, suggest a much weaker claim:

> Proponents of accuracy-centered epistemology will want to ... [maintain] that all facts about justification are interpreted as facts about the rational pursuit of doxastic accuracy. This would make it a truism (on the level of "evidence for X is evidence for X's truth") that believers are justified in holding credences exactly to the extent that their evidence makes it reasonable for them to expect those credences to be accurate (in the aggregate).[56]

This passage suggests that, perhaps, Joyce is only claiming this: for any norm, one can construct an argument for that norm that has the form of a scoring rule argument. This is a claim that I think virtually everyone would agree with. After all, similar claims have been made in a number of places (e.g., see Stalnaker (2002)), and have been allowed to pass without challenge. And this claim seems clearly true: given any choice of utility functions, and any choice of decision rules, one *can* construct an argument for any set of prescriptions one wants. Indeed, we don't even need this much—merely granting one free choice of decision rules is enough.[57]

If this is the claim that Joyce has in mind, then none of the arguments offered in this chapter are a threat to it. But this claim is uninteresting. For it doesn't bear on any substantive issues regarding justification, epistemic rationality, or epistemic norms.

In any case, questions regarding views like the All-Accuracy Account are interesting, regardless of who adopts them. This chapter has offered a critical look at such views. In light of this, one might conclude that views like the All-Accuracy Account are irreparably flawed, and should be rejected. Or one might just conclude that there are a number of issues that proponents of views like the All-Accuracy Account need to address. Either way, the tension between Veritism and evidential norms has yet to be resolved.[58]

References

Christensen, D. (1991). Clever Bookies and Coherent Beliefs. *Philosophical Review*, 100(2), 229–47.

Dunn, J. (2010). *Bayesian Epistemology and Having Evidence*. Ph.D. thesis, University of Massachusetts, Amherst, NY.

---

[56] Joyce (MS), p. 18.

[57] To see this, note that given any utility function, one can construct a decision rule which effectively ignores that utility function and yields the prescriptions one would get by applying decision rule X to utility function Y (for any X and Y). (How can the rule figure out these prescriptions if they rely on the assignments of utility function Y, and the rule has some other utility function $Z \neq Y$ as an argument? Well, note that a free choice of decision rules entails a free choice of what the arguments of the decision rule are. So one can construct a decision rule whose arguments include whatever one needs to deduce what Y's assignments would be.)

[58] I'd like to thank Jeff Dunn, Kenny Easwaran, Maya Eddon, and Richard Pettigrew for helpful comments and discussion.

Easwaran, K. (2013). Expected Accuracy Supports Conditionalization—and Conglomerability and Reflection. *Philosophy of Science*, 80(1), 119–42.

Easwaran, K. (2014). Decision Theory Without Representation Theorems. *Philosophers' Imprint*, 14(27).

Easwaran, K., and Fitelson, B. (2012). An 'Evidentialist' Worry about Joyce's Argument for Probabilism. *Dialetica*, 66(3), 425–33.

Goldman, A. (2002). The Unity of the Epistemic Virtues. In *Pathways to Knowledge* (pp. 51–72). New York: Oxford University Press.

Greaves, H., and Wallace, D. (2006). Justifying Conditionalization: Conditionalization Maximizes Expected Epistemic Utility. *Mind*, 115(459), 607–32.

Hedden, B. (2015). *Reasons without Persons: Rationality, Identity, and Time*. Oxford: Oxford University Press.

Howson, C., and Urbach, P. (1993). *Scientific Reasoning: The Bayesian Approach*. Chicago, IL: Open Court.

Joyce, J. M. (1998). A Nonpragmatic Vindication of Probabilism. *Philosophy of Science*, 65(4), 575–603.

Joyce, J. M. (2009). Accuracy and Coherence: Prospects for an Alethic Epistemology of Partial Belief. In Franz Huber and Christoph Schmidt-Petri (eds) *Degrees of Belief*, vol. 342 (pp. 263–297). Synthese. Dordrecht: Springer.

Joyce, J. M. (MS). Why Evidentialists Need Not Worry about the Accuracy Argument for Probabilism. http://www-personal.umich.edu/~jjoyce/papers/APA201.pdf.

Leitgeb, H., and Pettigrew, R. (2010b). An Objective Justification of Bayesianism II: The Consequences of Minimizing Inaccuracy. *Philosophy of Science*, 77(2), 236–72.

Leitgeb, H., and Pettigrew, R. (2010a). An Objective Justification of Bayesianism I: Measuring Inaccuracy. *Philosophy of Science*, 77(2), 201–35.

Levinstein, B. A. (2012). Leitgeb and Pettigrew on Accuracy and Updating. *Philosophy of Science*, 79(3), 413–24.

Lewis, D. (1980). A Subjectivist's Guide to Objective Chance. In R. C. Jeffrey (ed.) *Studies in Inductive Logic and Probability*, vol. 2 (pp. 83–132). Berkeley, CA: University of California Press.

Lewis, D. (1996). Elusive Knowledge. *Australasian Journal of Philosophy*, 74(4), 549–67.

Meacham, C. J. G. (2010). Unravelling the Tangled Web: Continuity, Internalism, Non-uniqueness and Self-locating Beliefs. In T. S. Gendler and J. Hawthorne (eds) *Oxford Studies in Epistemology*, Vol. 3, (pp. 86–125). Oxford: Oxford University Press.

Meacham, C. J. G. (2016). Understanding Conditionalization. *Canadian Journal of Philosophy*, 45(5–6), 767–97.

Moss, S. (forthcoming). Time-slice Epistemology and Action under Indeterminacy. In J. Hawthorne, and T. S. Gendler (eds.) *Oxford Studies in Epistemology*, Vol. 5.

Neta, R. (2008). What Evidence Do You Have? *British Journal for the Philosophy of Science*, 59(1), 89–119.

Nozick, R. (1974). *Anarchy, State, and Utopia*. New York: Basic Books.

Pettigrew, R. (2012). Accuracy, Chance, and the Principal Principle. *Philosophical Review*, 121(2), 241–75.

Pettigrew, R. (2013a). A New Epistemic Utility Argument for the Principal Principle. *Episteme*, 10(1), 19–35.

Pettigrew, R. (2013b). Accuracy and Evidence. *Dialectica*, 67(4), 579–96.
Pettigrew, R. (2013c). Epistemic Utility and Norms for Credences. *Philosophy Compass*, 8(10), 897–908.
Pettigrew, R. (2014). Accuracy, Risk, and the Principle of Indifference. *Philosophy and Phenomenological Research*, 91(1), 35–59.
Schoenfield, M. (Forthcoming). Conditionalization Does Not (in General) Maximize Expected Accuracy. *Mind*.
Stalnaker, R. (2002). Epistemic Consequentialism: Robert Stalnaker. *Aristotelian Society Supplementary Volume*, 76(1), 153–68.
Strevens, M. (1999). Objective Probability as a Guide to the World. *Philosophical Studies*, 95(3), 243–75.
van Fraassen, B. C. (1995). Belief and the Problem of Ulysses and the Sirens. *Philosophical Studies*, 77(1), 7–37.
Williamson, T. (2000). *Knowledge and its Limits*. Oxford: Oxford University Press.

8
A Problem for Credal Consequentialism

Michael Caie

Beliefs, we'll assume, come in degrees. As a short-hand, we'll refer to these graded doxastic attitudes as **credences**, and to the totality of an agent's credences as their **credal state**.

Plausibly, there are certain epistemically good-making features that an agent's credal state may have. Credences, for example, may be closer or further from the truth, and it is at least prima facie plausible that the closer an agent's credences are, on average, to the truth the better such credences are epistemically.[1]

Given an appropriately well-defined notion of the epistemic good for credal states, it is tempting to think that the facts concerning which credal states are rationally permissible or obligatory for an agent may be grounded in facts about the extent to which such credal states appear, by the lights of the agent, to be conducive to the attainment of the epistemic good.[2] Call this sort of view **credal consequentialism**. For example, it is tempting to think that an agent ought rationally to adopt those credences that, by her lights, would be most conducive to the attainment of the epistemic good. Credal rationality, on this picture, consists in maximizing the expected epistemic utility of one's credal state.

Like consequentialist accounts in ethics, credal consequentialism has the virtue of being simple and principled. However, like consequentialist accounts in ethics, credal consequentialism has some surprising consequences that are at odds with our pre-theoretic judgments. First, given plausible accounts of the epistemic good for credal states, this account councils the acceptance of so-called epistemic bribes; in certain

---

[1] See Joyce (1998) and Joyce (2009) for an assessment of different ways of developing the idea that the principal good-making feature for credal states consists in their closeness to the truth. For alternative proposals according to which the principal good-making feature of credal states consists in their closeness to chances see Hájek (n.d.), Pettigrew (2012), and Caie (2015).

[2] See, however, Konek and Levinstein (forthcoming) for an account that attempts to ground facts about credal rationality in facts about the epistemic good for credal states in a distinctively non-consequentialist manner.

cases, by adopting apparently irrational credences in particular propositions an agent may ensure that their other credences have certain epistemic good-making features, and so, in certain cases, an agent may maximize their *overall* epistemic utility by adopting credences in particular propositions that seem irrational.[3] Second, given plausible accounts of the epistemic good for credal states, this account entails that in certain cases an agent may be rationally required to have probabilistically incoherent credences.[4] And, finally, given plausible accounts of the epistemic good for credal states, this account entails that in certain cases a rational agent should update their credences in a manner that violates conditionalization and its natural generalizations.[5]

Some may take these consequences to provide decisive refutation of credal consequentialism. I'm less certain. In the ethical case, it seems to me that, given the simplicity and principled character of consequentialist theories, the fact that such theories appear to provide the right judgments in a large range of central cases makes it a delicate question—one without any obvious answer—whether those cases in which consequentialist theories are at odds with our pre-theoretic judgments should be seen as counterexamples or as surprising discoveries. Similarly, I think that *if* credal consequentialism is able to provide us with an account that delivers apparently reasonable judgments in a sufficiently large number of central cases, then it becomes a delicate question whether epistemic rationality may in fact sanction epistemic bribes, or demand probabilistic incoherence or violations of updating by conditionalization.

In what follows, though, I'll argue that credal consequentialism is at odds with our pre-theoretic judgments in a much wider class of cases than has so far been acknowledged. In particular, I'll show that there are a great number of cases in which, intuitively, there may be a non-trivial distinction between credences that are rationally permissible and those that are impermissible, but that in such cases credal consequentialism either entails that every possible credal state is rationally permissible, or that every possible credal state is rationally impermissible, or that credal states, in such cases, cannot be assessed as rationally permissible or impermissible. The picture of credal rationality that emerges from credal consequentialism, then, is one that would seem to bear little resemblance to our pre-theoretic picture.

8.1 Causal Decision Theory

The guiding thought behind credal consequentialism is that epistemic rationality requires that an agent adopt those credences that, by her lights, would be most conducive to the attainment of the epistemic good. This intuitive idea can be sharpened up with the tools of causal decision theory.

In this section, I'll outline some of the basic elements of causal decision theory. In §8.1.1, I'll provide a characterization of causal expectation values. In §8.1.2, I'll show

---

[3] For arguments to this effect see, for example, Jenkins (2007), Greaves (2013), and Berker (2013).
[4] For cases of this sort see Caie (2013). [5] For cases of this sort see Carr (n.d.).

how such expectation values may be used to yield deontic verdicts concerning the possible options available to an agent. In particular, I'll argue that any adequate version of causal decision theory will entail, given certain cases in which an agent lacks well-defined expectation values for the utility of certain options available to them, that every option available to them is rationally permissible, or that every option available to them is rationally impermissible, or that every option available to them is not apt for rational assessment.

In §8.2, I'll show how the machinery of causal decision theory, outlined in this section, may be used to provide a precise characterization of credal consequentialism. I'll then show that in a large class of cases agents will lack well-defined expectation values for the credal options available to them in such a manner that, given credal consequentialism, it follows that every credal option available to them is rationally permissible, or that every credal option available to them is rationally impermissible, or that every credal option available to them is not apt for rational assessment.

There are a number of different ways of developing the core ideas behind causal decision theory. In what follows, I'll focus on a version of causal decision theory inspired by, though in certain details distinct from, versions presented in Gibbard and Harper (1978) and Lewis (1981). While some of the details of the arguments that follow will depend on this particular choice, all the main points that I'll make could be made equally, mutatis mutandis, given alternative formulations.

8.1.1 Causal expectation values

Let W be the set of epistemically possible worlds, i.e., ways that the world might be that cannot be ruled out a priori. We say that a set $P \subseteq W$ is a **proposition**. We say that a set of propositions **A** is a σ-**algebra** just in case **A** is closed under complementation and finite and countable unions.[6] And we say that a σ-algebra **A** is **atomic** just in case **A** is such that there exists some **At** $\subset$ **A** such that (i) each $P \in$ **At** is non-empty, (ii) **At** partitions W, and (iii) for each $P \in$ **At**, there is no non-empty set $Q \in$ **A** such that $Q \subset P$.[7] We'll say that the members of **At** are the **atoms** of **A**.

Let $\mathbf{A}_i^t$ be an atomic σ-algebra of propositions and let $Cr_i^t(\cdot) : \mathbf{A}_i^t \to \mathbb{R}$ be a function mapping members of $\mathbf{A}_i^t$ to real numbers. We take $Cr_i^t(\cdot)$ to represent an agent i's credences at some time t. The members of $\mathbf{A}_i^t$ are those propositions that i is able to entertain at t, and $Cr_i^t(\cdot)$ represents how likely i at t thinks it is that each such proposition is true.[8] We let $\mathbf{At}_i^t \subset \mathbf{A}_i^t$ be the set of atoms of $\mathbf{A}_i^t$.

---

[6] That is: if $P \in \mathbf{A}$, then $W - P \in \mathbf{A}$, and if I is a finite or countable set of integers and $P_i \in \mathbf{A}$, for each $i \in I$, then $\cup \{P_i : i \in I\} \in \mathbf{A}$.

[7] We say that a set of propositions **P partitions** W just in case $\cup \mathbf{P} = W$ and, for each $P, Q \in \mathbf{P}, P \cap Q = \emptyset$.

[8] Note that all of the main points that follow could be made equally well if, instead of taking the objects of credence to be propositions, we took them to be **centered-propositions**, i.e., sets of world, time, individual triples. Such objects are appropriate, given agents who have essentially self-locating credences. See, for example, Lewis (1979b). For simplicity, however, we'll ignore this possible complication.

Let $u_i^t(\cdot) : W \to \mathbb{R}$ be a function mapping members of W to real numbers. We take $u_i^t(\cdot)$ to represent i's values at t. We have, then, that $u_i^t(w) \geq u_i^t(w')$ just in case, given i's values at t, w is at least as desirable as w'.[9]

Let $\mathbf{O}_i^{t'}$ be a set of propositions that partitions W. We assume that, for each $O \in \mathbf{O}_i^{t'}$, it is within i's power at t' to realize O and that, for each $O \in \mathbf{O}_i^{t'}$, there is no $O' \subset O$ such that it is within i's power at t' to realize O'. The members of $\mathbf{O}_i^{t'}$, then, constitute the strongest propositions that i is able to make true at t'. We'll refer to this set as i's **options** at t'.

Let P be a set such that, for some $x \in \mathbb{R}$, $P = \{w \in W : u_i^t(w) = x\}$. We'll call such a set a **t-value proposition**, and we'll denote such a proposition by $[V_i^t = x]$, and the class of such propositions by $\mathbf{V}_i^t$.

Let $P \,\square\!\!\rightarrow\, Q$ be the non-backtracking counterfactual proposition that says that were P the case, Q would be the case.[10] Given some $O \in \mathbf{O}_i^{t'}$ and some $[V_i^t = x] \in \mathbf{V}_i^t$, $O \,\square\!\!\rightarrow\, [V_i^t = x]$, then, is the set of worlds w such that, at w, were i to realize O at t', then the result would be a situation of utility x, given i's values at t.

Consider, then, a set that contains, for each $O \in \mathbf{O} \subseteq \mathbf{O}_i^{t'}$, a unique proposition of the form $O \,\square\!\!\rightarrow\, [V_i^t = x]$, and no other propositions. We'll say that a non-empty intersection of such a set is a **t-value dependence hypothesis for O**. A t-value dependence hypothesis for $\mathbf{O}$, then, tells us, for each $O \in \mathbf{O}$, how matters that i values at t depend counterfactually on i realizing O at t'. We'll denote the set of t-value dependence hypotheses for $\mathbf{O} \subseteq \mathbf{O}_i^{t'}$, $\mathbf{D}(\mathbf{O}, u_i^t)$. We'll assume that, in general, this set partitions W.[11]

For each $O \in \mathbf{O}_i^{t'}$ and each $D \in \mathbf{D}(\mathbf{O}_i^{t'}, u_i^t)$, there will be a unique $x \in \mathbb{R}$ such that $(O \,\square\!\!\rightarrow\, [V_i^t = x]) \cap D \neq \emptyset$. We let $U(O \cap D)$ be this unique x.

---

[9] Note that, if we like, we can take $u_i^t(\cdot) : W \to \mathbb{R}$ to be derivative from a function $v_i^t(\cdot) : \mathbf{At}_i^t \to \mathbb{R}$. In particular, given such a $v_i^t(\cdot)$ we can say that, for each $P \in \mathbf{At}_i^t$ and each $w \in P$, $u_i^t(w) = v_i^t(P)$. Thus, even if an agent's conceptual resources don't allow her to distinguish w from other worlds in P we can still talk about the value of the world for that agent. Note, though, that we cannot do the same for $Cr_i^t(\cdot)$ if we want to allow that such functions may be measures and so additive.

[10] Roughly speaking, a non-backtracking counterfactual $P \,\square\!\!\rightarrow\, Q$ is one that evaluates whether Q would have been true, had P been true, holding fixed as much of the past as is compatible with the truth of P. See Lewis (1973) and Lewis (1979a) for the distinction between backtracking and non-backtracking counterfactuals.

[11] This, it should be stressed, is a controversial assumption. Given plausible principles governing $\,\square\!\!\rightarrow\,$ this will follow if we assume, in addition, the principle of Conditional Excluded Middle (CEM): $(\phi \,\square\!\!\rightarrow\, \psi) \vee (\phi \,\square\!\!\rightarrow\, \neg\psi)$. However, (CEM) is a notoriously controversial principle. David Lewis famously rejected it, while Robert Stalnaker endorsed it. (See Lewis (1973), Stalnaker (1981b), and Stalnaker (1981a) for some of the early controversy.) And those cases that have led some to reject (CEM) have also led people to reject the claim that, in general, the t-value dependence hypotheses for $\mathbf{O} \subseteq \mathbf{O}_i^{t'}$ form a partition of W. (For arguments to this effect see Joyce (1999).) For what it's worth, I'm inclined to accept (CEM). (For some recent defenses of this principle see Williams (2010) and Goodman (n.d.).) If, however, one rejects (CEM), and so too the assumption that the t-value dependence hypotheses for $\mathbf{O} \subseteq \mathbf{O}_i^{t'}$ form a partition of W, then one will want to endorse an alternative formulation of causal decision theory. (See, for example, Joyce (1999).) However, let me note again that the main points that follow won't essentially depend upon this particular formulation of causal decision theory, and so won't depend essentially on the controversial assumption that t-value dependence hypotheses for $\mathbf{O} \subseteq \mathbf{O}_i^{t'}$ form a partition of W.

We want to provide a characterization of the extent to which i at t expects that good results would be brought about were they to realize O at t'. A standard way of doing this assumes that $\mathbf{D}(\mathbf{O}_i^{t'}, u_i^t) \subseteq \mathbf{A}_i^t$ and then takes an agent i's expectation value at t of the causal utility of realizing an option O at t' to be given by:[12]

ECU (Preliminary 1): $ECU_i^t(O) = \sum_{D \in \mathbf{D}(\mathbf{O}_i^{t'}, u_i^t)} Cr_i^t(D) U(O \cap D).$

This characterization of expected causal utility is perfectly fine, *given* the assumption that $\mathbf{D}(\mathbf{O}_i^{t'}, u_i^t) \subseteq \mathbf{A}_i^t$. However, even if an agent isn't able to entertain each proposition in $\mathbf{D}(\mathbf{O}_i^{t'}, u_i^t)$, they may still have a well-defined causal expectation value for some $O \in \mathbf{O}_i^{t'}$. For while an agent may not be able to consider, for each $O \in \mathbf{O}_i^{t'}$, each of the different ways in which outcomes may depend upon the realization of that option, it may nonetheless be that the agent is able to consider such dependencies for some $O \in \mathbf{O}_i^{t'}$.

To see this, consider some arbitrary $O \in \mathbf{O}_i^{t'}$. Given such an O, we can coarse-grain $\mathbf{D}(\mathbf{O}_i^{t'}, u_i^t)$ by taking unions of the members of $\mathbf{D}(\mathbf{O}_i^{t'}, u_i^t)$ that agree about what utility would result were O to be realized. If an agent has credences defined over an algebra containing such a coarse-graining of $\mathbf{D}(\mathbf{O}_i^{t'}, u_i^t)$, then the agent should be taken to have a well-defined expectation for the causal utility of O, even if the agent does not have a well-defined expectation value for the causal utility of each member of $\mathbf{O}_i^{t'}$.

More generally, it may be that, while it's not the case that $\mathbf{D}(\mathbf{O}_i^{t'}, u_i^t) \subseteq \mathbf{A}_i^t$, there is some $\mathbf{O} \subset \mathbf{O}_i^{t'}$, such that $\mathbf{D}(\mathbf{O}, u_i^t) \subseteq \mathbf{A}_i^t$.[13] In this case, the agent should be taken to have a well-defined expectation value for the causal utility for each $O \in \mathbf{O}$. ECU (Preliminary 1), though, is silent about such cases. We need, then, a more general characterization of causal utility expectation values.

To this end, we can extend our characterization of $U(\cdot)$. In particular, let us say, for each $O \in \mathbf{O}_i^{t'}$ and each $P \subseteq \mathbf{A}_i^t$, that $U(O \cap P) = x$ if $(O \boxright [V_i^t = x]) \cap P = P$, and otherwise $U(O \cap P)$ is undefined. $U(O \cap P)$, then, is well defined just in case each world in P agrees about what utility would result were O to be realized. And, if $U(O \cap P)$ is well defined, then this value is exactly the utility value that each member of P agrees would result were O to be realized.

---

[12] If the set of dependence hypotheses, $\mathbf{D}(\mathbf{O}_i^{t'}, u_i^t)$, is uncountable, then we have instead:

$$ECU_i^t(O) = \int_{D \in \mathbf{D}(\mathbf{O}_i^{t'}, u_i^t)} U(O \cap D) dCr_i^t(D).$$

Further qualifications of this sort will be required at various points throughout. To avoid tedium, though, from now on I will, for the most part, leave such qualifications implicit.

[13] In typical cases, if $\mathbf{O} \subset \mathbf{O}_i^{t'}$, then $\mathbf{D}(\mathbf{O}, u_i^t)$ will be a coarse-graining of $\mathbf{D}(\mathbf{O}_i^{t'}, u_i^t)$. And so, an agent may have credences defined over an algebra that contains the former though not the latter.

Given this characterization of $U(\cdot)$, we can define the following quantity:

Def. $G_i^t(O) =_{df} \sum_{A \in At_i^t} Cr_i^t(A)U(O \cap A).$

A natural way to try to address the limitation of our preceding characterization of expected causal utility is to take the expected causal utility of an option O for an agent i at t to be given by $G_i^t(O)$. Thus:

ECU (Preliminary 2): $ECU_i^t(O) = G_i^t(O).$

Unlike **ECU (Preliminary 1)**, this allows that an agent may have well-defined causal utility expectation values for some, though perhaps not all, $O \in \mathbf{O}_i^{t'}$. This may, for example, be true if, for some $\mathbf{O} \subset \mathbf{O}_i^{t'}$, $\mathbf{At}_i^t = \mathbf{D}(\mathbf{O}, u_i^t)$. It may also be true if, for some $\mathbf{O} \subset \mathbf{O}_i^{t'}$, $\mathbf{At}_i^t$ is a fine-graining of $\mathbf{D}(\mathbf{O}, u_i^t)$ which is not equal to $\mathbf{D}(\mathbf{O}_i^{t'}, u_i^t)$.

This characterization, though, is also too restrictive. For, given **ECU (Preliminary 2)**, $ECU_i^t(O)$ will be undefined as long as there is some $A \in \mathbf{At}_i^t$ and some $x \neq y$, such that, for some $w \in A$, $O \square\!\!\rightarrow [V_i^t = x]$ obtains at w, and, for some $w' \in A$, $O \square\!\!\rightarrow [V_i^t = y]$ obtains at w'. For, given such an $A \in \mathbf{At}_i^t$, $U(O \cap A)$ will be undefined. It seems to me, though, that even if there are some $A \in \mathbf{At}_i^t$ that are not homogeneous with respect to which utility would result were O to be realized, if the agent's credal state rules out each such atom, then the agent should be taken to have a well-defined expectation value for the causal utility of O.

For example, suppose that an agent is certain that were O to be realized, then a certain utility x would result. In this case, it is clear that the agent has a well-defined expectation value for the casual utility of O, viz., x. But it's compatible with an agent being certain that were O to be realized, then a certain utility x would result, that there be certain ways in which utility may depend upon the realization of O that the agent is not able to consider, and so some $A \in \mathbf{At}_t^{t'}$ that are not homogeneous about which utility would result were O to be realized.

In light of this, we will take the expected causal utility, for i at t, of an option $O \in \mathbf{O}_i^{t'}$ to be characterized as follows. Let $\mathbf{Z}_{Cr_i^t} = \{A \in \mathbf{At}_i^t : Cr_i^t(A) \neq 0\}$.[14] Then we say:

ECU: $ECU_i^t(O) = \sum_{A \in \mathbf{Z}_{Cr_i^t}} Cr_i^t(A)U(O \cap A).$

It is worth pausing to comment on how we should think about those cases in which $ECU_i^t(O)$ is well defined but $G_i^t(O)$ is not.

Let us say that an agent with credences $Cr_i^t(\cdot)$ is **quasi-opinionated** about $\mathbf{D}(\{O\}, u_i^t)$ just in case there is some $\mathbf{D} \subset \mathbf{D}(\{O\}, u_i^t)$ such that $\cup \mathbf{Z}_{Cr_i^t} \subseteq \cup \mathbf{D}$. If an agent is quasi-opinionated about $\mathbf{D}(\{O\}, u_i^t)$ then they are certain that the utility value

---

[14] Note that if $\mathbf{At}_i^t$ is uncountable, then in the above characterization we should take $Cr_i^t(\cdot)$ to be a density function.

that would obtain were O to be realized is amongst some proper subset of the set of a priori epistemically possible utility values that could be realized were O to obtain.

Now, if $G_i^t(O)$ is not well-defined but $ECU_i^t(O)$ is, then $Cr_i^t(\cdot)$ must be quasi-opinionated about $\mathbf{D}(\{O\}, u_i^t)$. In such cases, the agent's conceptual resources do not allow them to entertain all of the different ways in which O might result in outcomes of differing utility. However, despite not being able to entertain all such dependencies, the agent is able to entertain *some* such dependencies, and, moreover, the agent lumps all of their credence on some subclass of $\mathbf{At}_t^{t'}$ that serve to characterize such dependencies. By being opinionated and ruling out certain dependence hypotheses for O, an agent may have a well-defined expectation value for O, even if the agent cannot entertain all of the ways in which utility may result were O to be realized.

A consequence of this is that if i is not quasi-opinionated about $\mathbf{D}(\{O\}, u_i^t)$, and there are some dependence hypotheses for O that i cannot entertain, then i cannot have a well-defined expectation value for the causal utility of O. This fact will play an important role in what follows.

8.1.2 From expectations to deontic verdicts

According to causal decision theory, if there are options that maximize an agent's expected causal utility, then the agent ought to realize one of those options. As it stands, though, this claim is ambiguous. For the expected causal utility of an option depends on an agent's utilities and credences. But an agent's utilities and credences are time-relative. We need, then, a more precise characterization of how the deontic statuses of an agent's options at some time t' may be determined by the causal expectation values of those options.

To help avoid inessential and potentially distracting complications, in what follows, we'll impose a simplifying restriction on the class of decision problems with which we'll be concerned. We'll assume that, in a given decision problem, an agent has stable credences and utilities throughout some temporal interval leading up to t'. Thus, we assume that, in a given decision problem, there is some $t'' < t'$, such that, for each $t_1, t_2 \in (t'', t')$, $Cr_i^{t_1}(\cdot) = Cr_i^{t_2}(\cdot)$ and $u_i^{t_1}(\cdot) = u_i^{t_2}(\cdot)$. For present purposes, this assumption involves no important loss of generality.

Given this, let us define the following, perhaps partial, function from $\mathbf{O}_i^{t'}$ to $\mathbb{R}$:

Def. $ECU_i(O) = x$ just in case, for all $t \in (t'', t')$, $ECU_i^t(O) = x$.

Note that, given our simplifying assumption, $ECU_i(O)$ will be well defined as long as $ECU_i^t(O)$ is well defined for some $t \in (t'', t')$.

We can now provide the following precisification of the guiding idea behind causal decision theory:

Maximization: Let M be the set of $O \in \mathbf{O}_i^{t'}$ such that, for each $O' \in \mathbf{O}_i^{t'}$, $ECU_i(O) \geq ECU_i(O')$. If M is non-empty, then, for each $O \in M$, it is rationally permissible for i to realize O, and it is rationally required for i to realize some $O \in M$.[15]

Maximization tells us (for an agent with stable credences and utilities leading up to t') which options are rationally permissible and which rationally impermissible at t', given that there is a non-empty set of options M that maximize expected causal utility. This, however, leaves open the deontic status of such an agent's t'-options in those cases in which the set of options that maximize expected causal utility *is* empty. There are two important classes of such cases.

One way in which this type of case may arise is as follows. Given a credal state $Cr_i^t(\cdot)$ and utility function $u_i^t(\cdot)$, it may be that, for each option O, there is some option O',

---

[15] The natural generalization of **Maximization** is:

Diachronic Maximization: Let M be the set of $O \in \mathbf{O}_i^{t'}$ such that, for some $t'' < t'$, $ECU_i^t(O) \geq ECU_i^t(O')$, for every $O' \in \mathbf{O}_i^{t'}$ and every $t \in (t'', t')$. If M is non-empty, then, for each $O \in M$, it is rationally permissible for i to realize O, and it is rationally required for i to realize some $O \in M$.

An alternative way of precisifying the core idea behind causal decision theory is:

Synchronic Maximization: Let M be the set of $O \in \mathbf{O}_i^{t'}$ such that, for each $O' \in \mathbf{O}_i^{t'}$, $ECU_i^{t'}(O) \geq ECU_i^{t'}(O')$. If M is non-empty, then, for each $O \in M$, it is rationally permissible for i to realize O, and it is rationally required for i to realize some $O \in M$.

I'm inclined to think that **Diachronic Maximization**, and its special case **Maximization**, provide a better account than **Synchronic Maximization** of how the deontic status of an agent's options at t' may be determined by the agent's expectations of causal utility. In support of this, let me note two worries for **Synchronic Maximization**. First, it is natural to think that the credences and utilities of an agent that determine the expectation values that rationalize certain options for the agent should, at least sometimes, also be the things that cause the agent to realize some option that is so rationalized. However, it is hard to see how this could be so if the expectation values that rationalize an agent's options are determined by the credences and utilities that they have at the time that the option is realized.

Second, there is good reason to think that **Synchronic Maximization** is incompatible with a plausible ought-implies-can principle. For there are cases in which, given a set of options, each option O is such that if the agent learns that she has realized O, then, given this information, expected causal utility will be maximized by some option other than O. (For a case with this structure see Death in Damascus in Gibbard and Harper (1978).) But consider, then, an agent who is perfectly introspective about their own choices, so that it's guaranteed that at t they are aware of their choice at t. Such an agent will be guaranteed to realize an option at t that fails to maximize expected utility given their utilities and credences at t. Given **Synchronic Maximization**, then, such an agent will be guaranteed to be in violation of certain practical requirements of rationality. One might naturally think, though, that practical rationality should not preclude an agent from making a rational choice simply given that the agent manifests certain epistemic virtues, such as being aware of their own choices.

It's worth noting, though, that all of the main points that I'll make have natural analogues given the natural alternative version of causal decision theory that endorses **Synchronic Maximization**.

It's also worth noting that neither **Synchronic Maximization** nor **Diachronic Maximization** nor its special case **Maximization** are usually considered in presentations of decision theory. Instead, it's typically taken that there is some particular time of deliberation $t < t'$ that is relevant to the deontic status of one's t'-options. Taken literally, though, this seems to me completely implausible. A more charitable interpretation is that the assumption that there is some particular time prior to the time of choice that is specially relevant to the deontic status of one's later choices is simply a fiction used to simplify the decision-theoretic models. Insofar, though, as one thinks that it is not the expected utilities at t' that are relevant to the deontic status of one's t'-options, then it seems to me that **Maximization**, and more generally **Diachronic Maximization**, present a natural account of how the expected utilities of one's t'-options at earlier times serve to determine deontic statuses for such options.

such that $ECU_i^t(O') > ECU_i^t(O)$.[16] And so it may be that, given an agent with stable credences and utilities throughout some interval leading up to t', for each option O, there is some option O', such that $ECU_i(O') > ECU_i(O)$.

Another way in which this type of case may arise is if, given the agent's stable credences and utilities leading up to t', there are no well-defined causal expectation values for at least some of the members of $\mathbf{O}_i^{t'}$.

In what follows, our main concern will be with what we should say concerning certain cases of the second sort. It will help us, however, in addressing this question to first consider what we should say about the first type of case. There are, I think, three principled options for treating such cases, and, between these three options, one seems to me to be clearly preferable. The three principled ways of treating such cases are:

Global Dominance Permissivism: If, for each option O, there is some option O', such that $ECU_i(O') > ECU_i(O)$, then, for each $O \in \mathbf{O}_i^{t'}$, it is rationally permissible for i to realize O.

Global Dominance Prohibitionism: If, for each option O, there is some option O', such that $ECU_i(O') > ECU_i(O)$, then, for each $O \in \mathbf{O}_i^{t'}$, it is rationally impermissible for i to realize O.

Global Dominance Conservatism: If, for each option O, there is some option O', such that $ECU_i(O') > ECU_i(O)$, then, for each $O \in \mathbf{O}_i^{t'}$, it is neither rationally permissible nor rationally impermissible for i to realize O.

Granting that we should treat alike all cases in which, for each option that's available to an agent, there is another more attractive option, to reject each of these claims, one must maintain that, in such cases, some options are rationally permissible while others are impermissible. How might one distinguish, in such cases, between those options that are permissible and those that are impermissible?

One option would be to appeal to certain ordinal facts. For example, suppose that the ordering amongst an agent's options is isomorphic to the ordering amongst the natural numbers. Then one might maintain that there is some value n such that if O's expected utility is better than less than n other options then O is rationally impermissible, but if O's expected utility is better than n or more other options then O is rationally permissible.

Another option would be to appeal to some threshold value for $ECU_i(\cdot)$, so that, for some x, O is rationally permissible just in case $ECU_i(O) \geq x$.

The problem with these and other ways of trying to effect some non-trivial distinction between the class of permissible and impermissible options in such cases is that they seem completely unprincipled when combined with **Maximization**. And **Maximization** is extremely plausible.

---

[16] For cases of this sort see Pollock (1983).

Consider the threshold view. If there is some threshold for expected causal utility that suffices for an option to be rationally permissible in cases in which, for each option that's available to an agent, there is another more attractive option, then it becomes a mystery why there is not a similar threshold in cases in which there are some options that maximize expected utility. But it certainly seems that if there are some options that maximize expected utility then it is rationally impermissible to realize any other such option. Of course, one could simply maintain that, as a brute fact, there is threshold rationalization of options when, but only when, there are no maximal options. But this seems to me to be objectionably ad hoc.

Similar considerations could be adduced against the claim that certain ordinal facts serve to effect a non-trivial distinction between the permissible and impermissible options in cases in which there are no options that maximize expected utility.

The more general point is that **Maximization** would seem to require that we assign the same deontic status to options that are alike with respect to the existence of some expected utility dominating alternative. If this principle is to be respected in those cases in which, for each option that's available to an agent, there is another more attractive option, then one must endorse either **Global Dominance Permissivism**, **Global Dominance Prohibitionism**, or **Global Dominance Conservatism**.

Which of these, though, should one endorse?

I don't have a compelling argument against **Global Dominance Conservatism**. Still, I think it should be considered the option of last resort. For while I'm perfectly happy to say that, in cases in which an agent doesn't have an appropriate view concerning the expected utility of their options, one cannot assess the realization of an option by the agent as rationally permissible or impermissible, it seems to me that rationality should not remain silent in cases in which an agent does have a view concerning the expected utility of all of their options. At the very least, if there is a sufficiently attractive option that allows for rational verdicts in such cases, then such an option should be preferred to **Global Dominance Conservatism**. And I think that there is a sufficiently attractive alternative.

Let's turn, then, to **Global Dominance Prohibitionism**. There is a pretty straightforward argument for this principle that is at least initially compelling. For, in the cases to which **Maximization** applies, the existence, for some option O, of an expected utility dominating alternative entails that O is rationally impermissible. And this principle, applied generally, entails **Global Dominance Prohibitionism**.

There is, however, a serious problem with **Global Dominance Prohibitionism**. For consider the following plausible principle:

Possible Permissibility: If, for each $O \in \mathbf{O}_i^{t'}$, $ECU_i(O)$ is well-defined, and if i is not guilty of any antecedent rational failing, then there must be some $O \in \mathbf{O}_i^{t'}$ that is rationally permissible.

192 A PROBLEM FOR CREDAL CONSEQUENTIALISM

Now it seems to me completely implausible to maintain that an agent is irrational simply in virtue of having credences and utilities that entail that, for any option O, there is some other option O' such that $ECU_i(O') > ECU_i(O)$. Given this, it follows that **Possible Permissibility** is incompatible with **Global Dominance Prohibitionism**. **Possible Permissibility**, though, seems to me to be much more plausible than **Global Dominance Prohibitionism**. In light of this incompatibility, then, I think we should reject **Global Dominance Prohibitionism**.

Finally, let's consider **Global Dominance Permissivism**. We can also provide an argument for this principle by appeal to **Maximization**. To see this, note that both **Maximization** and **Global Dominance Permissivism** share the following natural property. In the cases in which they issue verdicts, each is the most conservative principle with respect to rational permissibility that is compatible with **Possible Permissibility** and that treats alike options that are alike with respect to the existence of some expected utility dominating alternative. We can see both of these principles, then, as being motivated by the following more general principle of rationality:

> **Permissible Dominance Symmetry:** Given an agent with stable credences and utilities for some interval leading up to t' that determine a well-defined expected causal utility for each of their available t'-options, there must be an available rational option, but only so many as are required in order not to draw deontic distinctions amongst cases that are alike with respect to the existence of dominating alternatives.

This strikes me as a plausible principle. The fact, then, that **Global Dominance Permissivism** follows from a plausible general principle from which **Maximization** also follows, gives us, I think, good reason to accept the former principle, in addition to the latter.

Let's now consider the second type of case in which **Maximization** leaves open the deontic status of an agent's options. In such cases, there are some $O \in \mathbf{O}_i^{t'}$ for which $ECU_i(\cdot)$ is not well defined. Given our purposes in this paper, we'll want to consider, more specifically, what we should say about those cases in which there are an *infinite* number of $O \in \mathbf{O}_i^{t'}$ for which $ECU_i(\cdot)$ is not well defined.

Let $\mathbf{O}^U \subseteq \mathbf{O}_i^{t'}$ be the class of the agent's t'-options for which $ECU_i(\cdot)$ is not well defined. And let $\mathbf{O}^D =_{df} \mathbf{O}_i^{t'} - \mathbf{O}^U$, so that $\mathbf{O}^D$ is the class of the agent's t'-options for which $ECU_i(\cdot)$ is well defined. I claim:

> **No Distinctions:** If $ECU_i(\cdot)$ is not well defined for an infinite $\mathbf{O}^U \subseteq \mathbf{O}_i^{t'}$, then, for each $O \in \mathbf{O}_i^{t'}$, it is rationally permissible for i to realize O, or, for each $O \in \mathbf{O}_i^{t'}$, it is rationally impermissible for i to realize O, or, for each $O \in \mathbf{O}_i^{t'}$, it is neither rationally permissible nor rationally impermissible for i to realize O.

In support of this, I'll argue that *if* there are non-trivial deontic distinctions amongst an agent's options in cases in which $\mathbf{O}^U$ is non-empty, then if $ECU_i(\cdot)$ is not well defined for an infinite $\mathbf{O}^U \subseteq \mathbf{O}_i^{t'}$, then, for each $O \in \mathbf{O}_i^{t'}$, it is rationally permissible for i to realize O. This claim entails **No Distinctions** and so the argument for the former serves as an argument for the latter.

Let us ask, then: how one might draw non-trivial deontic distinctions amongst an agent's options in cases in which $\mathbf{O}^U$ is non-empty? It seems clear that whatever we say about the deontic status of an agent's options in such a case, we should take each member of $\mathbf{O}^U$ to have the same deontic status. Given this constraint, here's a view one might find initially attractive:

> **Impermissible Undefinedness:** For each $O \in \mathbf{O}^U$, it is rationally impermissible for i to realize O. Let $\mathbf{O}^M \subseteq \mathbf{O}^D$ be the set of options that maximize expected causal utility amongst the members of $\mathbf{O}^D$. If $\mathbf{O}^M \neq \emptyset$, then it is rationally obligatory that one realize some option in $\mathbf{O}^M$. And if $\mathbf{O}^M = \emptyset$, then each $O \in \mathbf{O}^D$ is rationally permissible.

The guiding thoughts behind this principle are, first, that an agent ought not realize an option about which they have no view concerning its expected utility, and, second, that, having ruled out such options, we may then apply to the agent's remaining options those principles that apply in cases in which an agent has well-defined expectation values for all of the options that are available to them, treating the remaining options as the total set of options.

While this may seem at least prima facie plausible, it doesn't, I think, hold up under scrutiny. The problem with **Impermissible Undefinedness** is that, given **Maximization** and **Global Dominance Permissivism**, what would seem to matter for determining the permissibility or impermissibility of an agent's options is how attractive the options appear *relative* to one another. If, though, $ECU_i(\cdot)$ is not well defined for some $O \in \mathbf{O}_i^{t'}$, then, for every $O' \in \mathbf{O}^D$, there will be no well-defined relation of relative attractiveness between O and O'. There is, then, a symmetry with respect to the well definedness of the relative attractiveness of any $O \in \mathbf{O}^U$ and any $O' \in \mathbf{O}^D$. And, given this symmetry and the assumption that what matters for determining the permissibility or impermissibility of an agent's options is how attractive the options appear *relative* to one another, it is hard to see why each member of $\mathbf{O}^U$ should be ruled out as impermissible, while the same is not true of $\mathbf{O}^D$.

It seems to me, then, that a reasonable constraint on any principle that serves to draw non-trivial deontic distinctions amongst an agent's options in cases in which $\mathbf{O}^U$ is non-empty is that such a principle respect these sorts of symmetries with respect to the well definedness of the relative attractiveness of an agent's options. Since **Impermissible Undefinedness** fails to satisfy this constraint, we have, I think good reason to reject this principle.

In cases in which $\mathbf{O}^U$ is empty, an agent's credences and utilities determine a complete ordering amongst the members of $\mathbf{O}_i^{t'}$ that captures the relative attractiveness of these options by the light's of the agent.[17] In cases, though, in which $\mathbf{O}^U$ is non-empty,

---

[17] Strictly speaking these determine a complete *pre*-ordering. I'll, however, drop the prefix throughout this discussion.

while an agent's credences and utilities determine an ordering amongst the members of $\mathbf{O}^D$ that captures the relative attractiveness of these options by the lights of the agent, such credences and utilities leave open how attractive the members of $\mathbf{O}^U$ are both relative to one another and relative to the members of $\mathbf{O}^D$. In such cases, we can think of there being a non-empty non-singleton *set* of orderings amongst the agent's options that correspond to the different orderings capturing the relative attractiveness of the agent's options that are left open given their credences and utilities.

A principle that draws non-trivial deontic distinctions amongst an agent's options in cases in which $\mathbf{O}^U$ is non-empty, then, should tell us which options are rationally permissible and which rationally impermissible given such a set of orderings amongst the members of $\mathbf{O}_i^{t'}$.

There are, furthermore, two natural constraints on such principles that I think we should endorse. First, in determining the deontic status of an option, I think that no ordering that is left open given the agent's credences and utilities should be privileged over any other. This, I take it, is part of what respecting the symmetries with respect to the well-definedness of the relative attractiveness of an agent's options involves. Second, I think we should take it that, given a set of orderings amongst the members of $\mathbf{O}_i^{t'}$, the deontic status of some option O should be a function of the deontic status that O would have, relative to each ordering amongst the set, were that ordering to be the unique ordering given the agent's credences and utilities.

Given these two constraints, there are two principled ways that I can see of potentially drawing non-trivial deontic distinctions in cases in which $\mathbf{O}^U$ is non-empty, and, between these two options, one option seems to me to be clearly preferable.

We'll say that a function $ECU_i^*(\cdot) : \mathbf{O}_i^{t'} \to \mathbb{R}$ is an **extension** of $ECU_i(\cdot)$ just in case, for each $O \in \mathbf{O}^D$, $ECU_i^*(O) = ECU_i(O)$. Given, then, an agent i with stable credences and utilities leading up to t', let $\mathcal{E}_i$ be the set of $ECU_i^*(\cdot) : \mathbf{O}_i^{t'} \to \mathbb{R}$ that extend the function $ECU_i(\cdot)$ defined by their stable credences and utilities. Consider, then, the following principles for determining the deontic status of the agent's t'-options:

Deontic Supervaluationism: An option $O \in \mathbf{O}_i^{t'}$ is permissible just in case it is permissible given each $ECU_i^*(\cdot) \in \mathcal{E}_i$.

Deontic Subvaluationism: An option $O \in \mathbf{O}_i^{t'}$ is permissible just in case it is permissible given some $ECU_i^*(\cdot) \in \mathcal{E}_i$.

Both **Deontic Supervaluationism** and **Deontic Subvaluationism** allow for non-trivial deontic distinctions in certain cases in which $\mathbf{O}^U$ is non-empty.[18] Moreover, these seem to me to be the only principled ways of deriving such a distinction that satisfy the above constraints.

---

[18] To see this in the case of **Deontic Subvaluationism**, suppose that O^U is finite and that there is some subset of O^D that is maximal given $ECU_i(\cdot)$. Then, given **Deontic Subvaluationism** the only permissible options will be the members of O^U and the maximal members of O^D. Below, I'll consider a case in which **Deontic Supervaluationism** provides for non-trivial deontic distinctions given non-empty $\mathbf{O}^U$.

There is, however, good reason to reject **Deontic Supervaluationism**. For **Deontic Supervaluationism** together with **Maximization** and **Global Dominance Permissivism** entail that if $\mathbf{O}^U$ is singleton and, for each $O \in \mathbf{O}^D$, there is some $O' \in \mathbf{O}^D$, such that $ECU_i(O') > ECU_i(O)$, then one is rationally required to realize the unique $O \in \mathbf{O}^U$.[19] This consequence is, I take it, a reductio of the conjunction of these three views. For surely an agent should not be rationally required to realize the unique option about which they lack a view regarding its expected causal utility. Given the plausibility of **Maximization** and **Global Dominance Permissivism**, then, this provides us with good reason to reject **Deontic Supervaluationism**.

I don't think, though, that we have any such clear reason to reject **Deontic Subvaluationism**. There would seem, then, to be a defensible view on which non-trivial deontic distinctions may sometimes be drawn amongst an agent's options even if the agent lacks well-defined expectation values for some of their available options. Importantly, though, given **Global Dominance Permissivism**, such non-trivial distinctions can only be drawn when $\mathbf{O}^U$ is finite. For **Global Dominance Permissivism** and **Deontic Subvaluationism** entail that if $ECU_i(\cdot)$ is not well defined for an infinite $\mathbf{O}^U \subseteq \mathbf{O}_i^{t'}$, then, for each $O \in \mathbf{O}_i^{t'}$, it is rationally permissible for i to realize O.[20]

Since **Deontic Subvaluationism** is the only reasonable way of drawing non-trivial deontic distinctions in certain cases in which $\mathbf{O}^U$ is non-empty that satisfies certain plausible constraints, and since we have good reason to accept **Global Dominance Permissivism**, we have, then, good reason to think that if there is a way of drawing non-trivial deontic distinctions in certain cases in which $\mathbf{O}^U$ is non-empty, then if $ECU_i(\cdot)$ is not well defined for an infinite $\mathbf{O}^U \subseteq \mathbf{O}_i^{t'}$, then, for each $O \in \mathbf{O}_i^{t'}$, it is rationally permissible for i to realize O.

A consequence of this conditional is that if there is a way of drawing non-trivial deontic distinctions in certain cases in which $\mathbf{O}^U$ is non-empty, such distinctions can only be drawn when $\mathbf{O}^U$ is finite. And so it follows that any case in which $\mathbf{O}^U$ is infinite will be such that either each option is permissible, or each option is

---

[19] To see this, let O^* be the unique member of $\mathbf{O}^U$. Given that O^* is the unique member of $\mathbf{O}^U$ and that, for each $O \in \mathbf{O}^D$, there is some $O' \in \mathbf{O}^D$, such that $ECU_i(O') > ECU_i(O)$, it follows that (i) there exists some $ECU_i^*(\cdot) \in \mathcal{E}_i$ such that $ECU_i^*(O^*) > ECU_i^*(O)$, for each other $O \in \mathbf{O}_i^{t'}$, and (ii) every $ECU_i^*(\cdot) \in \mathcal{E}_i$ that does not satisfy the preceding condition is such that, for each $O \in \mathbf{O}_i^{t'}$, there is some $O' \in \mathbf{O}_i^{t'}$, such that $ECU_i^*(O') > ECU_i^*(O)$. Given **Deontic Supervaluationism** and **Maximization**, it follows from (i) that every $O \in \mathbf{O}^D$ is impermissible. And given **Deontic Supervaluationism**, **Maximization**, and **Global Dominance Permissivism**, it follows from (i) and (ii) that O^* is permissible. And so, since O^* is the unique permissible option amongst $\mathbf{O}_i^{t'}$, given **Deontic Supervaluationism**, **Maximization**, and **Global Dominance Permissivism**, it follows, given these principles, that it is rationally obligatory that i realize O^*.

[20] To see this, assume that $\mathbf{O}^U$ is infinite. Then it follows that there is some $ECU_i^*(\cdot) \in \mathcal{E}_i$, such that, for each $O \in \mathbf{O}_i^{t'}$, there is some $O' \in \mathbf{O}_i^{t'}$, such that $ECU_i^*(O') > ECU_i^*(O)$. And so, given **Global Dominance Permissivism**, each $O \in \mathbf{O}_i^{t'}$ is permissible relative to $ECU_i^*(\cdot)$. And so, given **Deontic Subvaluationism**, it follows that each $O \in \mathbf{O}_i^{t'}$ is permissible.

impermissible, or each option is not apt for rational evaluation. Thus, we have **No Distinctions**.

Now, if one thinks that non-trivial deontic distinctions can be drawn at least in certain cases in which $\mathbf{O}^U$ is non-empty, then the preceding also provides us with an argument that if $ECU_i(\cdot)$ is not well-defined for an infinite $\mathbf{O}^U \subseteq \mathbf{O}^{t'}_i$, then, for each $O \in \mathbf{O}^{t'}_i$, it is rationally permissible for i to realize O. But one might reject the claim that non-trivial deontic distinctions can ever be drawn in cases in which $\mathbf{O}^U$ is non-empty, and so reject this argument for the claim that when $\mathbf{O}^U$ is infinite each option available to the agent is rationally permissible. For example, one may maintain that if $\mathbf{O}^U$ is non-empty, then each option available to the agent is not apt for rational assessment. Or one may maintain that if $\mathbf{O}^U$ is non-empty, then each option available to the agent is rationally impermissible. We need not, though, consider how plausible any of these particular claims are. For **No Distinctions** itself will suffice for our purposes in what follows.

8.2 Credal Consequentialism

According to credal consequentialism, the deontic status of an agent's credal options is determined by the degree to which the agent takes such options to be conducive to the epistemic good. In this section, we'll sharpen up this intuitive idea and look more closely at the picture of credal rationality that it provides.

In §8.2.1, I'll outline, by appeal to the machinery of causal decision theory, a precise version of credal consequentialism. In §8.2.2, I'll show that, given plausible auxiliary assumptions, this theory has the undesirable consequence that in a vast range of cases no deontic distinctions can be drawn amongst an agent's credal options. In §8.3, I'll then consider two ways in which one might try to avoid this result.

8.2.1 Credal consequentialism precisified

We'll assume that there is an objective notion of the epistemic good for credal states that may be represented by a ternary function $eu(\cdot, \cdot, \cdot) : I \times T \times W \to \mathbb{R}$. Here I is the set of possible individuals, T is the set of possible times, and W is the set of epistemically possible worlds. Given an individual i, a time t, and a world w, $eu(i, t, w)$, then, tells us the epistemic utility of i's credal state at w and t. As a short-hand, we'll let $eu^t_i(\cdot) = eu(i, t, \cdot)$.[21]

---

[21] A few points. First, note that the notion of utility appealed to here is not tied to an agent's subjective values. Nonetheless, we will assume that it can be known a priori that the epistemic good may be represented by $eu(\cdot, \cdot, \cdot)$. For, otherwise, it is hard to see how $eu(\cdot, \cdot, \cdot)$ could have the deontic bearing that it has according to the version of credal consequentialism under consideration.

Second, one might worry about those cases in which i does not exist at w and t. There are two ways of dealing with such cases. Either we could take $eu(\cdot, \cdot, \cdot)$ to be a partial function that is only defined when i exists at w and t, or we could take the epistemic utility of having no credal state to be some particular value. Assuming that there is a minimal epistemic utility that one could have were one to have a credal state, a

Let $\mathbf{C}_i^{t'}$ be the partition of W consisting of i's **credal options** at t'. We'll assume that the agent's conceptual resources at t' are an exogenous factor, outside of their control, at least in the sense that is relevant for credal decision problems. Thus, we'll assume that there is a fixed algebra $\mathbf{A}_i^{t'}$ such that the agent's credal options at t' concern possible credal states defined over $\mathbf{A}_i^{t'}$, and that this algebra is the same algebra over which the agent's stable credences leading up to t' are defined, so that for some $t'' < t'$, for each $t \in (t'', t')$, $\mathbf{A}_i^t = \mathbf{A}_i^{t'}$.

Even given these constraints, it turns out to be a somewhat delicate matter how we should think of the elements of $\mathbf{C}_i^{t'}$. A natural thought is that the elements of $\mathbf{C}_i^{t'}$ will be propositions uniquely characterizing i's credal distribution, at t', over $\mathbf{A}_i^{t'}$. In this section, we'll operate under this assumption. In section 8.2.2, though, we'll consider the possibility that the members of $\mathbf{C}_i^{t'}$ may consist of coarse-grainings of this space of propositions, so that each $C \in \mathbf{C}_i^{t'}$ may be thought of as a union of propositions characterizing i's credal distribution over $\mathbf{A}_i^{t'}$ at t'.[22]

Let P be a set such that, for some $x \in \mathbb{R}$, $P = \{w \in \mathbf{W} : eu_i^{t'}(w) = x\}$. We'll call such a set an **epistemic value proposition** (for i at t'), and we'll denote such a proposition by $[EV_i^{t'} = x]$, and the class of such propositions by $\mathbf{EV}_i^{t'}$. Given some $C \in \mathbf{C}_i^{t'}$ and some $[EV_i^{t'} = x] \in \mathbf{EV}_i^{t'}$, $C \square\!\!\rightarrow [EV_i^{t'} = x]$, then, is the set of worlds w such that, at w, were i to realize C at t', then the result would be a situation of epistemic utility x.

We'll say that a non-empty intersection of a set that contains, for each $C \in \mathbf{C} \subseteq \mathbf{C}_i^{t'}$, a unique proposition of the form $C \square\!\!\rightarrow [EV_i^{t'} = x]$, and no other propositions, is an **epistemic-value dependence hypothesis for C**. We'll denote the set of epistemic-value dependence hypotheses for $\mathbf{C} \subseteq \mathbf{C}_i^{t'}$, $ED(\mathbf{C})$.

---

natural option, here, would be to take the epistemic utility of failing to have any credal state whatsoever to be a value less than this minimal value. For our purposes, it won't really matter which of these options we choose. To simplify the exposition, though, I'll ignore this complication in what follows.

Third, while we will assume that the notion of the epistemic good that is relevant to credal consequentialism is objective and independent of any agent's values, it should be clear that almost all of the main points that follow could be made equally well given a more subjective version of credal consequentialism. Typically, though, insofar as pursuit of the epistemic good is thought to be relevant to epistemology, it is an objective notion of the good that is taken to be so relevant.

[22] A worry: given this way of characterizing $\mathbf{C}_i^{t'}$, it wouldn't seem that this set will be a *partition* of W. For, in addition to all the worlds in which i has some credal state defined over $\mathbf{A}_i^{t'}$ at t', there are all sorts of other worlds in which i does not have a credal state at t' defined over $\mathbf{A}_i^{t'}$.

To get around this worry, we weasel. Let $\mathbf{C}^*$ be the set of propositions describing various possible credal states that i may have at t' over $\mathbf{A}_i^{t'}$, or a set of disjoint unions of such propositions the union of which is equivalent to the union of all of the propositions in the former set. Now pick an arbitrary $C \in \mathbf{C}^*$. Then $\mathbf{C}^* - \{C\}$ is the set of propositions in $\mathbf{C}^*$ with C removed. And so $(W - \cup (\mathbf{C}^* - \{C\}))$ is the proposition that is true just in case it's not the case that any of the propositions in $\mathbf{C}^* - \{C\}$ are true. Now let $\mathbf{C}_i^{t'} = (\mathbf{C}^* - \{C\}) \cup (W - \cup (\mathbf{C}^* - \{C\}))$. $\mathbf{C}_i^{t'}$, then, is the result of replacing C in $\mathbf{C}^*$ with the proposition that none of the other propositions in $\mathbf{C}^*$ obtain. $\mathbf{C}_i^{t'}$, so characterized, will be guaranteed to be a partition of W. And, given that the agent is certain that, at t', they will have credences defined over $\mathbf{A}_i^{t'}$, C and $(W - \cup (\mathbf{C}^* - \{C\}))$ will play the same role in the agent's credal state.

This being said, I'll ignore this complication in what follows and speak of the members of $\mathbf{C}_i^{t'}$ as if they characterize (perhaps disjunctively) the agent's credences at t' over $\mathbf{A}_i^{t'}$.

198 A PROBLEM FOR CREDAL CONSEQUENTIALISM

Let us say, for each $C \in \mathbf{C}_i^{t'}$ and each $P \subseteq \mathbf{A}_i^t$, that $EU(C \cap P) = x$ if $(C \,\square\!\!\rightarrow [EV_i^{t'} = x]) \cap P = P$, and otherwise $EU(C \cap P)$ is undefined. Given this characterization of $EU(\cdot)$, we can define the following quantity:

Def. $EG_i^t(C) =_{df} \sum_{A \in \mathrm{At}_i^t} Cr_i^t(A) EU(C \cap A).$

For the reasons canvassed in §8.1, we won't, in general, want to identify an agent's expectation value for the casual epistemic utility of some option C with $EG_i^t(C)$. Nonetheless, this quantity will play an important role in what follows, and so we single it out.

We'll instead take the expected epistemic causal utility, for i at t, of an option $C \in \mathbf{C}_i^{t'}$ to be characterized as follows:

EECU: $EECU_i^t(C) = \sum_{A \in \mathbf{Z}_{Cr_i^t}} Cr_i^t(A) EU(C \cap A).$

And, given this characterization of expected epistemic utility, we can then define the following, perhaps partial, function from $\mathbf{C}_i^{t'}$ to $\mathbb{R}$:

Def. $EECU_i(C) = x$ just in case, for all $t \in (t'', t')$, $EECU_i^t(C) = x$.

Again, given our assumption that, in a given credal decision problem, there will be some $t'' < t'$, such that, for each $t_1, t_2 \in (t'', t')$, $Cr_i^{t_1}(\cdot) = Cr_i^{t_2}(\cdot)$, $EECU_i(C)$ will be well defined as long at $EECU_i^t(C)$ is well defined for some $t \in (t'', t')$.

The core idea behind credal consequentialism, I take it, is that one should try to realize a credal option that will bring about the best epistemic consequences. Or, rather, *if* there are credal options that maximize an agent's expected epistemic utility, then the agent ought to realize one of those options. As with the core idea behind causal decision theory, there are a few ways in which this idea may be precisified. In what follows, we'll work with the following natural precisification:

Credal Maximization: Let M be the set of $C \in \mathbf{C}_i^{t'}$ such that, for each $C' \in \mathbf{C}_i^{t'}$, $EECU_i(C) \geq EECU_i(C')$. If M is non-empty, then, for each $C \in M$, it is rationally permissible for i to realize C, and it is rationally required for i to realize some $C \in M$.[23]

---

[23] The natural generalization of **Credal Maximization** is:

Diachronic Credal Maximization: Let M be the set of $C \in \mathbf{C}_i^{t'}$ such that, for some $t'' < t'$, $EECU_i^t(C) \geq ECU_i^t(C')$, for every $C' \in \mathbf{C}_i^{t'}$ and every $t \in (t'', t')$. If M is non-empty, then, for each $C \in M$, it is rationally permissible for i to realize C, and it is rationally required for i to realize some $C \in M$.

An alternative way of precisifying the core idea behind credal consequentialism is:

Synchronic Credal Maximization: Let M be the set of $C \in \mathbf{C}_i^{t'}$ such that, for each $C' \in \mathbf{C}_i^{t'}$, $EECU_i^{t'}(C) \geq EECU_i^{t'}(C')$. If M is non-empty, then, for each $C \in M$, it is rationally permissible for i to realize C, and it is rationally required for i to realize some $C \in M$.

Earlier, I noted some reasons to prefer **Maximization** to its synchronic alternative **Synchronic Credal Maximization**. There are also, I think, corresponding reasons to prefer **Credal Maximization** to

Credal Maximization, of course, leaves open the deontic status of an agent's credal options in two important classes of cases. First, it leaves open the deontic status of an agent's credal options when, for each credal option, there is another credal option with greater expected causal epistemic utility. Second, it leaves open the deontic status of an agent's credal options when there is no well-defined causal expectation value for at least some credal options.

The arguments presented in §8.1, though, tell us what the proponent of credal consequentialism ought to say about the first class of cases and at least a subclass of the second class of cases. In particular, the arguments presented in §8.1 tell us that, in addition to **Credal Maximization**, the proponent of credal consequentialism should endorse:

Global Credal Dominance Permissivism: If, for each credal option C, there is some option C', such that $EECU_i(C') > EECU_i(C)$, then, for each $C \in \mathbf{C}_i^{t'}$, it is rationally permissible for i to realize C.

No Credal Distinctions: If $EECU_i(\cdot)$ is not well-defined for an infinite $\mathbf{C}^U \subseteq \mathbf{C}_i^{t'}$, then, for each $C \in \mathbf{C}_i^{t'}$, it is rationally permissible for i to realize C, or, for each $C \in \mathbf{C}_i^{t'}$, it is rationally impermissible for i to realize C, or, for each $C \in \mathbf{C}_i^{t'}$, it is neither rationally permissible nor rationally impermissible for i to realize C.

For, in §8.1, we argued that, given **Maximization**, one should endorse **Global Dominance Permissivism**. And this argument may be repurposed, mutatis mutandis, to show that, given **Credal Maximization**, one should endorse **Global Credal Dominance Permissivism**. And, in §8.1, we argued that, given **Global Dominance Permissivism**, one should endorse **No Distinctions**. And this argument may be repurposed, mutatis mutandis, to show that, given **Global Credal Dominance Permissivism**, one should endorse **No Credal Distinctions**.

8.2.2 A problem for credal consequentialism

I'll now argue that, in a large class of cases, credal consequentialism entails that no non-trivial deontic distinctions can be drawn amongst an agent's credal options. The problem, in essence, is that, given a typical algebra $\mathbf{A}_i^{t'}$, there are simply more—indeed infinitely many more—dependence hypotheses for the different credal states over $\mathbf{A}_i^{t'}$ that an agent i might adopt at t' than there are atoms of $\mathbf{A}_i^{t'}$. Given that i has credences defined over $\mathbf{A}_i^{t'}$, leading up to t', the agent, then, simply can't form an appropriate view about the expectation values for the various credal states that they may adopt at t' over $\mathbf{A}_i^{t'}$—or at least they can't do so without ruling out infinitely many a priori possible epistemic dependence hypotheses. And given this consequence it follows from **No Credal Distinctions** that, in all but some very unusual cases, unless an agent rules

---

Synchronic Credal Maximization. However, deciding between these different ways of precisifying the guiding thought behind credal consequentialism need not detain us here. For all of the main points that I'll make have natural analogues given the natural alternative version of credal consequentialism that endorses **Synchronic Credal Maximization** instead of **Credal Maximization**.

out an infinite number of a priori possible epistemic dependence hypotheses, credal consequentialism will entail that no non-trivial deontic distinctions can be drawn amongst an agent's credal options.

The first point to note is that, in any case in which an agent has credences defined over an algebra of propositions that don't concern their own credal states, it follows, given **No Credal Distinctions**, that no non-trivial deontic distinctions can be drawn amongst an agent's credal options.

Let me briefly sketch why this is so by appeal to a toy case:

Rain: Let $R = \{w : \text{It is raining in } w \text{ at } t'\}$ and $\mathbf{A}^R = \{R, W - R, \emptyset, W\}$. $\mathbf{A}^R$, then, is the smallest algebra containing R. And let $\mathbf{C}^R$ be the set of propositions that uniquely characterize the possible credal distributions that i may have at t' over $\mathbf{A}^R$.

> **Claim:** Given **No Credal Distinctions**, no non-trivial deontic distinctions can be drawn amongst the agent's different credal options in **Rain**.

Justification: Each $C \in \mathbf{C}^R$ is compatible with both the truth of R and the falsity of R. Moreover, given any plausible account of epistemic value, we should expect that the class of $C \in \mathbf{C}^R$ for which the epistemic utility of C given the truth of R does not differ from the epistemic utility of C given the falsity of R will be quite small.[24] In particular, given that there is an infinite number of $C \in \mathbf{C}^R$, we should expect that this set will, at the very least, be non-cofinite. Thus, the class of $C \in \mathbf{C}^R$ for which the epistemic utility of C given the truth of R does differ from the epistemic utility of C given the falsity of R is infinite. Furthermore, we should expect that, for each $C \in \mathbf{C}^R$, in addition to the mundane worlds in R, in which $C \square\!\!\rightarrow R$ holds, there will also be some rather odd worlds in which $C \square\!\!\rightarrow (W - R)$ holds. Similarly, we should expect that, for each $C \in \mathbf{C}^R$, in addition to the mundane worlds in $W - R$, in which $C \square\!\!\rightarrow (W - R)$ holds, there will also be some rather odd worlds in which $C \square\!\!\rightarrow R$ holds. It follows, then, that for an infinite number of $C \in \mathbf{C}^R$ both $EU(C \cap R)$ and $EU(C \cap (W-R))$ will be undefined. And so we have that $EECU_i(\cdot)$ is not well defined for an infinite $\mathbf{C}^U \subseteq \mathbf{C}^R$. Thus, given **No Credal Distinctions**, it follows that for each $C \in \mathbf{C}^R$, it is rationally permissible for i to realize C, or, for each $C \in \mathbf{C}^R$, it is rationally impermissible for i to realize C, or, for each $C \in \mathbf{C}^R$, it is neither rationally permissible nor rationally impermissible for i to realize C.

While I think that this consequence is quite undesirable, there are a few responses available to the proponent of credal consequentialism. For example, they may maintain that epistemic rationality requires an agent to form an appropriate view about the expected epistemic utility of their own credences. In this way, they may try to justify the claim that, in this sort of case, all of an agent's credal options are rationally impermissible. Or they may maintain that, in order to assess an agent's credal state

---

[24] The sorts of symmetries that give rise to cases in which the epistemic utility of a credal state may be invariant given such differences in truth-value are further discussed below.

as being rationally permissible or impermissible, the agent must form an appropriate view about the expected epistemic utility of their own credences. In this way, they may try to justify the claim that, in this sort of case, none of the agent's credal options can be assessed as either being rationally permissible or rationally impermissible.

For this sort of move to be at all persuasive, though, there must be a sufficiently large class of cases in which non-trivial deontic distinctions may be drawn, given credal consequentialism. In this section, I'll argue, however, that this condition isn't satisfied. To this end, I'll argue that, given **No Credal Distinctions**, in all but some unusual cases, we have:

> **Opinionation:** No non-trivial deontic distinctions can be drawn amongst an agent's credal options, unless i is quasi-opinionated about $\mathbf{ED}(\{C\})$, for an infinite number of $C \in \mathbf{C}_i^{t'}$, in the stable interval leading up to t'.

To argue for this claim, I'll first argue that, in all but some unusual cases, we have:

> **Undefinedness:** If $\mathbf{C}_i^{t'}$ is the set of propositions characterizing i's possible credal distributions, at t', over $\mathbf{A}_i^{t'}$, then there will be some infinite $\mathbf{C} \subseteq \mathbf{C}_i^{t'}$ such that, for each $C \in \mathbf{C}$, there is some $A \in \mathbf{At}_i^{t'}$, for which $EU(C \cap A)$ is undefined.

Given **Undefinedness**, it follows that, for each t in the stable interval leading up to t', $EG_i^t(C)$ will be undefined for each $C \in \mathbf{C}$. And from this it follows that, unless, in the stable interval leading up to t', i is quasi-opinionated about $\mathbf{ED}(\{C\})$, for an infinite number of $C \in \mathbf{C}_i^{t'}$, $EECU_i(\cdot)$ will not be well defined for an infinite $\mathbf{C}^U \subseteq \mathbf{C}_i^{t'}$. And so, given that **Undefinedness** holds in all but some unusual cases, it follows, given **No Credal Distinctions**, that **Opinionation** holds in all but some unusual cases.

In support of the claim that **Undefinedness** holds in all but some unusual cases, I'll first argue that, in all but some unusual cases, the following two claims will both hold:

> **Bifurcation:** Let $\mathbf{C}_{\geq 2}(\mathbf{C}_i^{t'}) \subseteq \mathbf{C}_i^{t'}$ be the set of $C \in \mathbf{C}_i^{t'}$ such that $|\mathbf{ED}(\{C\})| \geq 2$. If $\mathbf{C}_i^{t'}$ is the set of propositions uniquely characterizing i's possible credal distributions over $\mathbf{A}_i^{t'}$, then $|\mathbf{C}_{\geq 2}(\mathbf{C}_i^{t'})|$ will be infinite and will be such that $|\mathbf{C}_{\geq 2}(\mathbf{C}_i^{t'})| \geq |\mathbf{A}_i^{t'}|$.
>
> **Exponentiation:** For each $\mathbf{C} \subseteq \mathbf{C}_{\geq 2}(\mathbf{C}_i^{t'})$, $|\mathbf{ED}(\mathbf{C})| \geq 2^{|\mathbf{C}|}$.

As we'll show, given that both of these claims hold in all but some unusual cases, it follows that **Undefinedness** will hold in all but some unusual cases.

Let's begin with **Bifurcation**. To see why it is plausible that this claim holds in typical cases, it will be helpful to first consider an unusual case in which the set of credal options, $\mathbf{C}_{T(*)}$, is such that $|\mathbf{C}_{\geq 2}(\mathbf{C}_{T(*)})| = 0$.[25]

---

[25] This sort of case is considered in detail in Caie (2013) and Caie (2014). For further discussion of such cases see Campbell-Moore (2015). And for a treatment of such cases in a non-classical setting see Caie (2012).

Anti-Expert: Consider the following interpreted sentence. (∗) **It's not the case that i's credence at t' that (∗) is true is greater than or equal to 0.5.** We can represent this as: (∗) $\neg Cr_i^{t'} T(*) \geq 0.5$. Let $\mathbf{A}_{T(*)} = \{T(*), W - T(*), \emptyset, W\}$. $\mathbf{A}_{T(*)}$, then, is the smallest algebra containing $T(*)$. Let $\mathbf{C}_{T(*)}$ be the set of propositions that uniquely characterize the possible credal distributions that i may have at t' over $\mathbf{A}_{T(*)}$.

Now the following principle concerning epistemic utility seems to me to be quite plausible:

Truth-Value Supervenience: For every $w, w' \in W$, $t, t' \in T$, and $i, i' \in I$, if $\mathbf{A}_i^t = \mathbf{A}_{i'}^{t'}$, $Cr_i^t(\cdot) = Cr_{i'}^{t'}(\cdot)$, and the truth-value distribution at w over $\mathbf{A}_i^t$ is the same as the truth-value distribution at w' over $\mathbf{A}_{i'}^{t'}$, then $eu(i, t, w) = eu(i', t', w')$.

> **Claim:** Given **Truth-Value Supervenience**, it follows that, in Anti-Expert, for each $C \in \mathbf{C}_{T(*)}$, there is a particular epistemic utility value such that necessarily that value would result were C to be realized. That is, given **Truth-Value Supervenience**, $\mathbf{C}_{\geq 2}(\mathbf{C}_{T(*)}) = \emptyset$.

Justification: Given **Truth-Value Supervenience**, it follows that, for each $C \in \mathbf{C}_{T(*)}$, there exist some $x \in \mathbb{R}$, such that $C \square\!\!\rightarrow [EV_i^{t'} = x]$ holds at w, for each $w \in W$. For note that as an instance of the T-schema, we have: $T(*) \leftrightarrow \neg Cr_i^{t'} T(*) \geq 0.5$. Since this proposition is both necessary and a priori knowable, it will obtain at every point in W.[26] And, given that $T(*) \leftrightarrow \neg Cr_i^{t'} T(*) \geq 0.5$ obtains at each $w \in W$, it follows that, for each $Cr(\cdot) : \mathbf{A}_{T(*)} \rightarrow \mathbb{R}$, each $w \in W$ will agree about what the truth-value distribution would be over $\mathbf{A}_{T(*)}$ were i at t' to have credal state $Cr(\cdot)$. And so, given **Truth-Value Supervenience**, it follows that each $w \in W$ will agree, for each $Cr(\cdot) : \mathbf{A}_{T(*)} \rightarrow \mathbb{R}$, about how much epistemic utility would result were i at t' to have credal state $Cr(\cdot)$. And so, given this plausible principle concerning epistemic utility, it follows that there is a single epistemic-value dependence hypothesis for $\mathbf{C}_{T(*)}$, viz., W. And so, we have $\mathbf{C}_{\geq 2}(\mathbf{C}_{T(*)}) = \emptyset$.

It's worth stressing, though, that the pair of $\mathbf{C}_{T(*)}$ and $\mathbf{A}_{T(*)}$ have a very unusual property. For each member of $\mathbf{C}_{T(*)}$ *entails* a particular truth-value distribution over $\mathbf{A}_{T(*)}$. Given a typical algebra, $\mathbf{A}$, though, there will be no agent i and time t' such that each proposition that describes i's credal distribution over $\mathbf{A}$ at t' entails a particular truth-value distribution over $\mathbf{A}$. Indeed, for a typical algebra, $\mathbf{A}$, any agent i and time t' will be such that no proposition that describes i's credal distribution over $\mathbf{A}$ at t' will entail a particular truth-value distribution over $\mathbf{A}$.

Thus, suppose that to $\mathbf{A}_{T(*)}$ we add the proposition $R = \{w : \text{It is raining in } w \text{ at } t'\}$ and close under negation and disjunction. Let $\mathbf{A}_{T(*)}^R$ denote the resulting algebra, and

---

[26] See Caie (2013) for a defense of the claim that this proposition is both necessary and a priori.

let $\mathbf{C}^R_{T(*)}$ be the set of propositions that characterize the possible credal distributions that i may have at t' over $\mathbf{A}^R_{T(*)}$. Then, unlike with $\mathbf{C}_{T(*)}$ and $\mathbf{A}_{T(*)}$, no member of $\mathbf{C}^R_{T(*)}$ entails a particular truth-value distribution over $\mathbf{A}^R_{T(*)}$. For while each $C \in \mathbf{C}^R_{T(*)}$ will entail a truth-value distribution over the sub-algebra $\mathbf{A}_{T(*)}$, each $C \in \mathbf{C}^R_{T(*)}$ is compatible with both the truth and the falsity of R.

Now we can't, I think, conclude from this fact that *every* $C \in \mathbf{C}^R_{T(*)}$ may result in more than one possible epistemic utility. For, while each $C \in \mathbf{C}^R_{T(*)}$ is compatible with at least two distinct truth-value distributions over $\mathbf{A}^R_{T(*)}$, given plausible principles concerning epistemic utility, for some $C \in \mathbf{C}^R_{T(*)}$ there will be symmetries that ensure that the same epistemic utility will result given C and any of the possible truth-value distributions over $\mathbf{A}^R_{T(*)}$ compatible with C. For example, suppose that C describes i at t' as having a probabilistically coherent credal state $Cr^{t'}_i(\cdot)$ such that $Cr^{t'}_i(T(*)) > 0.5$ and such that $Cr^{t'}_i(R) = Cr^{t'}_i(W - R) = 0.5$. In this case, there will be two possible truth-value distributions over $\mathbf{A}^R_{T(*)}$ compatible with C, viz., the truth-value distribution determined by the falsity of $T(*)$ and the truth of R, and the truth-value distribution determined by the falsity of $T(*)$ and the falsity of R. However, given that $Cr^{t'}_i(R) = Cr^{t'}_i(W - R) = 0.5$ and that $Cr^{t'}_i(\cdot)$ is probabilistically coherent, it seems quite reasonable to suppose that were C to obtain, the same epistemic utility would result, regardless of which of these two truth-value distributions obtained.[27]

I think, though, that this sort of symmetry will be the exception rather than the rule, given any plausible account of epistemic utility. Thus, for example, if C' describes i at t' as having a probabilistically coherent credal state $Cr^{t'}_i(\cdot)$ such that $Cr^{t'}_i(T(*)) > 0.5$ and such that $Cr^{t'}_i(R) > 0.5$, then, while the same two possible truth-value distributions that were compatible with C will be compatible with C', it seems that greater epistemic utility would result were the conjunction of C' and the truth-value distribution determined by the falsity of $T(*)$ and the truth of R to obtain, instead of the conjunction of C' and the truth-value distribution determined by the falsity of $T(*)$ and the falsity of R.[28] Given, then, a reasonable account of epistemic utility, we will have that the class of $C \in \mathbf{C}^R_{T(*)}$ for which there are special symmetries that ensure that there is only one epistemic utility value that could result were C to be realized will be relatively small. And, given that $\mathbf{C}^R_{T(*)}$ is infinite, this set will, at the very least, be non-cofinite. Thus, we have that the class of $C \in \mathbf{C}^R_{T(*)}$ for which more than one possible epistemic utility value may result were C to obtain will be infinite.

---

[27] This, for example, will hold if, in cases in which an agent i at w and t has a credal state defined over a finite algebra, we take $eu(t, i, w)$ to be given by the negative Brier score. Let $Cr(\cdot)$ give the agent's credences at w and t over an n-membered algebra $\mathbf{A}$. And let $w(\cdot) : \mathbf{A} \to \{0, 1\}$ be such that $w(P) = 1$ just in case P is true at w. Then, the negative Brier score for i's credences at w and t is given by:

$$1 - [(1/n) \sum_{P \in \mathbf{A}} (Cr(P) - w(P))^2].$$

[28] Again, this will hold if, in cases in which an agent i at w and t has a credal state defined over a finite algebra, we take $eu(t, i, w)$ to be given by the negative Brier score.

The preceding considerations, moreover, readily generalize. In all but some very strange cases, each $C \in \mathbf{C}_i^{t'}$ will be compatible with at least two possible truth-value distributions over $\mathbf{A}_i^{t'}$. This, for example, will be assured if, like $\mathbf{A}_{T(*)}^R$, $\mathbf{A}_i^{t'}$ contains at least one proposition that is logically independent of any credal state over $\mathbf{A}_i^{t'}$ that i might have at t'. And, in such cases, with the exception of a relatively small, non-cofinite, number of $C \in \mathbf{C}_i^{t'}$ for which there are special symmetries, there will be at least two possible epistemic utilities that may result given that C obtains.

Now given an algebra $\mathbf{A}_i^{t'}$, the cardinality of the class of possible credal functions over $\mathbf{A}_i^{t'}$ will be equal to $|\mathbb{R}|^{|\mathbf{A}_i^{t'}|}$. Since $|\mathbb{R}|^{|\mathbf{A}_i^{t'}|}$ is infinite and is greater than $|\mathbf{A}_i^{t'}|$, we have that, given any algebra $\mathbf{A}_i^{t'}$, the cardinality of the class of possible credal functions over $\mathbf{A}_i^{t'}$ is guaranteed to be infinite and greater than $|\mathbf{A}_i^{t'}|$. And so, if $\mathbf{C}_i^{t'}$ is the set of propositions uniquely characterizing i's possible credal distributions over $\mathbf{A}_i^{t'}$, it follows that $|\mathbf{C}_i^{t'}|$ will be infinite and will be greater than $|\mathbf{A}_i^{t'}|$.

Putting these pieces together, then, given that, in general, $|\mathbf{C}_i^{t'}|$ will be infinite and will be greater than $|\mathbf{A}_i^{t'}|$, and that, in all but some unusual cases, with the exception of a relatively small, non-cofinite, number of $C \in \mathbf{C}_i^{t'}$ for which there are special symmetries, there will be at least two possible epistemic utilities that may result given that C obtains, we should expect that, in all but some unusual cases, $|\mathbf{C}_{\geq 2}(\mathbf{C}_i^{t'})|$ will be infinite and will be such that $|\mathbf{C}_{\geq 2}(\mathbf{C}_i^{t'})| \geq |\mathbf{A}_i^{t'}|$. And so, we have that, in all but some very unusual cases, **Bifurcation** will hold.

Now let's turn to **Exponentiation**. In support of the claim that, in all but some very unusual cases, **Exponentiation** will hold, consider the following modal recombination principle:

Value Recombination: Let $\mathbf{C}_i^{t'}$ be a set of credal options for i at t'. Let $\mathbf{B}$ be a set of propositions of the form $C \square\!\!\rightarrow [EV_i^{t'} = x]$, where $C \in \mathbf{C}_i^{t'}$, and, for each $C \in \mathbf{C}_i^{t'}$, there is at most one such proposition in $\mathbf{B}$. If, for each $C \square\!\!\rightarrow [EV_i^{t'} = x] \in \mathbf{B}$, there is some $w \in W$ such that $C \square\!\!\rightarrow [EV_i^{t'} = x]$ obtains at w, then there is some $w' \in W$ such that $\cap \mathbf{B}$ obtains at w'.

To see why this principle is at least prima facie plausible, recall that W is the set of *epistemic* possibilities, i.e., maximally specific possibilities that cannot be ruled out a priori. **Value Recombination**, then, claims that if one cannot rule out a priori any member of some set of propositions of the form $C \square\!\!\rightarrow [EV_i^{t'} = x]$, where $C \in \mathbf{C}_i^{t'}$, and there is at most one such proposition in the set for each $C \in \mathbf{C}_i^{t'}$, then one cannot a priori rule out the conjunction of such propositions. At first glance, at least, this seems to me to be quite plausible. For it's hard to see what sort of a priori discernible connection there might be amongst a class of propositions of the form $C \square\!\!\rightarrow [EV_i^{t'} = x]$, given that their antecedents are incompatible, that would allow one to rule out the combination of such counterfactuals without ruling out some particular counterfactual.

There is, however, at least some reason to not endorse this principle in an unrestricted form. For assuming that the space of epistemically possible worlds forms a set, it follows that in certain cases it may be that the space of epistemic possibilities is simply not large enough for this recombination principle to be satisfied.[29] However, it is worth stressing that in order for this to be so, the algebra over which the members $\mathbf{C}_i^{t'}$ are defined must be *extremely* fine-grained.

To see this, let $\mathcal{B}$ be the set of sets such that each $\mathbf{B} \in \mathcal{B}$ is such that, for each $C \in \mathbf{C}_i^{t'}$, there is exactly one proposition of the form $C \mathbin{\square\!\!\rightarrow} [EV_i^{t'} = x]$ in $\mathbf{B}$, where $C \mathbin{\square\!\!\rightarrow} [EV_i^{t'} = x]$ holds at some w, and nothing else is in $\mathbf{B}$. If, then, the space of epistemically possible worlds W forms a set and is large enough to accommodate the modal recombinations required by the instance of **Value Recombination** for $\mathbf{C}_i^{t'}$ it must be that $|W| \geq |\mathcal{B}|$.

Under what conditions, then, will it be the case that $|\mathcal{B}| > |W|$? We can determine an upper bound on the value of $|\mathcal{B}|$ as follows. Suppose that, for each $C \in \mathbf{C}_i^{t'}$ and each proposition of the form $[EV_i^{t'} = x]$, there is some w at which $C \mathbin{\square\!\!\rightarrow} [EV_i^{t'} = x]$ holds. (Now, in fact we shouldn't expect this to be the case. However, since the actual value of $|\mathcal{B}|$ will be at least as great as its value under this supposition, by determining the cardinality of $\mathcal{B}$ under this supposition we can set an upper bound for this value.) Since the cardinality of propositions of the form $[EV_i^{t'} = x]$ is $|\mathbb{R}|$, it follows, given our assumption, that $|\mathcal{B}| = |\mathbb{R}|^{|\mathbf{C}_i^{t'}|}$. And since, $|\mathbf{C}_i^{t'}| \geq |\mathbb{R}|$, we have $|\mathbb{R}|^{|\mathbf{C}_i^{t'}|} = 2^{|\mathbf{C}_i^{t'}|}$.[30] Thus, given that $|\mathbf{C}_i^{t'}| = |\mathbb{R}|^{|\mathbf{A}_i^{t'}|}$, we have that $|\mathcal{B}| = 2^{|\mathbb{R}|^{|\mathbf{A}_i^{t'}|}}$. And so, in general, we will have that $|\mathcal{B}| \leq 2^{|\mathbb{R}|^{|\mathbf{A}_i^{t'}|}}$.

Now, for present purposes, the key point to note is that, while, on the assumption that W forms a set, there will certainly be algebras $\mathbf{A}_i^{t'}$ such that $|W| < 2^{|\mathbb{R}|^{|\mathbf{A}_i^{t'}|}}$, for any algebra that an actual agent might entertain we should, I think, expect that $2^{|\mathbb{R}|^{|\mathbf{A}_i^{t'}|}}$, and so $|\mathcal{B}|$ will be *vastly* smaller than $|W|$. We should, then, expect that, in all but some unusual cases, the space of epistemic possibilities will be large enough to accommodate the combinatorial possibilities demanded by **Value Recombination**. And so, given its prima facie plausibility, I think that we should expect that in typical cases, in which the members $\mathbf{C}_i^{t'}$ are not defined over extremely fine-grained algebras, **Value Recombination** will hold.

> **Claim:** **Exponentiation** follows from **Value Recombination**.

Justification: Here is a sketch of how this result may be proved. We want to show that, given **Value Recombination**, we have that for each $\mathbf{C} \subseteq \mathbf{C}_{\geq 2}(\mathbf{C}_i^{t'})$,

---

[29] See Chalmers (2011), though, for an argument that the space of epistemically possible worlds is too large to form a set.
[30] In general, if $2 \leq \kappa \leq \lambda$ and λ is infinite, then $\kappa^\lambda = 2^\lambda$. See Jech (2000) Lemma 5.6.

$|\mathbf{ED}(\mathbf{C})| \geq 2^{|\mathbf{C}|}$. Now $2^{|\mathbf{C}|} = |\{f : f : \mathbf{C} \to \{0,1\}\}|$. To show that, for each $\mathbf{C} \subseteq \mathbf{C}_{\geq 2}(\mathbf{C}_i^{t'})$, $|\mathbf{ED}(\mathbf{C})| \geq 2^{|\mathbf{C}|}$, it suffices then to show that, for each $\mathbf{C} \subseteq \mathbf{C}_{\geq 2}(\mathbf{C}_i^{t'})$, there is an injective function $g : \{f : f : \mathbf{C} \to \{0,1\}\} \to \mathbf{ED}(\mathbf{C})$.

Let $\mathbf{C}$ be an arbitrary subset of $\mathbf{C}_{\geq 2}(\mathbf{C}_i^{t'})$. To show that there is such a function for $\mathbf{C}$, let $r(\cdot) : \mathbf{C} \to \cup\{\mathbf{ED}(\{C\}) : C \in \mathbf{C}\} \times \cup\{\mathbf{ED}(\{C\}) : C \in \mathbf{C}\}$ be a function such that $r(C) = \langle C \mapsto [EV_i^{t'} = x], C \mapsto [EV_i^{t'} = y]\rangle$, where $C \mapsto [EV_i^{t'} = x]$, $C \mapsto [EV_i^{t'} = y] \in \mathbf{ED}(\{C\})$. We let $\mathbf{R} = \{r(C) : C \in \mathbf{C}\}$. Let $\mathbf{Q}$ be the set of functions mapping elements of $\mathbf{R}$ to elements of $\cup\{\mathbf{ED}(\{C\}) : C \in \mathbf{C}\}$ that satisfy the condition that, for each $R \in \mathbf{R}$, $q(R) \in R$. Given **Value Recombination**, we have that for each $q \in \mathbf{Q}$, there is a non-empty set $P_q = \cap\{q(r(C)) : C \in \mathbf{C}\}$. Let $\mathbf{S} = \{P_q : q \in \mathbf{Q}\}$.

Now there is clearly a bijection from $\{f : f : \mathbf{C} \to \{0,1\}\}$ to $\mathbf{Q}$. And so there is a bijection from $\{f : f : \mathbf{C} \to \{0,1\}\}$ to $\mathbf{S}$. Let us pick an arbitrary bijection of this sort and call it h.

For each $S \in \mathbf{S}$, there will be a unique $\mathbf{D}_S \subseteq \mathbf{ED}(\mathbf{C})$ such that $\cup \mathbf{D}_S = S$. Moreover, for each $S, S' \in \mathbf{S}$, $\mathbf{D}_S \cap \mathbf{D}_{S'} = \emptyset$. Let $m : \mathbf{S} \to \mathbf{ED}(\mathbf{C})$ be such that $m(S) \subseteq S$. Given that, for each $S, S' \in \mathbf{S}$, $\mathbf{D}_S \cap \mathbf{D}_{S'} = \emptyset$, this function will be injective, i.e., one-to-one.

Now we let $f = m \circ h$. This function will be an injection from $\{f : f : \mathbf{C} \to \{0,1\}\}$ to $\mathbf{ED}(\mathbf{C})$.

Since **Exponentiation** follows from **Value Recombination**, and since we should expect that, in all but some unusual cases, **Value Recombination** holds, we should expect, then, that, in all but some unusual cases, **Exponentiation** holds. And, given our previous arguments, we have that, in all but some unusual cases, **Bifurcation** holds. Furthermore, since the situations in which either of these principles might fail are, I think, *highly* unusual, we should in addition expect that, in all but some unusual cases, both **Bifurcation** and **Value Recombination** will hold.

We can now show that, given that both **Bifurcation** and **Value Recombination** hold in all but some unusual cases, it follows that, if $\mathbf{C}_i^{t'}$ is the set of propositions uniquely characterizing i's possible credal distributions over $\mathbf{A}_i^{t'}$, then, in all but some very unusual cases, there will be some infinite $\mathbf{C} \subseteq \mathbf{C}_i^{t'}$ such that, for each $C \in \mathbf{C}$, there is some $A \in \mathbf{At}_i^{t'}$, for which $EU(C \cap A)$ is undefined, i.e., in all but some unusual cases **Undefinedness** holds.

> **Claim:** Bifurcation and Exponentiation entail Undefinedness.

Justification: To see this, first note that, if $\mathbf{C} \subseteq \mathbf{C}_i^{t'}$, and, for every $C \in \mathbf{C}$ and every $A \in \mathbf{At}_i^{t'}$, $EU(C \cap A)$ is well defined, then either $\mathbf{At}_i^{t'} = \mathbf{ED}(\mathbf{C})$, or $\mathbf{At}_i^{t'}$ is a fine-graining of $\mathbf{ED}(\mathbf{C})$. It follows that if $\mathbf{C} \subseteq \mathbf{C}_i^{t'}$, and, for every $C \in \mathbf{C}$ and every $A \in \mathbf{At}_i^{t'}$, $EU(C \cap A)$ is well defined, then $|\mathbf{At}_i^{t'}| \geq |\mathbf{ED}(\mathbf{C})|$.

Now suppose that $|\mathbf{C}_{\geq 2}(\mathbf{C}_i^{t'})|$ is infinite and is such that $|\mathbf{C}_{\geq 2}(\mathbf{C}_i^{t'})| \geq |\mathbf{A}_i^{t'}|$. We'll show that, given this assumption, it follows from **Exponentiation**, that there will be some infinite $\mathbf{C} \subseteq \mathbf{C}_i^{t'}$ such that, for each $C \in \mathbf{C}$, there is some $A \in \mathbf{At}_i^{t'}$, for which $EU(C \cap A)$ is undefined.

Let $\mathbf{C}' \subseteq \mathbf{C}_{\geq 2}(\mathbf{C}_i^{t'})$ be the set of $C \in \mathbf{C}_{\geq 2}(\mathbf{C}_i^{t'})$ such that $EU(C \cap A)$ is well defined, for every $A \in \mathbf{At}_i^{t'}$. Then we have that $|\mathbf{At}_i^{t'}| \geq |\mathbf{ED}(\mathbf{C}')|$. And, by **Exponentiation**, we have that $|\mathbf{ED}(\mathbf{C}')| \geq 2^{|\mathbf{C}'|}$. And so we have $|\mathbf{C}_{\geq 2}(\mathbf{C}_i^{t'})| \geq |\mathbf{At}_i^{t'}| \geq 2^{|\mathbf{C}'|}$. In general, though, if $|\Sigma|$ is infinite and $\Delta \subseteq \Sigma$ is such that $2^{|\Delta|} \leq |\Sigma|$, then $|\Sigma - \Delta|$ is infinite. If, then, we let $\mathbf{C} = \mathbf{C}_{\geq 2}(\mathbf{C}_i^{t'}) - \mathbf{C}'$, it follows that $|\mathbf{C}|$ is infinite. But, by definition, we have that for each $C \in \mathbf{C}$, there is some $A \in \mathbf{At}_i^{t'}$, such that $EU(C \cap A)$ is undefined.

Given, then, that $|\mathbf{C}_{\geq 2}(\mathbf{C}_i^{t'})|$ is infinite and is such that $|\mathbf{C}_{\geq 2}(\mathbf{C}_i^{t'})| \geq |\mathbf{A}_i^{t'}|$, it follows, given **Exponentiation**, that there will be some infinite $\mathbf{C} \subseteq \mathbf{C}_i^{t'}$ such that, for each $C \in \mathbf{C}$, there is some $A \in \mathbf{At}_i^{t'}$, for which $EU(C \cap A)$ is undefined.

Given **Bifurcation**, though, if $\mathbf{C}_i^{t'}$ is the set of propositions uniquely characterizing i's possible credal distributions over $\mathbf{A}_i^{t'}$, then $|\mathbf{C}_{\geq 2}(\mathbf{C}_i^{t'})|$ will be infinite and will be such that $|\mathbf{C}_{\geq 2}(\mathbf{C}_i^{t'})| \geq |\mathbf{A}_i^{t'}|$. It follows, then, given **Exponentiation** and **Bifurcation**, that if $\mathbf{C}_i^{t'}$ is the set of propositions uniquely characterizing i's possible credal distributions over $\mathbf{A}_i^{t'}$, then there will be some infinite $\mathbf{C} \subseteq \mathbf{C}_i^{t'}$ such that, for each $C \in \mathbf{C}$, there is some $A \in \mathbf{At}_i^{t'}$, for which $EU(C \cap A)$ is undefined. And so we have **Undefinedness**.

Given, then, that both **Bifurcation** and **Exponentiation** hold in all but some unusual cases, we have that if $\mathbf{C}_i^{t'}$ is the set of propositions uniquely characterizing i's possible credal distributions over $\mathbf{A}_i^{t'}$, then, in all but some very unusual cases, there will be an infinite $\mathbf{C} \subseteq \mathbf{C}_i^{t'}$ such that, for each t in the stable interval leading up to t', $EG_i^t(C)$ will be undefined for each $C \in \mathbf{C}$.

In §8.1, we noted that if $G_i^t(O)$ is not well defined but $ECU_i^t(O)$ is, then $Cr_i^t(\cdot)$ must be quasi-opinionated about $\mathbf{D}(\{O\}, u_i^t)$, i.e., the agent must be certain that the utility value that would obtain were O to be realized is amongst some proper subset of the set of a priori epistemically possible utility values that could be realized were O to obtain. The same principle applies in cases in which $EG_i^t(C)$ is not well defined but $EECU_i^t(O)$ is. In such cases, i must have a credal state $Cr_i^t(\cdot)$ that is quasi-opinionated about $\mathbf{ED}(\{C\})$, so that i is certain that the epistemic utility value that would obtain were C to be realized is amongst some proper subset of the set of a priori epistemically possible epistemic utility values that could be realized were C to obtain.

Given, then, that **Undefinedness** holds, in all but some unusual cases, we have that, in all but some unusual cases, if, in the stable interval leading up to t', i is not quasi-opinionated about $\mathbf{ED}(\{C\})$, for an infinite number of $C \in \mathbf{C}_i^{t'}$, then $EECU_i(\cdot)$ will not be well defined for an infinite $\mathbf{C}^U \subseteq \mathbf{C}_i^{t'}$. Given this, though, it follows from **No Credal Distinctions** that, in all but some very unusual cases, if, in the stable interval leading up to t', i is not quasi-opinionated about $\mathbf{ED}(\{C\})$, for an infinite number of $C \in \mathbf{C}_i^{t'}$, then no non-trivial deontic distinctions can be drawn amongst an agent's credal options. And so we have that, in all but some unusual cases, **Opinionation** holds.

This strikes me as a very bad result for credal consequentialism. To appreciate why this is so, it's worth stepping back and considering the general picture of rationality that a credal consequentialist theory provides.

The principle that captures the core thought behind credal consequentialism, **Credal Maximization**, is a *diachronic* principle of rationality. This principle tells us what sort of credal state it is rationally permissible or obligatory for an agent to have at a time t' given certain facts about the agent's credal state prior to t'. And the same is true of the other principles of credal consequentialism that we've considered, such as **Global Credal Dominance Permissivism**. These principles impose certain constraints on which patterns of credal states over time count as rationally permissible and which count as rationally impermissible.

It's natural to think that such diachronic principles should be supplemented by certain boundary conditions. Let us call the credal state that an agent has at the beginning of their epistemic life their **initial credal state**. It's natural, then, to think that the diachronic principles of rationality provided by credal consequentialism should be supplemented by principles that tell us which initial credal states are rationally permissible and which are rationally impermissible.

Now one prima facie plausible constraint on such boundary conditions is:

Dependence Hypothesis Neutrality: If an agent i has an initial credal state at some time t, then, for any $t' > t$, it is rationally permissible for i's credal state to be such that, for each $C \in \mathbf{C}_i^{t'}$, i is not certain that the epistemic utility value that would obtain were C to be realized is amongst some proper subset of the set of a priori epistemically possible epistemic utility values that could be realized were C to obtain.

This claim follows from a very plausible general principle that says that an agent should not be rationally required to have an initial credal state that makes them certain of some proper subset of the set of a priori epistemic possibilities.[31]

Given this plausible principle, though, we can see that the picture of credal rationality that results from credal consequentialism has some deeply implausible consequences.

Let t be the time at which i has their initial credal state. Now, given **Dependence Hypothesis Neutrality** and the dynamic principles of rationality endorsed by the proponent of credal consequentialism, for any algebra $\mathbf{A}_i^{t'}$, it should, in general, be possible for an agent to have an initial credal state at t, $Cr(\cdot)_i^t$, defined over this algebra

---

[31] Note that if the space of epistemic possibilities for an agent is uncountable in size, then it's certainly true that the agent will not be able to assign positive credence to each such possibility. What this general principle requires in such cases, though, is simply that the agent's credal density function be spread out over the whole space of epistemic possibilities and not restricted to some proper subspace.

such that there is some time $t' > t$, for which the following two conditions obtain. First, given $Cr(\cdot)_i^t$, for each $C \in \mathbf{C}_i^{t'}$, i is not certain that the epistemic utility value that would obtain were C to be realized is amongst some proper subset of the set of a priori epistemically possible epistemic utility values that could be realized were C to obtain. Second, it is rationally permissible for i to maintain $Cr(\cdot)_i^t$ as their credal state through the half-closed interval $[t, t')$.

To see this, note first that, given **Dependence Hypothesis Neutrality**, i need not be irrational in virtue of $Cr(\cdot)_i^t$ satisfying the first condition. Second, note that the diachronic principles of rationality endorsed by the proponent of credal consequentialism, such as **Credal Maximization** and **Global Credal Dominance Permissivism**, impose no constraints on i's credal state for any time $t'' < t'$, given the assumption that i's credal state satisfies the first condition. And so the diachronic principles of rationality endorsed by the proponent of credal consequentialism do not rule out $Cr(\cdot)_i^t$ satisfying the second condition, given that it satisfies the first. Of course, one might impose further conditions to rule out such cases. But it's hard to see what conditions one might appeal to here that would serve to rule out the rationality of maintaining one's initial credences in these sorts of cases that wouldn't serve to, in general, rule out the rationality of an agent maintaining their credal state over any positive interval of time. But the proponent of credal consequentialism should surely reject any such general prohibition. For principles such as **Credal Maximization** and **Global Credal Dominance Permissivism** require such stable credal states to issue any verdicts at all. The proponent of credal consequentialism, then, should allow, given **Dependence Hypothesis Regularity**, that, for any algebra $\mathbf{A}_i^{t'}$, an agent may have a credal state $Cr(\cdot)_i^t$ satisfying both of the above conditions.

We've seen, though, that, in all but a few cases, if an agent i has stable credences leading up to some time t' and i is not quasi-opinionated about $\mathbf{ED}(\{C\})$, for an infinite number of $C \in \mathbf{C}_i^{t'}$, then, for each $C \in \mathbf{C}_i^{t'}$, it is rationally permissible for i to realize C, or, for each $C \in \mathbf{C}_i^{t'}$, it is rationally impermissible for i to realize C, or, for each $C \in \mathbf{C}_i^{t'}$, it is neither rationally permissible nor rationally impermissible for i to realize C.

It follows, then, that for almost any algebra $\mathbf{A}_i^{t'}$ and agent i, there are possible situations in which, for some time t', (a) the agent starts out with rational credences defined over $\mathbf{A}_i^{t'}$ and at t' the agent may rationally adopt any possible credal state defined over $\mathbf{A}_i^{t'}$, or (b) the agent starts out with rational credences defined over $\mathbf{A}_i^{t'}$ and at t' the agent is rationally prohibited from adopting any credal state defined over $\mathbf{A}_i^{t'}$, or (c) the agent starts out with rational credences defined over $\mathbf{A}_i^{t'}$ and at t' any credal state defined over $\mathbf{A}_i^{t'}$ that the agent may adopt has no deontic status attaching to it.

Each of these options seems to me to lead to a deeply distorted picture of credal rationality. Option (a) leads to an overly permissive picture of credal rationality. According to this option, for almost every algebra $\mathbf{A}_i^{t'}$ and agent i, there are rational paths that allow an agent to adopt any credences they like no matter how bizarre.

Option (b) leads to an overly prohibitive picture of credal rationality. According to this option, for almost every algebra $\mathbf{A}_i^{t'}$ and agent i, there are rational dead-ends, whereby, given no antecedent irrationality, an agent is left with no rational options available to them. Finally, option (c) leads to a overly reticent picture of credal rationality. According to this option, for almost every algebra $\mathbf{A}_i^{t'}$ and agent i, there are gappy paths whereby a rational initial segment is guaranteed to lead to a point that simply cannot be classified as rationally permissible or impermissible.

None of these claims seems to me to be remotely plausible. We have, then, reason to be quite skeptical of the picture of credal rationality that results given the commitments of credal consequentialism.

8.3 Two Responses

I've argued that, given some plausible assumptions, credal consequentialism leads to a highly unattractive picture of credal rationality. I now want to consider two ways of resisting this argument.

8.3.1 Coarse-grained credal options

A key assumption in the preceding argument is that $\mathbf{C}_i^{t'}$—i.e., the set of propositions characterizing i's credal options—is the set of propositions uniquely characterizing i's possible credal distributions over $\mathbf{A}_i^{t'}$. For the preceding argument relied on the claim that, in typical cases, $|\mathbf{C}_{\geq 2}(\mathbf{C}_i^{t'})|$ will be infinite and will be such that $|\mathbf{C}_{\geq 2}(\mathbf{C}_i^{t'})| \geq |\mathbf{A}_i^{t'}|$. And this claim is plausible given that $\mathbf{C}_i^{t'}$ is the set of propositions uniquely characterizing i's possible credal distributions over $\mathbf{A}_i^{t'}$. For, as we noted, the set of possible credal distributions over $\mathbf{A}_i^{t'}$ will have a cardinality equal to $|\mathbb{R}|^{|\mathbf{A}_i^{t'}|}$, and so will be guaranteed to be infinite and greater than the cardinality of $\mathbf{A}_i^{t'}$. And, in typical cases, we should expect $\mathbf{C}_{\geq 2}(\mathbf{C}_i^{t'})$ to contain all but a small, non-cofinite, subset of $\mathbf{C}_i^{t'}$.

If, however, we take the members of $\mathbf{C}_i^{t'}$ to be *unions* of propositions uniquely characterizing i's possible credal distributions over $\mathbf{A}_i^{t'}$, then, at least in principle, we may restrict the size of $\mathbf{C}_i^{t'}$ so that it isn't the case that $|\mathbf{C}_{\geq 2}(\mathbf{C}_i^{t'})|$ is infinite and greater than $|\mathbf{A}_i^{t'}|$. In this way, then, one can block the preceding argument for the claim that there will be some infinite $\mathbf{C} \subseteq \mathbf{C}_i^{t'}$ such that, for each $C \in \mathbf{C}$, there is some $A \in \mathbf{At}_i^{t'}$, for which $EU(C \cap A)$ is undefined. Indeed, if the cardinality of $\mathbf{C}_i^{t'}$ is appropriately restricted, then it is easy to show that, in certain cases, the cardinality of $\mathbf{A}_i^{t'}$ may be large enough to allow that $EU(C \cap A)$ is well defined, for each $C \in \mathbf{C}_i^{t'}$ and each $A \in \mathbf{At}_i^{t'}$.[32]

---

[32] Here's a simple way of seeing this. Suppose that we take there to be two members of $\mathbf{C}_i^{t'}$. Call these C_1 and C_2. Given that we are taking epistemic utility values to be real numbers, it follows that $|\mathbf{ED}(\{C_1\})| \leq |\mathbb{R}|$ and $|\mathbf{ED}(\{C_2\})| \leq |\mathbb{R}|$. But, then, it follows that $|\mathbf{ED}(\mathbf{C}_i^{t'})| \leq |\mathbf{ED}(\{C_1\})| \times |\mathbf{ED}(\{C_2\})| \leq |\mathbb{R}|$. Thus, as

Let's consider, then, the possibility that $\mathbf{C}_i^{t'}$ may be a set of *unions* of propositions that uniquely characterize i's possible credal distributions over $\mathbf{A}_i^{t'}$. I'll argue that, while this way of developing a credal consequentialist account may allow one to block the preceding argument, it also has some undesirable consequences.

Let **C** be a set of credal options in a putative credal decision problem. We'll call a set of unions of the members of **C** a set of **coarse-grainings** of **C**, and we'll call **C** a set of **fine-grainings** of this set of unions.

Given a putative credal decision problem with a set of options **C**, we can construct an alternative credal decision problem involving a coarse-graining of this set of options. To see this, consider the following toy model:

Fine-Grained Decision: Let $\mathbf{C} = \{C_1, C_2, C_3, C_4\}$. And we let $\mathbf{ED(C)} = \{D_1, D_2\}$ where $D_1 = [C_1 \square\!\!\rightarrow [EV_i^{t'} = 5]] \cap [C_2 \square\!\!\rightarrow [EV_i^{t'} = 3]] \cap [C_3 \square\!\!\rightarrow [EV_i^{t'} = 1]] \cap [C_4 \square\!\!\rightarrow [EV_i^{t'} = 7]]$, and $D_2 = [C_1 \square\!\!\rightarrow [EV_i^{t'} = 6]] \cap [C_2 \square\!\!\rightarrow [EV_i^{t'} = 4]] \cap [C_3 \square\!\!\rightarrow [EV_i^{t'} = 2]] \cap [C_4 \square\!\!\rightarrow [EV_i^{t'} = 8]]$.

We can represent this as follows:

	D_1	D_2
C_1	5	6
C_2	3	4
C_3	1	2
C_4	7	8

Now, suppose that one claims that the credal options available to i at t' are really coarse-grainings of **C** and that, in particular, $\mathbf{C}_i^{t'} = \{C_1 \cup C_2, C_3 \cup C_4\}$. There is a straightforward way of taking the preceding credal decision problem and converting it into a credal decision problem for this new coarse-grained set of options. To do this, we divide up each of D_1 and D_2 into disjoint subspaces that determine which of the options C_1 and C_2 the agent would realize were they to realize $C_1 \cup C_2$ and which of the options C_3 and C_4 the agent would realize were they to realize $C_3 \cup C_4$.

Coarse-Grained Decision: Let $S_1 = [C_1 \cup C_2 \square\!\!\rightarrow C_1] \cap [C_3 \cup C_4 \square\!\!\rightarrow C_3]$, $S_2 = [C_1 \cup C_2 \square\!\!\rightarrow C_1] \cap [C_3 \cup C_4 \square\!\!\rightarrow C_4]$, $S_3 = [C_1 \cup C_2 \square\!\!\rightarrow C_2] \cap [C_3 \cup C_4 \square\!\!\rightarrow C_3]$, $S_4 = [C_1 \cup C_2 \square\!\!\rightarrow C_2] \cap [C_3 \cup C_4 \square\!\!\rightarrow C_4]$. Then we can let $\mathbf{ED}(\mathbf{C}_i^{t'}) = \{D_1 \cap S_1, D_1 \cap S_2, D_1 \cap S_3, D_1 \cap S_4, D_2 \cap S_1, D_2 \cap S_2, D_2 \cap S_3, D_2 \cap S_4\}$.

We can now represent the new credal decision problem for the coarse-grained set of options as follows:

---

long as $|\mathbf{At}_i^{t'}| \geq |\mathbb{R}|$, it is at least in principle possible that, for each $C \in \mathbf{C}_i^{t'}$ and each $A \in \mathbf{At}_i^{t'}$, $EU(C \cap A)$ is well defined.

	$D_1 \cap S_1$	$D_1 \cap S_2$	$D_1 \cap S_3$	$D_1 \cap S_4$	$D_2 \cap S_1$	$D_2 \cap S_2$	$D_2 \cap S_3$	$D_2 \cap S_4$
$C_1 \cup C_2$	5	5	3	3	6	6	4	4
$C_3 \cup C_4$	1	7	1	7	2	8	2	8

It's important to note that these two credal decision problems are not mere notational variants. Indeed, it may be that, given the second sort of credal decision problem, the coarse-grained option that maximizes expected epistemic utility will not include the fine-grained option that maximizes expected epistemic utility, given the first sort of credal decision problem.[33]

The key fact here is that in converting a credal decision problem involving fine-grained options into one involving coarse-grained options, one must take it that which of the fine-grained options the agent would realize were they to realize one of the coarse-grained options is an exogenous factor about which the agent may have credences but over which the agent has no control, and which serves to partly characterize the epistemic dependence hypotheses for the coarse-grained options.

Now it's a subtle and difficult question in what sense exactly it is within an agent's power to realize their credal options. If, though, one wants to maintain that an agent's credal options should be thought of as *unions* of propositions that uniquely characterize i's possible credal distributions over $\mathbf{A}_i^{t'}$, then there must be some normatively relevant sense in which it may be within an agent's powers to realize which of these unions obtains, but not within their power to realize which of the particular propositions that uniquely characterizes their credal distribution obtains.

It is, I think, far from obvious that there is any clear sense in which an agent's credal options are within their power that would allow us to draw a principled distinction here. But let us suppose that such a distinction can be drawn and so $\mathbf{C}_i^{t'}$ is a set of *unions* of propositions that uniquely characterize i's possible credal distributions over $\mathbf{A}_i^{t'}$. I'll now argue that, even given this assumption, credal consequentialism has undesirable consequences.

Assuming that $\mathbf{C}_i^{t'}$ is a set of *unions* of propositions that uniquely characterize i's possible credal distributions over $\mathbf{A}_i^{t'}$, a credal consequentialist account will, in the first instance, result in verdicts concerning which coarse-grained credal options are rationally permissible or impermissible to realize. Given such deontic verdicts, though, it is natural to ask whether one can extract deontic verdicts concerning the

---

[33] To see this consider the two toy credal decision problems outlined above. Since C_4 dominates all other options it is guaranteed to have the highest expected epistemic utility given the fine-grained credal decision problem. However, since C_3 is dominated by all the other options, if i gives sufficient credence to $S_1 \cup S_3$, i.e., to the claim that were C_3 or C_4 to be realized, C_3 would be realized, then, given the coarse-grained credal decision problem, $C_1 \cup C_2$ may maximize expected epistemic utility.

more fine-grained space of propositions uniquely characterizing i's possible credal distributions over $\mathbf{A}_i^{t'}$. I'll argue that the answer to this question is 'no'.

To this end, let me begin by considering a more specific question. Let $\mathbf{C}^P \subseteq \mathbf{C}_i^{t'}$ be the set of coarse-grained credal options that it is rationally permissible for the agent to realize. And let $\mathbf{F}^P$ be the set of propositions uniquely characterizing i's possible credal distributions over $\mathbf{A}_i^{t'}$ that fine-grain the members of $\mathbf{C}^P$. Let us, then, begin by focusing on the question of whether, given the permissibility of the members of $\mathbf{C}^P$, we can extract deontic verdicts concerning the members of $\mathbf{F}^P$. I'll argue that the answer to this question is 'no'.

First, note that if we are to extract deontic verdicts for the members of $\mathbf{F}^P$ from the deontic status of the members of $\mathbf{C}^P$, then it would seem that the only principled option is to treat all of the members of $\mathbf{F}^P$ as having the same deontic status. Thus, if we are to extract deontic verdicts for the members of $\mathbf{F}^P$ from the deontic status of the members of $\mathbf{C}^P$, then either all of the members of $\mathbf{F}^P$ must be rationally permissible to realize, or all of the members of $\mathbf{F}^P$ must be rationally impermissible to realize. However, given that $\mathbf{C}^P$ is the set of rationally permissible credal options, and that if one realizes some member of $\mathbf{C}^P$, then one must realize some member of $\mathbf{F}^P$, we should not maintain that all of the members of $\mathbf{F}^P$ are rationally impermissible to realize. If, then, we are to extract deontic verdicts for the members of $\mathbf{F}^P$ from the deontic statuses of the members of $\mathbf{C}^P$, it must be that all of the members of $\mathbf{F}^P$ are rationally permissible to realize.

There is, however, good reason to reject the claim that, given that each of the members of $\mathbf{C}^P$ is rationally permissible to realize, each of the members of $\mathbf{F}^P$ is rationally permissible to realize. And so, given this, there is good reason to think that we cannot extract deontic verdicts for the members of $\mathbf{F}^P$ from the deontic statuses of the members of $\mathbf{C}^P$.

The problem with maintaining that each of the members of $\mathbf{F}^P$ is rationally permissible to realize, given that each of the members of $\mathbf{C}^P$ is rationally permissible to realize, is that this commits us, in certain cases, to claiming that some $F \in \mathbf{F}^P$ is rationally permissible, at least in part, in virtue of the fact that i takes it to be sufficiently likely that were they to realize some coarse-grained credal option $C = F \cup \ldots$, they would not realize F, but would instead realize some other option that would result in greater epistemic utility.

To see this, suppose, as the account under consideration maintains, that the members of $\mathbf{F}^P$ are rationally permissible in virtue of the fact that each of the members of $\mathbf{C}^P$ is rationally permissible and the members of $\mathbf{F}^P$ are the fine-grainings of these permissible coarse-grained options. Now, in standard cases, the members of $\mathbf{C}^P$ will be rationally permissible in virtue of the fact that their expected epistemic utility is at least as great as any other option. But note that, amongst the fine-grainings of some $C \in \mathbf{C}^P$, there may be credal options that do very poorly with respect to epistemic utility in various circumstances. Nonetheless, it may be that C has high expected epistemic utility because i expects that were they to realize C they would not realize F, but would instead realize some other option that results in greater epistemic utility.[34] Since, then, C has high expected epistemic utility in virtue of the fact that i expects that were they to realize C they would not realize F, and since C is rationally permissible, at least in part, in virtue of the fact that it has sufficiently high expected epistemic utility, if we, in addition, say that F is rationally permissible in virtue of the fact that C is rationally permissible, we seem to be forced to say that F is rationally permissible, at least in part, in virtue of the fact that i expects that were they to realize C they would not realize F, but would instead realize some epistemically superior option.

But surely taking it to be likely that were one to realize C one would not realize F but instead would realize some epistemically superior option can't be the sort of fact that serves, even in part, to rationalize F. I think, then, that this shows that we can't, in any plausible manner, extract verdicts about the deontic status of the members of $\mathbf{F}^P$, given the permissibility of the members of $\mathbf{C}^P$, or more generally, given the deontic status of the agent's coarse-grained options.

This, of course, leaves open the question about whether we can extract verdicts concerning the deontic status of those fine-grained credal options that are not members of $\mathbf{F}^P$, given verdicts about the deontic status of various coarse-grained options. Similar considerations, though, may be used to argue that the answer to this question is also 'no'.

Let $\mathbf{C}^I = \mathbf{C}_i^{t'} - \mathbf{C}^P$ and let $\mathbf{F}^I$ be the set of propositions uniquely characterizing i's possible credal distributions over $\mathbf{A}_i^{t'}$ that fine-grain the members of $\mathbf{C}^I$. $\mathbf{C}^I$, then, is the set of coarse-grained credal options that would be rationally impermissible for i to realize, and $\mathbf{F}^I$ are the fine-grainings of this set of options.

If we are to extract deontic verdicts for the members of $\mathbf{F}^I$ from the deontic status of the members of $\mathbf{C}^I$, it would seem that the only principled option is to treat all of the members of $\mathbf{F}^I$ as having the same deontic status. If, then, we are to extract deontic verdicts for the members of $\mathbf{F}^I$ from the deontic status of the members of $\mathbf{C}^I$, then either all of the members of $\mathbf{F}^I$ must be rationally permissible to realize, or all of the members of $\mathbf{F}^I$ must be rationally impermissible to realize. However, given that $\mathbf{C}^I$ is the set of rationally impermissible credal options, and that if one realizes some member of $\mathbf{C}^I$, then one must realize some member of $\mathbf{F}^I$, we should not maintain that all of the members of $\mathbf{F}^I$ are rationally permissible to realize. If, then, we are to extract deontic verdicts for the members of $\mathbf{F}^I$ from the deontic status of the members of $\mathbf{C}^I$, then it must be that all of the members of $\mathbf{F}^I$ are rationally impermissible to realize.

---

[34] As an example of this consider the toy credal decision problem outlined earlier in this section. In this case, C_3 results in worse epistemic utility than all of the other fine-grained credal options. Nonetheless, since C_4 results in greater epistemic utility than all of the other fine-grained credal options, the coarse-grained option $C_3 \cup C_4$ could maximize expected epistemic utility if i assigns sufficiently low credence to $S_1 \cup S_3$, i.e., to the claim that were C_3 or C_4 to be realized, C_3 would be realized.

There is, however, good reason to reject the claim that, given that each of the members of $\mathbf{C}^I$ is rationally impermissible to realize, each of the members of $\mathbf{F}^I$ is rationally impermissible to realize. And so, given this, there is good reason to think that we cannot extract deontic verdicts for the members of $\mathbf{F}^I$ from the deontic status of the members of $\mathbf{C}^I$.

The problem with maintaining that each of the members of $\mathbf{F}^I$ is rationally impermissible to realize, given that each of the members of $\mathbf{C}^I$ is rationally impermissible to realize, is that this commits us, in certain cases, to claiming that some $F \in \mathbf{F}^I$ is rationally impermissible, at least in part, in virtue of the fact that i takes it to be sufficiently likely that were they to realize some coarse-grained credal option $C = F \cup \ldots$, they would not realize F, but would instead realize some other option that would result in lesser epistemic utility.

To see this, suppose, as the account under consideration maintains, that the members of $\mathbf{F}^I$ are rationally impermissible in virtue of the fact that each of the members of $\mathbf{C}^I$ is rationally permissible and the members of $\mathbf{F}^I$ are the fine-grainings of these impermissible coarse-grained options. Now, in standard cases, the members of $\mathbf{C}^I$ will be rationally impermissible in virtue of the fact that there is some set of options that maximize expected epistemic utility and the expected epistemic utility of the members of $\mathbf{C}^I$ are all less than this maximal value. But note that, amongst the fine-grainings of some $C \in \mathbf{C}^I$, there may be a credal option F that does very well with respect to epistemic utility in various circumstances. Nonetheless, it may be that C has low expected epistemic utility because the agent expects that were they to realize C they would not realize F, but would instead realize some other option that results in greater epistemic utility. Since, then, C has low expected utility in virtue of the fact that i expects that were they to realize C they would not realize F, and since C is rationally impermissible, at least in part, in virtue of the fact that it has sufficiently low expected epistemic utility, if we, in addition, say that F is rationally impermissible in virtue of the fact that C is rationally impermissible, we seem to be forced to say that F is rationally impermissible, at least in part, in virtue of the fact that i expects that were they to realize C they would not realize F, but would instead realize some epistemically inferior option.

I think, though, that taking it to be likely that were one to realize C one would not realize F but instead would realize some epistemically inferior option can't be the sort of fact that serves, even in part, to make the realization of F rationally impermissible. Now this claim may be less obvious than the claim that taking it to be likely that were one to realize C one would not realize F but instead would realize some epistemically superior option can't be the sort of fact that serves, even in part, to make the realization of F rationally permissible. But it seems to me that there is a common principle behind both of these claims that is simply more starkly illustrated in the latter case. For just as it seems plausible that an expectation that were one to realize some fine-grained option in some class, one would not realize some option F but instead some other option with certain good-making features, can't itself be the sort of good-making feature that would make the realization of *F* rationally permissible, so too should we think that an expectation that were one to realize some fine-grained option in some class, one would not realize some option *F* but instead some other option with certain bad-making features, can't itself be the sort of bad-making feature that would make the realization of *F* rationally impermissible. For in neither case does the fact in question seem to bear on *F* in the right way to either rationally support or impugn its realization.

Given the preceding, then, we should conclude that we can't, in any plausible manner, extract verdicts about the deontic status of the members of $\mathbf{F}^I$, given the permissibility of the members of $\mathbf{C}^I$, or more generally given the deontic status of the agent's coarse-grained options.

Since $\mathbf{F}^P$ and $\mathbf{F}^I$ collectively exhaust the fine-grained credal options available to an agent, and since in neither case can one extract verdicts about the deontic status of the members of these classes, given the deontic status of the agent's coarse-grained options, we should conclude that, in general, one cannot extract deontic verdicts about an agent's fine-grained credal options given deontic verdicts about the agent's coarse-grained credal options. If, then, one is a credal consequentialist and one takes $\mathbf{C}_i^{t'}$ to be a set of *unions* of propositions uniquely characterizing *i*'s possible credal distributions over $\mathbf{A}_i^{t'}$, it seems to me that one must maintain that which particular credal state one has is not something that can be assessed as rationally permissible or impermissible.

This strikes me as a bad consequence. For, at least prima facie, it would seem that an adequate theory of credal rationality should provide deontic verdicts for the particular credal states that an agent may have and not merely for classes of such states.

While, then, a proponent of credal consequentialism can block the argument presented in §8.2.2 for the claim that, in a large class of cases, no deontic distinctions can be drawn amongst an agent's credal options, by taking $\mathbf{C}_i^{t'}$ to be a set of *unions* of propositions uniquely characterizing *i*'s possible credal distributions over $\mathbf{A}_i^{t'}$, this move itself comes with significant costs.

8.3.2 *Credal quasi-consequentialism*

I've argued that the proponent of credal consequentialism should endorse **No Credal Distinctions**, given that they endorse **Credal Maximization**. The argument for this claim took the following form. First, I argued that, given **Maximization**, one should endorse **Global Dominance Permissivism**, and that, given the latter principle, one should endorse **No Distinctions**. I then noted that these arguments may be repurposed, mutatis mutandis, to argue first that, given **Credal Maximization**, one should endorse **Global Credal Dominance Permissivism**, and second that, given the latter principle, one should endorse **No Credal Distinctions**.

Now, given our characterization of credal consequentialism, we should, I think, accept this argument. For, as I've understood it here, credal consequentialism is the view that, in general, the deontic status of an agent's credal options is determined by the degree to which the agent takes such options to be conducive to the epistemic good. Given this characterization, then, the proponent of credal consequentialism should take it that the principles governing credal rationality will be the same *formally* as the principles governing practical rationality, and will differ only *materially* with respect to the relevant notion of utility and the relevant options whose deontic status is under consideration.

It is worth noting, however, that there are other views of credal rationality that may have consequentialist elements, but that don't take all credal norms to follow from a more basic norm that enjoins an agent to try to adopt credences that have the best epistemic outcomes. And, given this sort of theory of credal rationality, one might in principle accept **Credal Maximization** while rejecting **No Credal Distinctions**.

For example, consider the following theory. On this view, there are two interacting components that determine the rationality of an agent's credal state, one consequentialist, one evidential. In those cases in which an agent has an appropriate expectation value for the epistemic utility of all of their possible credal states at some time t', an agent ought, according to this theory, to adopt a credal state that maximizes this expectation value (if there are such credal states). In those cases, though, in which an agent lacks appropriate expectation values for the epistemic utility of some of their possible credal states at t', then, according to this theory, the basic norms governing the agent's credences at t' are evidential. In particular, in such cases, an agent ought to have whatever credences are mandated by the agent's evidence.

On this two-tiered view, then, **Credal Maximization** holds, but if the agent lacks appropriate expectation values for the epistemic utility of an infinite number of credal states that they may adopt at t', it need not follow that no non-trivial deontic distinctions can be drawn for such credal states. For, in such cases, facts about the agent's evidence may serve to determine non-trivial deontic distinctions. This view, then, rejects **No Credal Distinctions**, while endorsing **Credal Maximization**.

Now I think it's far from obvious that this sort of two component theory is at all plausible. For present purposes, though, the point to note is simply that, while such views may endorse **Credal Maximization** and reject **No Credal Distinctions**, strictly speaking, they are not credal consequentialist views. For, on these views, not all norms follow from a basic norm enjoining pursuit of the epistemic good.

A theory of credal rationality that appeals to consequentialist considerations, then, may avoid the arguments presented in this chapter. Doing so, however, requires rejecting the ambitious idea that credal rationality can be understood fully in consequentialist terms.

8.4 Conclusion

When we look closely at the picture of rationality provided by credal consequentialism, the results appear to be very much at odds with our pre-theoretic judgments. Not only does this account, in certain circumstances, sanction probabilistic incoherence or the acceptance of epistemic bribes, but, given plausible assumptions, in a vast range of cases, this account fails to draw any interesting deontic distinctions. This makes for a very strange and implausible picture of credal rationality.

The problem stems from the fact that, given an account of credal rationality, the most natural bearers of deontic properties—namely, the particular credal states that an agent might adopt at some time—are, given the conceptual resources available to an agent who might adopt such credal states, simply not the sorts of things about whose epistemic value an agent can, in general, have well-defined expectation values. This, I suggest, is a deep structural weakness with credal consequentialism.[35]

References

Berker, Selim. Epistemic teleology and the separateness of propositions. *The Philosophical Review*, 122: 337–93, 2013.

Caie, Michael. Belief and indeterminacy. *The Philosophical Review*, 121(1): 1–54, 2012.

Caie, Michael. Rational probabilistic incoherence. *The Philosophical Review*, 122(4): 527–75, 2013.

Caie, Michael. Calibration and probabilism. *Ergo*, 1(1): 13–38, 2014.

Caie, Michael. Credence in the image of chance. *Philosophy of Science*, 82(4): 626–48, 2015.

Campbell-Moore, Catrin. Rational probabilistic incoherence? A reply to Michael Caie. *The Philosophical Review*, 124(3): 393–406, 2015.

Carr, Jennifer. Accuracy or coherence. MS, n.d.

Chalmers, David. The nature of epistemic space. In Andy Egan and Brian Weatherson, editors, *Epistemic Modality*, pages 60–107. Oxford: Oxford University Press, 2011.

Gibbard, Allan and William Harper. Counterfactuals and two kinds of expected utility. In C. Leach, E. McClennen, and C. Hooker, editors, *Foundations and Applications of Decision Theory*, pages 125–62. Dordrecht: D. Reidel, 1978.

Goodman, Jeremy. Consequences of conditional excluded middle. MS, n.d.

Greaves, Hilary. Epistemic decision theory. *Mind*, 122(488): 915–52, 2013.

Hájek, Alan. A puzzle about degree of belief. MS, n.d.

Jech, Thomas. *Set Theory*. Dordrecht: Springer Press, 2000.

Jenkins, C. S. Entitlement and rationality. *Synthese*, 157: 25–45, 2007.

Joyce, James. A non-pragmatic vindication of probabilism. *Philosophy of Science*, 65: 575–603, 1998.

Joyce, James. *The Foundations of Causal Decision Theory*. Cambridge: Cambridge University Press, 1999.

Joyce, James. Accuracy and coherence: Prospects for an alethic epistemology of partial belief. In F. Huber and C. Schmidt-Petri, editors, *Degrees of Belief*, pages 263–98. Dordrecht: Synthese Library, 2009.

Konek, Jason and Ben Levinstein. The foundations of epistemic decision theory. *Mind*, forthcoming.

---

[35] Thanks to the editors, Jeffrey Dunn and Kristoffer Ahlstrom-Vij, and to the anonymous referees of this volume. Special thanks to Jason Konek and Cian Dorr for very helpful comments on a draft of this chapter.

Lewis, David. *Counterfactuals*. Cambridge, MA: Harvard University Press, 1973.
Lewis, David. Counterfactual dependence and time's arrow. *Noûs*, 13(4): 455–76, 1979a.
Lewis, David. Attitudes de dicto and de se. *The Philosophical Review*, 88(4): 513–43, 1979b.
Lewis, David. Causal decision theory. *Australasian Journal of Philosophy*, 59: 5–30, 1981.
Pettigrew, Richard. Accuracy, chance, and the principal principle. *The Philosophical Review*, 121(2): 241–75, 2012.
Pollock, John L. How do you maximize expectation value? *Noûs*, 17(3): 409–21, 1983.
Stalnaker, Robert. A defense of conditional excluded middle. In W. L. Harper, G. A. Pearce, and R. Stalnaker, editors, *Ifs*, pages 87–104. Dordrecht: Springer, 1981a.
Stalnaker, Robert. A theory of conditionals. In W. L. Harper, G. A. Pearce, and R. Stalnaker, editors *Ifs*, pages 41–55. Dordrecht: Springer, 1981b.
Williams, J. R. G. Defending conditional excluded middle. *Noûs*, 44(4): 650–68, 2010.

9
Making Things Right
The True Consequences of Decision Theory in Epistemology

Richard Pettigrew

In his 1998 paper, 'A Nonpragmatic Vindication of Probabilism', James M. Joyce introduced a new style of argument by which he hoped to establish the principles of rationality that govern our credences (Joyce, 1998).[1] In that paper, he used this new style of argument to offer a novel vindication of Probabilism, the principle that says that it is a requirement of rationality that an agent's credence function—which takes each proposition about which she has an opinion and assigns to it her credence in that proposition—is a probability function.[2]

Joyce's argument might be reconstructed as follows. According to Joyce, there is just one epistemically relevant source of value for credences: it is their accuracy, where we say that a credence in a true proposition is more accurate the higher it is, while a credence in a false proposition is more accurate the lower it is. Following Alvin Goldman (1999), we might call this claim *credal veritism*. Joyce then characterizes the legitimate ways of measuring the accuracy of a credence function at a given world. And he proves a mathematical theorem that shows that, whichever of the legitimate ways of measuring accuracy we use, if a credence function violates Probabilism—that is, if it is not a probability function—then there is an alternative credence function that assigns credences to the same propositions and that is more accurate than the original credence function at every possible world. Joyce then appeals to the decision-theoretic principle of dominance, which says if one option has greater value than another at every possible world, then the latter option is irrational. In combination

---

[1] An agent's credence in a proposition is the strength of her belief in that proposition; it is her degree of belief or level of confidence in it.
[2] A credence function is a probability function if (i) it assigns 0 to contradictions and 1 to tautologies, and (ii) the credence it assigns to a disjunction is the result of summing the credence it assigns to each disjunct and subtracting the credence it assigns to their conjunction.

with the mathematical theorem and the monist claim about the epistemically relevant sources of value for credences, which we have called credal veritism, the dominance principle entails Probabilism.

Thus, Joyce's argument has two substantial components besides the mathematical theorem: (i) a precise account of the epistemically relevant value of credal states; and (ii) a decision-theoretic principle. This suggests a general argument strategy: pair a mathematically precise account of epistemically relevant value for credences with a decision-theoretic principle and derive principles of credal rationality. Since that original paper, this argument strategy has been adapted to provide arguments for other principles, such as Conditionalization and the Reflection Principle (Greaves and Wallace, 2006; Easwaran, 2013; Huttegger, 2013), the Principal Principle (Pettigrew, 2012, 2013), and the Principle of Indifference (Pettigrew, 2014). For an overview, see Pettigrew (2016). In each case, the first premise—that is, the account of epistemically relevant value for credences—remains unchanged, but the second premise—the decision-theoretic principle—changes.

In this chapter, I'd like to consider an objection to Joyce's argument strategy that was raised originally by Hilary Greaves (2013).[3] In section 9.1, I state Greaves' objection; in section 9.2, I consider what I take to be the most promising existing response to it, given by Konek and Levinstein (forthcoming), and conclude that it doesn't work; in section 9.3, I offer my own response to the objection.

9.1 Greaves' Objection to Joyce

There are essentially two stages to Greaves' objection. The first stage claims that the scope of Joyce's argument—and indeed, all arguments that use the same strategy—is much more limited than he takes it to be. One response to this might be simply to limit the ambitions of this style of argument so that their conclusions fit within the scope that Greaves delineates. The second stage of the objection seeks to remove the possibility of that response: it claims that the argument strategy itself fails; it shows this by giving other versions of the argument strategy that establish intuitively wrong conclusions about credal rationality.

Let us begin with the first part of Greaves' objection. Its target is the following decision-theoretic principle, upon which Joyce's argument for Probabilism turns. We state it in full generality:

Naive Dominance Suppose $\mathcal{O}$ is a set of options, $\mathcal{W}$ is the set of possible worlds, and $\mathfrak{U}$ is a utility function, which takes an option o from $\mathcal{O}$ and a world w from $\mathcal{W}$

---

[3] It is related to an objection that Roderick Firth raised against Alvin Goldman's reliabilism (Firth, 1998). That objection has been refined and deployed against other positions by Jenkins (2007), Berker (2013a, b), Carr (2017), and Jenkins and Elstein (forthcoming).

and returns the utility $\mathfrak{U}(o, w)$ of o at w. Now, suppose o, o' are options in $\mathcal{O}$. Then, if $\mathfrak{U}(o, w) < \mathfrak{U}(o', w)$, for all w in $\mathcal{W}$, then o is irrational.

In standard practical decision theory, the options will be the actions that are available to the agent. For us, the options will be the possible credence functions. In other contexts, they might be scientific theories, for instance, as for Maher (1993). The framework is general enough to cover many different sorts of thing the rationality of which we would like to assess.

Now, in practical decision theory—where the options are actions—it is well known that Naive Dominance does not hold in full generality. It holds only when the options in question do not influence the way the world is. Here's an example to show why it needs to be restricted in this way:

Driving Test My driving test is in a week's time. I can choose now whether or not I will practise for it. Other things being equal, I prefer not to practise. But I also want to pass the test. Now, I know that I won't pass if I don't practise, and I will pass if I do. Here is my decision table:

	Pass	Fail
Practise	10	2
Don't Practise	15	7

According to Naive Dominance, it is irrational to practise, because whether I pass or fail, I will prefer not practising. But that's clearly bad reasoning. And it is bad reasoning because the options themselves determine which world will end up holding, and each option determines that a different world will hold. Thus, instead of comparing the two options at each world, we should compare them *at each world at which they are adopted*. Thus, we should compare the utility of practising at a world at which I pass— that is, 10 utiles—with the utility of not practising at a world at which I fail—that is, 7 utiles. Since the former exceeds the latter, it is irrational not to practise.

The point is that, in situations like this, the following decision-theoretic principle applies:

Causal Dominance Suppose $\mathcal{O}$ is a set of options, $\mathcal{W}$ the set of worlds, and $\mathfrak{U}$ the utility function, as before. Now, suppose o, o' are options in $\mathcal{O}$. And suppose X and X' are the strongest propositions such that $o \Rightarrow X$ and $o' \Rightarrow X'$.[4] Then, if $\mathfrak{U}(o, w) < \mathfrak{U}(o', w')$, for all worlds w in which X is true and w' in which X' is true, then o is irrational for an agent who knows both of the subjunctive conditionals.

---

[4] Here, we write '$A \Rightarrow B$' to mean *If A were the case, then B would be the case*. That is, '$\Rightarrow$' is the subjunctive conditional.

That is, an option is ruled irrational if there is another option that is guaranteed to bring about more utility.

Now, the restricted version of Naive Dominance—the version on which we apply the principle only to options that do not influence the states of the world—follows from Causal Dominance. For in the cases to which the restricted version applies, the strongest proposition that o makes true is the tautology, and similarly for o'—if o does not influence the state of the world, nothing follows about the world when we make the supposition that o is adopted. Thus, Naive Dominance applies in that restricted situation. And, Greaves concludes, Joyce's argument will thus also have this limited range of application. That is, it will establish Probabilism only for agents whose credences have no influence on the way the world is that is relevant to the truth values of the propositions to which they assign credences.

Thus, the first part of Greaves' objection is simply this: Joyce's argument establishes Probabilism only in certain cases, namely, those in which the credal state of the agent does not influence the truth of the propositions on which her credences are defined. Now, if this were the full extent of the objection, we might be willing to bite the bullet. After all, in nearly all cases of interest, the condition is satisfied. Much Bayesian epistemology is carried out in the interests of understanding rational principles for reasoning in science; and there our credences have no impact upon the truth of the propositions to which we assign those credences.

However, there is a second part to Greaves' objection. Joyce's strategy is to give an account of epistemically relevant value—it is accuracy and only accuracy—and then apply decision-theoretic principles to establish principles of credal rationality. The second part of Greaves' objection is that this strategy cannot establish any such principles because, when applied to certain situations—situations of the sort to which Causal Dominance applies, but Naive Dominance does not—it produces conclusions that are counterintuitive and therefore false. The idea is that a particular instance of an argument strategy cannot on its own establish a conclusion if other instances of that same argument strategy have conclusions that are false. It's a proves-too-much objection. Compare: naive utilitarianism entails that a wealthy European should give money to charity, but it does not establish this conclusion. Why? Because naive utilitarianism also entails that you should harvest the organs of a single innocent person to save the lives of some number of people, and you should not do that. Here's the sort of example that Greaves has in mind—this particular case is adapted from an example given by Michael Caie (2013).

Basketball 1   Rachel has credences only in two propositions, B and its negation $\overline{B}$, where $B = $ *There will be a basketball in the garage five minutes from now*. But Rachel's mischievous older sister Anna, who is in possession of the only basketball in the vicinity, is out to thwart her younger sister's accuracy. Anna will put a basketball in the garage five minutes from now if, and only if, Rachel's current credence that there will be a basketball in the garage five minutes from now is less than 0.5. That is, Anna will make it so that B is true iff Rachel's credence in B is less than 0.5.[5] And Rachel knows all of this.

This example is an epistemic analogue of Driving Test. Suppose c and c' are two possible credence functions, both defined on B and $\overline{B}$, that Rachel might adopt. Then, just as we should not assess the utility of the possible actions *Practise* and *Don't Practise* at both the *Pass*-world and the *Fail*-world and then ask whether one is better than the other at both, it seems that we also should not assess the accuracy of c and c' at both the B-world and the $\overline{B}$-world and ask whether one is more accurate than the other at both. After all, just as practising my driving rules out the *Fail*-world and not practising rules out the *Pass*-world, so Rachel having credence function c will rule out one of the worlds—it will rule out the B-world if $c(B) \geq 0.5$, and it will rule out the $\overline{B}$-world if $c(B) < 0.5$. And similarly for c'. So, instead, we should compare the accuracy of c at *the world it leaves open if adopted* with the accuracy of c' *at the world it leaves open if adopted*. Thus, we are not in one of the situations in which the restricted version of Naive Dominance applies; we should instead use Causal Dominance. Or so says Greaves' objection.

Now, it is easy to see that, in this case, Causal Dominance entails that all but the following credence function are irrational for Rachel: $c^\dagger(B) = 0.5$, $c^\dagger(\overline{B}) = 1$. The reason is that the set up of the case ensures that, however Rachel picks her credence in B, she knows whether it is less that 0.5 or not, and so she can then set her credence in $\overline{B}$ in such a way as to make it perfectly accurate. So, to maximize the accuracy that her credence function will bring about, she need only find a way to pick her credence in B so that it will be as accurate as it can be. The set up of the case prevents her from having a credence in B that enjoys full accuracy, but setting her credence in B to 0.5 provides greatest accuracy amongst the options available to her—any higher and B would still be false, but her credence in it would be higher; any lower and B would then be true, but then the credence would be further from 1 than 0.5 is from 0.[6]

However, $c^\dagger$ violates Probabilism: the credences it assigns to B and $\overline{B}$ sum to 1.5, whereas Probabilism demands that they sum to 1. So, by Joyce's mathematical theorem, it is accuracy dominated: that is, there is an alternative credence function c^* that is more accurate than $c^\dagger$ whether or not there is a basketball in the garage.[7] However, just as the fact that not practising in Driving Test has greater utility than practising whether or not I pass does not render practising irrational, so the fact that c^* is more accurate than $c^\dagger$ whether or not there is a basketball in the garage does not render $c^\dagger$ irrational. After all, any such accuracy-dominating credence function is less accurate at any world *in which it is Rachel's credence function* than $c^\dagger$ is at any world *in*

---

[5] Thus, if c_R is Rachel's credence function, we have: (i) $c_R(B) < 0.5 \Rightarrow B$; and (ii) $c_R(B) \geq 0.5 \Rightarrow \overline{B}$.
[6] This conclusion is based on very minimal assumptions about measures of accuracy: (i) only credence 1 in a truth or 0 in a falsehood have maximal accuracy; (ii) the accuracy of credence r in a truth is the same as the accuracy of credence $1 - r$ in a falsehood.
[7] If we measure accuracy using the Brier score, then the credence function $c^*(B) = 0.25$, $c^*(\overline{B}) = 0.75$ is one of the many that accuracy dominate $c^\dagger$.

which it is Rachel's credence function. So the decision-theoretic principle that applies in this situation—namely, Causal Dominance—does not rule $c^\dagger$ out as irrational, while it does in fact rule c^* out as irrational, and similarly for all other credence functions besides $c^\dagger$.

Now, according to Greaves, $c^\dagger$ is intuitively rationally prohibited, while c^* is intuitively rationally permitted. Thus, this particular application of Joyce's argument strategy issues in a conclusion that is intuitively wrong. For this reason, Greaves concludes that, absent a principled distinction between this instance of Joyce's argument strategy and the sort of instance to which Joyce appeals, no such instance of that strategy establishes its conclusions, including the instances mentioned in the introduction that purport to establish Probabilism, Conditionalization, the Reflection Principle, the Principal Principle, and the Principle of Indifference.[8]

9.2 Konek and Levinstein's Response to Greaves

Konek and Levinstein (forthcoming) offer a response to Greaves' objection. According to them, whether we must restrict the Naive Dominance principle or not depends on the nature of the options whose rationality we are using it to assess. If those options are possible practical actions—such as the actions of practising or not practising, as in Driving Test—then, they say, we are right to restrict its application to those cases in which the options do not influence the way the world is. Indeed, in those cases, they say, it is correct to use Causal Dominance instead. If, on the other hand, the options whose rationality we are assessing are credal states, as in Basketball 1, then there is no need to restrict Naive Dominance—it applies, Konek and Levinstein contend, even when the credal states we are assessing influence the state of the world. Thus, they say that, in Basketball 1, $c^\dagger$ is irrational, because, as Joyce's mathematical theorem shows, there are credence functions—such as c^*—that are more accurate than $c^\dagger$ regardless of whether B is true or false.

To justify their different treatment of practical actions, on the one hand, and credal states, on the other, Konek and Levinstein point to the well-known thesis that beliefs—indeed, doxastic states more generally—have a different "direction of fit" from desires—or, at least, actions as the mechanism by which we try to fulfil those desires. Beliefs, so this thesis goes, have a mind-to-world direction of fit, whereas desires and the actions that seek to fulfil them have a world-to-mind direction of fit (Anscombe, 1957). As it stands, this slogan is too metaphorical. Konek and Levinstein make it precise by giving it the sort of evaluative reading that Anscombe herself suggests. We evaluate actions according to their success at changing the world to bring it into line with the desires that they attempt to fulfil; but we evaluate beliefs according to their success at representing the world as it is. That is, we consider an

---

[8] The instances of the argument strategy that purport to establish these principles do not appeal to Naive Dominance; but they do appeal to other decision-theoretic principles that, like Naive Dominance, are only true in those cases in which the options involved do not influence the way the world is.

action to have done better the closer it has brought the world in line with our desires; but we consider a belief to have done better the closer it has brought itself in line with the way the world is.

Condensing Konek and Levinstein's discussion a little, this claim is spelled out formally as follows. Suppose I have probability function p, and I am evaluating option o from the doxastic point of view represented by that probability function. We know the value of o relative to a given possible world w—it is $\mathfrak{U}(o, w)$. But what about its value relative to p? If o is an option, such as an action, that has world-to-mind direction of fit, Konek and Levinstein say that I should assign it value as follows:

$$V_p^{CDT}(o) := \sum_{w \in \mathcal{W}} p(w \,||\, o) \mathfrak{U}(o, w)$$

where $p(w \,||\, o)$ is the probability of world w under the subjunctive supposition that o is chosen. The reason is that I value option o for its ability to bring about good outcomes—that's why I weight the utility of o given some possible world w by $p(w \,||\, o)$, which we might think of as the power of o to bring about w. Now, notice that this is the causal decision theorist's account of the value of an option o relative to a probability function p, hence the 'CDT' in the subscript (Joyce, 1999). We will call this the *CDT Account of Value* (or CDT for short).

Now, given an account of the value of options relative to probability functions—any such account, the casual decision theorist's or some other—we have a basic principle of decision theory that relates those values to ascriptions of (ir)rationality:

Value-Rationality Principle Suppose $\mathcal{O}$ is a set of options, $\mathcal{W}$ the set of worlds, and $\mathfrak{U}$ the utility function, as before. And suppose p is a probability function. Now suppose o, o' are options in $\mathcal{O}$. Then, if the value of o relative to p is less than the value of o' relative to p, then o is irrational for an agent with credence function p.

Now, notice that the principle Causal Dominance that we introduced above is a consequence of Value-Rationality Principle + CDT. If our agent knows that $o \Rightarrow X$, and X is false at w, then $p(w \,||\, o) = 0$; so the utility of o at w makes no contribution to $V_p^{CDT}(o)$. Thus, if o has lower utility at all worlds that it doesn't rule out than o' has at all worlds that it doesn't rule out, then for any probability function p that reflects the known causal structure of the situation, $V_p^{CDT}(o) < V_p^{CDT}(o')$. So o is irrational for someone with credence function p. And thus o is irrational, regardless of credence function. This is Konek and Levinstein's account of the value of an option relative to a probability function for options that have world-to-mind direction of fit.

Next, here is Konek and Levinstein's account of the value of an option for options that have mind-to-world direction of fit. If o is such an option, and p is my probability function, I should assign it value as follows:

$$V_p^{NDT}(o) := \sum_{w \in \mathcal{W}} p(w) \mathfrak{U}(o, w).$$

In this account of value, the ability of the option to bring about worlds is not taken into account. The reason is that, given their evaluative reading of the direction-of-fit considerations, option *o* is not valued for its ability to bring about better outcomes; it is valued for its ability to reflect the way the world is. This is the naive decision theorist's account of the value of an option, which we call the *NDT Account of Value* (or NDT for short). In this case, we note that unrestricted Naive Dominance is a consequence of Value-Rationality Principle + NDT.

Thus, Konek and Levinstein's claim that Naive Dominance need not be restricted when the options are credence functions or other doxastic states follows from their different accounts of how to value options with different directions of fit—namely NDT and CDT—together with their claim that doxastic states, such as credences, have mind-to-world direction of fit. If they are right, both parts of Greaves' objection are answered: we need not restrict the application of Naive Dominance in Joyce's vindication of Probabilism, and thus we need not restrict the conclusion; and the apparently counterintuitive consequences of certain instances of Joyce's argument strategy are not consequences of those instances after all, whether or not they are counterintuitive.

Unfortunately, I don't think Konek and Levinstein can be right. This is for two reasons. The first might be called *the stoicism objection*; the second *the normative force objection*. Let's begin with the stoicism objection. According to Konek and Levinstein, actions have world-to-mind direction of fit: that is, an action is evaluated in accordance with its success at bringing the world into line with the agent's desires. But, while this is a rough-and-ready rule, there are philosophers who take it to have exceptions. Consider, for instance, the Stoic. She thinks that, at least sometimes, we should evaluate acts in accordance with their success at bringing our desires into line with the world. That is, sometimes, we should aim to change our desires to fit the world, rather than trying to change the world to fit our desires. If I live in Bristol and have a strong desire for sun, I might move to a sunnier city; but I might equally change my desire so that I come to desire copious rain and relentless cloud cover. Similarly, even if I don't currently desire the changes in my life that would result if I were to adopt a child, I might nonetheless adopt a child in the knowledge that, having done so, my desires will change in such a way that I will come to value those changes in my life that currently I do not desire (Paul, 2014). And indeed there will be cases in which changing my desires is the rational thing to do (Bykvist, 2006; Pettigrew, 2015). If I consider my current desires and my potential future desires both to be within the realms of the permissible, and if I know that I will be better able to fulfil my potential future desires than I will be able to fulfil my current desires, then it seems that I might be rationally compelled to change my desires to the potential future desires. The upshot of these considerations is this: desires and the actions that attempt to bring them to fulfilment can sometimes have mind-to-world direction of fit, contrary to the slogan to which Konek and Levinstein appeal. But if that's the case, what reason is there to think that, in cases such as Basketball 1, the credal states in question do not have world-to-mind direction of fit, and are thus appropriately evaluated using V^{CDT} rather than V^{NDT}? If sometimes we should shape our desires in order to make them easier to satisfy in the world we inhabit, perhaps sometimes we should shape the world we inhabit in order to make it possible to represent it more accurately using our doxastic state.

So much, then, for the stoicism objection. It claims that, *at least sometimes*, it is rationally required to have credal states that bend the world to our representation of it, just as it is sometimes rationally required to perform actions that bend our desires to the world's ability to fulfil them. In those situations, it is rationally required to evaluate credal states using V^{CDT} rather than V^{NDT}. According to the second objection, which is an amalgamation of objections raised first by Jennifer Carr (2017) and Brian Talbot (2014), it is *always* rationally required to evaluate credal states using V^{CDT} rather than V^{NDT}.

Here's one way to state the objection, which draws on Jennifer Carr's work. If we evaluate credal states using V^{NDT}, and if we follow the Value-Rationality Principle, then our principles of rationality will violate the following plausible meta-normative principle:

> *The Irrelevance of Impossible Utilities* The rational status of an option—whether it is rationally permissible, prohibited, or mandated—does not depend upon its utility or the utilities of other options at worlds at which those options could not possibly be adopted.

If, on the other hand, we evaluate credal states using V^{CDT}, and if we follow the Value-Rationality Principle, then our principles of rationality will not violate The Irrelevance of Impossible Utilities. The problem with the account of rationality that grows out of Value-Rationality Principle + NDT is that, whichever credence function Rachel adopts in Basketball 1, its rational status will depend crucially on the accuracy that her credal state enjoys at worlds at which she could not possibly have that credal state. Suppose, for instance, she has credence function $c^\dagger$. (Recall: $c^\dagger(B) = 0.5$; $c^\dagger(\overline{B}) = 1$.) Then, as noted above, according to Naive Dominance—which is a consequence of Value-Rationality Principle + NDT, and advocated by Konek and Levinstein—her credal state is accuracy dominated by c^*. That is, c^* is more accurate than $c^\dagger$ if B is true and $\overline{B}$ is false; and c^* is more accurate than $c^\dagger$ if B is false and $\overline{B}$ is true. But this fact depends on the particular accuracy of $c^\dagger$ at a B-world, where it could not possibly be adopted, and the particular accuracy of c^* at a $\overline{B}$-world, where it could not possibly be adopted. Thus, if we conclude from this that $c^\dagger$ is irrational, that conclusion depends on the utilities of $c^\dagger$ and c^* at worlds at which they could not possibly be adopted—if their utilities at those worlds were different, it may be that c^* would not dominate $c^\dagger$. And that violates our meta-normative principle.

Now, I think that there is a way of reading Konek and Levinstein's account that avoids this objection. However, as we will see, the adaptation runs into a further problem. They draw a distinction between *epistemic acts* and *epistemic states*, and they hold that these should be evaluated in different ways. Epistemic acts, such as Rachel's act of adopting $c^\dagger$ in Basketball 1, for instance, have world-to-mind direction of fit—as indeed do all acts—and thus should be evaluated using V^{CDT}. On the other hand, epistemic states, such as the credal state $c^\dagger$, have mind-to-world direction of fit and should be evaluated using V^{NDT}. Now, this can't be quite right. After all, it is not the act of adopting a credal state c with $c(B) < 0.5$ that causes Anna to put the basketball in the garage, thereby making B true. It is simply Rachel being in that credal state, *however she ended up like that*, that has the causal effect. So, if simply being in the credal state has the causal power itself, then it should be evaluated using V^{CDT}, in line with our meta-normative principle, The Irrelevance of Impossible Utilities. However, there is a further distinction to be drawn between the epistemic state *as instantiated* in a particular agent, such as Rachel, at a particular time, such as the time at which Anna reads her mind and determines whether or not to put the basketball in the garage, on the one hand, and the epistemic state *itself*, considered abstractly, perhaps as a property that might be possessed by any number of agents and is at the moment possessed by Rachel, on the other. Now, this latter entity—the abstract state itself, perhaps considered as a property, or perhaps considered in some other way—does not have any causal power: only its instances have causal power. Thus, it is in keeping with The Irrelevance of Impossible Utilities to evaluate it using V^{NDT}. Indeed, since it has no causal powers, there is no difference between evaluating it using V^{NDT} or using V^{CDT}: if c is taken to be the abstract credal state, rather than an instance of it, then $p(w \mid\mid c) = p(w)$ for any world w. Thus, we might understand Konek and Levinstein's account as follows, in line with The Irrelevance of Impossible Utilities. What we primarily evaluate for rationality is the abstract credal state. Since this is an abstract state, it does not on its own influence the way the world is. So it is appropriate to apply Naive Dominance. This tells us that the abstract state corresponding to $c^\dagger$ is accuracy dominated by the abstract state corresponding to c^*, and thus $c^\dagger$ is irrational. Having evaluated the rationality of the abstract state corresponding to $c^\dagger$, we are now in a position to evaluate the rationality of one of its instances, namely, Rachel's instantiation of that state in Basketball 1. To do this, we use a bridge principle, which says that it is irrational to instantiate an abstract credal state that is itself irrational. However, to borrow Brian Talbot's terminology, the problem with such an account of rationality is that it lacks "normative force" (Talbot, 2014). While it might well issue in pronouncements on rationality that accord well with our intuitions—and Konek and Levinstein argue that their account does give the intuitive answer in each case that they consider—it is hard to see on this account why an agent should care about being rational in this sense. Suppose Rachel's credence function is $c^\dagger$. Why should she care that there is another credence function c^* such that the abstract state corresponding to c^* is guaranteed to be more accurate than the abstract state corresponding to $c^\dagger$? What she cares about is the accuracy of her own credal state, not the accuracy of the abstract credal of which it is a particular instance. Another way to make this point: we would never wish to give an analogous account of the rationality of an action. For any action

I might perform, there is an abstract action—the property, perhaps, of performing the action. Suppose that I suggested that we assess the rationality of an agent's action by first assessing the rationality of the abstract action that corresponds to it; and suppose that I suggested that we assess the rationality of that abstract correlate by comparing its utility to the utility of other abstract correlates of particular actions. You would recognize that this allows me to categorize particular actions by particular agents in particular situations as rational or not. But it would immediately drain the resulting notion of rationality of any normative force—why should I care about the utility of the abstract correlate of my action? This, then, is the *normative force objection* against Konek and Levinstein's proposal.

What's more, independent of considerations of normative force, the foregoing reveals a disanalogy between the epistemic case and the practical case that cannot be accounted for by appealing to considerations of direction of fit. Why, in the epistemic case, should we evaluate the rationality of an agent indirectly, by first evaluating the rationality of the abstract credal state she instantiates, while, in the practical case, we evaluate the rationality of an agent performing an action directly, via an evaluation of the abstract act of which her concrete action is an instance? Konek and Levinstein's account must explain this asymmetry, and direction-of-fit considerations do not seem to speak to it.

9.3 An Error Theory for our Intuitions

Konek and Levinstein's proposed response to Greaves' objection to Joyce's argument strategy is, I think, the best available. However, it fails. It is based on considerations of direction of fit that don't seem compelling enough to support the conclusion—this is the stoicism objection. And, once adapted to avoid that objection, it issues in a notion of rationality about which we have little reason to care—this is the normative force objection. Thus, we must seek another response to Greaves' objection.

The second stage of Greaves' objection has two parts: the first says that, in cases such as Basketball 1, Joyce's argument strategy issues in certain conclusions; the second says that those conclusions are counterintuitive and therefore false. Konek and Levinstein's response denies the first objection; my response denies the second. Now, I do not deny that the conclusions are counterintuitive; rather, I deny that we should infer from this that they are false. Since I wish to say that our intuitions are wrong in this case, I need to give an error theory. And that is what I will try to provide in this section.

9.3.1 *The requirements of an error theory*

An error theory for a class of intuitive judgments consists of two components: first, the claim that those judgments are mistaken; second, an explanation of why we make them all the same. However, first, let me address a natural initial reaction to my offer to provide an error theory for our intuitive judgments about the rational status of particular credal states in specific situations. Why does the fact that those judgments are mistaken call for explanation in the first place? After all, no one demands an explanation when I claim that our intuitive judgments about certain fundamental features of the physical universe are mistaken—our intuitive judgment that every event must have a cause, for instance, or that there is no action at a distance, or that, for every physical entity and every physical property, it is a determinate matter of fact whether the entity does or does not have that property. We simply accept that science is hard. It requires detailed and elaborate empirical investigation of the world, as well as ingenious formulation of hypotheses that explain the results of that investigation—no wonder intuitive judgments are sometimes wildly wrong! Surely the same is true of our intuitive judgments about the rationality of particular credal states in specific situations. Credal epistemology is hard: it requires extensive theorizing about what grounds facts about the rational status of certain states, and how to describe those grounds precisely enough that we might derive substantial conclusions from the description. This is certainly true. However, the intuitive judgments I am claiming to be mistaken do not concern the grounds of facts about rationality. They concern particular judgments concerning rationality in specific cases. And these sorts of intuitive judgment we should expect ourselves to get right, at least most of the time. Likewise, we don't expect ourselves to be able to intuit the fundamental features of the physical universe, but we do expect to be reliable in our intuitive judgments about what will happen in specific physical cases, such as when I release a rubber ball at the top of an incline, or a cat pushes a glass of water off a table onto a concrete floor. The reason we expect to be right in our particular judgments concerning rationality in specific cases is that we take ourselves to be, on the whole, rational creatures; or, at least, we take ourselves to adopt the rational response to a situation with reasonable reliability, given sufficient time to consider it. If that is correct, then my claim that we are mistaken in our intuitive ascriptions of rational status to the various possible credal states in Basketball 1 calls for explanation. How can we reliably adopt rational responses to the situations we encounter whilst making incorrect judgments in cases such as Basketball 1?

The error theory I will offer shares certain structural features with the error theories that are offered for our flawed intuitive judgments in the literature on cognitive fallacies and bias, such as implicit bias, base rate fallacy, etc. (Kahneman and Tversky, 1972). In particular, I will claim that we employ a *heuristic* when we make intuitive judgments about the rational status of credal states in given situations. That is, instead of assessing the rationality of such a state by considering the true grounds for rationality and basing our judgment on the results of that consideration, we instead base our judgment on some other consideration that is not directly related to the true ground. However, if the heuristic is a good one, the judgments to which it gives rise track the correct judgments in a large proportion of the cases we encounter most often. And if positing the heuristic is going to help provide an error theory for the mistaken judgments, it will have to track our incorrect intuitive judgments in those cases as well. Thus, when we provide an error theory by positing a heuristic, we must do three things:

1. Establish that the heuristic gives the correct judgment in all the cases in which our intuitive judgments are correct.
2. Establish that the heuristic gives the same incorrect judgment that we give in all the cases in which our intuitive judgments are mistaken.
3. Establish that employing the heuristic has advantages over the strategy of simply basing our judgments on a consideration of the true grounds of rationality; and establish that those advantages outweigh the disadvantages of issuing mistaken judgments in the cases covered by (2).

9.3.2 The evidentialist heuristic

We begin by describing the heuristic, which I call the *evidentialist heuristic*:

> *Evidentialist heuristic*   When we assess the rationality of an agent's credal state in a given situation, we ask whether each credence she assigns matches the extent to which her evidence supports the proposition to which she assigns it. If it does, the credal state is rationally permissible; if not, it is prohibited. In some cases, the extent to which the evidence supports a proposition is vague, with a number of different acceptable precisifications: in these cases, any credal state whose credences match the degrees of evidential support encoded in one of those precisifications is rationally permissible.

Thus, our heuristic posits something like the evidential or logical probabilities that have been championed in a tradition beginning with Keynes and leading through Carnap to Timothy Williamson and Patrick Maher (Keynes, 1921; Carnap, 1950; Williamson, 2000; Maher, 2006). These are thought to provide an objective measure of the degree to which one proposition or set of propositions supports another. For these authors and, I think, for the measure that undergirds the heuristic we use when we make assessments of rationality, the degree of evidential support is a function only of the body of evidence and the proposition whose support we are measuring—the degree does not depend on the agent whose body of evidence it is. The idea is that this notion of evidential probability or degree of evidential support is taken to be primitive; but there are a number of basic principles that, intuitively, we take to hold of this notion, and they guide us in our assessments of the rationality of an agent's credal state in a given evidential situation. For instance, we think that, if evidence E supports X more strongly than it supports Y, then E supports $\overline{Y}$ more strongly than it supports $\overline{X}$. And we think that, if E entails that the chance of X is r, and entails nothing more about X, then E supports X to degree r. And so on. Intuitively, we take these basic principles to support certain general principles of credal rationality, such as Probabilism, the Principal Principle, the Principle of Indifference, and so on. It seems natural to say that tautologies receive maximal evidential support from any body of evidence; and contradictions receive minimal evidential support; and it seems natural to say that the disjunction to two mutually exclusive propositions receives as evidential support the sum of the support that each of its disjuncts receive. And this gives us Probabilism. And so on. None of these arguments is watertight, of course—but that is the nature of heuristics used for intuitive judgments. And in any case, the notion of evidential support to which they ascribe these properties is taken to be primitive; so it would not be possible to give a watertight argument from more basic principles. On this view, principles such as Probabilism, the Principal Principle, etc. are judged to be general principles of rationality because they hold regardless of the nature of the evidence that the agent has. Thus, any agent with any evidence whatsoever will be judged irrational by the lights of the evidentialist heuristic if she violates any one of these principles.

9.3.3 The evidentialist heuristic in the normal cases

Now, let's turn to tasks (1), (2), and (3) from above. To complete (1), we need to explain why appeal to the evidentialist heuristic will give the correct verdicts in the normal cases, namely, those in which the agent's credal state does not influence the world in any way that affects the accuracy of that credal state. This is not obvious. Indeed, it might be seen as the conclusion of the past fifteen years of work on the consequences of Joyce's argument strategy. As mentioned above, during that period, instances of Joyce's argument strategy have been given in favour of various intuitively plausible principles of rationality, such as Probabilism, the Principal Principle, the Principle of Indifference, etc. What's more, what is sometimes surprising about those results is that the principles in question seem to be those that are most naturally justified on the basis of evidentialist considerations, rather than the veritistic considerations deployed in the instances of Joyce's argument strategy. Indeed, they are precisely the rules of thumb to which I said our evidentialist heuristic would appeal when assessing the rationality of a credal state. Now, of course, in line with the Value-Rationality Principle + CDT, which I take to provide the correct account of the rationality of an agent's credal state, the instances of Joyce's argument strategy establish Probabilism, the Principal Principle, etc. only in the normal cases, where the agent's credal state does not influence the world. But those are exactly the cases we are considering under (1) here. Thus, we can see this string of results as showing that evidentialist considerations of the sort that our heuristic endorses match up with the consequences of credal veritism, at least in the normal cases. And this strongly supports (1).

We gain further support for (1) when we consider cases where the body of evidence is large and diverse. Take, for instance, the proposition that Hillary Clinton will become the 45th President of the United States. I have a vast and extremely varied body of evidence that bears on this proposition: it comes from polls, the outcomes of past elections, the content of Clinton's speeches, the content of her opponent's speeches, the reactions on social media, whom she chooses as her running mate, and so on. The rules of thumb listed above give me only weak guidance when I try to pin down the range of credences that are supported by this evidence; and other rules of thumb do not provide much further help—there are no very precise rules concerning how to weigh different sorts of evidence (testimonial, statistical, first-hand) against each other. As a result, the evidentialist heuristic is difficult to apply in this case—it will not give an unequivocal answer. Thus, if I am right that it is this heuristic that we use to assess the rationality of a credal attitude to that proposition, we should expect that it would be equally difficult to come to a settled judgment about the rationality of any such attitude. And that is, in fact, exactly what we find. We find people debating furiously over exactly such judgments of rationality: people will accuse their evidential peers of having 'unrealistic', or 'unreasonable', or 'overly optimistic', or 'overly pessimistic' attitudes towards Clinton's prospects. And all of these are rationality judgments. That is, just as my error theory predicts, there is widespread disagreement over the rationality of credal states in cases of substantial and diverse evidence.[9]

9.3.4 *The evidentialist heuristic in the pathological cases*

What about (2)? Of course, it is difficult to establish that the heuristic described above agrees with our intuitive judgments in every case in which the credal state of the agent influences the way the world is. But I will consider three such cases in which it does return the correct answer. I take these to be representative. The first case is Basketball 1, which we have already described; the second and third are two sequels to Basketball 1. Here is the first sequel—it is analogous to Greaves' Leap case (Greaves, 2013, 916):

> *Basketball 2*   It is two hours later. Rachel now has credences only in one proposition: $B =$ *There will be a basketball in the garage five minutes from now*. She has lost interest in its negation. Rachel's younger brother Josh, today less mischievously disposed than their sister Anna, is now in possession of the basketball in question. He is keen to help his sister's accuracy. Josh is more likely to put the basketball in the garage five minutes from now the more strongly Rachel believes that it will be in the garage at that time. More precisely, for any $0 \leq r \leq 1$, the chance of B is r iff Rachel's credence in B is r. Rachel knows all of this.

Our intuitive reaction to Basketball 2 is this: any credence $0 \leq r \leq 1$ in B is rationally permissible for Rachel. However, the verdict of credal veritism together with Value-Rationality Principle + CDT is that all but credence 0 and 1 are rationally prohibited for her. After all, by having credence 0 in B, she thereby makes the chance that it is true 0, so she is guaranteed to be maximally accurate. And similarly, if she has credence 1 in B, she thereby makes the chance that it is true 1, so again she is guaranteed to be maximally accurate. On the other hand, if she has

---

[9] Thanks to Jeff Dunn for urging me to consider cases of large and diverse bodies of evidence.

credence $0 < r < 1$ in B, then she guarantees that her credence is not maximally accurate.

In this case, it is clear that our evidentialist heuristic agrees with our intuitions and not with the consequences of credal veritism here. In the case in question, and indeed in all cases in which the agent's credences influence the way the world is, the agent's credal state itself creates some of the agent's evidence. By adopting credence r in B, she creates the evidence that the chance of B is r. But recall that she thereby guarantees that her credence in B matches the strength of support given to B by her newly created evidence, in line with the Principal Principle. Thus, if all that matters is that an agent has credences that match the degree of support provided by her evidence, then picking any credence $0 \leq r \leq 1$ will be rationally permissible.

Here is the second sequel to Basketball—it is analogous to Greaves' Imps case:

Basketball 3 It is now four hours later. Josh is standing in front of Rachel. Rachel has credences in five propositions: $J = $ *Josh is standing in front of me*; $B_g = $ *There will be a basketball in the garage*; $B_b = $ *There will be a basketball in the bedroom*; $B_d = $ *There will be a basketball in the dining room*; $B_l = $ *There will be a basketball in the lounge*. Anna is being mischievous again and this time she has four basketballs. If Rachel has credence greater than 0 in J, then Anna will flip a fair coin for each of the basketball propositions about which Rachel has an opinion, and she will use this coin toss to decide whether or not to make that proposition true by placing a basketball in the room in question. On the other hand, if Rachel has credence 0 in J, then Anna will ensure that all four propositions about the basketballs are true by placing a basketball in each room. Rachel knows all of this.

Our intuitive reaction to Basketball 3 is this: we should have some high credence in J, and then credence 0.5 in each of the propositions concerning the basketballs. However, given many of the standard measures of accuracy, credal veritism, together with the Value-Rationality Principle + CDT, entails that the credences recommended by our intuition are in fact irrational, because there are other credences Rachel might have that are guaranteed to be more accurate. They are these: she assigns credence 0 to J and 1 to each of the basketball propositions. Now, while her credence of 0 in J will be maximally inaccurate, since Josh is indeed standing in front of her, her credences in each of the basketball propositions will be maximally accurate. On the other hand, if she follows our intuitive judgment and assigns high credence to J, then that will be very accurate, but then her credences of 0.5 in each basketball proposition will not be maximally accurate, and on many of the popular measures of accuracy, this will result in less overall accuracy than the alternative suggested above.

Again, it is clear that our evidentialist heuristic agrees with our intuitions and not with the causal decision theorist. After all, Rachel's perceptual evidence of Josh standing in front of her strongly supports J; so, if she assigns credence 0 to J, her credence will not match the degree of support given by her evidence to that proposition.

So, in the two sequels to Basketball 1, our intuitions match those that would be given by the heuristic that I claim guides them. Let's now consider Basketball 1. Here, I think our intuitions are a little more tentative. Basketball 2 and 3 are unusual sorts of cases—we don't encounter them very often in our epistemic life. But Basketball 1 is of an extremely rare kind. So I think we're less sure of our judgments in that case. But my feeling is that our intuitions are as follows: every credence function in that case is irrational for Rachel. However, credal veritism together with the Value-Rationality Principle + CDT disagrees: it claims that credence function $c^\dagger$ is permissible.

Again, it is clear that our intuitions agree with the verdict of the evidentialist heuristic. Here's why: given the set up of the case, Rachel's choice of credence in B creates evidence about the propositions B and $\overline{B}$. The problem is that, whichever credence she adopts for B will create evidence such that that very credence cannot then match the support that this evidence gives to B. If she adopts a credence in B of less than 0.5, that creates conclusive evidence in favour of B; if she adopts a credence in B of at least 0.5, that creates conclusive evidence against B. Thus, in the way that Rachel's credences in Basketball 2 create evidence that they thereby respect, her credences in Basketball 1 create evidence that they thereby do not respect. So the evidentialist heuristic agrees with our intuitions that there is no rationally permissible credal state that Rachel might adopt in Basketball 1.

The conclusion of the preceding paragraphs is that the evidentialist heuristic that I posit agrees with our intuitions and not with the credal veritist in three kinds of cases: a case of self-defeating credences (Basketball 1), a case of self-supporting credences (Basketball 2), and a case in which we are offered the opportunity to trade off our match with the evidence in order to obtain greater accuracy (Basketball 3). These three cases are representative of many of the sorts of case that arise when an agent's credal state influences the way the world is. That our evidentialist heuristic agrees with our intuitions in those three sorts of case goes a long way to establishing that it does so in all such cases, and this is what is required by (2).

9.3.5 *The advantages of our heuristic*

Finally, we turn to (3). Clearly, the posited heuristic has a major disadvantage when compared with the alternative process of simply calculating which credal state will produce the most accuracy, which is what the credal veritist claims is required by rationality: the disadvantage is that it produces the wrong verdicts in the sorts of cases considered under (2) above, whereas the alternative does not. Thus, to establish (3), we must describe an advantage that this heuristic has over the alternative that explains why we have adopted the heuristic instead of the alternative as the basis for our intuitive judgments of rationality.

One advantage that this heuristic had over the alternative until recently is simply that it was available! While it has long been acknowledged and intuitively accepted that accuracy is a virtue of credences, it is not until Joyce's work that this has been made precise enough that it could be used to establish specific principles of credal rationality, such as Probabilism or the Principal Principle. And of course even now and for many years to come, this will not be part of the commonly accepted folklore of rationality in a way that will allow it to form the basis of many people's intuitive judgments. In the absence of a precise understanding of this central source of value for credences, our intuitive judgments about the rationality of credal states had to be based on other considerations. The evidentialist heuristic provides such alternative considerations.

Another advantage of the evidentialist heuristic is the limited and clearly defined range of considerations that it needs to take into account, and its resulting ease of use. It takes the agent's total evidence and it takes the propositions to which she assigns credences and it discerns facts about the degree of support provided for the latter by the former in accordance with certain rules of thumb, such as Probabilism, the Principal Principle, etc. In contrast, like all consequentialist methods of assessment, the alternative—which considers the different amounts of accuracy that different credal states might bring about and rules irrational those for which there is another that is expected to bring about more accuracy—must taken into account not only the agent's evidence, which helps to fix the subjunctive probabilities $p(w \,||\, o)$ by which we assign value to the different options, but also all of the accuracy-related consequences of those options. As Selim Berker puts it—though he endorses the verdicts of our intuitive judgments, whereas I do not—the evidentialist considerations are only *backward* and *sideways* looking, whereas the assessments required by credal veritism must also look *forward* to the consequences of adopting those credences (Berker, 2013b, 377). And of course weighing all of those consequences is a difficult and costly task. Indeed, in ethics, the demand by consequentialism that we do this when choosing which action to perform in a particular situation in order to ensure that it is, morally speaking, permissible is sometimes thought to count against that moral theory (Lenman, 2000; Burch-Brown, 2014).

The sorts of cases in which the heuristic gives a mistaken verdict is small—on the whole, when we assess the rationality of our credal states or those of others, we are concerned with states that have no influence on the way the world is that will affect their own accuracy. Thus, the disadvantage of giving incorrect verdicts in those cases is likewise small. It seems to me that it is easily outweighed by the advantage of an available heuristic that is more efficient because it takes into account fewer factors. The evidentialist heuristic provides that. This completes task (3) from above.

With this, we complete our error theory for our intuitive judgments of the rational status of particular credal states in certain situations in which the credal state influences the world in a way that affects its own accuracy. Those intuitive judgments are produced by the evidentialist heuristic: the outputs of this heuristic match our correct intuitions in those cases in which our credences do not influence the world; and they also match our incorrect intuitions in those cases in which our credences do influence the world.

9.4 Conclusion

Hilary Greaves worries that Joyce's argument for Probabilism cannot be correct because the argument strategy to which it belongs has instances whose conclusions are counterintuitive and thus false. As we have seen, *contra* Konek and Levinstein, those instances of the argument strategy really do have those consequences, at least if we are concerned with a notion of rationality about which an agent has some reason to care. However, as we have also seen, while these conclusions are counterintuitive, they are not false. Rather, it is the intuitions that are false. The intuitions are based on a heuristic that, while very reliable in the normal cases in which we usually assess agents for rationality, tends to fail in the sorts of cases that Greaves considers. I conclude, then, that Joyce's argument for Probabilism does indeed establish its conclusion, at least in those cases in which the agent's credences do not influence the way the world is. And similarly for the related arguments for Conditionalization, the Reflection Principle, the Principal Principle, and the Principle of Indifference.

References

Anscombe, G. E. M. (1957). *Intention*. Oxford: Basil Blackwell.

Berker, S. (2013a). Epistemic Teleology and the Separateness of Propositions. *Philosophical Review*, 122(3), 337–93.

Berker, S. (2013b). The Rejection of Epistemic Consequentialism. *Philosophical Issues (Supp. Noûs)*, 23(1), 363–87.

Burch-Brown, J. (2014). Clues for Consequentialists. *Utilitas*, 26(1), 105–19.

Bykvist, K. (2006). Prudence for Changing Selves. *Utilitas*, 18(3), 264–83.

Caie, M. (2013). Rational Probabilistic Incoherence. *Philosophical Review*, 122(4), 527–75.

Carnap, R. (1950). *Logical Foundations of Probability*. Chicago, IL: University of Chicago Press.

Carr, J. (2017). Epistemic Utility Theory and the Aim of Belief. *Philosophy and Phenomenological*, 95(3), 511–34.

Easwaran, K. (2013). Expected Accuracy Supports Conditionalization—and Conglomerability and Reflection. *Philosophy of Science*, 80(1), 119–42.

Firth, R. (1998). The Schneck Lectures, Lecture 1: Epistemic Utility. In J. Troyer (ed.) *In Defense of Radical Empiricism: Essays and Lectures*. Lanham, MD: Rowman and Littlefield, pp. 317–34.

Goldman, A. I. (1999). *Knowledge in a Social World*. Oxford: Clarendon Press.

Greaves, H. (2013). Epistemic Decision Theory. *Mind*, 122(488), 915–52.

Greaves, H., and Wallace, D. (2006). Justifying Conditionalization: Conditionalization Maximizes Expected Epistemic Utility. *Mind*, 115(459), 607–32.

Huttegger, S. M. (2013). In Defense of Reflection. *Philosophy of Science*, 80(3), 413–33.

Jenkins, C. S. (2007). Entitlement and Rationality. *Synthese*, 157, 25–45.

Jenkins, C. S., and Elstein, D. (forthcoming). The Truth Fairy and the Indirect Epistemic Consequentialist. In N. J. L. L. Pedersen, and P. Graham (eds) *Epistemic Entitlement*. Oxford: Oxford University Press.

Joyce, J. M. (1998). A Nonpragmatic Vindication of Probabilism. *Philosophy of Science*, 65(4), 575–603.

Joyce, J. M. (1999). *The Foundations of Causal Decision Theory*. Cambridge Studies in Probability, Induction, and Decision Theory. Cambridge: Cambridge University Press.

Kahneman, D., and Tversky, A. (1972). Subjective Probability: A Judgment of Representativeness. *Cognitive Psychology*, 3(3), 430–54.

Keynes, J. M. (1921). *A Treatise on Probability*. London: Macmillan.

Konek, J., and Levinstein, B. A. (forthcoming). The Foundations of Epistemic Decision Theory. *Mind*.

Lenman, J. (2000). Consequentialism and Cluelessness. *Philosophy and Public Affairs*, 29, 342–70.

Maher, P. (1993). *Betting on Theories*. Cambridge Studies in Probability, Induction, and Decision Theory. Cambridge: Cambridge University Press.

Maher, P. (2006). The Concept of Inductive Probability. *Erkenntnis*, 65(2), 185–206.

Paul, L. A. (2014). *Transformative Experience*. Oxford: Oxford University Press.

Pettigrew, R. (2012). Accuracy, Chance, and the Principal Principle. *Philosophical Review*, 121(2), 241–75.

Pettigrew, R. (2013). A New Epistemic Utility Argument for the Principal Principle. *Episteme*, 10(1), 19–35.

Pettigrew, R. (2014). Accuracy, Risk, and the Principle of Indifference. *Philosophy and Phenomenological Research* 92(1), 35–59.

Pettigrew, R. (2015). Transformative Experience and Decision Theory. *Philosophy and Phenomenological Research*, 91(3), 766–74.

Pettigrew, R. (2016). *Accuracy and the Laws of Credence*. Oxford: Oxford University Press.

Talbot, B. (2014). Truth Promoting Non-Evidential Reasons for Belief. *Philosophical Studies*, 168, 599–618.

Williamson, T. (2000). *Knowledge and its Limits*. Oxford: Oxford University Press.

10

Accuracy, Ratification, and the Scope of Epistemic Consequentialism

James M. Joyce

The accuracy argument for probabilism[1] invokes considerations of *credal accuracy* to establish probabilistic coherence as a norm of epistemic rationality. It is meant to serve as both a starting point and an exemplar for an *accuracy-centered epistemology* (ACE) that enshrines "closeness to the truth" as the cardinal epistemic good, and sees its rational pursuit as the most basic epistemic duty. Michael Caie (2013) has recently alleged that the accuracy argument is invalid, and that "considerations of accuracy, instead of motivating probabilism, support the claim that . . . in certain cases a rational agent's credences ought to be probabilistically incoherent" (p. 528). In a similar vein, Hilary Greaves (2013) has presented examples in which ACE seems to recommend violations of the Principal Principle. Both criticisms are predicated on the idea that ACE is a form of *epistemic consequentialism*. According to this view, we can determine whether a certain credal state is permissible by asking whether it would be rational for a believer to *choose* to hold it. The rationality of such "epistemic choices" is to be assessed in much the same way that standard decision theory assesses practical choices, except with "epistemic utility" replacing ordinary practical utility. I will explain why ACE should not be construed this way, and will show that both Caie's and Greaves' criticisms fail when the theory is elaborated within a more sophisticated consequentialist framework that includes a *ratifiability principle*. This more nuanced framework recognizes that consequentialist reasoning is valid in epistemology only when agents are committed to using the credences they choose to do the sorts of things that credences are characteristically supposed to do, e.g., making estimates of truth-values or setting prices for bets. This commitment is lacking in the sorts of cases that Caie and Greaves present, where credal states are treated as *final ends* rather than as instruments for making estimates, pricing bets, and the like. The position I ultimately

[1] Joyce (1998) and (2009).

arrive at has similarities to the view defended by Jason Konek and Ben Levinstein in their (forthcoming), but it is motivated in a very different way and differs in some significant respects.[2]

10.1 A Sketch of Accuracy-Centered Epistemology

To illustrate the basics of ACE,[3] consider a set of propositions $\Omega = \{T, A, \neg A, \neg T\}$, where $T = A \vee \neg A$. A *credence function* on Ω is a mapping b of elements of Ω to real numbers. These numbers represent a believer's degrees of confidence in Ω-propositions on a scale where 1 represents complete certainty and 0 represents total incredulity. Assuming (inessentially) that the believer is certain of the tautology and incredulous of the contradiction, so that $b(T) = 1$ and $b(\neg T) = 0$, each credence function is a pair of numbers $\langle b(A), b(\neg A) \rangle = \langle a, \tilde{a} \rangle$. The consistent truth-value assignments for Ω can be thought of as the maximally opinionated credence functions, w_1 and w_0, which assign the values $w_1(A) = w_0(\neg A) = 1$ and $w_1(\neg A) = w_0(A) = 0$. w_1 is the assignment in which A is true. w_0 is the assignment in which A is false.[4]

In this simple framework ACE boils down to four main theses:

(I) *Estimation.* Credences are used to make *estimates* of truth-values and quantities that depend on them. A believer's estimate of a proposition's truth-value coincides with her credence for that proposition.

An *estimate* is a forecast of the value of a quantity that is assessed for accuracy on a gradational (closeness counts) scale that measures the degree of *divergence* between the forecast and the actual value of the estimated quantity. Someone who offers an estimate of $a < 1$ for a's truth-value will not simply be deemed wrong if A turns out to be true, but will be judged as more or less accurate depending upon how close or far a is from 1.

(II) *Accuracy.*[5] A credal state is accurate to the extent that it sanctions accurate estimates. In particular, the accuracy of a credence function is a matter of how little its values (truth-value estimates) diverge from the actual truth-values.

---

[2] I thank Maria Lasonen-Aarnio, Brad Armendt, Boris Babic, Kevin Blackwell, Gordon Belot, Richard Bradley, Mike Caie, Catlin Campbell-Moore, Jeff Dunn, Jason Konek, Simon Huttegger, Ben Levinstein, Shyam Nair, Richard Pettigrew, and Brian Skyrms for useful advice.

[3] ACE should be distinguished from the "accuracy first" epistemology defended in Pettigrew (2016). The key difference is that, whereas Pettigrew believes that every legitimate epistemic norm can be *derived* from the duty to pursue accuracy, ACE requires only that all such norms be consistent with the thesis that accuracy is the cardinal epistemic good and that its pursuit is the overriding epistemic duty.

[4] Truth-values are coded with truth represented by 1 and falsity represented by 0. Nothing hangs on this choice. See (Joyce 2015) for further discussion.

[5] The name is taken from Joyce (2009): "A person's credences determine her best estimates of the sorts of quantities that, from a purely epistemic perspective, it is important to be right about. The accuracy of a system of credences can be assessed by looking at how closely its estimates are to the actual values of these quantities" (p. 267–8).

(III) *Scoring.* The divergence of credences from truth-values can be measured with an *inaccuracy score* I that associates each credal function b and truth-value assignment ω with a real number $I_\omega(b) \geq 0$ which measures b's inaccuracy when ω is actual.

In the simple case at hand, each inaccuracy score can be decomposed into two functions: $I_1(b)$ gives b's inaccuracy when A holds; $I_0(b)$ gives its inaccuracy when $\neg A$ holds. Inaccuracy is measured on a scale where zero means perfection, so that $I_1(\omega_1) = I_0(\omega_0) = 0$, and where larger numbers reflect greater divergences from the truth.

While no single inaccuracy score is universally recognized as correct, the following constitute the minimum requirements that all such scores should meet:[6]

Truth-Directedness. Moving credences uniformly closer to truth-values improves accuracy.

Extensionality. The inaccuracy of a credence function b relative to a truth-value assignment ω is solely a function of the values of b and ω.

Continuity. Inaccuracy scores are continuous.

Propriety. If b obeys the laws of probability, then b uniquely minimizes *expected* inaccuracy when expectations are computed relative to b itself.[7]

Infinitely many scoring rules satisfy these requirements. One is the *quadratic score* of Brier (1950), which sets $I_1(a, \tilde{a}) = \frac{1}{2}[(1-a)^2 + \tilde{a}^2]$ and $I_0(a, \tilde{a}) = \frac{1}{2}[a^2 + (1-\tilde{a})^2]$. For another example, the *simple logarithmic score* sets $I_1(a, \tilde{a}) = -\log(a)$ and $I_0(a, \tilde{a}) = -\log(\tilde{a})$. We will use the Brier score as our exemplar, but the structure of the argument is the same for any accuracy score that meets the above conditions.

The final principle of ACE ties accuracy to evidence.

(IV) An epistemically rational believer will always seek to occupy a credal state, among those available to her, that minimizes *estimated* inaccuracy in light of her total evidence.

To appreciate what this entails we need to understand what it is for a credal state to "minimize estimated inaccuracy in light of the believer's total evidence." The rough idea is that a believer's evidence about propositions is also evidence about how inaccurate various truth-value estimates are likely to be. (IV) says that a believer should only occupy a particular credal state when, given her evidence, it is reasonable for her to expect that state to be among the most accurate she can occupy. This is

---

[6] For justifications of these claims see Joyce (2009).
[7] That is, for any credence function $c \neq b$ it must be true that $Exp_b(I(c)) > Exp_b(I(b))$ where $Exp_b(I(\bullet)) = b(A) \cdot I_1(\bullet) + (1 - b(A)) \cdot I_0(\bullet)$.

admittedly vague, but part of the substance of ACE lies in identifying clear norms as instances of (IV).

We will consider three such norms for purposes of illustration.

1. *Accuracy Non-dominance.* Following Joyce (1998) we regard a credal state as rationally defective whenever there is another state that is certain to be more accurate under *every* possible truth-value assignment. More precisely,
   - An epistemically rational believer will never occupy a credal state b when there is another available credal state c that is sure to be more accurate than b under every logically possible truth-value assignment.

   The point here is that b cannot minimize estimated inaccuracy relative to *any* body of evidence when it is accuracy dominated. This is because the principles of rational estimation require one to assign a higher estimated value to X than to Y whenever X is certain to have a higher actual value than Y.

2. *Chance Estimation* (CE). Second, following Pettigrew (2013), we regard a credal state as defective when there is an available alternative with a lower objective expected inaccuracy in light of known chances.
   - If an epistemically rational believer knows the chance $ch(\omega)$ of each world ω, and if she has no inadmissible information,[8] then she will never occupy a credal state b when there is another available state with a lower objective expected inaccuracy, i.e., a state c with $\Sigma_\omega ch(\omega) \cdot I_\omega(b) > \Sigma_\omega ch(\omega) \cdot I_\omega(c)$.

   The idea is that one cannot reasonably estimate b's inaccuracy to be lower than c's when one knows the chances favor c.

3. *The Value of Learning.* Imagine an agent who assigns an intermediate probability $b(E_k)$ to each member of a partition $\{E_1, E_2, \ldots, E_K\}$. She is about to learn which E_k obtains, and is considering an *update rule* that produces a "posterior" (post-learning) credence function b^k with $b^k(E_k) = 1$ in the event she learns E_k. Proponents of ACE will say that the agent should not update using $b \to b^k$ unless she expects it to increase accuracy, so that, when computed from her *pre-learning* perspective, the expected inaccuracy of her pre-learning credences should exceed the expected inaccuracy of her post-learning credences. Formally:

$$\Sigma_k \Sigma_{\omega \in E_k} b(\omega) \cdot I_\omega(b) > \Sigma_k \Sigma_{\omega \in E_k} b(\omega) \cdot I_\omega(b^k).$$

The quantity on the left is the agent's current expectation of inaccuracy for her current credences, and the one on the right is her current expectation of inaccuracy for her post-learning credences.[9]

---

[8] This is information about the truth-values of the ω that is not screened off by knowledge of the chances. In typical cases inadmissible information is direct evidence about future chances that makes the current chances irrelevant.

[9] This might seem to contradict Propriety, but it does not. Propriety says that b expects itself to be more accurate than any *specific* alternative credence function c. The Value of Learning requirement compares

Each of these rules of estimation underwrites a substantive epistemic norm. Accuracy Non-dominance vindicates *probabilistic coherence*. In our simple case, b satisfies the laws of probability when $b(A) + b(\neg A) = 1$. As a number of authors have shown, anyone who violates this condition runs afoul of Accuracy Non-dominance. The relevant result is this:[10]

> *Accuracy Theorem.* If inaccuracy is measured using a score I that satisfies the four conditions listed above, then:
>
> i. Every credence function that violates the laws of probability is accuracy-dominated by some credence function (indeed by one that obeys the laws of probability), and
> ii. No probability function is dominated by anything.

Since dominated credences are forbidden, this derives a prohibition against incoherence from the duty to rationally pursue accuracy.

As shown in Pettigrew (2013), Chance Estimation requires believers to align their credences with known chances, thereby vindicating the *Principal Principle* of Lewis (1980).

> *Principal Principle*: A believer (who has no "inadmissible" information regarding A) should satisfy $b(A \mid ch(A) = x) = x$ for every x in $[0, 1]$.

Propriety ensures that the chance function minimizes objective expected inaccuracy, so that, for all $b \neq ch$, one has $\Sigma_\omega ch(\omega) \cdot I_\omega(b) > \Sigma_\omega ch(\omega) \cdot I_\omega(ch)$. Chance Estimation then rules out any credence function that does not agree the known chances.

The requirement that learning should increase expected accuracy can be used to derive a version of the famous Ramsey/Good "value of learning theorem." The basic insight, which is found in Skyrms (1990) and insightfully discussed in Oddie (1997) and Myrvold (2012), is that a learner who conditions on the true E_k, so that $b^k(\bullet) = b(\bullet \mid E_k)$, will satisfy the Value of Learning requirement, and this is the only way to do it in general.[11]

These are paradigm successes of the accuracy-centered approach. In each, a widely accepted epistemic norm is shown to be integral to the pursuit of accuracy. The norms in question, which (in these three cases) do not depend on the specifics of the I-score,

---

b not to a specific alternative, but to a *generic* one: the agent's credence upon learning which E_k is true, whatever that might be. Since different b^k are the posterior under different conditions, it will be true that $\Sigma_\omega b(\omega) \cdot I_\omega(b) < \Sigma_\omega b(\omega) \cdot I_\omega(b^k)$ for every k, were ω ranges over all worlds, and that $\Sigma_k \Sigma_{\omega \in E_k} b(\omega) \cdot I_\omega(b) > \Sigma_k \Sigma_{\omega \in E_k} b(\omega) \cdot I_\omega(b^k)$, since the latter inequality assumes that each b^k is the posterior only in the E_k worlds.

[10] Interestingly different versions of the Accuracy Theorem can be found in Joyce (1998), Joyce (2009), Lindley (1982), Predd et al. (2009), and Schervish et al. (2009).

[11] Proof Sketch: when $b^k(\bullet) = b(\bullet \mid E_k)$ the propriety of I guarantees that for each k we will have $\Sigma_{\omega \in E_k} b^k(\omega) \cdot I_\omega(b^k) < \Sigma_{\omega \in E_k} b^k(\omega) \cdot I_\omega(b)$. Multiplying both sides by $b(E_k)$ yields $\Sigma_{\omega \in E_k} b(\omega) \cdot I_\omega(b^k) < \Sigma_{\omega \in E_k} b(\omega) \cdot I_\omega(b)$, and summing over k yields the Value of Information result.

are meant to be general requirements of epistemic rationality to which all believers are answerable. According to ACE, if a person's credences violate the laws of probability or the Principal Principle, then the person is holding credences that, in light of her evidence, she cannot reasonably estimate to be among the most accurate that she could hold. Similar things can be said about believers who fail to update by Bayesian conditioning (in contexts where the method applies), and perhaps even about subjects who form their credences using objectively unreliable methods. We are thus left with a picture in which the rational pursuit of accuracy sits at the heart of a broadly Bayesian epistemology for credences.

10.2 Epistemic Consequentialism and the Caie and Greaves Objections

This pretty picture has recently been challenged by Michael Caie (2013) and Hilary Greaves (2013), who argue, in different ways, that ACE is committed to a brand of *epistemic consequentialism*, and that, when so construed, its flagship successes—the accuracy-based vindications of probabilism and of the Principal Principle—break down. Caie argues that, "considerations of accuracy, instead of motivating probabilism, support the claim that... in certain cases a rational agent's credences ought to be probabilistically incoherent" (p. 528). He presents an example in which the pursuit of accuracy seems to require believers to invest credence $1/2$ in a proposition and credence 1 in its negation. Greaves offers examples in which ACE seems to generate similarly troublesome results. When modified slightly, one of these appears to show that ACE requires believers to violate the Principal Principle.

It is crucial to both objections that ACE be a species of *epistemic consequentialism*. Greaves describes the position thus:

Epistemic consequentialism is the analogue of prudential or ethical consequentialism... It recognize[s] a notion of *epistemic value*, analogous to utility or ethical value: a state of affairs is one of high epistemic value for a given agent just in case it is a state of affairs in which there is a good degree of fit between that agent's beliefs and the truth. Where prudential consequentialists evaluate acts such as carrying umbrellas for prudential rationality, the epistemic consequentialist evaluates "epistemic acts"—acts such as... adopting particular credence functions... Such acts count as epistemically rational to the extent to which they do, or could reasonably be expected to, bring about states of high epistemic value... This suggests the project of developing an... epistemic decision theory... in which an epistemic utility function makes quantitative the extent to which the agent has "achieved a state of high epistemic value", and according to which, in any given epistemic predicament, the epistemically rational (epistemic) "act" is the one that "tends to maximize epistemic utility".

(Greaves 2013, p. 919)

Greaves' picture is thus one in which credences are evaluated by asking whether it would have been rational to *choose* them over other potential credal states in a hypothetical "epistemic decision" whose goal is to maximize epistemic utility. This leaves us with a kind of decision-theoretic acid-test for when it is permissible to occupy a credal state.

> E-CON: To determine whether it would be epistemically permissible for a believer to occupy a credal state at time t we should imagine, perhaps contrary to fact,[12] that she is able at some earlier time t_0 to *choose* among all the credal states that she could occupy at t. It is permissible to hold the credal state in question at t only if its choice maximizes expected t_0 epistemic utility in this imaginary competition.

If we conjoin this with the natural idea that inaccuracy scores function like epistemic *dis*utility functions, it follows that believers are epistemically rational only insofar as they hold credences that minimize expected inaccuracy in hypothetical epistemic choice problems.

As Greaves notes, *E-CON* is quite plausible for "pure observers" whose beliefs about a proposition P "do not causally influence the truth of P," and for whom "the fact that [she] believes that P on the basis of evidence E is not itself additional evidence in favour of, or against, P" (p. 915). Epistemic decision theory is clear-cut in such cases: it is standard decision theory applied to the choice of credences.

Things sour quickly if a believer can influence either the truth-values of propositions to which she attaches credences or the evidence on which those credences are based. To see how, let's start by considering Caie's startling claim that the pursuit of accuracy requires believers to hold incoherent credences. After that, we will look at an example, inspired by Greaves, which suggests that ACE requires violations of the Principal Principle.

In Caie's case, the truth-value of a proposition is tied, causally or logically, to a believer's level of confidence in its truth. Here are two examples:

- Consider the proposition # that a believer would express using the self-referential sentence:

    At time t, if I have a definite credence in the proposition expressed by this very sentence then that credence will be less than ½.

    Note that # will be true when it is assigned a credence below ½ at t (or not assigned any credence at all), and false when assigned a credence of ½ or more.

- Imagine an archer who will shoot an arrow at time t, and who can be in one of two belief states with respect to the proposition $ expressed by this sentence:

    My shot at time-t will hit the bullseye.

---

[12] One might balk at the idea of *choosing* credences. Epistemic consequentialists seek to allay such worries by suggesting that the actual ability to choose credences is inessential. One can think of credal states being evaluated in the way they would if the agent *could* choose them.

Our archer can be in a "confident" state in which she assigns $ a credence of at least ½ at t or she can be in the "dubious" state of assigning $ a credence of less than ½ at t (or not assigning it any credence at all). The archer also knows that being in the confident state will cause her to miss the bullseye, while being in the dubious state will cause her to hit it.

In both cases the believer knows that adopting a credence of less than ½ will make the target proposition true, while adopting a credence of ½ or more will make it false. As long as she has epistemic access to her time-t credences at t (as we assume throughout, following Caie), she cannot be rationally confident in either the proposition's truth (since high confidence would be conclusive evidence of falsity), or its falsity (since low credence would be conclusive evidence of truth).

To generalize a bit, say that a *Caie proposition* is any claim U such that:

- The believer knows that being in a credal state with $b_t(U) < ½$ or in which $b_t(U)$ is indeterminate will cause or logically necessitate U's truth.
- The believer knows that being in a credal state with $b_t(U) \geq ½$ will cause or logically necessitate U's falsehood.

The relevant inaccuracy relations for Caie propositions are summarized in Figure 10.1:

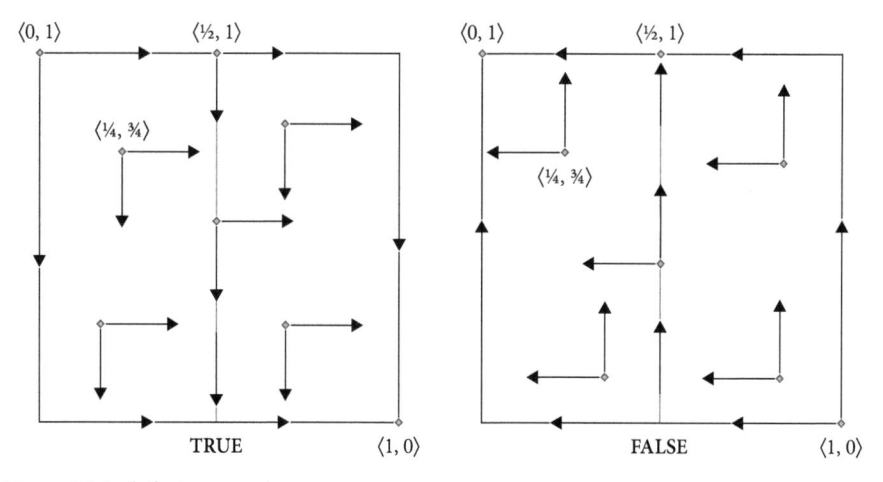

Figure 10.1 *de facto* accuracies
Arrows point to greater accuracy. The diagram on the left reflects the situation in which the believer's time-t credence for U is not greater than or equal to ½, and the inaccuracy of each pair $\langle b_t(U), b_t(\neg U) \rangle = \langle u_t, \tilde{u}_t \rangle$ is $I_1(u_t, \tilde{u}_t)$. In the diagram on the right the believer's time-t credence for U is ½ or greater, so that the inaccuracy of each pair $\langle u_t, \tilde{u}_t \rangle$ is $I_0(u_t, \tilde{u}_t)$.

To obtain these diagrams, we suppose our believer is in some definite credal state $\langle b_t(U), b_t(\neg U) \rangle = \langle u_t, \tilde{u}_t \rangle$ at t, and ask how accurate other credal states will be *on that supposition*. These *de facto* accuracies measure divergence from the truth relative to a *fixed* truth-value for U. For future reference, note that if I = Brier, then $\langle ¼, ¾ \rangle$

has a lower *de facto* inaccuracy than $\langle 1/2, 1 \rangle$ whether U is true or false, i.e., $\langle 1/4, 3/4 \rangle$ accuracy dominates $\langle 1/2, 1 \rangle$.

Despite this, Caie argues for the surprising conclusion that $\langle 1/2, 1 \rangle$ is "the credal state that has the highest possible [Brier] accuracy" (p. 550). He reasons thus: consider any point $\langle u_t, \tilde{u}_t \rangle$ in the unit square, and suppose the believer were to choose it as her credal state. If $u_t < 1/2$, then U is true and the Brier inaccuracy of any time-t credence x for U is $(1-x)^2$. In particular, the inaccuracy of u_t itself is $(1-u_t)^2$. Likewise, if $u_t \geq 1/2$, then U is false and the Brier accuracy of the assignment x is x^2. In particular, the inaccuracy of u_t is u_t^2. So, if we map the Brier accuracy of investing credence u_t in U at t we get Figure 10.2:

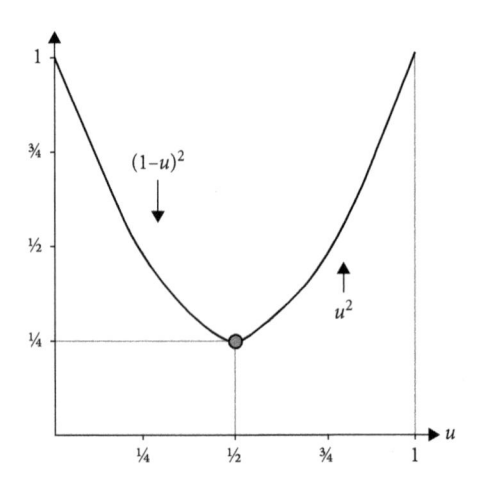

Figure 10.2
As the credence for U approaches $1/2$ from the left, the Brier score of each assignment is $(1-u)^2$. This quantity declines monotonically to an (unrealized) limit of $1/4$. As the credence for U approaches $1/2$ from the right, the Brier score of each assignment u is u^2. This declines monotonically to a (realized) limit of $1/4$.

Caie concludes that, independent of the credence that a believer invests in $\neg U$, $1/2$ is the least inaccurate credence she can have for U. Since U is false when $b_t(U) = 1/2$, the right credence for $\neg U$ is 1. Thus, Caie concludes, accuracy considerations mandate $\langle 1/2, 1 \rangle$ as the uniquely permissible credal state.

This might seem puzzling given that a believer who adopts $\langle 1/2, 1 \rangle$ as her time-t credences makes it true that other *identifiable* credences are more accurate. Since adopting $\langle 1/2, 1 \rangle$ makes U false, every inaccuracy score will deem any pair $\langle u, 1 \rangle$ with $u < 1/2$ more accurate than $\langle 1/2, 1 \rangle$. In fact, $\langle 1/2, 1 \rangle$ is accuracy dominated according to every inaccuracy score! (For Brier, $\langle 1/4, 3/4 \rangle$ is a dominating alternative; other scores generate other alternatives.) So, one might wonder how Caie can say that a believer "would be more accurate were she to have the probabilistically incoherent credal state $\langle 1/2, 1 \rangle$ than were she to have [any] probabilistically coherent credal state" (p. 548). The answer is that Caie does *not* mean this false thing: the accuracy of $\langle 1/2, 1 \rangle$ when $\langle 1/2, 1 \rangle$ is held exceeds the accuracy of any alternative when $\langle 1/2, 1 \rangle$ is held. He means this true thing: the accuracy of $\langle 1/2, 1 \rangle$ when $\langle 1/2, 1 \rangle$ is held exceeds the accuracy of any alternative *when that alternative is held.*

Some terminology will help. Define a time-t credal state's *self-inaccuracy* as its inaccuracy *on the assumption that the believer holds it*. More formally, $I^{self}(u_t, \tilde{u}_t) = I_1(u_t, \tilde{u}_t)$ when $u_t < 1/2$ and $I^{self}(u_t, \tilde{u}_t) = I_0(u_t, \tilde{u}_t)$ when $u_t \geq 1/2$. Figure 10.3 conveys the relevant facts about self-accuracy for Caie propositions.

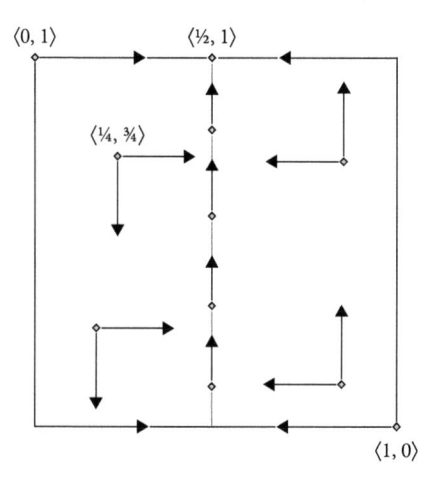

Figure 10.3
Arrows indicate increasing *self*-accuracy. On the left half of the square (excluding the segment $u = 1/2$) inaccuracy is measured on the assumption that U is true. On the right (including $u = 1/2$) inaccuracy is measured on the assumption that U is false.

Caie claims that what matters is $\langle 1/2, 1 \rangle$'s advantage in self-inaccuracy, not $\langle 1/4, 3/4 \rangle$'s dominant position in *de facto* accuracy.

To see why Caie thinks so, consider his critique of the accuracy-dominance argument for probabilism found in (Joyce 1998, 2009). Here is that argument seen through the lens of epistemic consequentialism:

Suppose a believer, who aims to minimize Brier inaccuracy, faces a kind of *epistemic decision* in which she can *choose* (at $t_0 < t$) her time-t credal state $\langle u_t, \tilde{u}_t \rangle$. Here are the Brier inaccuracies of her various choices, with $\langle 1/2, 1 \rangle$ and $\langle 1/4, 3/4 \rangle$ highlighted:

	U	$\neg U$
Choose $\langle 1/4, 3/4 \rangle$	$9/16$	$1/16$
Choose $\langle 1/2, 1 \rangle$	$10/16$	$2/16$
Choose $\langle u, \tilde{u} \rangle$	$1/2 - u + 1/2(u^2 + \tilde{u}^2)$	$1/2 - \tilde{u} + 1/2(u^2 + \tilde{u}^2)$

Since the believer sees U and $\neg U$ as live epistemic possibilities,[13] and since $\langle 1/4, 3/4 \rangle$ has the lower Brier score both when U is true and when U is false, choosing $\langle 1/2, 1 \rangle$ commits the believer to

---

[13] Maybe this is too strong since the believer's credence of 1 for $\neg U$ might be taken to show that U is not an epistemic possibility for her after all. While it is hard to make sense of a person who is both maximally uncertain about U and certain of $\neg U$, we can say this: either she regards both U and $\neg U$ as epistemic possibilities or she sees only the latter as a possibility. Either way she is committed to credences that are less accurate than $\langle 1/4, 3/4 \rangle$ in every world she sees as possible.

credences that are sure to be less accurate than $\langle 1/4, 3/4 \rangle$ in every possible world. By Accuracy Non-dominance this is irrational. So, it is irrational to choose $\langle 1/2, 1 \rangle$ when $\langle 1/4, 3/4 \rangle$ is an option.

Caie notes, quite correctly, that dominance reasoning is only valid when states of the world are *causally independent* of acts. This is not the case here since choosing $\langle 1/4, 3/4 \rangle$ makes U true and choosing $\langle 1/2, 1 \rangle$ makes U false. So, when these causal dependencies are taken into account, the relevant epistemic decision is really this (where Ø represents impossibility):

	U	$\sim U$
Choose $\langle 1/4, 3/4 \rangle$	$9/16$	Ø
Choose $\langle 1/2, 1 \rangle$	Ø	$2/16$
Choose $\langle u, \tilde{u} \rangle, u < 1/2$	$1/2 - u + 1/2(u^2 + \tilde{u}^2)$	Ø
Choose $\langle u, \tilde{u} \rangle, u \geq 1/2$	Ø	$1/2 - \tilde{u} + 1/2(u^2 + \tilde{u}^2)$

Since the agent can simply *decide* her accuracy, $\langle 1/2, 1 \rangle$ is the rational epistemic choice, despite being dominated by $\langle 1/4, 3/4 \rangle$. For Caie the conclusion is clear: an accuracy-centered epistemic consequentialism must jettison Accuracy Non-dominance and with it the accuracy-centered argument for probabilism.

A similar objection can be raised against Chance Estimation and ACE's argument for the Principal Principle. Consider the following example, which is taken from Greaves (though we make different use of it here):

Promotion: At t_0 you choose your time-t credence for X. Things have been arranged so that X's objective chance at t is sure to be $1 - x_t$ if you choose x_t.

Assume that at t you will know both your credence for X (having chosen it) and X's objective chance (which you infer from your choice). Assume also that any other evidence you have about X at t is "admissible," i.e., is screened off by your knowledge of $ch_t(X)$. Given all this, what credence should you choose to invest in X? There look to be three potential answers:

Decide like Savage. Choose the time-t credences that minimize expected inaccuracy relative to your time-t_0 credences. This requires $x_t = b_0(X)$.

Satisfy the Principal Principle. Align your time-t credence with X's time-t objective chance. This requires you to set $x_t = 1/2$, the only value for which $x_t = 1 - x_t$.

Minimize Objective Expected Self-inaccuracy. Choose your credences to minimize objective time-t expected inaccuracy conditional on being chosen, i.e., minimize

$$Exp(I(x_t) \mid b_t(X) = x_t) = (1 - x_t) \cdot (1 - x_t)^2 + x_t \cdot x_t^2.$$

This too requires you to choose $x_t = 1/2$.

The first suggestion is a non-starter. Since you know your choice will affect X's time-t chance, and since this knowledge screens off your time-t_0 evidence, your t_0 credences will be out of date as soon as you choose them. The second and third suggestions seem more promising. The second applies Chance Estimation. By picking any x_t other than ½ you fail to minimize objective expected inaccuracy at t. The third suggestion reflects the consequentialist idea that one should minimize *self*-accuracy. By this reckoning, $x_t = \frac{1}{2}$ is the best choice.

Since the last two suggestions agree about $x_t = \frac{1}{2}$, it might not seem terribly pressing to resolve the issue between them. Unfortunately, they conflict in nearby cases. Suppose choosing x_t causes X's time-t chance to be $(1 - x_t)^2$ rather than $1 - x_t$. To satisfy the Principal Principle you must adopt $x_t = 0.382$ to guarantee $x_t = (1-x_t)^2$. But, to minimize expected self-inaccuracy[14] you must set $x_t = 0.423$, which puts X's chance at roughly 0.333. We thus have a conflict between Chance Estimation and the consequentialist requirement to minimize objective expected self-inaccuracy. Things get even worse if choosing x_t sets X's chance to $(1 - x_t)^{1/2}$. It is now *impossible* to satisfy the Principal Principle since this requires $x_t^2 - x_t + 1 = 0$, an equation without a real solution. E-CON, on the other hand, recommends $x_t = 0.357$, which uniquely minimizes objective expected self-accuracy but puts the chance at 0.77.[15]

Call this last scenario the *Chance Paradox*. It is an exact analogue of Caie's example. Each has the following features:

(i) There is a unique "epistemic choice" that minimizes estimated self-inaccuracy, partly as a result of manipulating the truth-value or objective chance of the proposition whose credence is being chosen.

(ii) Every possible choice, *including the one that minimizes self-inaccuracy*, produces evidence that undermines the chosen credence. In Caie's example a choice produces either conclusive evidence for thinking U is true or conclusive evidence for thinking U is false. Either way, the agent can identify other time-t credal states that are more accurate than her own. In the Chance Paradox the choice gives the agent evidence that enables her, at t, to identify alternative credal states whose objective expected inaccuracies are lower than the objective expected inaccuracy of her own.

Epistemic consequentialism thus leaves the believer in a position at t where she can truly say both "no matter what credence I might have chosen at t_0, I could not then have expected to be more accurate," and "I know that, objectively speaking, my current credences are not likely to be as accurate as some others I can name."

This leaves friends of ACE with a dilemma. By embracing epistemic consequentialism, with inaccuracy scores in the role of epistemic disutilities, they can bring rational choice theory to bear on problems of credal epistemology. This has striking benefits,

---

[14] Here, expected self-accuracy is $Exp(I(x_t) \mid b_t(X) = x_t) = (1 - x_t)^2 \cdot (1 - x_t)^2 + (1 - (1 - x_t)^2) \cdot x_t^2$.
[15] Here, expected self-accuracy is $Exp(I(x_t) \mid b_t(X) = x_t) = (1 - x_t)^{1/2} \cdot (1 - x_t)^2 + (1 - (1 - x_t)^{1/2}) \cdot x_t^2$.

especially in the area of belief updating. But, these benefits come at a high cost since ACE must give up two of its major successes: its dominance rationale for probabilism, and its rationale for the Principal Principle based on Chance Estimation.

It is tempting to simply dismiss this as a philosopher's worry (in the pejorative sense). After all, epistemic decision theory works quite well when the choice of a credence for A does not affect A's truth-value or alter the evidence for A. Fantastical scenarios involving propositions whose truth-values or chances are tied to how strongly they are believed seem peripheral to substantive epistemology. After all, one could just append a rider to ACE—*provided that the chances of propositions do not depend on the credences they are assigned*—and it will get the right answers in all cases we actually care about. Would it really be so bad if ACE's arguments for probabilism or its rationale for the Principal Principle only applied to non-fantastical cases?

While I am sympathetic to this dismissive response, it concedes too much. It grants both that ACE is a brand of epistemic consequentialism and that *E-CON* identifies the right credences to hold in Caie's case, the Chance Paradox, or other problems in which choosers are not "mere observers." In fact, *E-CON* gets these cases wrong: anyone who chooses to hold credences of $\langle 1/2, 1 \rangle$ in Caie's example is making a mistake, as is anyone with credence $x_t = 0.357$ in the Chance Paradox. These mistakes stem not from the idea that credences should be judged on the basis of accuracy, but from the idea that "epistemic choices" always reveal the most rational credences to hold. To get things right, ACE must be divorced from *E-CON*!

10.3 Why Epistemology Is Not Decision Theory

The core thesis, and main mistake, of epistemic consequentialism is the idea that one can always identify the best credal state to *hold* by finding the best credal state to *choose*. In the fantastical scenarios we've been considering, an epistemic agent is given a perverse incentive to choose credences that she will regard as rationally defective from the moment she chooses them. As a result, her choice of these credences has the side effect of creating evidence that makes it unreasonable for her to rely on them to do the jobs that credences are characteristically meant to do. She will not want to use them to estimate truth-values, price bets, or estimate the value of any other random variable because the evidence her choice creates shows that credences other than the ones she choose are likely to do a better job. As long as she knows what she chose, the agent will have this view at the moment of choice and every time thereafter. Even while the chosen credences are being held she will regard them as suboptimal for purposes of truth-value estimation, pricing bets, and so on. In the jargon of decision theory, the choices of $u_t = 1/2$ in Caie's example or $x_t = 0.357$ in the Chance Paradox are *unratifiable*. They minimize expected self-inaccuracy, but fail to minimize expected inaccuracy in light of the evidence that will become available once they are chosen. Unlike ordinary practical acts, which can be perfectly rational even when unratifiable, I claim that epistemic acts must be ratifiable if the decision-theoretic approach is to tell us anything useful about rational belief. The reason, in a nutshell, is that, in contrast with the practical case, the rational epistemic agent who chooses a credal state for her future self will not regard the occupation of that state as a *final end*, but will see it as an instrument for making estimates, pricing bets, and doing all the other things that credences are characteristically used to do.

In practical decision theory the outcomes associated with acts are supposed to encompass everything, desirable or undesirable, which those acts might cause. Once outcomes are specified all relevant questions of value are resolved. Imagine an agent deciding whether to take a simple bet on the toss of a coin that pays [$5 if heads, –$2 if tails]. By writing down $5 and –$2 as outcomes we imply that these values can be treated as *final ends* that capture everything that matters to the agent in the context. Strictly speaking, this will be true only for *misers* who care exclusively about the size of their fortunes. Most of us, of course, value money as a means to other ends. Hence, to adequately describe our predicaments these other ends would have to be elaborated, so that the outcomes include not merely the amount of money won or lost, but also any further goods that the money might be used to secure. If, say, we will use our winnings to buy ice cream, the outcomes should have been, "win $5 and buy chocolate, if available," "win $5 and buy vanilla, if available," and so on. If losing $2 makes it impossible for us to take the bus, then that outcome should be "lose $2 and walk home." In practice, it is often possible to ignore such niceties since in well-developed markets one's fortune can be treated as an approximation of the amount of happiness one can buy. But, strictly speaking, actions aim at final outcomes, and the danger lies in mistaking intermediate results for final ones.

To illustrate the point, and to set the table for future developments, consider a famous decision situation that was introduced and analyzed by Bruno de Finetti (1937/1964):

The Prevision Game. Some target proposition A is specified, and a miser is given $1 on the understanding that (i) at t_0 she must announce two real numbers a and $\tilde{a}$ as her "previsions" for A and $\neg A$, and (ii) she must repay $\$^1\!/\!_2[(1-a)^2 + \tilde{a}^2]$ if A is true and $\$^1\!/\!_2[a^2 + (1-\tilde{a})^2]$ if A is false. With outcomes as *penalties* (Brier scores *of previsions*), her choice is this, with $\langle 1/4, 3/4 \rangle$ and $\langle 1/2, 1 \rangle$ emphasized:

	A	$\sim A$
Announce $\langle 1/4, 3/4 \rangle$	$9/16$	$1/16$
Announce $\langle 1/2, 1 \rangle$	$10/16$	$2/16$
Announce $\langle a, \tilde{a} \rangle$	$1/2 - a + 1/2(a^2 + \tilde{a}^2)$	$1/2 - \tilde{a} + 1/2(a^2 + \tilde{a}^2)$

As de Finetti recognized,[16] this game has two noteworthy features when A is a garden-variety proposition whose truth is not influenced by what previsions are chosen.

---

[16] Classic references are de Finetti (1974) and Savage (1971).

First, a rational decision-maker will never report incoherent previsions since they are always dominated in the way $\langle 1/2, 1\rangle$ is dominated by $\langle 1/4, 3/4\rangle$. Second, a coherent agent minimizes her expected penalty by reporting previsions that reveal her true credences.[17] If she reports a and $\tilde{a}$, then we can be sure that at t_0 she believes A to degree a and $\neg A$ to degree $\tilde{a}$.

In light of these two facts, the problem of choosing credences for A and $\neg A$ seems like a version of the prevision game in which the valuable quantity, money or practical utility, has been replaced by accuracy or epistemic utility. Since previsions reveal credences, choosing credences with the aim of minimizing Brier inaccuracy seems no different from reporting previsions in de Finetti's game: the common goal is to minimize average squared-distances from truth-values.[18]

Things change when the target proposition's truth-value is affected by the previsions that the agent reports. Consider the Caie-type proposition:

O The o-component of the previsions $\langle o, \tilde{o}\rangle$ announced for the proposition expressed by this very sentence is *not* $1/2$ or more.

Clearly, O is true if $o < 1/2$ is reported, and O is false if $o \geq 1/2$ is reported. So, the agent's decision looks like this:

	O	$\neg O$
Announce $\langle 1/4, 3/4\rangle$	$9/16$	$\emptyset$
Announce $\langle 1/2, 1\rangle$	$\emptyset$	$2/16$
Announce $\langle o, \tilde{o}\rangle, o < 1/2$	$1/2 - o^2 + 1/2(o^2 + \tilde{o}^2)$	$\emptyset$
Announce $\langle o, \tilde{o}\rangle, o \geq 1/2$	$\emptyset$	$1/2 - \tilde{o} + 1/2(o^2 + \tilde{o}^2)$

Two things are immediate. First, a profit maximizer should report $\langle o, \tilde{o}\rangle = \langle 1/2, 1\rangle$, since this choice uniquely minimizes her *self-penalty*. Second, the neat alignment of previsions and credences breaks down. In reporting the $\langle 1/2, 1\rangle$ previsions the agent is *not* revealing her time t_0 credence for o. From the moment she settles on $o = 1/2$ she knows O is false and assigns it *zero* credence. She reports $1/2$ only as a way of jointly manipulating her prevision and O's truth-value so as to bring the two as close together as possible (consistent with the structure of the game, which thwarts perfect agreement). So, o is *not* the report of a credence.

To drive the point home, suppose that, in addition to reporting previsions, our agent is required to announce a second pair of numbers $\langle n, \tilde{n}\rangle$ that she must use to

---

[17] This follows from the propriety of the Brier score.
[18] There are obvious similarities between the prevision game and the accuracy argument for probabilism. In fact, de Finetti's work inspired the argument, which is really just his general approach recast in epistemic terms. The key difference between the two is that de Finetti could simply assume that his agent wanted money, and so had an incentive to minimize her penalty. In the accuracy argument one needs to argue for the idea that accuracy, as measured by a scoring rule, is desirable from an epistemic perspective.

evaluate any bets she might be offered at t. By announcing $\langle n, \tilde{n} \rangle$ she commits to buying (selling) [$x if O, $0 if $\neg O$] for a price up to (no less than) $$n \cdot x$, and commits to buying (selling) [$0 if O, $y if $\neg O$] for a price up to (no less than) $$\tilde{n} \cdot y$. Since this is the way she would bet with credences of $b_t(O) = n$ and $b_t(\neg O) = \tilde{n}$, the agent is, in effect, being asked to say which credences she would most like to bet with *after* reporting her previsions. Obviously, $\langle o, \tilde{o} \rangle$ and $\langle n, \tilde{n} \rangle$ will never agree: if $o \geq 1/2$ then $n = 0$, and if $u < 1/2$ then $n = 1$. So, insofar as credences determine betting prices, our agent does not see her choice of a prevision for O as anything like the choice of a credence. Interestingly though, since her choice of $\tilde{n}$ does not causally influence O's truth-value, if she reports previsions of $\langle o, 1 \rangle$ with $o \geq 1/2$, or previsions of $\langle o, 0 \rangle$ with $u < 1/2$, then $\tilde{o} = \tilde{n}$. Thus, in reporting previsions of $\langle 1/2, 1 \rangle$ our agent does not announce her credence for O but does announce her credence for $\neg O$. We know that this is so by her unwillingness (willingness) to use the $o = 1/2$ ($\tilde{o} = 1$) assignment in the characteristic way that a credence is used in pricing bets.

The trouble with adhering to an unsophisticated epistemic consequentialism in the face of Caie-type examples is that it portrays a believer as choosing credences even though she would not endorse using them in the way credences are characteristically used. An epistemic agent who chooses $\langle 1/2, 1 \rangle$ in Caie's example achieves *two* things: she obtains the lowest self-inaccuracy score that can be secured given her powers at t_0, and she saddles herself with the $u_t = 1/2$ credence. However laudable the former achievement might be, the latter commits her to a truth-value estimate that no rational agent will want to make. From the moment she chooses $u_t = 1/2$ the agent knows that the $\langle 0, 1 \rangle$ pair sanctions perfectly accurate estimates of all quantities that depend on U's truth value. The fact that she could not have made her time-t credences more accurate by choosing $\langle 0, 1 \rangle$ at t_0 does nothing to mitigate this. She knows, at t_0 and ever after, that the chosen $u_t = 1/2$ credence should not be *used* if the goal is to make accurate truth-value estimates. Unfortunately, she leaves herself no option: by selecting $u_t = 1/2$ at t_0 she commits to using $1/2$ as her time-t estimate of U's truth-value (in ACE that's what it means to have a credence at t), even though the evidence produced by the choice is certain to show that this estimate is far from optimally accurate. So, in the same way that an ordinary agent will not want to bet on O using her stated prevision, so too an epistemic agent facing Caie's case will not want to use the credence for U that she would choose at t_0 as her time-t estimate of U's truth-value. The same holds for those who minimize objective expected self-inaccuracy in the Chance Paradox. My view, which I will defend in the next section, is that an epistemic agent who cannot say, "these credences I am choosing now are the ones I will want to use as a basis for truth-value estimation at t (assuming I remain rational and acquire no new information between t_0 and t)," does not see himself as choosing *credences* at all.

Standing back a bit, an agent who chooses time-t credences with the goal of minimizing self-inaccuracy, and without considering how those credences will look from the perspective of her time-t self, is treating the accuracy of the chosen credences the way misers treat money, i.e., as a final end.[19] This marks the key difference between evaluating $\langle 1/2, 1\rangle$ based on the effects of *choosing* it or based on the effects of committing to *using* it. In the first kind of evaluation the issue is: "what alternative credal states could I choose at t_0 that would produce more accurate estimates at t?" In the second the question is "irrespective of what I could have done at t_0, can I count on my time-t credences to generate accurate estimates in light of the evidence my earlier choice produced?" Epistemic consequentialists mistakenly focus on the first question, but only the second matters to epistemology. An agent who chooses $u_t = 1/2$ to secure a time-t credal state that minimizes self-inaccuracy is trying to align her credence for U as closely as possible with U's truth-value by manipulating *both* quantities. This is exactly what she should do if the final goal is to choose a $\langle u_t, \tilde{u}_t \rangle$ pair with a low self-inaccuracy score, or, to put it differently, to create a world in which her time-t credences are as accurate as she can make them at t_0. But, proponents of ACE should *not* recognize this as the final goal. The final goal is to hold time-t credences that allow the agent to make truth-value estimates that she can expect to be (*de facto*) accurate in light of what she will know at t, *not* in light of what she can do at t_0. The choice of a credal state at t_0 is merely a means to the end of producing credences that the chooser will be happy to *use* at t. But, as long as the agent remembers what she chooses, from time t_0 onward she will see it as a *mistake*, from the perspective of inaccuracy minimization, to use $1/2$ as her estimate of U's truth-value, and this is true even though she could not have *chosen* anything better.

This distinction between treating credences as final ends and treating them as a basis for estimation is related to a distinction that Jason Konek and Ben Levinstein draw in their (forthcoming) paper between treating a credence function as an epistemic choice and treating it as an epistemic state to be occupied. While Konek and Levinstein motivate their distinction differently than I do, by appeal to considerations of *direction of fit*, their picture and mine are similar in many respects. In speaking about Caie and Greaves-type cases, they rightly say:

When the act of adopting a credal state can influence the world, which epistemic acts an agent wants to perform can come apart from which credal state she would most like to occupy. That is, an agent can prefer to [choose credences c over credences c'] while preferring to be in epistemic state c' to state c.   (Konek and Levinstein forthcoming)

An agent with credal state c is epistemically irrational iff she prefers or, given her evidence, ought to prefer, some alternative credal state b to her own... Epistemic rationality... tells you when you have landed in a bad spot... It tells you where or where not to be, not what to do.
(Konek and Levinstein forthcoming)

---

[19] When I speak of "the chosen credences" I have in mind the *entire* credal state. It is consistent with treating the entire credal state as a final end that an agent treats parts of it as means to that end. Indeed, this is what happens in Caie's case. The agent chooses $u = 1/2$ partly as a way of ensuring that U is false, and allows him to assign a perfectly accurate credence to $\neg U$, thus guaranteeing a low inaccuracy score for the entire credal state. Likewise, in Greaves' "Imps" case the epistemic consequentialist will choose to assign one proposition a highly inaccurate credence as a means to the end of having a total credal state that is highly accurate. The final end is the highly accurate total state. Thanks to Jeff Dunn for encouraging me to clarify this point.

While Konek and Levinstein justify this conclusion on the basis of "direction of fit" considerations, I would trace it back to the characteristic role that credences play in estimation (see section 10.4). But, our messages are similar:[20] the genesis of the time-t credences is of little or no importance when it comes to epistemic evaluation. When assessing a believer's credences we do not care what other credences she might have been able to choose at some other time or in some different information state. Rather, we want to know how well or poorly the credences will serve her when she uses them as the basis for making accurate truth-value estimates. The fact that there was or was not a way for her to ensure a more accurate set of estimates at some earlier time is irrelevant. Credences are for *using*, not for *choosing*, and must be evaluated accordingly. Thus, we must reject E-CON, and with it the idea that we can always determine the best time-t credences for a believer to hold by asking which credal state she should have chosen at t_0 if her goal at that time was to minimize the inaccuracy of the time-t credences.

I think Konek and Levinstein will agree with me here, but they will go one step further. They see epistemic actions as being part of a "fit-the-world-to-the-attitude" regime, and epistemic states as part of a "fit-the-attitude-to-the-world" regime. As a result, they reject the idea that any decision-theoretic considerations will be relevant to questions about the rationality of occupying various epistemic states. "Epistemic acts, like actions more generally," they write, "are good to the extent that they make the world desirable. Epistemic states are not" (p. 11). I am more optimistic about the possibility of using decision theory for these purposes. While the unbridled consequentialism of *E-CON* cannot be maintained, a more restricted consequentialist approach has promise.

10.4 When Decision Theory Is Like Epistemology

There is a different connection between decision theory and epistemology than the one *E-CON* envisions. The basic problem in the Caie/Greaves cases is that the choice of a credal state at t_0 produces evidence that prevents the agent from seeing the chosen credences as a suitable basis for making estimates of truth-values and quantities that depend on truth-values. When no such evidence is produced, a consequentialist model can be a useful guide. This suggests that decision theory can contribute to epistemology if it is buttressed with a *ratifiability maxim*. Following Jeffrey (1983), say that an act is *ratifiable* just when it maximizes expected utility in light of the evidence that it is chosen. Translating this into the current context, say that the choice of credal state b_t at t_0 is *epistemologically ratifiable* exactly when the expected inaccuracy of b_t given that b_t is chosen is less than the expected inaccuracy of any alternative c given that b_t is chosen. Here t is a time immediately after the choice at which the only new evidence that the agent has acquired is that she has chosen b_t. Also, the expected inaccuracies in question are the ones that the agent will compute at t_0 when she

---

[20] Though, see the discussion of "Leap" later for one way in which our views differ.

supposes that she will choose b_t. To capture the idea that epistemic choices should be ratifiable, I propose the following necessary (but not sufficient) condition on epistemic permissibility:

> E-RAT:[21] To determine whether it would be epistemically permissible for a believer to occupy a particular credal state at t we can imagine, perhaps contrary to fact, that she is able at some earlier time t_0 to *choose* among all credal states that she can occupy at t. It is permissible to hold the state in question at t only if that state is both (i) epistemologically ratifiable at t_0, and (ii) its choice minimizes time-t_0 expected inaccuracy *among the epistemologically ratifiable options*.

I see E-RAT as distinguishing genuine epistemic choices, those in which the agent sees herself as choosing *real* credences, from *sham*-epistemic choices, in which she sees herself choosing *sham* "credences." The hallmark of real credences is that the believer is happy to use them as the basis for making estimates of truth-values and quantities that depend on truth-values, the characteristic things credences are meant to do. In contrast, believers with sham "credences" will not want to use them to do these jobs, but will instead aim to switch to alternative credences before making estimates of truth-values, evaluating bets, etc. As I see it, consequentialist considerations only apply when one is choosing among real credences. The fact that adopting one set of sham "credences" will have better consequences for credal accuracy than adopting another is of no interest to epistemology.

Choices among unratifiable "credences" are shams in this way. When the choice of some credal state b_t is unratifiable the agent knows, before she chooses, that (a) her choice of b_t will create evidence that is relevant to questions about accuracies of truth-value estimates, and (b) that by her current (t_0) lights that evidence will show that b_t sanctions truth-value estimates that are inferior in expected accuracy to others she can hold at t. (Note: I do *not* say "to others she could have previously chosen to hold.") In particular, the chooser will think that her post-choice self should not start making estimates until she takes the evidence that her choice has produced into account. In Caie's case, the t_0 chooser, having selected $\langle 1/2, 1 \rangle$, will not want her time-t self to make any truth-value estimates until she updates on $u_t = 1/2$, and lowers her credence for U from ½ to zero. So, ½ is a sham "credence" for U, and the fact that it minimizes self-inaccuracy is moot. Likewise, the agent who chooses $x_t = 0.357$ in the chance paradox will not want her post-choice self to start making estimates until she updates on the

---

[21] Though it will not matter much here, I think of this principle as being attached to a *casual* version of decision theory, as in Weirich (1985) or Harper (1986).

new evidence that $ch(X) = 0.77$. So, $x_t = 0.357$ is a sham "credence" for X, and the fact that it minimizes self-inaccuracy is moot.[22]

Before trying to rationalize *E-RAT* and to explain why it is relevant to an accuracy-centered epistemology, let's see how it handles some problem cases (most taken from Greaves (2013)).

- *Caie.* Here there are no ratifiable acts: the choice of $u_t < {}^1\!/_2$ makes $\langle 1, 0 \rangle$ the most accurate credal state; the choice of $u_t \geq {}^1\!/_2$ makes $\langle 0, 1 \rangle$ most accurate; and, if one can actually choose not to have time-t credences, doing so would make $\langle 0, 1 \rangle$ most accurate. So, what credences should one choose? This is a nonsense question: since there are no ratifiable options one is not choosing among real credences. As such, an epistemic decision theory should not provide an answer. What sham "credences" should one choose? I'm not sure since I do not know what the point of choosing sham "credences" would be. Perhaps one should choose the sham "credences" that, when updated on the evidence their choice produces, generate the most accurate real credences. In that case, any $\langle u_t, \tilde{u}_t \rangle$ pair would be equally good since each will generate perfectly accurate credences, either $\langle 1, 0 \rangle$ or $\langle 0, 1 \rangle$. Maybe one might want to use $\langle {}^1\!/_2, 1 \rangle$'s minimal self-inaccuracy as a tie-breaker. This is fine, but it does not indicate, in any way, that those are the best credences to adopt, epistemically speaking. Self-inaccuracies of credal states whose choices cannot be ratified are irrelevant to epistemology.
- *Promotion.* Here the time-t_0 choice of a credence of x_t for X causes $ch_t(X) = (1 − x_t)$. The only ratifiable choice is $x_t = {}^1\!/_2$.
- *Promotion Squared.* Here the time-t_0 choice of x_t for X causes $ch_t(X) = (1−x_t)^2$. The sole ratifiable option is $x_t = 0.382$, the one that satisfies the Principal Principle.
- *Chance Paradox.* Here the time-t_0 choice of x_t for X causes $ch_t(X) = (1 − x_t)^{1/2}$. There are no ratifiable choices, and the situation is the same as in *Caie*.
- *Leap.* Here assigning a credence of x_t to X causes $ch_t(X) = x_t$. This makes all $\langle x, 1 − x \rangle$ pairs ratifiable. Among these, $\langle 1, 0 \rangle$ and $\langle 0, 1 \rangle$ minimize objective expected inaccuracy. None of the other ratifiable actions may be chosen.

    On this last point I differ from Konek and Levinstein. They see every $\langle x, 1 − x \rangle$ as a rationally permissible state for the agent to occupy, despite the fact that the choice of $\langle 1, 0 \rangle$ or $\langle 0, 1 \rangle$ will maximize expected accuracy from the t_0 perspective. Since beliefs, unlike acts, have a world-to-attitude direction of fit, it matters not a whit whether a believer can cause her credences to be more accurate by choosing

---

[22] Let me stress that I am *not* advocating that we evaluate epistemic choices using some more comprehensive epistemic utility function, one that includes both the self-accuracy of the chosen credences as well as their suitability for making estimates at t and beyond. My thesis, and the intent of the *E-RAT*, is that, by itself, the self-accuracies of credal states count for *nothing* in epistemic evaluations. Thanks to Jason Konek for encouraging me to clarify this point.

⟨0, 1⟩ than by choosing ⟨³/₄, ¹/₄⟩. A person who ends up occupying ⟨³/₄, ¹/₄⟩ as a result of choosing it has made no epistemic error since her credences agree with the chances her choice produced.

I agree that there is nothing anyone can say that should *convince* someone who occupies the ⟨³/₄, ¹/₄⟩ state that she made a mistake by choosing it. She made a mistake nonetheless. I agree with E-CON to this extent: if accuracy truly is the central epistemic good then choosing to occupy ⟨³/₄, ¹/₄⟩ rather than, say, ⟨0, 1⟩ amounts to choosing a worse state over a better one, when nothing but accuracy distinguishes the two. Evidentially speaking, the two are on a par—each minimizes expected inaccuracy by its own lights—but equating ⟨³/₄, ¹/₄⟩ with ⟨0, 1⟩ seems to imply that ending up with beliefs that are ideally well supported by one's evidence is enough, all by itself, to make it reasonable to hold those beliefs, so that evidential considerations can render accuracy considerations irrelevant. This ACE must deny.

- *Imps*, Greaves (2013). At t_0, the chances of four logically independent propositions W, X, Y, Z are known to be ⟨1, ¹/₂, ¹/₂, ¹/₂⟩, respectively. By choosing time-t credences of ⟨0, 1, 1, 1⟩ one can force the time-t chances to be ⟨1, 1, 1, 1⟩. Other choices leave them at ⟨1, ¹/₂, ¹/₂, ¹/₂⟩. While ⟨0, 1, 1, 1⟩ maximizes self-accuracy (according to Brier), it is unratifiable since, conditional on its choice, ⟨1, 1, 1, 1⟩ maximizes objective expected utility. The only ratifiable choice is ⟨1, ¹/₂, ¹/₂, ¹/₂⟩, the one that minimizes objective expected inaccuracy at t_0. Thus, E-RAT does not allow one to "trade off" the accuracy of one's credence in W as a means to the end of increasing the accuracy of one's credences in X, Y, and Z. However, the reason has nothing to do with any doctrine of "separateness of propositions," as in Berker (2013). It has to do with the fact that you cannot really be choosing a *credence* of 0 for X when you know that it will be maximally inaccurate.[23]

As a first step toward justifying E-RAT and explaining its role in ACE, let's see how it differs from ratifiability principles that have been proposed in practical decision theory, e.g., by Paul Weirich (1985) and Bill Harper (1986). I have argued against such principles in (Joyce 2012). I will not recap my reasoning here, but it will be instructive to consider an example. Suppose a miser is made to play the prevision game with the Caie-like proposition O (which, recall, says that the agent will not choose a *prevision* above ¹/₂). It is part of the deal that after announcing previsions of ⟨o, $\tilde{o}$⟩,

---

[23] On one variant of Imps I have heard, the agent chooses to mislead herself about W's truth by, e.g., taking a pill that will make her think, incorrectly, that she has conclusive evidence for $\neg W$. This would not make any difference to my answer. Remember that E-RAT has us evaluate the agent's choice on the basis of the evidence she has *while choosing* augmented by the supposition that she will make the choice in question. She will therefore not condition on the misleading evidence that she will provide to her future self.

she must bet at time t as if these are her credences, i.e., she is obliged to pay $\$o \cdot x$ for [$\$x$ if O, $\$0$ if $\neg O$] and $\$\tilde{o} \cdot y$ for [$\$0$ if O, $\$y$ if $\neg O$]. Imagine also that, at some past time, a perfectly reliable predictor made a forecast of the previsions the agent would announce. If he predicted she would announce $o \geq \frac{1}{2}$ he arranged that she should be offered [$\$1/o$ if O, $\$0$ if $\neg O$] for $\$1$. If he predicted she would announce $o < \frac{1}{2}$ he arranged that she should be offered [$\$0$ if O, $\$1/\tilde{o}$ if $\neg O$] for $\$1$. Unfortunately, our agent must pay $\$1$ for whichever bet she is offered. Since she is sure the predictor will be right, she will see this as a form of robbery: whatever previsions she chooses at t_0, at t she will be forced to fork over $\$1$ for a bet that pays $\$0$. Since her immediate profit from announcing her previsions is less than $\$1$, she ends up losing money.

What's the best thing to do? Two answers suggest themselves. First, one might think that, since the time-t bet is a sure $\$1$ loss, the agent should aim to maximize profit by announcing previsions that minimize the initial penalty. This makes $\langle \frac{1}{2}, 1 \rangle$ the only rational choice since it has the minimum penalty of $\$1/8$. Alternatively, one might see this as a "rational dilemma" in which no $\langle o, \tilde{o} \rangle$ pair may be rationally chosen. Ratificationists like Harper and Weirich take this second line since no acts are ratifiable here, including $\langle \frac{1}{2}, 1 \rangle$.

I think the first diagnosis is correct: the fact that $\langle \frac{1}{2}, 1 \rangle$ is unratifiable in this *practical* context does not reflect badly on it at all. Indeed, I do not think that the *bare* fact that an act is unratifiable ever tells against its choiceworthiness. In general, the knowledge that one will come to rue some action after choosing it is only a reason for avoiding that act if the knowledge engages *currently* available reasons for expecting that some other choice will better serve one's ends. When I reflect on the fact that, in the morning I will regret staying up late, this should make me more inclined to go to bed only to the extent that it makes it salient to me that I *now* have good reasons for going to bed early and being well rested in the morning. Nothing like that occurs here. Here, the agent does not get the crucial evidence that leads her to regret her action (i.e., the information that she'll be offered the particular bet she is offered) until after she *irrevocably* makes her decision, at which point she has no more control over her fate. Before she decides what to do she cannot be sure what the predictor has predicted, and so cannot be sure what bet she will be offered.[24] This information becomes available only after a *final* outcome has been determined, at which point it is immaterial that other choices might have been better responses given the bet the agent actually faced. So, in the practical sphere the unratifiability of an action either serves to show an agent that she already has reasons not to do it, or it is irrelevant to what she should do.

Epistemic choices (insofar as they exist) work differently. As stressed above, when an epistemic agent chooses a credal state she is *not* choosing a final end. She is choosing the beliefs she will use, starting at t, to confront the future, process new information, and estimate truth-values and other quantities. Real credences are

---

[24] This is slightly misleading since, during her deliberation, she will make some inferences about what the predictor predicted, and thus about what bet she is likely to be offered.

essentially forward looking: by choosing them one is choosing to live with their downstream effects. As a result, epistemic choices, unlike practical choices, must be ratifiable. When the choice of a credal state generates information that is relevant to assessing that state's post-choice accuracy, an epistemic agent needs to ask whether the choice makes sense in light of that information. If not, she should not make it.

We can get a better grip on why this is so by tweaking the prevision game one last time so that the agent chooses *credences* directly. This is now an *epistemic* decision. Let's focus first on its potential practical consequences, and then draw morals about its epistemic consequences. Suppose our agent is asked, at t_0, to state previsions for the Caie propositions U and $\neg U$, where (as before) U says that her time-t credence for U will not be less than ½. The new wrinkle is that the agent has taken a pill that will cause her time-t credence for U to match whatever previsions she reports at t_0. So, reporting $\langle u, \tilde{u} \rangle$ has two effects: it produces a penalty of $\$^{1}/_{2}[(1-u)^2 + \tilde{u}^2]$ if $u < 1/2$ or of $^{1}/_{2}\$[u^2 + (1-\tilde{u})^2]$ if $u \geq 1/2$, and causes the agent to hold the credences $\langle u, \tilde{u} \rangle$ at t. For example, reporting $\langle 1/2, 1 \rangle$ has the immediate practical effect of producing the minimum penalty of \$1/8, so that the agent will have earned \$7/8 when she arrives at t, but it also forces her to occupy the $\langle 1/2, 1 \rangle$ credal state at t.

This second effect has bad consequences that can entirely negate the good consequences of the first. Since a person's credences at t affect her choices at t, we cannot gauge the *total* practical impact of this epistemic choice unless we consider both its intermediate impact at t_0 and its impact on practical choices made down the road. These downstream effects can be quite pernicious since the agent will happily pay to buy bets at t that are sure losers. In fact, her time-t credences can lead her to give away everything she earns from her t_0 choice. The following table tells the tale (where the wagers are purchased at t for stated prices):

Prevision	Intermediate (t_0) Profit	Wager	Price	Net
$\langle u, \tilde{u} \rangle, u \geq 1/2$	$\$w = 1/2 + \tilde{u}^2 - 1/2(u^2 + \tilde{u}^2)$	[\$w/u if U, \$0 else]	\$w	\$0
$\langle u, \tilde{u} \rangle, u < 1/2$	$\$v = 1/2 + u^2 - 1/2(u^2 + \tilde{u}^2)$	[\$v/$\tilde{u}$ if $\neg U$, \$0 else]	\$v	\$0

There is something wrong with such decision-making. Even if it makes sense to choose some $\langle u, \tilde{u} \rangle$ pair at t_0, the agent should *not* want to bet with the credences that choice produces since, no matter which pair she chooses, there will be bets she finds fair or attractive that lead her to give away whatever money she might have acquired as a result of the t_0 choice. Moreover, she knows all this at t_0 when she chooses her credences. It is thus unclear that there are *any* practical advantages to choosing $\langle 1/2, 1 \rangle$. Even though doing so will maximize the agent's intermediate profit, it will also lead her to squander it, so that nothing is actually gained. $\langle 1/2, 1 \rangle$ looks best if we treat the intermediate profit as a final end, but not when we factor in its downstream effects. The root of the problem, of course, is that the initial practical benefits of *choosing* $\langle 1/2, 1 \rangle$ are entirely eclipsed by potential practical costs of *using* $\langle 1/2, 1 \rangle$ in the way credences are used, e.g., to price bets. This is true for any $\langle u, \tilde{u} \rangle$ pair. So, no choice can be rational since all lead the agent to spend good money to buy bets that are sure losers.

One can imagine two rejoinders here. Some might object that I unfairly assume a worst-case scenario in which (a) the agent is sure to be offered bets at t that will result in the loss of her t_0 winnings, and (b) she will take *any* bet that she judges to be fair or favorable at t. Why assume either thing? Maybe no "Dutch bookie" is around to exploit the agent. Even if one is, can't she protect her profits by, e.g., refusing bets on U or by sequestering some of her t_0 winnings? If she can "tie herself to the mast" in one of these ways then she can make more by choosing $\langle 1/2, 1 \rangle$ than by choosing any alternative.

This rejoinder seeks to justify the choice of self-undermining credences by supposing that the agent is prevented from choosing options that her credences portray as fair or advantageous, so that she is unable to use her time-t "credences" in the way credences are characteristically used. The status of $\langle 1/2, 1 \rangle$ as the best credal state to choose at t_0 then depends on restricting the agent's freedom of action to prevent her from squandering her t_0 profits by acting as her time-t credences recommend. Followers of F. P. Ramsey (1931), who understand credence "qua basis of action" (p. 169), will deny that the agent is choosing *credences* at all because her choice is predicated on the idea that she will *not* use them in practical decision-making. These sham "credences" lack the ordinary connection to action. As such, their choice tells us nothing about the properties that real credences should possess.

As a second rejoinder, it might seem that I am making a moot point since, as long as the agent remembers what she chose at t_0, she won't be able to act on the $\langle 1/2, 1 \rangle$ credences simply for lack of time! In addition to producing an immediate $7/8 profit, choosing $\langle 1/2, 1 \rangle$ produces conclusive evidence for $\neg U$, evidence the agent will have at t. But, an agent with such evidence will immediately update her beliefs so that her credence for U goes to *zero* the instant after t. Of course, the pill and her choice force her to adopt the $½$ credence at t, but she will revert instantly to $u_s = 0$ for all times s thereafter. As a result, any decision she faces will be assessed using the $\langle 0, 1 \rangle$ credences. The $½$ time-t credence for U, being entirely ephemeral, has no detrimental effects! So, it looks like the $\langle 1/2, 1 \rangle$ choice will maximize total payoff without the need for any "tying to the mast" strategies or any scarcity of bookies!

This is incorrect. First, one might wonder why the agent must update on the evidence about her t_0 choice *before* evaluating bets at t. If her credence for U really is $½$, shouldn't that be the source of her time-t evaluations? Indeed, it's not even clear that she can see herself as having conclusive evidence against U at t. At t she (a) thinks U is as likely as not to be true, and (b) knows U is true iff she chose a credence of less than $½$ for U at t_0. So, does she actually know what credence she chose at t_0? Not obviously, though it is hard to say what she knows given that she is also certain U is false. But, leaving this aside, suppose the agent does update on her t_0 choice before making decisions at t. The earlier problem re-arises. If the agent's rationale for choosing $u_t = 1/2$ requires it to be so fleeting that she will never use it to evaluate acts then, to the extent that credences are essentially tied to action, she will see this as a sham "credence."

There are three morals to be drawn here. First, in practical terms, an agent who has the ability to choose her future credences will *only* choose incoherent ones (or ones that violate the Principal Principle) if she is certain that they will not affect her subsequent choices in a way that undoes the goods obtained in her initial choice, either because she is never offered problematic choices, or because she ties herself to the mast, or because her future credences are ephemeral. Second, the choices that tend to produce these decision-theoretically inert "credences" are those in which the agent has an incentive to choose a credal state that will *not* be justified in light of the evidence the choice produces. These choices are unratifiable, which makes it unreasonable for the agent to employ the chosen credences in decision-making. Third, these decision-theoretically inert attitudes do not deserve to be called "credences" at all: we should see them as shams, at least insofar as we see credences as essentially tied to the production of action.

The epistemic analogy should be clear. The initial payment in the prevision game is like the self-accuracy score. If we treat this aspect of the choice as a final end, as E-CON advises, then choosing $\langle 1/2, 1 \rangle$ in Caie's example (or setting $x_t = 0.423$ in the Chance Paradox) makes good sense. If, however, we consider the downstream accuracy-related consequences of holding the chosen credences at t—sanctioning truth-value estimates that are known to be inaccurate—the alleged accuracy benefits of the t_0 choice vanish. This is because the choice produces evidence which makes it unreasonable to use the chosen "credences" as truth-value estimates, thus undermining their ability to play one of the characteristic epistemic roles of credences. As a result, it is only rational for an epistemic agent to choose $\langle 1/2, 1 \rangle$ in Caie's case, or to set $x_t = 0.423$ in the Chance Paradox, if she has some way of preventing their use in making estimates at t. This makes the chosen attitudes sham "credences."

The root of the problem is the unratifiability of the t_0 choices. By creating evidence that makes it impossible for the agent to see her time-t credences as accurate truth-value estimates, the t_0 choice undermines its own status as a guide to rational belief at t. To see the point, it helps to contrast U with $\neg U$. Since the agent manipulates U's truth-value by her choice of u_t, the value she chooses at t_0 reflects more than just her assessment of U's likely truth: it is also the product of strategic considerations that give her incentives to force her time-t self to hold a credence that she sees as a lousy estimate of U's truth-value (at t_0 and ever after). So, her choice of $u = 1/2$ at t_0 cannot be an endorsement of the use of her time-t credence as a basis for truth-value estimation. Absent such an endorsement, the agent is choosing a sham "credence." By way of contrast, the agent's choice of $\tilde{u} = 1$ *is* an endorsement of this credence as an estimate of $\neg U$'s truth-value. Since $\neg U$ is *not* affected by $\tilde{u}$, the agent is encouraged to choose a credence for $\neg U$ that she is happy to use as the basis for estimating $\neg U$'s truth-value and the values of quantities that depend on it. In particular, since U's truth-value depends on $\neg U$'s truth-value, when she chooses $\langle 1/2, 1 \rangle$ she endorses 0 as the best estimate for U's truth-value, i.e., the one that will minimize estimated inaccuracy in light of the evidence she knows her choice will produce.[25] Thus, as the contrast between U and $\neg U$ illustrates, epistemic choices can reliably reveal rational credences for propositions that are not causally tied to those choices, but not for propositions that are so tied. The key is epistemic ratifiability. Hypothetical epistemic choices can be useful guides to what one should believe when one is choosing among ratifiable options, but not otherwise. There is a role for decision theory in epistemology, but not a theory that treats credal states as final ends in the way that crude forms of epistemic consequentialism suggests.[26]

References

Berker, Selim, 2013. 'Epistemic Teleology and the Separateness of Propositions'. *Philosophical Review* 122(3): 337–93.
Brier, George W., 1950. 'Verification of Forecasts Expressed in Terms of Probability'. *Monthly Weather Review* 78: 1–3.
Caie, Michael, 2013. 'Rational Probabilistic Incoherence'. *Philosophical Review* 122(4): 527–75.
Campbell-Moore, Catrin, 2015. 'Rational Probabilistic Incoherence? A Reply to Michael Caie'. *Philosophical Review* 124(3): 393–406.
de Finetti, Bruno, 1937/1964. 'Foresight: Its Logical Laws, Its Subjective Sources'. In *Studies in Subjective Probability*: 93–158, edited by H. Kyburg and H. Smokler, New York: John Wiley.
de Finetti, Bruno, 1974. *Theory of Probability*, vol. 1, New York: John Wiley and Sons.
Greaves, Hilary, 2013. 'Epistemic Decision Theory'. *Mind* 122(488): 915–52.
Harper, William, 1986. 'Mixed Strategies and Ratifiability in Causal Decision Theory'. *Erkenntnis* 24(1): 25–36.
Jeffrey, Richard, 1983. *The Logic of Decision* (2nd revised edition). Chicago, IL: University of Chicago Press.
Jeffrey, Richard, 1986. 'Probabilism and Induction'. *Topoi* 5: 51–8.
Joyce, James M., 1998. 'A Non-Pragmatic Vindication of Probabilism'. *Philosophy of Science* 65: 575–603.
Joyce, James M., 2009. 'Accuracy and Coherence: Prospects for an Alethic Epistemology of Partial Belief'. In *Degrees of Belief*: 263–98, edited by Franz Huber and Christoph Schmidt-Petri, Amsterdam: Springer (*Synthese Library*, 342).

---

[25] This assumes that the agent really does have a definite credence for U at t (as she would in the "pill" version of the prevision game). If she chooses only a *sham* credence of ½ then, as I would read things, U is *true* because at t she does not invest a *credence* of less than ½ in it. (Sham credences are not credences.) In such a case, $\langle ½, 0 \rangle$, rather than $\langle ½, 1 \rangle$, would minimize self-inaccuracy and $\langle 1, 0 \rangle$ would give the agent's actual truth-value estimates. Thus, the 0 in $\langle ½, 0 \rangle$ would be a genuine credence, and the ½ would be a sham credence. Thanks to Shayam Nair for helping me clarify this point.

[26] Readers may have noticed that the rationale I have given for *E-RAT* works just as well whether we think of credences in Ramsey's way, qua basis of action, or in ACE's way, in terms truth-value estimation. Nothing in *E-RAT* ties it essentially to an accuracy-centered approach. Any account that assesses credences on the basis of the effects of *using* them will see the "credences" that result from epistemologically unratifiable choices as shams. ACE is one such theory. There may be others. But, all will reject any version of epistemic consequentialism that fails to include a ratifiability requirement.

Joyce, James M., 2012. 'Regret and Instability in Causal Decision Theory'. *Synthese*, 187(1): 123–45.
Joyce, James M., 2015. 'The Value of Truth: A Reply to Howson'. *Analysis* 75(3): 413–24.
Konek, Jason and Ben Levinstein, forthcoming. 'The Foundations of Epistemic Decision Theory'. *Mind*.
Lewis, David, 1980. 'A Subjectivist's Guide to Objective Chance'. In *Studies in Inductive Logic and Probability 2*: 263–94, edited by R. Jeffrey, Berkeley, CA: University of California Press.
Lindley, David, 1982. 'Scoring Rules and the Inevitability of Probability'. *International Statistical Review* 50: 1–26.
Myrvold, Wayne, 2012. 'Epistemic Values and the Value of Learning'. *Synthese* 187(2): 547–56.
Oddie, Graham, 1997. 'Conditionalization, Cogency, and Cognitive Value'. *The British Journal for the Philosophy of Science* 48: 533–41.
Pettigrew, Richard, 2013. 'A New Epistemic Utility Argument for the Principal Principle'. *Episteme* 10(1): 19–35.
Pettigrew, Richard, 2016. *Accuracy and the Laws of Chance*. Oxford: Oxford University Press.
Predd, J., R. Seiringer, E. H. Lieb, D. Osherson, V. Poor, and S. Kulkarni, 2009. 'Probabilistic Coherence and Proper Scoring Rules'. *IEEE Transactions on Information Theory* 55(10): 4786–92.
Ramsey, Frank, 1931. 'Truth and Probability'. In *The Foundations of Mathematics and other Logical Essays*: 156–98, edited by R. B. Braithwaite, London: Kegan, Paul, Trench, Trubner & Co.
Savage, Leonard J., 1971. 'Elicitation of Personal Probabilities'. *Journal of the American Statistical Association* 66: 783–801.
Schervish, Mark J., Teddy Seidenfeld, and Joseph B. Kadane, 2009. 'Proper Scoring Rules, Dominated Forecasts, and Coherence'. *Decision Analysis* 6(4): 202–21.
Skyrms, Brian, 1990. *The Dynamics of Rational Deliberation*, Cambridge, MA: Harvard University Press.
Weirich, Paul, 1985. 'Decision Instability'. *The Australasian Journal of Philosophy* 63: 465–72.

PART III

Epistemic Consequentialism Applied

11

Epistemic Value and the Jamesian Goals

Sophie Horowitz

William James (1897) famously argued that rational belief aims at two goals: *believing truth* and *avoiding error*. What it takes to achieve one goal is different from what it takes to achieve the other. Believing *everything* secures the first goal but not the second; believing *nothing* secures the second but not the first. In the middle, we could plausibly favor one goal or the other in less extreme ways, by drawing stronger or weaker conclusions on the basis of our evidence.

Is there more than one *rational* way to weight the relative importance of these two goals? If there is, James's observation seems to support an argument for epistemic permissivism. For our purposes, I'll define permissivism as follows:

Permissivism: For at least some bodies of evidence, there are many different total credal states that different rational agents can have in response to that evidence.[1]

If there are different rationally permissible epistemic values or goals, then there should be different rationally permissible responses to a given body of evidence, corresponding to those values.

The Jamesian argument for permissivism will be my focus here.[2] Is this argument sound? And in particular, does Jamesian reasoning support permissivism about rational *credence*? Remarks from several contemporary epistemologists, as well as parallels between the epistemic and practical realms, suggest that the argument

---

[1] There are many subtly different ways that one could define "permissivism." Often it is defined in the literature as the negation of another principle, "uniqueness," which can also be spelled out in a number of subtly different ways. See Titelbaum and Kopec (MS) and Meacham (MS) for further exploration of these issues. For my current purposes, I will stick to the principle above, but will note when these authors' further distinctions seem particularly relevant.

[2] The "Jamesian" argument rather than "James's" argument: the aim of this chapter is not James scholarship. Instead, for better or worse, I will look at arguments inspired by his remarks, most of which cite "The Will to Believe" in passing just as I have. However, as I'll note along the way, the Jamesian argument may be more plausible if we accept it in the form in which James presents it.

should work. And a popular branch of formal epistemology, which sees epistemic rationality as a matter of maximizing expected "epistemic utility," seems to provide the perfect setting for spelling out a degreed-belief version of James's thought in a Bayesian setting. However, I will argue, Jamesian Permissivism about rational credence is false.

The rest of the chapter will proceed as follows. In section 11.1, I will narrow down the particular form of the Jamesian argument that I'm interested in, and look at some of the motivations for that argument. In section 11.2, I will look at how we might try to use epistemic utility theory to spell out the Jamesian argument, and show why this strategy fails. In section 11.3, I will consider the possibility of revising epistemic utility theory so that the argument goes through; this strategy, I will suggest, incurs significant costs. Finally, in section 11.4, I will consider another interpretation of James's "goals," which associates them with aspects of our prior or initial credences. I will end by suggesting a couple of pessimistic conclusions for the would-be Jamesian Permissivist. First, there is likely no plausible, distinctively Jamesian argument for permissivism about rational credence. And second, a decision-theoretic understanding of epistemic rationality is likely misguided.

11.1 Motivating the Jamesian Argument

I'll begin by focusing on the central idea that is often attributed to James: we *want* to believe truth, and we *want* to avoid error. These are, quite literally, desires or goals, and they influence what is rational for us to believe.[3] The argument for permissivism comes in once we consider the possibility that there might be different rational ways to balance the two Jamesian goals. If permissivism about epistemic value is true, then permissivism about rational credence should follow. The Jamesian Argument, then, is distinctive in the following way: it is an argument *from* permissivism about epistemic value *to* permissivism about rational credence.

A major motivation for the Jamesian Argument is the fact that a similar line of thought seems to work in the practical realm. What we value or desire influences what it is practically rational for us to do. There are (plausibly) many different desires or practical values that one could have, compatible with practical rationality. As a result, there are cases in which different practical values rationalize different choices: practical permissivism is true. For instance:

---

[3] Many epistemologists speak of epistemic rationality as goal-oriented in this manner. See Berker (2013) for an extensive overview of "goal" talk in recent epistemology, and for an argument against this sort of "epistemic teleology." I will not try to argue, as Berker does, that everyone who appeals to the Jamesian goals really commits herself to the consequentialist project. However, this chapter will be much in the spirit of Berker's, in that I will be discussing (and criticizing) the type of epistemic consequentialism that takes this talk of "goals" literally.

Snack: You and I are at the diner, and there are two items on the menu: French fries or ice cream. You prefer salty snacks to sweet ones. I prefer sweet snacks to salty ones. What should we each order?

The answer in this case is obvious: I should order the ice cream (and not the fries), and you should order the fries (and not the ice cream). This is explained by our different values; if we somehow swapped values, we should swap snacks as well.[4] It's also clear that, in cases like this, we are justified in taking a certain liberal attitude towards one another's choices at the diner. While I would never want to order the fries for myself, I can understand why that's the right choice for you. And you can understand why ice cream is the right choice for me. Indeed, if you asked me what to order, I might reasonably recommend the fries—even while admitting that I like ice cream better.

If the Jamesian Argument is right, then there should be purely epistemic cases that work just like Snack. And in fact, in addition to James himself, many contemporary epistemologists have suggested that such cases exist. For instance, Kelly (2014) discusses a case along the following lines (my paraphrase):[5]

Election: We both have the same evidence regarding the upcoming presidential election, and we agree that on balance it favors D: the hypothesis that the Democrat will win. But I weight believing truth more highly than you do, while you weight avoiding error more highly. As a result, my credence in D is .7, and yours is .6.

Kelly suggests that in cases like Election, different epistemic values might underwrite different rational responses to our evidence. Furthermore, he finds it plausible that a liberal attitude towards one another's credences, like the one we saw in Snack, might be justified here as well:

If I learned that we differed in our cognitive goals in this way, I would be disinclined to conclude that the manner in which you are responding to our shared evidence is unreasonable, even though it differs from my own. In fact, I might even think that if you were responding to the evidence in any other way than you are, then that would be unreasonable, given your cognitive goals. Moreover, notice that making such a judgment has no tendency to make me insecure in my conviction that I am also responding to the evidence in a reasonable way, given my cognitive goals. The upshot: subtly different ways of responding to the same body of evidence seem equally reasonable, given corresponding differences in the weights that we give to our shared cognitive goals. (Kelly, 2014, p. 302)

---

[4] Snack is *inter*personally, but not *intra*personally, permissive; there is only one rational option for each person. This is the kind of permissive case I am interested in. Of course, there are also practical cases that are *intra*personally permissive: for instance, when two or more options are equally valuable or desirable for an agent. I will set those cases aside for now, and focus on the interpersonal ones. This restriction should be welcome to many epistemic permissivists. See, for instance, Kelly (2014), Schoenfield (2013), and Meacham (2014) for endorsements of interpersonal, but not intrapersonal, epistemic permissivism.

[5] See especially pp. 299–300.

Kelly does not fully endorse the argument sketched above, but he puts it forward as a plausible route to epistemic permissivism, about both rational belief and rational credence.[6]

Others mention similar ideas in passing. For instance, Ben Levinstein (2015, p. 346) writes that, "in a degree-of-belief model, agents can avoid massive inaccuracy by having credences close to .5, but they thereby sacrifice the potential epistemic good of being highly accurate. Plausibly, rationality permits a range of different attitudes toward epistemic risk. If Alice and Bob have different risk-profiles, then they can rationally maintain disagreement." The suggestion here is, of course, that these "different risk-profiles" might justify Alice and Bob in having different credences.

A third instance of this idea comes from Jonathan Kvanvig, who cites an earlier paper of Kelly's. Kvanvig draws this lesson from Kelly:

Some people find it easier to risk being wrong than others, while others reveal a deeper horror at the thought of making a mistake. At the extremes, each of these character traits can lead to irrational attitudes, but in between, Kelly suggests, is an area where the tolerance of differences should be shown by our theories of rationality.[7]

Kvanvig's idea is that different levels of risk tolerance might "lead to" different attitudes. Extreme risk-aversion or risk-seeking is irrational, and will "lead to irrational attitudes." But in the middle, where we should be "toler[ant] of differences," presumably that tolerance should extend both to differences in risk profiles, and differences in the credences that they rationalize.

Finally, writing in somewhat different terms, here is Hartry Field (2000, p. 141):

We recognize that a slight modification of our goals—an increase in the relative value of reliability over power—would lead to a preference for [another] system, and we regard the alternative goals as well within the bounds of acceptability. Consequently we make no very strong claims for the preferability of our system over the alternative: the alternative is slightly less good than ours given our precise goals, but slightly better on alternative goals that are by no means beyond the pale.

According to this line of thought, different epistemic goals justify different epistemic "systems," or ways of responding to our evidence. And Field seems to agree that the goal-relativity of rational belief justifies the liberal attitude toward one another's beliefs as well.[8]

---

[6] There may be important differences between the full-belief setting and the credence setting. Kelly writes a few pages later that he used to find "the James point" plausible for full beliefs, but *not* for credences. But now, he says, he has come around to viewing the argument as compelling in both cases. "To the extent that it works at all," he writes, "the Jamesian route to vindicating a permissive epistemology sketched in this section works just as well in a framework that employs credences instead of all or nothing beliefs" (p. 303).

[7] See Kvanvig (2014, p. 140). Both Levinstein and Kvanvig cite Kelly on this point, though Kvanvig cites an older remark of Kelly's that isn't as explicitly tied to the Jamesian goals.

[8] Field writes about "reliability" and "power" rather than the Jamesian goals, but the upshot is similar. I will not get into the question of how reliability and power might *differ* from the Jamesian goals, but notice

None of these authors defends a Jamesian argument for permissivism in any kind of detail (or, necessarily, at all—Levinstein mentions the idea but does not endorse it, and Kelly presents the idea as plausible but does not endorse it either). But their remarks show that the Jamesian line of thought is interesting and at least prima facie plausible. To make things more precise, here is the argument that I am interested in, which I take to be a straightforward way of crystallizing the thought expressed in the passages above. I'll call this the "Jamesian Argument" and the kind of permissivism that it supports "Jamesian Permissivism."

The Jamesian Argument
P1. If there are many different rationally acceptable epistemic values, then, for at least some bodies of evidence, there are many different total credal states that different rational agents can have in response to that evidence.
P2. There are many different rationally acceptable epistemic values.
C. For at least some bodies of evidence, there are many different total credal states that different rational agents can have in response to that evidence.

Two quick clarifications. First, this argument is of course just one route to permissivism. There are other ways to defend the argument's conclusion, even if P1 and P2 turn out to be false; I won't discuss those here. This argument assumes a certain type of framework on which values are relevant to beliefs. Some permissivists might reject that entire framework, and consequentialism about rationality more generally; such permissivists are not "Jamesian permissivists" in my sense. (There may also be other ways to understand the Jamesian thought expressed by Kelly and others; I will generally not discuss those in this chapter, either.)

Second, many permissivists hold that some bodies of evidence are *impermissive* with respect to some propositions. For instance, if evidence E entails P, then arguably it is not rational for someone with evidence E to have any credence in P other than 1. Or if you know that I am about to flip a fair coin, then arguably it is not rational for you to have any credence other than .5 that my coin will come up heads. The version of Jamesian Permissivism that I am interested in is compatible with this sort of restriction—hence the caveat, "for at least some bodies of evidence"—but it also takes value-based differences in rational credences to be a quite widespread phenomenon. Jamesian Permissivism, of the sort I am interested in, is not restricted to cases of entailment or known objective chances, "forced and momentous" choices, or to particular circumscribed domains. If Jamesian Permissivism is true, our values influence our reasoning in ordinary inductive cases, like Election, as well.

---

that there is a natural way of understanding them to be quite similar. A belief system is "reliable" insofar as it avoids accepting falsehoods, and "powerful" insofar as it attains truth.

11.2 Epistemic Utility Theory and Jamesian Permissivism

We should by now have a handle on the general line of thought behind Jamesian Permissivism. But it would be helpful to give some more substance to the idea of epistemic value. As it happens, there is a well-developed account of epistemic value on offer, coming from a popular branch of formal epistemology: epistemic utility theory. Epistemic utility theory (EUT) treats epistemic rationality as analogous to practical rationality understood in decision-theoretic terms. Epistemically rational agents are taken to maximize expected accuracy in their credences just as practically rational agents maximize expected utility in their actions. If the Jamesian Argument works, EUT seems like a natural framework to use to fill in the details.

So let's turn now to EUT itself.[9] EUT gives a decision-theoretic understanding of rational credence, where what credence an agent ought to have is partly a matter of her "epistemic utility" function, or "scoring rule." Scoring rules are functions that take the distance between a degree of credence and a state of the world as input, and output a value. Scoring rules are often used to measure accuracy (and inaccuracy), and plausible accuracy scoring rules assign higher value to an agent's credence in a given proposition the closer that credence is to the proposition's truth-value. So, if the proposition is true, one's credence gets more and more valuable as it gets closer to 1; if the proposition is false, one's credence gets more and more valuable as it gets closer to 0. EUT therefore (canonically) uses scoring rules as measures of accuracy and understands accuracy as a *good* that we ought to pursue in our credences.

Different people might have different conceptions of this epistemic good, however, in just the way James described. One person might prioritize *believe truth* and have a scoring rule that rewards credences in larger increments as they get closer to the truth—so the difference between .8 and .9 credence in a true proposition, for instance, would count for more than the difference between .7 and .8. A scoring rule like this would, intuitively, reward a believer for having more opinionated or extreme credences. Another person might prioritize *avoid error*, and have a scoring rule that rewards credences in smaller increments as they become more extreme. This scoring rule would reward epistemic caution. A particular agent's scoring rule, then, encodes her own personal tradeoff between the two Jamesian goals.[10]

---

[9] For a few canonical papers developing the approach I'm interested in here, see Joyce (1998; 2009), Greaves and Wallace (2006), and Leitgeb and Pettigrew (2010a; 2010b). Not all epistemic utility theorists see themselves as engaged in the kind of decision-theoretic project I will be describing. However, since this is the most straightforward interpretation of their formalism—and since at least some people *do* see the project this way—I will focus on that understanding here. For simplicity, I will also talk about "accuracy measures" here, though in fact EUT more often discusses *in*accuracy measures, and the requirement to minimize expected inaccuracy.

[10] See Joyce (2009, p. 281) for the thought that scoring rules encode the Jamesian goals in this way; see also Pettigrew (2016) for explicit ties to the Jamesian goals, and an explicit endorsement of the consequentialist understanding of EUT.

But not all such tradeoffs are rational, and an important project for EUT is to identify which are and which are not. As we have already noted, someone who *only* cared about believing truth would not be rational, and her lopsided weighting of the epistemic goals would not make it rational for her to assign credence 1 to everything. Part of the problem with this epistemic extremist is that she violates a plausible coherence norm concerning which credences can be rational, or can be supported by a body of evidence. One way in which we can narrow down the range of acceptable scoring rules, then, is by looking at which structural constraints on credences are compatible with which scoring rules.

The scoring rules commonly accepted as rational, by EUT, form a narrow class: the "strictly proper" ones. An advantage of these rules is that they are compatible with three plausible rational coherence requirements: immodesty, probabilistic coherence, and conditionalization. The second two are familiar parts of the Bayesian framework, and give, respectively, synchronic and diachronic coherence constraints on an agent's credences.[11] Immodesty is a different kind of coherence, which holds between a rational agent's credences and her way of assessing accuracy (in this case, her scoring rule). The general idea is that, insofar as you are rational, you will adopt the credences that you take to be the most accurate response to your evidence. (It would be *irrational* to regard some other, particular credences in P as *more* accurate than your own credence in P, but hold onto your own anyway. Similarly, it would be irrational to have some credence in P while regarding another particular credence in P as *equally accurate*.) As understood by EUT, being immodest means having credences that uniquely maximize expected accuracy, by the lights of your own credences and scoring rule.

Let's call this popular, though not uncontroversial, view "Simple EUT." Simple EUT holds that rational agents have both credences and a scoring rule, or epistemic utility function, and that they are rationally required to maximize expected accuracy in their credences. The rationally acceptable scoring rules are just those that are strictly proper. And agents who maximize expected accuracy, according to those rationally acceptable scoring rules, will be probabilistically coherent, will update by conditionalization, and will be immodest.[12]

---

[11] Whether requirements like conditionalization are best understood as truly diachronic is a matter of current debate. I will set that question aside for now, and go along with the simple view here that they are diachronic. See, for instance, Hedden (2015) and Moss (2015) for further discussion.

[12] The dialectical relationship between strictly proper scoring rules and these three coherence requirements is not always presented in the same way. Epistemic utility theorists often treat probabilism as the conclusion of their arguments, rather than a reason to hold strictly proper scoring rules; however, critics complain that the assumptions of those arguments come close to presupposing probabilism (see, for instance, Maher (2003)). Immodesty (and more generally, a prohibition on self-undermining) is more often taken as a starting point. Greaves and Wallace (2006) argue that conditionalization maximizes expected accuracy, starting from the assumption that the Brier score is rational. (Their argument, however, doesn't rely on the particular features of the Brier score itself, other than strict propriety.) But while practitioners of EUT do not always argue for strict propriety with these coherence constraints as premises, some do; see, for instance, Arntzenius (2008) (though Arntzenius argues against thinking of scoring rules as "purely

Simple EUT might seem like the perfect formal setting in which to spell out the Jamesian Argument. It says that rational agents should maximize expected accuracy, by the lights of their own scoring rules. And it says that there are many different scoring rules that one could rationally have. Sure, the acceptable scoring rules have been narrowed down somewhat, but only enough to vindicate a few structural requirements on rational credence. Imposing structural requirements on acceptable practical utility functions, such as transitivity and independence of irrelevant alternatives, is still compatible with a broadly Humean view of rational preference, and permissivism in cases like Snack. So it might seem as though Simple EUT should be compatible with Jamesian Permissivism, and should explain permissivism in cases like Election.

However, it does neither; given Simple EUT, the Jamesian Argument fails. That's because, on Simple EUT, Premise 1 of the Jamesian Argument is false:

> P1. If there are many different rationally acceptable epistemic values, then, for at least some bodies of evidence, there are many different total credal states that different rational agents can have in response to that evidence.

Though there *are* many different permissible values, for Simple EUT, they *do not* make a difference to which credences we should have.

The Jamesian Argument fails because of immodesty and conditionalization. Conditionalization ensures that the only factors that determine a rational agent's credences are her prior credences and her evidence, and that her posterior credences depend on those factors in a particular way. Strictly proper scoring rules all agree that this *particular* update procedure is rational. So no matter which permissible *scoring rule* a rational agent has, it will not make a difference to which *credences* are rational for her. Furthermore, because of immodesty, Simple EUT does not justify the liberal attitude that Field and Kelly's arguments suggest.

To illustrate these points more concretely, think back to Election, where the Jamesian argument looked initially promising:

> *Election*: We both have the same evidence, E, regarding the upcoming presidential election, and we agree that on balance it favors D: the hypothesis that the Democrat will win. But I weight believing truth more highly than you do, while you weight avoiding error more highly. As a result, my credence in D is .7, and yours is .6.

Think back to earlier in this story, before the evidence comes in, and suppose that we have different strictly proper scoring rules. I have scoring rule S1, you have scoring rule S2. Now we see the evidence, and I accommodate it by maximizing

---

epistemic") and Swanson (2008) for arguments against improper scoring rules on the grounds that they encourage bad updating policies. A more neutral way to put it: vindicating these coherence constraints is certainly a *benefit* or *advantage* of strictly proper scoring rules, and makes EUT an overall more attractive picture.

expected epistemic utility according to S1. Because S1 is strictly proper, it recommends conditionalization. What if I had had S2 instead? Well, since S2 is also strictly proper, it will *also* recommend conditionalization. From my perspective, then, it does not matter whether I have S1 or S2. And the same, of course, is true from your perspective: your strictly proper scoring rule will recommend conditionalization. But mine would have, too.

This means that if we end up with different posterior credences in Election, it is *not* because of the difference in our epistemic values. Since we both conditionalize, the only factors that could make a difference are our prior credences and our evidence. By hypothesis, our evidence is shared. So our disagreement must be due to different priors. If our different credences are both rational, it is because we have different rational priors—not because we have different rational scoring rules.[13]

Furthermore, since both S1 and S2 respect immodesty, I will regard my credences as optimal, given *both* S1 and S2. And likewise, you will regard *your* credences as optimal. So we can't sensibly adopt the liberal attitude similar to the one in Snack; we won't say, "I see why you believe as you do: your epistemic values are different from mine." If any liberal attitude like this is justified, it is one based on priors. We *can* say, "I can see why you believe as you do: you regarded it as antecedently more (or less) likely that the Democrat would win, given this information." But this is different; rather than liberalism about credences based on liberalism about values, it is liberalism about credences based on liberalism about other, past credences.

These observations show that Election—at least, as interpreted by Simple EUT—is very different from Snack. We can also see now that, given Simple EUT, value does not play a substantive role in determining our rational credences. That's because for any rational agent, acceptable scoring rules will always agree about what her credence should be. So given Simple EUT, there is not a sound, value-based argument for permissivism.

Before moving on, I would like to look at one possible objection, which looks at another place in the Simple EUT framework where value might play a substantive role. That objection says: "sure, *in cases like Election*, strictly proper scoring rules will all agree on which credences are rational for a given agent. That's because they all agree on which options *maximize* expected accuracy. But different strictly proper scoring rules *disagree* on something else, namely, how they rate those options that *do not* maximize expected accuracy. Won't there be cases where those disagreements make a difference?"

Note that in abandoning cases like Election, this objection gives up a lot of the original Jamesian view! But let's consider the more limited form of Jamesian Permissivism that the objection suggests. In order for this view to work, we need to find cases where

---

[13] The fact that our priors do so much work here might make some people suspicious of the Bayesian framework more generally. See, for instance, Marley-Payne (MS). However, I won't pursue that line of thought here.

different views about suboptimal, non-expected-accuracy-maximizing, options make a difference to which credence an agent should have. Sarah Moss (2011, pp. 1063–4) suggests a few cases that fit this pattern.[14] Here is one example (my paraphrase):

> *Evil Scientist*: An evil scientist is going to change your credence in P. Currently, your credence is .7. The scientist will change it to either .6 or .8, and you can choose. Which should you choose?

In Evil Scientist, supposing you start off rational, any strictly proper scoring rule you have will agree that your current credence, .7, is the one that maximizes expected accuracy. (Notice that the evil scientist is just changing your credence, not providing you with new evidence.) But in your current situation, credence .7 is off the menu; your options are restricted, and you have to choose between the suboptimal options of credence .6 and .8. As it happens, different strictly proper scoring rules will disagree about which of .6 and .8 is better. So, the objection goes, maybe we could use Evil Scientist to construct a scenario like Snack. Suppose both of us are in the lab, facing the same decision, but we have different scoring rules; should we therefore make different choices between the two credences that the scientist is offering? And doesn't this therefore give us a (limited) illustration of Jamesian Permissivism?

I am doubtful that cases like Evil Scientist can resurrect the Jamesian Argument. As we noted before, Jamesian Permissivism in this kind of case would not extend to ordinary disagreements like Election, which do not seem to involve restricted options.[15] Furthermore, notice that for Simple EUT, cases like Evil Scientist are epistemic dilemmas. Since we are prevented from maximizing expected accuracy (and prevented from conditionalizing), neither option is fully rational. (This is part of what makes the scientist so evil!) Cases like Evil Scientist are positioned to motivate a version of Jamesian Permissivism on which our "epistemic values" only make a difference under quite restricted circumstances.

As a final rejoinder, the objector might deny that cases like Evil Scientist are dilemmas. One way to do that is if we see epistemic rationality as a matter of maximizing expected accuracy *from among one's credal options*. Call this decision rule "Options-Sensitive." According to Options-Sensitive, conditionalization is only rationally required in the special case when your options are unlimited, and you have

---

[14] Alejandro Pérez Carballo (this volume) considers a case similar to Evil Scientist. Though Moss's main goal is not to argue for Jamesian Permissivism, she does present Evil Scientist and others as cases where different strictly proper scoring rules will license different choices. I find it most natural to interpret these cases as practical choices (between various actions we could take in our conversation with the scientist, made on practical grounds). However, to adapt the cases to the Jamesian's purposes, we can consider them as "purely epistemic" choices.

[15] The narrow Jamesian view, however, is arguably in line with what James himself defended, according to which our values only make a difference in cases where our choice is "forced."

all of the possible credence functions to choose from. Under less ideal circumstances, when your doxastic options are limited, you should just do the best you can. Options-Sensitive would make epistemic rationality much more similar to practical rationality, where having limited options does not automatically force us into a dilemma.

However, there is something odd about looking at epistemic rationality in an Options-Sensitive way. Doing so presupposes that our doxastic options are narrowed down in some non-arbitrary way. What would that be? In the practical realm, it's natural to understand our available options as just those that we are able to undertake voluntarily.[16] This goes along with the thought that for practical rationality, "ought" implies "can." But for epistemic rationality, "ought" does not imply "can," and the relevant "acts" are involuntary anyway.[17] It's often the case that we ought to adopt credences that aren't among our "available" actions. This makes it hard to see how Moss's cases are interestingly different from ordinary cases where we are unable to be rational, even without the interference of evil scientists. Without even a rough, non-arbitrary way of circumscribing options, Options-Sensitive is unmotivated. We should reject it, along with the circumscribed form of Jamesian Permissivism that it delivers.[18]

Let's sum up. Simple EUT fails to justify the Jamesian Argument. And the objection from cases of restricted options does not help. If we want to defend Jamesian Permissivism, we will need to give up at least some of Simple EUT.

---

[16] Of course, that's not to say that there is any agreed-upon, developed view of exactly what our practical options are. See Hedden (2012) for further discussion.

[17] It's unsurprising that doxastic involuntarism should be incompatible with an argument inspired by "The Will to Believe"!

[18] There are other ways we might vindicate a restricted kind of Jamesian Permissivism by extending Simple EUT. One is by looking at cases of uncertain evidence, where we don't assign our evidence probability 1. Leitgeb and Pettigrew (2010b) and Levinstein (2012) show that different proper scoring rules will recommend different results in these cases (assuming we should maximize expected accuracy). Interestingly, these authors do not take this observation to support a Jamesian view. Levinstein, in particular, argues that we should prefer logarithmic scoring rules over quadratic ones like the Brier score, because only the former is consistent with Jeffrey conditionalization in these cases, and there are problems with the update procedure consistent with the latter. (Levinstein's argument, then, explicitly argues for and against certain accounts of epistemic value on the basis of the update rules that they sanction.) However, it is controversial whether we should consider uncertain evidence in our overall theory. (Following Williamson (2000), some may argue that our evidence must be known.) And a Jamesian view where differences in value *only* showed up when our evidence was uncertain would be quite limited.

A second place where different strictly proper scoring rules might make a difference is in cases of "epistemic expansion," where we expand the domain of propositions to which we assign credences. See Carr (2015) and Pérez Carballo (this volume) for discussion of such cases, using the EUT framework. Again, extending EUT to such cases is a controversial move, and would vindicate Jamesian Permissivism only in a limited form.

I won't say more here about these extensions of EUT (and there may be others as well). It is enough to notice for now that such extensions do not explain ordinary cases like Election. So if Jamesian reasoning goes through only under these particular circumstances, the kind of Jamesian Permissivism we initially wanted to investigate is still false.

11.3 Revising Simple EUT?

The two commitments that made the Jamesian Argument fail, for Simple EUT, were immodesty and conditionalization. In this section I will consider the possibility that those commitments themselves are the problem. (The assumptions are distinct, but related, and have related consequences.) Could we make room for Jamesian Permissivism by dropping one of these assumptions?

11.3.1 Giving up immodesty?

If we give up immodesty, then some *merely proper*, or even *improper* scoring rules might be rational. Unlike strictly proper scoring rules, merely proper or improper scoring rules will not recommend sticking with your own credences (in the presence of no new evidence), and they will not recommend conditionalization (in the presence of new evidence). And different improper scoring rules will not agree with one another. Some will recommend becoming more confident, and some less.

Allowing improper scoring rules would open the door to both Jamesian Permissivism, and to the Jamesian liberal attitude towards one another's credences. However, this move would also incur significant costs.

First, maximizing expected accuracy according to an improper scoring rule has some odd effects on how one learns over time. The linear scoring rule, for instance, recommends moving all of one's somewhat-opinionated credences to the extremes, so that the only permissible credences in any proposition are 0, 1, and .5. Frank Arntzenius (2008) argues that someone who is uncertain (with credence other than .5) about what the world is like, but who uses the linear scoring rule, should just take a guess and stick with it—even if, prior to taking that guess, she knows that she will learn some more in an hour.[19] This seems irrational. Similar problems would result from other improper scoring rules. Eric Swanson (2008) considers the possibility that such a person should just wait until all the evidence is in, and maximize expected accuracy once at the end. This would allow her to accommodate new evidence in a more reasonable way, but is obviously a strange thing to do and runs counter to the thought that our epistemic utilities should guide our doxastic behavior *throughout* our lives.[20]

As both Arntzenius and Swanson bring out, in order to learn over time in a reasonable way *and* maximize expected accuracy according to an improper scoring rule, one would somehow have to keep "double books"—either by having two sets of credences, or by having a very complicated update rule that "undoes" the effects of accuracy-maximization at every step. Swanson also points out that, in order to follow this second suggestion, an agent must also keep track of *how many separate*

---

[19] Arntzenius's paper touches on many of the issues discussed here, though in a different setting.
[20] This is yet another conclusion that would not seem so odd to James himself, who argued that our values only make a difference when the choice is "momentous." Momentous choices are choices of great practical importance *that we only have one chance to make*.

times she has updated, in order to prevent that factor from influencing her credences. None of these options is very attractive. These considerations show that it is hard to have an improper scoring rule as one's measure of accuracy if one wants to believe accurately across time, *and* one wants that scoring rule to play a substantive role in one's doxastic life.

There are also more general, intuitive reasons to hold immodesty, motivated by looking at credences synchronically. David Lewis (1971) introduces the idea with the following example: *Consumer Reports* is rating consumer magazines, and picks one to recommend as the best. If it is to be trusted, Lewis argues, *Consumer Reports* has to recommend itself. Suppose it does not, and modestly recommends *Consumer Bulletin*—a magazine that makes different recommendations about other products— instead. You're in the market for a toaster, so you turn to *Consumer Reports* and see that it recommends the Toasty Plus. But on the next page you see that *Consumer Reports* recommends *Consumer Bulletin* as the best consumer magazine. *Consumer Bulletin*, in turn, recommends the Crispy Supreme. Which toaster should you buy? If you try to follow *Consumer Reports*' advice, you will be at a loss; the advice is inconsistent.

Lewis's point about magazines has similar force when carried over to the case of full belief. Suppose someone believes it will rain, but also takes that belief to be *inaccurate*—in her view, believing that it *won't* rain would be more accurate. This sort of belief, "P, but believing ¬P would be more accurate," seems straightforwardly inconsistent; it is hard to distinguish between modest belief and belief in a contradiction. (Compare modest belief to akratic belief: "P, but believing ¬P would be more rational." Akratic belief certainly seems odd and irrational, but it doesn't lead to inconsistency as immediately as modest belief.)

Why is modest belief so problematic? Here is a controversial, but plausible, hypothesis: belief has a constitutive aim. It's not just that beliefs *should* aim at the truth, to be rational; it's that they must, to even count as beliefs. If this hypothesis is right, there is an important asymmetry between belief and action in this respect. Actions can succeed or fail at being properly motivated, or oriented at the right goals. They might be imprudent or immoral if they fail, but they will still be actions. Beliefs, on the other hand, can't fail to aim at the truth. This is also why it seems so odd to treat truth as a "value" that we should try to "maximize" in our beliefs. There is not enough space between *believing* and *regarding as true* to treat the two as separate moving parts in one's epistemic system. Our notion of belief and our notion of accuracy need to line up.[21]

Though it's harder to see intuitively, I think this same line of thought should carry over to credences as well. If credences are genuine doxastic states, aiming to represent the world as it is, they should aim at accuracy in the same way beliefs aim at truth.

---

[21] The question of whether belief has a constitutive aim has been thoroughly debated in the literature: the Internet Encyclopedia of Philosophy article on the subject (http://www.iep.utm.edu/beli-aim/) has well over a hundred references. I will not attempt to discuss the question in any kind of detail here.

And whatever our notion of accuracy for credences is, it should reflect that fact by vindicating immodesty. There is something incoherent about having credence .7 in a proposition, but regarding credence .9 as more accurate. Whatever the right notion of accuracy turns out to be—scoring rules or something else—it should explain that incoherence. Immodesty should be a *constraint* on our account of accuracy; we should not give it up to save the Jamesian Argument.

11.3.2 Giving up conditionalization?

Conditionalization is the other reason that the Jamesian Argument failed, for Simple EUT. If rationality requires us to conditionalize, then the rational response to our evidence must depend on our prior credences in a particular way. There is no room for epistemic value to make a difference.

Notice that the real issue here is not conditionalization itself, but the more general fact that, for Simple EUT, there is only one rational way to update one's credences, and only one kind of diachronic coherence between one's past and present rational credences. (In this way, the argument here is not only relevant to Bayesianism, but also to any view on which there is a unique rational update rule.) If we gave up conditionalization but adopted a similar updating rule in its place, we would not have vindicated the Jamesian Argument.

To use this strategy to save the Jamesian Argument, then, we could give up conditionalization as a rational requirement, and instead adopt permissivism about *update rules*. We would need to defend a view on which different rules are rational for different people, and on which one's epistemic values determine which rule is rational for a given person. These different rules would then justify different credences in response to a body of evidence.[22]

One way to carry this project out is similar to the suggestion regarding improper scoring rules, discussed in section 11.3.1. For instance, a reasoner with an improper scoring rule might update by "conditionalization+" or "conditionalization−," conditionalizing and then giving her credences a little nudge in one direction or another to add or subtract a bit of epistemic risk (with that nudge depending on the scoring rule). If this view were right, it might explain cases like Election. I might say, "Sure, I see why your having credence .6 is rational: our shared evidence alone supported credence .65, and you just gave your credence a nudge down. I gave mine a nudge up. We disagree, but we're both rational, and I see how our values led to our disagreement."

However, as we saw in section 11.3.1, using an improper scoring rule, thus violating immodesty, leads to some serious problems. Moreover, the suggestion that it could be rational to update by "conditionalization+" or "conditionalization−" is fairly radical. The idea of giving one's credence a "nudge" after accommodating the evidence sounds a lot like going *beyond* the evidence. And while this might be just what James himself

---

[22] The dispute over uncertain evidence, mentioned above, illustrates this idea. See Leitgeb and Pettigrew (2010b) and Levinstein (2012).

had in mind (in claiming that, contra Clifford (1877/1999), it is sometimes fine to believe on insufficient evidence), more moderate permissivists should be reluctant to go so far. The thought behind our Jamesian Argument is not that our values might make it rational to go beyond our evidence, but that they might influence what our evidence supports.

To make this more moderate Jamesian strategy work—and to say something systematic about *how* it works—we would need an argument where different, independently plausible measures of epistemic value justify different, independently plausible update rules, coherence relations, and notions of evidential support. The lesson I take from this is that it is hard to keep some parts of our theory of rationality fixed (for instance, our notion of coherence and update rules) and make room for value to make a difference. The different overall epistemic systems, as a Jamesian Permissivist must defend them, will be different in *many* respects. This strikes me as a surprising and unwelcome conclusion for more conservative permissivists, who might have hoped to make the Jamesian argument without departing too much from orthodoxy elsewhere. However, it may be the most promising strategy for making sense of the Jamesian view.

Some may be willing to accept the costs of giving up either immodesty or conditionalization (or both). I will leave this open as a possibility for would-be Jamesians to explore. However, to endorse it, we have to give up plausible assumptions about how we should regard our own doxastic states, how we should respond to evidence, or both. That this balance is hard to strike may be surprising, but perhaps it should not be. After all, whether it can be rational to go beyond one's evidence was the subject of Clifford and James's original debate. We have seen here that Clifford and James's disagreement is deep, and compromise is not easy to find. It is hard to do justice to evidentialism without making epistemic value irrelevant to rational credence; similarly, it is hard to do justice to the Jamesian thought without giving up plausible tenets of evidentialism. For those with mainstream evidentialist leanings, the Jamesian Argument for permissivism does not come for free.[23]

11.4 Reinterpreting "Epistemic Value"

We can draw some lessons from the previous section. The Jamesian view that we started with aimed to make room for value-based, rational disagreements without departing too drastically from mainstream, plausible views about rational credence. The thought was that our epistemic values should make a difference to how we should interpret our evidence. But Simple EUT was unable to make sense of that

---

[23] This might seem obvious; on a strict form of evidentialism, justification supervenes (only) on evidence, so of course there is no room for things other than evidence to influence what one should believe. See Titelbaum and Kopec (MS, pp. 7–8) and Kopec and Titelbaum (2016, p. 193). However, I think it is still surprising that even a looser form of evidentialism, on which there are "a few different ways of interpreting one's evidence," also can't easily make sense of the Jamesian argument. Thanks to Matt Kopec for helpful comments here.

argument. This is because once Simple EUT is constrained so as to be consistent with various structural requirements on rational credence, value has no more work to do. So Simple EUT (and more generally, any view that endorses immodesty and conditionalization) does not vindicate Jamesian Permissivism. And giving up those structural requirements would be costly—or at least, it would represent a quite substantial departure from the mainstream!

In conversation I have often encountered the following response: the fact that EUT doesn't vindicate the Jamesian Argument shows that its conception of epistemic value is not right. Epistemic value is not embodied in *scoring rules*, objectors argue, but in our *priors*. Epistemic value (in the Jamesian Argument) is supposed to be something that makes a difference to what we should believe, and that can underwrite rational disagreements. Priors, unlike scoring rules, might plausibly fill that role. So we should think of our priors, not scoring rules, as embodying our epistemic values.[24]

The main advantage of this view is that it could make the Jamesian Argument work in cases like Election. Let's return to that story and fill in some details. Suppose that before arriving at our posterior credences in D (.7 for me, .6 for you), we both look at some polls. I think something like: "Trends are sticky. If the Democrat is ahead now, she'll be ahead six months from now too." You think something like: "Things can change. I see that she's ahead now, but a lot can happen in six months; I'm not quite so confident that she'll win." Suppose, plausibly, that those prior attitudes—"trends are sticky" versus "things can change"—show up in our conditional credences, $Pr(D|E)$, such that for me, $Pr(D|E) = .7$, and for you, $Pr(D|E) = .6$. If those prior conditional credences are both rational, our posterior credences in D—.7 for me, and .6 for you— are both rational too.[25]

The disadvantage of this view is that it is hard to make this an argument for *Jamesian* Permissivism in particular. The distinctive feature of the Jamesian Argument is supposed to be that it uses permissivism in one domain (epistemic value) to argue for permissivism in another domain (rational credence). If priors *are* values,

---

[24] A closely related view is that our scoring rules help us *choose* our priors. This is an interesting suggestion, which deserves further discussion, though I won't pursue it fully here. See Pettigrew (2014) and Pettigrew (2016) for implementation of a view like this. An interesting consequence of this strategy is that it requires agents to use different decision rules at different stages of their "epistemic lives." Simple EUT says we should maximize expected accuracy; but that is not something one can do without priors. So one would have to use another decision rule to pick one's priors, and then maximize expected accuracy afterwards. This type of view would, therefore, still be significantly different from practical views on which one's values influence one's choices in a consistent way *throughout* one's existence as a rational agent.

[25] Without committing ourselves to Bayesianism, we could make a similar argument regarding "standards," "background assumptions," or "inductive policies." Titelbaum and Kopec (MS), for instance, call our priors or initial credences "standards." Schoenfield (2013) also writes in terms of "standards"; though she does not commit herself to a Bayesian framework in that chapter, her notion of standards would be equivalent to initial credences or priors. In this paper I will not pursue non-Bayesian views, and how they might handle these arguments, and it may turn out that this choice makes a difference to my argument. I am sticking with Bayesianism in this chapter because it is a popular and well-developed view of rational credence. I leave it open to others to explore non-Bayesian options.

the argument has some potential force. But if priors are just more credences, the argument becomes much less interesting. Instead of offering a new, distinctive reason for permissivism, it would simply say that there are different rational credences at one time, and that those justify different rational credences later on.

In evaluating this response, then, a lot hangs on how we should understand priors. Perhaps in a very loose sense, we could describe someone as "valuing truth" in cases like Election if she draws a stronger conclusion on the basis of the evidence. Someone might "value" simplicity or explanatory power, in the same way, if she tends to favor simpler or more explanatory hypotheses. But talk of value seems to be more of a stretch in describing other aspects of an agent's inductive policy; do we really "value green" rather than grue? And in general, value talk does not go well with most plausible interpretations of what priors are. For instance, the most literal, flat-footed understanding of priors says that they just *are* credences—credences that we used to have. More neutrally, we might also think of them as representing the "inherent plausibility" of various hypotheses.[26] We might also think of them as hypothetical credences, ones that would be rational to have on the basis of no evidence, even if we recognize that there was no moment when we actually had those credences. None of these views, it seems to me, would be enough to let us make the Jamesian Argument in a non-question-begging way. The thesis that there are many permissible credences to start off with, or many different permissible inherent levels of plausibility, may well be true—but in this context, it is too close to what the Jamesian Permissivist is trying to prove.

My hunch is that the same will turn out to be true of many non-Bayesian articulations of similar ideas. Priors, standards, or inductive policies should themselves aim at truth, just like beliefs or credences; it does not make sense to reason inductively if you don't expect the future to be like the past, or to take appearances at face value if you don't expect your eyes to work. If that's right, differences in priors are best understood as disagreements about *what* is true or accurate rather than about what is epistemically valuable, or about the nature of truth or accuracy itself. I won't try to argue for this stronger view here, but will leave it as a challenge for Jamesian Permissivism: if priors, standards, or inductive policies themselves are the basis for the Jamesian Argument, we need a plausible way to understand them as non-doxastic entities.

11.5 Conclusion

Given certain plausible formal constraints on rational credence, different rational epistemic values do not justify different credences. This means that defending the Jamesian Argument comes at a high cost: in order to make room for value to make a difference, we have to give up some of these plausible constraints.

---

[26] Williamson (2000) characterizes his notion of "evidential probability" along these lines.

The failure of the Jamesian Argument should serve as a cautionary note for those who are attracted to the formal tools offered by EUT. We have seen here that scoring rules are very different from the practical utility functions used by decision theory. Though the formalism is similar, the two notions play very different roles. More generally, the failure of the Jamesian Argument illustrates the fact that, although we can represent epistemic rationality and practical rationality in formally analogous ways, conclusions from one realm may not carry over to the other. The disanalogies between epistemic value and practical value do not show that EUT is wrong or should be abandoned, but they do pose a challenge for EUT. If we are going to use this formal system, we need to know how to understand it. And we can't rely on a straightforward decision-theoretic reading.[27]

Without the straightforward decision-theoretic understanding of EUT, we need a new way to interpret the formalism. To that end, it may be helpful to think about a new practical analogy: "consequentialized" Kantian views in ethics. Many have argued that so-called "non-consequentialist" views of moral action can be accurately represented in consequentialist terms.[28] Suppose these people are right, and we develop the formal details of such a view; following Douglas Portmore (2009), let's call it "Kantsequentialism." Kantsequentialism will have a moral utility function (or maybe more than one) and a decision rule, designed together to always recommend doing what one ought to do, by the lights of Kantian morality. Kantsequentialism will, for instance, always recommend acts that respect others, or that are motivated by universalizable maxims, by (roughly) assigning those acts the highest utility. Kantsequentialism will be extensionally equivalent to its non-consequentialist counterpart, but will represent morality as a matter of (for example) maximizing expected utility.

Some claim that the difference between Kantian and Kantsequentialist views is not significant. James Dreier (2011), for instance, argues that consequentialized and non-consequentialized (extensionally equivalent) theories are mere "notational variants," and that defenders of each view are "not really disagreeing" with one another. However, a Kantian could complain (it seems to me, legitimately) that the consequentialist version of her theory, while not wrong, is nevertheless *not as explanatory* as the non-consequentialist version. The consequentialized version might tell us which actions are right, and when, but would not explain why they are right—at least not as well as the original, non-consequentialized version does.[29]

A certain kind of Kantian might also complain that putting the theory in consequentialist terms is misleading: it suggests that there is an independence between

---

[27] This observation is in line with some other recent work, arguing (for independent reasons) that EUT is importantly different from practical decision theory, and should not be interpreted as "epistemic decision theory." See Carr (forthcoming), and Konek and Levinstein (forthcoming).

[28] There is a large literature on this. See Portmore (2009) for an overview.

[29] See Portmore (2009, section 6). Portmore makes a stronger claim: that the two theories would *disagree about* why the actions are right. Dreier (2011) disputes this, arguing that consequentializers can agree (for example) that an action is wrong because it is a lie, and labeling lying as a particular kind of bad consequence. But it is plausible, to me, that two theories could be "mere notational variants" and yet one be more explanatory than the other. This weaker claim of explanatory asymmetry is the one I am suggesting here.

actions and values which does not exist. The Kantian I am imagining here is one who takes action to have constitutive conditions: acting in a way that disrespects another person's good will, or under a maxim that is not universalizable, does not count as an action at all. (It's "mere behavior," maybe.) Because action, for this view, has certain *constitutive* conditions, it is strange to think of it as also aiming towards a separate *goal*.[30] Again, the consequentialized view wouldn't get the wrong answers about what's moral; it would just be an unnatural and roundabout way of getting to those answers.

Perhaps EUT should be understood along these same lines, as an epistemic version of Kantsequentialism. Though it might not get the wrong answers, we might nevertheless have the same complaints that the Kantian has about Kantsequentialism. EUT may be simply less explanatory, and more misleading, than a non-consequentialized view would be. We should therefore be careful when using EUT. It should not lead us to think of epistemic rationality as decision-theoretic or consequentialist in any deep or informative sense.

If we give up the straightforward understanding of EUT, we are free to interpret James's insight in other ways, and find other places where differences in "epistemic values" might have interesting upshots. A plausible option is to take the Jamesian goals to be part of our *practical* values, showing up in rational action—especially action related to inquiry. Choosing whether and how to gather evidence is a natural candidate; this interpretation would make James's observation highly relevant to scientific practice, even if not to epistemic rationality itself.[31] The Jamesian goals may also make a difference to rational *belief*, on certain views that employ both beliefs and credences. If belief itself is action-like, and rationally responsive to both evidence and practical goals, perhaps it is sensitive to differences in "epistemic values" even if credence is not. We can pursue either of these understandings of the Jamesian goals without thinking of rational credence in a decision-theoretic way, and without understanding accuracy as a special kind of utility. Speaking of rational credence as "aiming" at these "twin goals," or any goals at all, is perhaps best understood as metaphorical.[32]

References

Arntzenius, Frank. 2008. "Rationality and Self-Confidence." In Tamar Szabó Gendler and John Hawthorne (eds), *Oxford Studies in Epistemology: Volume 2*. Oxford: Oxford University Press, 165–78.

---

[30] See Dreier (2010) for a similar argument, in defense of moral expressivism. Dreier argues that sometimes, even though a set of norms *in fact* furthers some goal, the goal nevertheless does not explain those norms. His example involves cases where the norms are constitutive of the activity in question.

[31] See Fallis (2007) for an example of an application of this approach.

[32] For helpful questions and comments, I am grateful to Jennifer Carr, David Christensen, Ryan Doody, Kevin Dorst, Jeffrey Dunn, Daniel Greco, Brian Hedden, Damien Rochford, and Miriam Schoenfield; and to audiences at MIT's Work in Progress series and SLACRR 2015. Special thanks to Matthew Kopec for very helpful comments on an earlier draft.

Berker, Selim. 2013. "Epistemic Teleology and the Separateness of Propositions." *Philosophical Review* 122(3): 337–93.

Carr, Jennifer. 2015. "Epistemic Expansions." *Res Philosophica* 92(2): 217–36.

Carr, Jennifer. forthcoming. "Accuracy or Coherence?." *Philosophy and Phenomenological Research*.

Clifford, William K. 1877/1999. "The Ethics of Belief." In William K. Clifford, *The Ethics of Belief and Other Essays*. Amherst, NY: Prometheus Books, 70–96.

Dreier, James. 2010. "When Do Goals Explain the Norms that Advance Them?" In Russ Shafer-Landau (ed.), *Oxford Studies in Metaethics*. Oxford: Oxford University Press, 5–153.

Dreier, James. 2011. "In Defense of Consequentializing." In Mark Timmons (ed.), *Oxford Studies in Normative Ethics: Volume 1*. Oxford: Oxford University Press, 97–119.

Fallis, Don. 2007. "Attitudes towards Epistemic Risk and the Value of Experiments." *Studia Logica* 86(2): 215–46.

Field, Hartry. 2000. "Apriority as an Evaluative Notion". In Paul A. Boghossian and Christopher Peacocke (eds), *New Essays on the A Priori*. Oxford: Oxford University Press, 117–49.

Greaves, Hilary, and David Wallace. 2006. "Justifying Conditionalization: Conditionalization Maximizes Expected Epistemic Utility." *Mind* 115(459): 607–32.

Hedden, Brian. 2012. "Options and the Subjective Ought." *Philosophical Studies* 158(2): 343–60.

Hedden, Brian. 2015. "Time-Slice Rationality." *Mind* 124(494): 449–91.

Joyce, James. 1998. "A Nonpragmatic Vindication of Probabilism." *Philosophy of Science* 65(4): 575–603.

Joyce, James. 2009. "Accuracy and Coherence: Prospects for an Alethic Epistemology of Partial Belief." In Franz Huber and Christoph Schmidt-Petri (eds), *Degrees of Belief*. Dordrecht: Springer, 263–97.

James, William. 1897. "The Will to Believe." In *The Will to Believe and Other Essays in Popular Philosophy*. New York: Longmans, Green, and Co., 1–15.

Kelly, Thomas. 2014. "Evidence Can Be Permissive." In Matthias Steup and John Turri (eds), *Contemporary Debates in Epistemology*. Chichester: Blackwell, 298–312.

Konek, Jason and Ben Levinstein. Forthcoming. "Foundations of Epistemic Decision Theory." *Mind*.

Kopec, Matthew and Michael Titelbaum. 2016. "The Uniqueness Thesis." *Philosophy Compass* 11(4): 189–200.

Kvanvig, Jonathan. 2014. *Reflection and Rationality*. Oxford: Oxford University Press.

Leitgeb, Hannes and Richard Pettigrew. 2010a. "An Objective Justification of Bayesianism I: Measuring Inaccuracy." *Philosophy of Science* 77(2): 201–35.

Leitgeb, Hannes and Richard Pettigrew. 2010b. "An Objective Justification of Bayesianism II: The Consequences of Minimizing Inaccuracy". *Philosophy of Science* 77(2): 236–72.

Levinstein, Ben. 2012. "Leitgeb and Pettigrew on Accuracy and Updating." *Philosophy of Science* 79(3): 413–24.

Levinstein, Ben. 2015. "Permissive Rationality and Sensitivity." *Philosophy and Phenomenological Research* 94(2): 342–70.

Lewis, David. 1971. "Immodest Inductive Methods." *Philosophy of Science* 38(1): 54–63.

Maher, Patrick. 2003. "Joyce's Argument for Probabilism." *Philosophy of Science* 69(1): 73–81.

Marley-Payne, Jack. MS. "Epistemic Ideals."

Meacham, Chris. 2014. "Impermissive Bayesianism." *Erkenntnis* 79(S6): 185–217.

Meacham, Chris. MS. "Dividing Uniqueness."
Moss, Sarah. 2011. "Scoring Rules and Epistemic Compromise." *Mind* 120(480): 1053-69.
Moss, Sarah. 2015. "Time-Slice Epistemology and Action under Indeterminacy." In John Hawthorne and Tamar Szabó Gendler (eds), *Oxford Studies in Epistemology: Volume 5*. Oxford: Oxford University Press, 172-94.
Pettigrew, Richard. 2014. "Accuracy, Risk, and the Principle of Indifference." *Philosophy and Phenomenological Research* 92(1): 35-59.
Pettigrew, Richard. 2016. "Jamesian Epistemology Formalised: An Explication of 'The Will to Believe.'" *Episteme* 13(3): 253-69.
Portmore, Douglas. 2009. "Consequentializing." *Philosophy Compass* 4(2): 329-47.
Schoenfield, Miriam. 2013. "Permission to Believe: Why Permissivism Is True and What It Teaches Us about Irrelevant Influences on Beliefs." *Noûs* 47(1): 193-218.
Swanson, Eric. 2008. "Note on Gibbard, 'Rational Credence and the Value of Truth.'" In Tamar Szabó Gendler and John Hawthorne (eds), *Oxford Studies in Epistemology: Volume 2*. Oxford: Oxford University Press, 179-89.
Titelbaum, Michael and Matthew Kopec. MS. "Plausible Permissivism."
Williamson, Timothy. 2000. *Knowledge and its Limits*. Oxford: Oxford University Press.

12
Epistemic Consequentialism and Epistemic Enkrasia

Amanda Askell

12.1 Introduction

Objective epistemic consequentialism is the view that whether it is right or wrong, or good or bad to adopt a given doxastic attitude depends entirely on the consequences of adopting that attitude. Subjective epistemic consequentialism is the view that whether it is right or wrong, or good or bad to adopt a given doxastic attitude depends entirely on the *expected* consequences of adopting that attitude. Both forms of epistemic consequentialism can be applied to different doxastic attitudes. For example, it may be right to adopt a given belief insofar as this leads the agent to adopt more true beliefs.[1] But epistemic consequentialism has primarily been applied to credences: subjective degrees of confidence in a proposition. One principle that has been proposed by subjective epistemic consequentialists who have focused on credences is that adopting a given credence is right if and only if adopting that credence maximizes expected accuracy—that is, if and only if the agent expects that adopting that credence will cause the agent to have a more accurate credal state overall.

Epistemic *enkrasia* principles say that an agent should not adopt an attitude that she takes to be irrational: she should not believe P if she thinks it is irrational to believe P. But how can we formulate such enkrasia principles for credences rather than outright beliefs? In this chapter I will argue that the most plausible epistemic enkrasia principle for credences largely coincides with the epistemic consequentialist principle of maximizing expected accuracy. Given this, I argue that epistemic consequentialism inherits some of the problems faced by those who defend epistemic enkrasia principles. In particular, I will argue that epistemic consequentialists face a trilemma: they must deny that we can be uncertain about what is epistemically valuable, or they must deny that this uncertainty can affect what attitudes agents ought to adopt, or they must adopt a highly subjective account of epistemic value. I argue that each of these

---

[1] See Berker (2013) for recent objections to this teleological account of the rightness of beliefs.

positions produce undesirable results for epistemic consequentialists. I refer to this as the problem of axiological uncertainty.

This chapter is composed of three further sections. In section 12.2 I will formulate an epistemic enkrasia principle for credences, and point out that this epistemic enkrasia principle seems to coincide with the consequentialist principle of maximizing expected accuracy. In section 12.3 I will outline both objective and subjective accounts of epistemic value, and argue that it seems plausible that we should sometimes be uncertain about the epistemic value of a given attitude under either account. In section 12.4 I will outline the problem of axiological uncertainty.

12.2 Epistemic Enkrasia and Epistemic Consequentialism

We will say that an agent's belief state is epistemically *akratic* if she adopts attitude A while thinking that A is irrational. For example, an agent who believes that she will pass a test but also thinks that she is irrational to believe that she will pass that test is said to be epistemically akratic. If an agent's belief state does not contain any such combination of attitudes then that belief state is epistemically *enkratic*.[2]

A plausible epistemic enkrasia principle for beliefs is not too difficult to formulate. Let us follow Titelbaum (2015: 259) in defining a situation as whatever features the true theory of rationality deems relevant to the permissibility or impermissibility of doxastic attitudes. For example, according to evidentialism, an agent's situation is just the agent's total evidence. According to reliabilism, the agent's situation also includes facts about the reliability of her belief-forming methods. We don't need to arbitrate such disputes here: instead, let us assume that S includes all features that could be relevant to the permissibility of her belief. This includes her evidence, her belief-forming methods, facts about the world, and so on.

Given this, the following is a plausible epistemic enkrasia principle for beliefs:

Belief Enkrasia: It is never permissible for an agent in situation S to jointly believe that attitude A is impermissible in S and to adopt attitude A in S.

Belief Enkrasia is a *wide scope* principle of rationality, rather than a narrow scope principle. Where O is the ought operator, B is a belief operator, and A is an attitude that one could adopt, narrow scope principles are of the form $B(O\neg(A)) \to O(\neg A)$. Wide scope principles are of the form $O(B(O\neg(A)) \to \neg A)$.[3] Narrow scope enkrasia principles say that if an agent believes that attitude A is impermissible then, even if this belief is *irrational*, she ought not to adopt attitude A. For example, suppose that

---

[2] 'Enkrasia' coming from the Greek meaning 'with power' and 'akrasia' meaning 'without power', the concept originally applied to actions and not beliefs. Our actions are akratic if they are not in accordance with our reason.

[3] For further discussion of the wide scope/narrow scope distinction see Broome (2007).

Susan believes that she would be irrational to believe that it is raining outside, even though she is actually irrational to believe that this belief is irrational. A narrow scope enkrasia principle would say that, given that she *does* believe that it would be irrational for her to believe that it's raining outside, Susan should not adopt the belief that it is raining outside. On the narrow scope reading, O(¬ A) follows from B(O¬(A)). And this is true even if the belief that attitude A is irrational would itself have been rational were it not for the agent's having adopted attitude A.

On the wide scope reading, it's possible for an agent to believe that she should not have attitude A, but for her to nonetheless be obligated to have attitude A because her belief about the normative status of attitude A is itself impermissible. In other words, it's possible for B(O¬(A)), O(B(O¬(A)) → ¬A), and O(A) to be true on the wide scope reading because O¬(B(O¬(A))). Wide scope principles say that an agent cannot jointly have attitude A and believe that attitude A is irrational, but if an agent irrationally adopts attitude A then she can satisfy the wide scope enkrasia principle by ceasing to adopt A.

The principle above suffices as an approximation of the kind of enkrasia principle we should endorse when it comes to outright beliefs. Of course, we might want to add several caveats or amendments to Belief Enkrasia. For example, perhaps we should talk not merely about the permissibility and impermissibility of akratic attitude states, but also the degrees of goodness and badness of these states. We might also worry that Belief Enkrasia will be less plausible in cases where what situation the agent is in is not obvious to her. But I will set aside these problems for Belief Enkrasia, and turn to enkrasia principles for credences.

It is more difficult to formulate an adequate enkrasia principle for credences than for outright beliefs. Credences are subjective degrees of confidence in propositions that lie in the [0,1] interval (with 0 meaning 'P is certainly false' and 1 meaning 'P is certainly true').[4]

A first attempt to formulate enkrasia principles for credences is as follows:

High Confidence Enkrasia: It is not permissible to adopt credence n in P and have a high credence that credence n in P is irrational.

Even if we set aside questions about what constitutes a 'high credence' that credence n in P is irrational, High Confidence Enkrasia is an implausible enkrasia principle for credences. To see this, consider a case in which an agent is not sure which credence between 0.6 and 0.7 it is rational for her to have in P. Suppose that she has the highest credence—a credence of 0.1—that credence of 0.65 in P is rational, with her remaining credence about which credences are rational forming a normal distribution around 0.65. In a case like this, the agent is highly confident (credence 0.9) that credence 0.65

---

[4] For now I will not assume that credence functions must be probability functions. I will return to this in the discussion of probabilism later in this section.

is irrational, and yet it does not seem epistemically akratic for her to adopt a credence of 0.65 in this case, since this is the credence that she is *most* confident is rational.

Given this, we might think that an agent is epistemically enkratic if there is no credence that she is more confident is rational than her current credence:

Comparative Confidence Enkrasia: It is not permissible to adopt credence *n* in P if there is some credence *m* in P such that the agent is more confident that credence *m* in P is rational than she is that credence *n* in P is rational.

However, Comparative Confidence Enkrasia fails in cases where the degrees of irrationality differ greatly between different attitudes. For example, consider the following case:

Amy and the Loaded Coin
Amy is a magician who uses a loaded coin in some of her magic tricks. Her loaded coin has a 90 per cent chance of landing heads. She isn't sure whether she packed her loaded coin or a regular coin. And she isn't sure about what it's rational for her to believe about whether the coin will land heads in these circumstances. She assigns a credence of 0.6 to the claim that she should have a credence 0.8 that this coin will land heads, and a credence of 0.4 to the claim that she should have a credence 0.7 that this coin will land heads. However, she is also highly confident that if she should have a credence 0.8 that this coin will land heads then her having a credence 0.7 that the coin will land heads would not be extremely disvaluable. But she is highly confident that if she should have a credence 0.7 that this coin will land heads then her having a credence 0.8 that the coin will land heads would be extremely disvaluable.[5]

In such circumstances, it does not seem like it would necessarily be epistemically akratic for Amy to have a credence other than 0.8 that the coin will land heads, even though she is more confident that a credence of 0.8 is rational than that anything else is, since the value of having a credence of 0.8 has higher variance: if it is irrational, then it's very epistemically disvaluable. Given that she has a high confidence that 0.8 is rational, however, she might not think it's best to have a credence of 0.7 either: instead, she might try to strike a compromise between these two credences. But for our purposes, all that matters is that a credence of 0.8 is not necessarily akratic in this case.

It seems like we care not only about our confidence that an attitude is rational or not, but also *how* epistemically valuable we think that attitude will be. It seems epistemically akratic for us to adopt credences that we expect to be less epistemically valuable than others. In the case above, it doesn't seem akratic to adopt a credence

---

[5] Amy's high confidence in these claims might strike us as irrational, but let us assume that Amy's credences about rationality have been formed on the basis of misleading testimony by an evil epistemology teacher.

other than 0.8 because even though the agent thinks that 0.8 is more rational than 0.7, she also thinks that if 0.8 is less rational than 0.7 then it is *much* less epistemically valuable than 0.7 would be. As Wedgwood (2013) argues, we can formulate epistemic enkrasia principles for credences by appealing to the expected epistemic value of the attitudes available to us in a given situation. In order to do this, let A_S represent an attitude A (e.g. a credence of n in a proposition P) in a situation S. Let S be the set of all situations that are epistemically possible for the agent. And let U be an agent's epistemic value function: a function from all possible attitudes in situations to a real number that represents the epistemic value of those attitudes in those situations. Given this, the expected epistemic value of an attitude can be defined as follows:

$$EU(A) = \Sigma_S Cr(S)U(A_S).$$

In other words, the expected epistemic value of attitude A is just the sum of the expected value that A will produce in all situations that are epistemically possible for her, weighted by the agent's confidence that she is in that situation. Using this formulation of expected epistemic value, we can formulate the following enkrasia principle for credences:[6]

Expected Value Enkrasia (EVE): It is never permissible for an agent to have credences such that $EU(A_2) < EU(A_1)$ and adopt attitude A_2.

In the case above, EVE says that since the expected value of credence 0.7 that the coin will land heads is greater than the expected value of credence 0.8 then, even though Amy is more confident that 0.8 is rational than that 0.7 is rational, she would not be enkratic if she adopted a credence of 0.8, since this is not the attitude that she expects to produce the most epistemic value in her current situation.[7] She is only permitted to adopt the credence that does best in terms of expected epistemic value: otherwise, she is epistemically akratic.[8]

Being epistemically enkratic is, essentially, doing well by your own lights. You could have misleading evidence about what attitudes are valuable or rational, but the key idea is that you should at least be doing the best that you can given your own evidence. EVE seems to capture this notion of 'doing well by your own lights' when it comes to credences rather than outright beliefs. If we accept a wide scope enkrasia principle like EVE then we can explain the intuitive irrationality of epistemic akrasia. Akratic

---

[6] This principle is closely related to the New Rational Reflection principle outlined in Elga (2013).

[7] If this kind of case is possible, then we must assume that the agent has an objective rather than a subjective notion of rationality in mind: i.e. that she believes that 0.8 can be rational even if the expected value of credence 0.8 is lower than that of some other attitude available to her. If we assume that this kind of case is not possible because rationality just *is* maximizing expected epistemic value, then EVE will not differ in its judgments from Comparative Confidence Enkrasia. But I don't wish to rule out cases in which agents are confident that rationality is objective and distinct from maximizing expected epistemic value.

[8] More than one credence might be best in terms of expected epistemic value. If this is the case, then EVE just says that the agent is enkratic as long as she chooses among these equally valuable credences.

attitudes violate a plausible view of the subjective epistemic ought: that you ought to adopt attitudes that maximize expected value, relative to the credences you ought to have in your current situation.[9]

Let us now turn from epistemic enkrasia principles to epistemic consequentialism. Epistemic consequentialism is, roughly speaking, the view that the deontic status (right/wrong) and axiological status (good/bad) of the attitudes that an agent can adopt in a given situation are determined by the epistemic value that they produce. A theory which says that you ought to proportion your beliefs to the evidence because 'proportion your beliefs to the evidence' is a fundamental norm of rationality is not a consequentialist theory. However, a theory which says that you ought to proportion your beliefs to the evidence because this will lead you to have more accurate or more well-calibrated beliefs *is* a consequentialist theory. Epistemic consequentialism does not entail any particular view about what constitutes epistemic value (except, perhaps, that it is a distinctly *epistemic* value).[10]

Maximizing epistemic consequentialists hold that we epistemically ought to adopt attitudes that minimize expected epistemic disvalue, and that therefore maximize expected epistemic value.[11] That is: if we treat the adoption of doxastic attitudes as an action, then they accept something like the following epistemic norm for doxastic actions, which is a variant of a principle found in Leitgeb and Pettigrew (2010: 207):

Accuracy (expected global): An agent ought to minimize the expected global inaccuracy (or: maximize the expected global accuracy) of her belief function relative to a legitimate measure of global inaccuracy.[12]

This assumes that epistemic value can be couched in terms of *accuracy*. Although epistemic consequentialists need not accept this account of epistemic value, it is a popular view in the literature. I will therefore assume an accuracy-based account of epistemic value, but much of what I say will apply to epistemic consequentialists who claim that something other than accuracy is of final epistemic value. We will return to the issue of what constitutes a 'legitimate' measure of inaccuracy in section 12.3.

---

[9] It is generally accepted that there is something irrational about epistemic akrasia. Perhaps, in part, because there seems to be something Moore paradoxical about statements of the form 'I believe P and I'm irrational to believe P'.

[10] Some epistemic consequentialists might have an account of final value that does not include epistemic value. For example, they might think that only moral or prudential values are final, and that 'epistemic value' is merely instrumental. These views may sometimes allow that an epistemically disvaluable attitude can be right on moral or pragmatic grounds. I find such views plausible, but in this chapter I will only be talking about epistemic consequentialists that treat epistemic value as final and not merely instrumental.

[11] Minimizing epistemic disvalue is perhaps a more natural formulation in this context, since zero typically represents a perfect score on the standard scoring rules used by epistemic value theorists.

[12] Pettigrew argues that Accuracy (expected global) can be defended on ought implies can grounds—i.e. that norms should not require more of an agent than she is capable of—and that it leads to an internalist account of justification. Both the nature of these ought implies can principles and the nature of the internalism they lead to will be discussed in section 12.3.

Leitgeb and Pettigrew differentiate between *local* and *global* inaccuracy measures. They state: 'a global inaccuracy measure is a mathematical function that takes a belief function b and a world w and gives a measure of G(w, b) the global inaccuracy of having belief function b at world w' (2010: 204). A local inaccuracy measure, on the other hand, is one that just takes a credence in a single proposition and the truth value of that proposition, and gives a measure of the local accuracy or inaccuracy of the relevant credence.

Expected epistemic value (EVE) given above can be formulated either as a local principle, one that looks at the value of attitudes relative to the agent's overall credence state, or as a global measure of that overall credal state. On the global reading of EVE, A_1 and A_2 are the agent's entire credal state. On the local reading of EVE, A_1 and A_2 are individual credences. Like Accuracy (expected global), EVE is a principle that asks us to minimize expected inaccuracy of our attitudes. So, plausible epistemic enkrasia principles for credences and epistemic consequentialist principles seem to coincide, at least to some degree. This is good news for epistemic consequentialists, insofar as enkrasia is often taken to be a fundamental requirement of rationality. However, EVE takes into account an agent's credences about her epistemic situation. More precisely, it takes into account her uncertainty about what is of epistemic value. Should epistemic consequentialists also take into account an agent's credences about her epistemic situation, if this includes her credences about epistemic value? This is the question I will consider in section 12.3.

12.3 Epistemic Axiological Uncertainty

From now on I will treat EVE as the central principle of both those who defend the view that epistemic enkrasia is rationally required, and as a proxy for the view of maximizing epistemic consequentialists, insofar as the former seem to coincide with the latter. There are known problems for those who defend the view that it is always epistemically impermissible to be akratic. An important class of problems for enkrasia principles are problems that arise out of an agent's axiological uncertainty: her uncertainty about what is of epistemic value.[13]

In order to motivate the axiological uncertainty problems for epistemic principles like EVE, we need to first argue that agents can be uncertain about the epistemic value of the attitudes available to them. Should epistemic consequentialists accept that agents can be rationally uncertain about what is of epistemic value? To answer this,

---

[13] Similar problems for enkrasia principles arise when agents are uncertain about what their evidence is, what situation they are in, what is of value, or what they ought to do. In some of these situations, akrasia can seem to be a rational attitude state. I think this is really a species of the problem I discuss here: agents cannot be both rationally uncertain about these things and also enkratic. And so in cases where it seems rational to be uncertain about these things, it seems that enkrasia is not a rational requirement. One option is to revise enkrasia principles so that an agent is enkratic if she does not think that an attitude state is irrational or epistemically impermissible *given the evidence that is accessible to her*, including evidence about what her evidence is, what situation she is in, and so on.

we need to say more about some of the accounts of epistemic value appealed to by epistemic consequentialists.

The two main types of epistemic value that have been considered by epistemic consequentialists who work with credences are calibrationist accounts and accuracy-based accounts. An agent's credence that an event will occur is *well calibrated* if it reflects the actual or hypothetical frequency that the event will occur. An agent's credence that an event will occur is *accurate* if it closer to 1 if the event occurs and closer to 0 if the event does not occur. For example, suppose a fair die is to be rolled and I have credence 1 that it will land on 4. As it happens the die does land on 4. So my credence that it will land on 4 was accurate in actual fact, even if it was not accurate in expectation, because the event did occur. But my credence was not well calibrated on the hypothetical calibrationist account, because the hypothetical frequency that a fair die will land on 4 is 1/6. In this chapter, however, I will focus on accuracy-based accounts of epistemic value and agents that are uncertain over different measures of inaccuracy.[14]

Various measures of epistemic accuracy have been proposed and defended by epistemic value theorists. The discussion has largely focused on strictly proper scoring rules like the log and Brier scores. Here are these scoring rules for a set of propositions **P** comprised of *n*-many propositions $p_1, ..., p_n$, where c_p is the credence that the agent assigns to a given p, and x_p is 1 if p is true and 0 if p is false:[15]

Log score: $\quad LS(c_P) = 1/n \Sigma^n (x_p (\ln(c_p)) + (1 - x_p)(\ln(1 - c_p)))$

Brier score: $\quad BS(c_P) = 1/n \Sigma^n (x_p - c_p)^2$

An agent's attitudes are more accurate, according to both scoring rules, the closer that they are to zero (this involves minimization on the Brier score and maximization on the log score). For example, a credence of 0.7 in a true proposition will receive a log score of about −0.36 and a Brier score of 0.09. A credence of 0.9 in the same true proposition will receive a log score of about −0.1 (closer to zero) and a Brier score of 0.01 (closer to zero).

The log and Brier scoring rules are both strictly proper. A scoring rule is strictly proper if and only if a coherent credence function expects itself to do better than any other credence function, with respect to that score.[16] These scoring rules have desirable properties that improper scoring rules lack. To see this, we can consider what is probably the most intuitively plausible improper scoring rule: the linear scoring rule.

---

[14] However, it seems that most agents should also be uncertain over calibrationist and accuracy-based measures of inaccuracy.
[15] It is possible to formulate the log score as the natural log of the agent's credence in the correct answer, but I have used this formulation for greater consistency with the Brier score. Although other scoring rules like the Spherical scoring rule are also strictly proper, the log and Brier scores have been the primary focus of epistemic value theorists.
[16] For a detailed account of proper scoring rules, see Gneiting and Raftery (2007).

The linear score (Lin) of a prediction is just the absolute difference between the agent's credences in propositions and the truth values of those propositions: so $\text{Lin}(c_P) = 1/n \Sigma_n |c_p - x_p|$. The linear scoring rule is not a proper scoring rule. To show this, let us take a variant of an example given in Joyce (2009). Imagine that you have three cups before you, and I place a ball under one of the cups before shuffling the cups with extraordinary speed so that you cannot possibly know which cup the ball is under. In this case, you can be certain that the ball is still under one of the cups, and so you should assign the claim 'the ball is under one of the cups' credence 1 according to the linear scoring rule. It might seem rational for you to adopt a credence of 1/3 that the ball is under any given cup. As the ball is under one of the cups, the average linear score of these credences will be $1/3(2/3 + 1/3 + 1/3) = 4/9$. But now consider what happens if, for any given cup, you adopt a credence of 0 that the ball is under that cup. Since the ball is under one of the cups, the average linear score of these credences will be $1/3(1 + 0 + 0) = 1/3$. And since $1/3 < 4/9$, the linear scoring rule deems having credence 0 that the ball is under any given cup more rational than having a credence of 1/3 that the ball is under any given cup. And it does so even though this overall credal state is probabilistically incoherent, since you have credence 1 that the ball is under one of the cups but credence 0 that it is under any given cup.

Can we be uncertain about whether different epistemic value functions are correct? For example, can we be uncertain about whether proper scoring rules like the log and Brier scoring rules, or improper scoring rules like the linear scoring rule are the correct measure of epistemic value? In order to answer this question, we need to say more about what we have in mind when we talk about epistemic value. We could be referring to an objective notion of epistemic value, or a subjective notion of epistemic value.

If epistemic value is objective, then the epistemic value that an attitude has is not relative to an agent's personal epistemic value function. For example, suppose that epistemic value of an attitude is objective and that epistemic value is, despite the problems above, captured by the linear scoring rule and not by the log scoring rule. Then, if an agent adopts a log scoring rule as her personal epistemic value function, her credences will *in fact* be worse than the credences of agents who adopt the linear scoring rule as their personal epistemic value function. This is because the agent who adopts the log scoring rule has a false view about epistemic value. Given this, she will do well by her own lights when she adopts a credence of 1/3 that the ball is under a given cup, but she will do badly in terms of objective epistemic value as captured by the linear scoring rule, because the linear scoring rule says that a credence of 0 that the ball is under any given cup is more epistemically valuable.

A subjective account of epistemic value, on the other hand, treats epistemic value functions as something akin to personal preferences. We may be able to place some restrictions on what kind of preferences are deemed rational—for example, intransitive preferences are usually thought to be irrational—but there may still be more than one rational preference function. And there are no facts of the form 'x is preferable to y' that exist independent of agents' preference functions. If we think that epistemic value is subjective in the same way that personal preference functions are, then we might think that there are several scoring rules that are acceptable epistemic value functions. If this is true then an agent who adopts one scoring rule might have different credences to an agent who adopts a different scoring rule. But if both of them minimize expected inaccuracy relative to their own epistemic value functions, then neither of them would have credences that are *objectively* better or worse than the attitudes adopted by the other.

Is epistemic value objective or subjective? In favor of an objective account of epistemic value, we might point out that epistemic value seems to be less like a personal preference function and more like objective accounts of moral value in ethics. There seems to be a genuine fact of the matter about how epistemically good an attitude is, given a certain body of evidence, one that doesn't change merely because an agent has a different view about what constitutes a good or bad attitude. It also seems difficult to justify some of the restrictions placed on an agent's epistemic value function by epistemic consequentialists if it is merely a subjective value function. Although some restrictions are placed on an agent's value function—that it is transitive, complete, and so on—these are usually structural restrictions, and not restrictions based on the plausibility of an agent's preference function. But some of the restrictions on epistemic value functions—for example, that she cannot have an epistemic value function that is falsity-directed, or that she cannot have an epistemic value function that is improper— do seem to be more than mere structural restrictions. To extend the analogy with subjective preferences: even if we think that an agent shouldn't prefer to be in pain because pain is objectively bad, an agent can still have a subjective preference for being in pain. If epistemic value functions are subjective measures of epistemic value, then why not think that she can similarly think that inaccurate attitudes are better than true ones?

In favor of the subjective account, we might think that an agent's epistemic value function is justified insofar as it serves her *prudential* interests. If we believe that agents merely want to satisfy their prudential preferences, and we can show that adopting attitudes that do better according to proper scoring rules will cause an agent to act in ways that satisfy more of her prudential preferences than adopting attitudes that do better according to improper scoring rules, then this would justify more robust restrictions on an agent's epistemic value function than mere structural constraints. The subjective account is also less metaphysically loaded than the objective account: it does not say that there is some objective epistemic value out there in the world. Instead, epistemic value is merely a result of either brute preferences for accuracy on the part of agents, or it falls out of the agent's non-epistemic preferences.

I won't try to take a position on whether the objective or subjective reading of epistemic value is correct. What is important for our purposes is whether an agent can be *uncertain* about the epistemic value that a given attitude has, on both the objective and subjective accounts of epistemic value.

It seems plausible that if epistemic value is objective then there is at least some important sense of 'rational' on which we can be rationally uncertain about epistemic value. This might not be true for sufficiently idealized accounts of epistemic rationality, but it does seem to be true of accounts of rationality that are sensitive to an agent's cognitive limitations. For example, suppose that an agent Sam has a highly respected epistemology professor who gives him some superficially excellent reasons for thinking that the linear scoring rule is superior to any strictly proper scoring rule. It seems that it would be rational for Sam to at least have a non-zero credence that the linear scoring rule is correct, based on the testimony of his professor. Moreover, whether we should adopt attitudes in accordance with proper scoring rules like the Brier and log score, or even improper scoring rules like the linear scoring rule, are not even settled issues amongst epistemologists. It therefore seems irrational for non-ideal agents like Sam to be *certain* that a scoring rule like the linear scoring rule is not a correct account of objective epistemic value. Even if we think that our credences that improper scoring rules like the linear scoring rule are correct should be low, it hardly seems plausible that they should be zero. So there seems to be an important sense in which agents can be rationally uncertain about epistemic value under the objective account.[17]

But what if we adopt a subjective account of epistemic value? Unlike the objective account, the subjective account says that epistemic value supervenes on the mental states of agents. And so it is not as easy to claim that epistemic value is something that we can be uncertain about on the subjective account. After all, we might think that, since subjective value functions supervene on our own mental states, we can access these sorts of value functions by introspection alone. But it seems plausible that agents will be uncertain about the nature of their own epistemic value function. Even if an agent's epistemic value function is in principle accessible to them under ideal introspection, since it supervenes on his or her individual mental states, most agents do not have ideal introspection with respect to their own mental states. And so they will lack access to facts about the nature of their own epistemic value function. They may suspect that their epistemic value function coincides with one of those outlined in section 12.2, but it seems implausible that they can rule out the hypothesis that their epistemic value function is, say, the Brier scoring rule rather than the log scoring rule or the linear scoring rule. They may have a negligible credence that their epistemic value function is the same as the Brier scoring rule, but all that is required is that they should not be absolutely certain about the nature of their epistemic value function.

---

[17] We might think that the correct account of epistemic value is knowable a priori. If so, we could argue that axiological certainty is a requirement of rationality in the same way that logical certainty is. But if we think that logical omniscience is a problem, then surely we should think that axiological omniscience is equally problematic. For a recent defense of the view that agents are rationally required to avoid having mistaken beliefs about rationality, see Titelbaum (2015).

Finally, it also seems plausible that agents will not always be uncertain only over epistemic value functions that lead to a proper scoring rule in expectation. By this I mean that she will not merely be uncertain across different proper scoring rules like the log scoring rule and the Brier scoring rule. Instead, she will have non-zero credence in improper scoring rules like the linear scoring rule. If this is the case, then she could end up with an improper scoring rule in expectation.[18] It also seems very unlikely that, for all improper scoring rules, the agent will have equal uncertainty in both the truth-directed and falsity-directed versions of those scoring rules, since truth-directed scoring rules are more inherently plausible, and since this kind of fortuitous credal equality seems independently unlikely to occur.[19]

But if agents can be uncertain about either what the objective epistemic value function is or what their own epistemic value function is, this creates important problems for epistemic consequentialists. The problem is this: in order to accept epistemic principles like EVE we need to either reject the sort of axiological uncertainty outlined above, or deny that agents cannot have introspective access to their epistemic utility function. In other words, epistemic consequentialists must either reject principles like EVE, or deny that we can be rationally uncertain in axiological facts. This problem will be the focus of section 12.4.

12.4 The Problem of Axiological Uncertainty

In section 12.2 I outlined epistemic enkrasia principles, and argued that these coincided with an epistemic consequentialist principle of maximizing expected epistemic value. And in section 12.3 I argued that agents can be uncertain about various normative and axiological matters. More precisely, I argued that agents can be uncertain about what is epistemically valuable: i.e. about what constitutes epistemic accuracy. In this section, I want to formulate a problem for epistemic consequentialists that arises when we combine both expected value maximization with axiological uncertainty: the problem of axiological uncertainty.

In order to present this problem more precisely, let $E_E U(A)$ be the expected value of A relative to an agent's empirical uncertainty only: that is, let us assume that an agent responding to $E_E U$ assigns credence 1 to all true axiological facts and credence 0 to all false axiological facts, but that she assigns non-extreme credences to empirical facts in accordance with her evidence. Let $E_T U(A)$ be the expected value of A relative to the agent's uncertainty across both empirical and axiological matters. So an agent

---

[18] Axiological uncertainty is less problematic for epistemic consequentialists if agents are only uncertain over different proper scoring rules, since any mixture of proper scoring rules will itself be a proper scoring rule (thanks to Ben Levinstein for pointing this out to me).

[19] If agents only ever assign non-zero credences to improper truth-directed scoring rules when they also assign non-zero credences to the falsity-directed versions of those scoring rules, then she may have a proper scoring rule in expectation if her credences in improper scoring rules all cancel one another out. But it seems unlikely that this will be the case.

responding to $E_T U$ assigns non-extreme credences to empirical and axiological facts in accordance with her evidence (assuming, of course, that an agent's evidence can support non-extreme credences in axiological claims if she is cognitively non-ideal).[20] Finally, let us assume that the following principle is true, based on the considerations of section 12.3:

> *Axiological Uncertainty*: It is permissible for an agent to be uncertain about the nature of the/her epistemic value function U, and her uncertainty can be such that, for any attitudes A_2 and A_1, $E_E U(A_2) < E_E U(A_1)$ does not entail that $E_T U(A_2) < E_T U(A_1)$.

Axiological Uncertainty says that agents can be uncertain about either the objective epistemic value function, or about their own subjective epistemic value function, in ways that lead $E_T U(A)$ to be non-identical with $E_E U(A)$. The claim that $E_T U(A)$ is not identical to $E_E U(A)$ is not quite sufficient for Axiological Uncertainty, however. Imagine that scoring rule S_1 is correct, and that S_1 assigns a perfect score of 0 to some attitude A and a score of 1 to some attitude B. Suppose that an agent is certain about all empirical matters, but uncertain over S_1 (Cr=0.8) and some other scoring rule S_2 (Cr=0.2). Suppose that S_2 assigns a score of 1 to attitude A and a score of 0 to attitude B (the opposite of score S_1). Then the expected score of A will be 0.2 and the expected score of B will be 0.8, if we appeal to a linear meta-scoring rule (discussed below). The expected epistemic accuracy of A is greater than the expected epistemic accuracy of B, just as it would be if the agent were certain that S_1 was the correct scoring rule.

But Axiological Uncertainty says that an agent can sometimes be axiologically uncertain in ways that alter the expected value of her attitudes and fail to preserve the *order* of her attitudes in terms of expected value. For example, imagine that an agent Sarah is in the cup and ball situation described in section 12.3: she sees a ball being placed under one of three cups that are then shuffled randomly. Suppose that she is permissibly uncertain over the Brier scoring rule and the linear scoring rule, and has a credence of 0.5 that each is correct (on the objective view of epistemic value) or that each is an accurate description of her personal epistemic utility function (on the subjective view of epistemic value). Suppose that the Brier score is either correct or does represent her personal epistemic utility function. Then, relative to $E_E U$, she should have a credence of 1/3 that the ball is under any given cup. But, relative to $E_T U$, she should have a credence in the (0, 1/3) interval that the ball is under any given cup. Axiological Uncertainty says that the scenario that Sarah finds herself in is possible.[21]

---

[20] This is at least in part an idealization, since it might not be so easy to separate axiological and empirical uncertainty. Although a more general account of expected epistemic value under uncertainty would include uncertainty about normative claims, what our evidence is, etc., I will assume that both $E_E U(\bullet)$ and $E_T U(\bullet)$ are not sensitive to the sort of uncertainty not covered by empirical and axiological uncertainty.

[21] Axiological Uncertainty says that this could be true of *any* two attitudes, but this requirement is stronger than what is actually needed. All that is required for a conflict with EVE (below) is that agent's

There are two ways of formulating the expected value enkrasia principle (EVE) given the distinction between expected epistemic value relative to empirical uncertainty only, and expected epistemic value relative to empirical and axiological uncertainty:

Empirical Enkrasia: It is never permissible for an agent to have credences such that $E_E U(A_2) < E_E U(A_1)$ and to adopt attitude A_2.

Total Enkrasia: It is never permissible for an agent to have credences such that $E_T U(A_2) < E_T U(A_1)$ and to adopt attitude A_2.

Empirical Enkrasia is sensitive to less of the agent's uncertainty, since Empirical Enkrasia is insensitive to the agent's axiological uncertainty. If epistemic consequentialists think that Empirical Enkrasia is the correct formulation of EVE, and that Axiological Uncertainty is true, then they will have to accept that an agent can be rationally uncertain about axiological facts *but* they will deny that this rational axiological uncertainty will have any impact on the credences that it is rational for the agent to adopt, because Empirical Enkrasia ignores the agent's axiological uncertainty altogether.

But if epistemic consequentialists accept Axiological Uncertainty, then their theory will run into trouble regardless of which of these two variants of EVE they adopt. To see why, suppose, firstly, that epistemic consequentialists accept Empirical Enkrasia and reject Total Enkrasia. If this is the case, then they must accept that agents can sometimes be uncertain about what is epistemically valuable, and that this uncertainty can be such that, given the agent's permissible axiological uncertainty, attitude A_2 is more expectedly epistemically valuable than A_1 is, and yet the agent is still required to adopt attitude A_1 and not attitude A_2. This seems inconsistent with the internalist spirit of epistemic consequentialism,[22] since it says that an agent ought adopt an attitude even if, given all of the information available to her, it is not the best attitude that she can adopt out of the options available to her. It may be useful to illustrate this kind of scenario with a case:

Emma and Pierre

Emma has good evidence that Pierre is the murderer, but she does not know how valuable it is for her to avoid error in her judgment. If it is very valuable for Emma to avoid error in her judgment then it is best for her to have a credence of 0.6 that Pierre is the murderer. If it is only mildly valuable for Emma to avoid error in her judgment then it is best for her to have a credence of 0.8 that Pierre is the murderer. Given all of her evidence, it is rational for Emma to think that it is only mildly valuable for her to avoid error and that 0.8 is the best credence for her to adopt in 'Pierre

---

uncertainty can sometimes be such that, for attitudes A_2 and A_1, $E_E U(A_2) < E_E U(A_1)$ does not entail that $E_T U(A_2) < E_T U(A_1)$, where A_1 maximizes expected epistemic value relative to her empirical uncertainty.

[22] See Leitgeb and Pettigrew (2010: section 3.3).

is the murderer'. However, Emma's evidence about epistemic value is misleading evidence: it is actually very valuable for her to avoid error.

It seems that it would reasonable for Emma to adopt a credence of 0.8 that Pierre is the murderer in this case. In fact, it would be intuitively unreasonable for Emma to simply ignore her evidence that it is only mildly valuable to avoid error and adopt the more cautious credence of 0.6. However, if epistemic consequentialists adopt a principle like Empirical Enkrasia, then they will end up saying that Emma is required to adopt a credence of 0.6 in this case.

This seems to violate a plausible picture of rationality, which says that if an agent responds rationally to all of the evidence available to her, then her attitudes cannot be irrational merely because of the way that the world is. Her attitudes may be *mistaken* or may lack some other important feature (for example, they may never attain the status of knowledge), but an agent that responds rationally to all of her evidence cannot be irrational. But if Empirical Enkrasia is the epistemic consequentialist norm of rationality, and agents can be rationally axiologically uncertain in the manner described by Axiological Uncertainty, then an agent can be irrational even if she has completely rational credences about axiological facts, simply because her uncertainty does not accurately reflect the axiological facts that are *true*.

One key reason that epistemic consequentialists have for formulating their norms in terms of *expected* epistemic value instead of epistemic value is presumably that the former, unlike the latter, is sensitive to an agent's limited information about her situation. If this is an important motive for the consequentialist, then it seems undesirable if their norms take into account the agent's rational uncertainty about empirical matters, but fail to take into account the agent's rational uncertainty about axiological matters.

In order to avoid these problems, the epistemic consequentialist could accept Axiological Uncertainty and endorse a version of the epistemic consequentialist EVE principle that takes into account an agent's axiological uncertainty: namely, Total Enkrasia. In the case of Emma and Pierre, Total Enkrasia will say that Emma ought to adopt the credence that will do expectedly best *given her uncertainty about epistemic value*. In other words, she should adopt a credence of 0.8 that Pierre is the murderer, since she is rationally confident that avoiding error is only mildly valuable. This seems to accord with our intuitions about the case, and with the epistemic consequentialist's original motivations for appealing to expected rather than actual epistemic value.

However, appealing to Total Enkrasia in this sort of case creates at least three problems for the epistemic consequentialist. The first problem is that Total Enkrasia requires the existence of a 'meta-scoring rule': a rule for aggregating the scores of different scoring rules. In the Emma and Pierre case we simply assumed that such a meta-scoring rule existed and that Emma was not uncertain over multiple meta-scoring rules. But suppose that Emma is uncertain about whether scoring rule A or scoring rule B is correct. Scoring rule A says that it is very valuable for her to avoid error in her judgments, and scoring rule B says that it is merely mildly valuable for her to avoid error in her judgments. How should we weigh up the badness of error on each of these scoring rules? Suppose, for example, scoring rule B is *bounded*—it says that a given attitude can only be finitely bad—while scoring rule A is *unbounded*—it says that a given attitude can be infinitely bad. In such cases should we weigh the badness of a bad attitude on A as equivalent to the badness of a bad attitude on B, or should we treat the badness of a bad attitude on A as much worse than the badness of a bad attitude on B? Without a clear answer to this question, it is not obvious how Emma should respond to her axiological uncertainty.[23]

The second problem is that any meta-scoring rule that we formulate will lead to a regress problem. We are not likely to achieve rational certainty in our answer to the question 'what is the correct meta-scoring rule?' and so we must presumably take our uncertainty about the nature of the meta-scoring rule into account when we assign value to attitudes. But in order to take this uncertainty into account we must have already settled what the meta-scoring rule consists in! To see this, suppose that Emma is uncertain across scoring rule A and scoring rule B. And suppose that she is also uncertain across meta-scoring rule C and meta-scoring rule D, which disagree about which first-order credence Emma should have, given her uncertainty across A and B. What first-order credence should Emma have in this situation? In order to answer this, we are going to need to appeal to a *meta meta-scoring rule* that can allow us to compare C and D and that can tell us what to do given our uncertainty in C and D. In other words, if we haven't settled what the meta meta-scoring rule is, then we won't have a way of calculating the expected value of attitudes under uncertainty about the nature of the meta-scoring rule.[24] But this process can presumably go on ad infinitum, unless there is some convenient stopping point—some high level meta-scoring rule in which we can be rationally certain. Insofar as we have reason to doubt that there exists a high level meta-scoring rule in which we can be rationally certain, we have reason to worry about the adopting of both Total Enkrasia and Axiological Uncertainty.[25]

The third problem is that, even if we find an adequate meta-scoring rule that avoids the regress problem, adopting Total Enkrasia will probably undermine most of the results that epistemic consequentialists have been able to derive thus far. For example, epistemic consequentialist arguments for probabilism,[26] the principal principle,[27] and updating by conditionalization[28] assume that the agent's scoring rule is *strictly proper*. But, as I argued earlier, it seems rationally permissible for agents to be

---

[23] This is a difficult problem, one that is closely related to the problem of intertheoretic comparisons that has been discussed in the literature on moral uncertainty. See, for example, MacAskill (2014: ch. 4).

[24] If we do settle on a meta-scoring rule, then it might be argued that we will end up denying that a certain form of axiological uncertainty can be rational: namely, uncertainty about what is rational *given one's uncertainty*. This is arguably an easier kind of axiological certainty to live with, although it does seem to require introspective infallibility.

[25] This regress problem is also closely related to a similar regress problem that has been discussed in the literature on moral uncertainty. See Sepielli (2014).

[26] Joyce (2009).   [27] Pettigrew (2013).   [28] Greaves and Wallace (2006).

rationally uncertain not only over different strictly proper scoring rules, but also over improper scoring rules like the linear scoring rule. And it seems that agents could be rationally uncertain over improper scoring rules in a way that is *asymmetric*: in other words, they need not be equally uncertain in the linear scoring rule that assigns a perfect score of 0 to credence 1 (0) in a proposition iff the proposition in question is true (false), and to an inverse linear scoring rule that assigns a perfect score of 0 to credence 1 (0) in a proposition iff the proposition in question is false (true). But if an agent is asymmetrically uncertain in some improper scoring rule, then it seems unlikely that the current arguments for probabilism, the principal principle, and conditionalization will succeed for this agent.[29] For example, suppose that the agent has a credence of 0.5 that the linear scoring rule is correct, and a credence of 0.5 that the Brier score is correct. It seems plausible that her meta-scoring rule will not be proper: some non-probabilistic credence functions will not be dominated by their probabilistic counterparts. For example, in the case of Sarah given above, it seems very unlikely that any plausible meta-scoring rule will give *no* weight to Sarah's credence in the linear scoring rule. But if it gives any weight to her credence in the linear scoring rule, then it will say that she ought to adopt a credence in the (0, 1/3) interval that the ball is under a given cup. This will mean that she has a credence of 1 that the ball is under one of the three cups, but a credence less than 1/3 that the ball is under any given cup. In other words, if a meta-scoring rule gives any weight to Sarah's uncertainty over an improper scoring rule, it is likely that this meta-scoring rule will itself be improper.

To summarize the problem facing epistemic consequentialists: epistemic consequentialists could accept Axiological Uncertainty and Empirical Enkrasia, since the latter says that agents ought to maximize expected epistemic accuracy relative to their empirical uncertainty only, even if they are axiologically uncertain. But it seems implausible that agents should be required to adopt attitudes that, given their axiological uncertainty, are in expectation worse than other attitudes available to them. Yet this is a consequence of adopting Empirical Enkrasia. Alternatively, epistemic consequentialists could accept Axiological Uncertainty and adopt the subjective principle Total Enkrasia, which says that agents ought to maximize expected value relative to their empirical and axiological uncertainty. But Total Enkrasia depends on the existence of a meta-scoring rule. This is not only difficult to formulate but also opens the door to the regress problem. It is also not clear that epistemic norms that have been derived from epistemic consequentialist principles under the supposition of axiological certainty will hold if we adopt a principle like Total Enkrasia. So, both objective and subjective versions of the consequentialist's EVE principle produce undesirable consequences under axiological uncertainty.

In order to avoid these problems, epistemic consequentialists could deny Axiological Uncertainty and argue that agents are rationally required to be axiologically

---

[29] Of course, this depends at least partly on the selection of the meta-scoring rule. However, it seems prima facie unlikely that the correct meta-scoring rule will support the existing conclusions.

certain. For example, they could argue that axiological facts are knowable a priori, and that we ought to be certain in these a priori facts in the same way that we ought to be certain in logical facts. But, as was discussed above, it seems implausible that non-ideal agents like ourselves can be expected to be certain about what is objectively or subjectively epistemically valuable.

However, the epistemic consequentialist could argue that either the correct scoring rule (on the objective value view) or the agent's actual scoring rule (on the subjective value view) will, regardless of the agent's empirical and axiological evidence, assign higher expected value to certainty in itself than to any credence distribution across possible scoring rules.[30] This means that the epistemic consequentialist needn't say that only certainty in true axiological claims has epistemic value. She can say that axiological uncertainty can have some epistemic value, in the same way that a credence of 0.7 that it will rain can have some epistemic value, even if a credence of 0.8 is more expectedly accurate. But on this view axiological uncertainty will never be *epistemically permissible*, because it will always be less expectedly accurate than axiological certainty.

In defense of this view, the epistemic consequentialist could argue that the rationality of an agent's credences in axiological claims depends entirely on her credence in the correct or actual scoring rule, since the correct or actual scoring rule will be self-supporting: it will assign a score to the agent's credal distribution as accurate to the degree that she is confident that it is the correct or actual scoring rule, and inaccurate to the degree that she is not. In other words, it could assign no epistemic value to credences in scoring rules other than itself.[31] If this is the case then an ideal epistemic agent will always be certain in the correct epistemic scoring rule (on the objective value view) or in the scoring rule that she actually has (on the subjective value view). Axiological uncertainty is never rationally permitted.

Suppose that, given an agent's *actual* but impermissible axiological uncertainty, $EU(A_1) < EU(A_2)$, but that if we assume axiological certainty, $EU(A_2) < EU(A_1)$. If axiological uncertainty is never rational, and an agent should always satisfy the wide scope version of EVE, then she should respond to this by correcting her credences about the axiological facts. In other words, instead of satisfying EVE by failing to adopt attitude A_1, she should satisfy EVE by failing to adopt credences such that $EU(A_1) < EU(A_2)$.

---

[30] Here we need to assume that the correct scoring rule (on the objective value view) or the agent's actual scoring rule (on the subjective value view) are not sensitive to the agent's axiological uncertainty. That is, an agent's axiological uncertainty cannot itself change which scoring rule she has or which scoring rule is correct.

[31] The epistemic consequentialist could even claim that—regardless of an agent's evidence—the correct scoring rule or the agent's actual scoring rule will assign extreme positive value to only itself, and extreme negative value to not just any credence in an alternative scoring rule, but to any state of axiological uncertainty. But this seems extremely gerrymandered.

Denying that axiological uncertainty can ever be rational will allow the epistemic consequentialist to avoid the three problems of axiological uncertainty that I have outlined above. The main worry for those who would deny that axiological uncertainty is ever rationally permissible is that it seems intuitively plausible that we can *in some important sense* be rationally uncertain about axiological facts.[32] As was pointed out in section 12.3, we might think that epistemically ideal agents cannot be uncertain about axiological facts, just as we might think that epistemically ideal agents cannot be uncertain about logical facts. But it seems that non-ideal agents like ourselves will not only find ourselves uncertain about axiological and logical facts, but that this uncertainty can be rational. Even if axiological facts are a priori, we don't seem to have the ability to access them with any certainty given our actual cognitive abilities. And we still see a great deal of disagreement about what the true axiological facts are (and whether such facts exist) among experts. If a non-ideal agent like ourselves were to be axiologically certain in these circumstances then, even if she is certain in the correct axiological theory, her certainty seems far from rationally justified.[33]

If there is an important sense in which axiological uncertainty can be rational, then we want to be able to say what an agent that is in this sense epistemically rational ought to do given this kind of uncertainty. In other words, we don't want to restrict the scope of epistemic consequentialism to agents that are cognitively ideal. If the epistemic consequentialist wants her theory to extend to non-ideal agents like ourselves, then she must try to find a way around the problems that arise when non-ideal agents are axiologically uncertain.

So epistemic consequentialists face the following problem: either they must deny that axiological uncertainty can ever be rational, or they must deny that axiological uncertainty can ever influence what attitudes it is permissible for us to adopt, or they must accept a more subjective notion of epistemic value that takes into account an agent's credences in different accounts of epistemic value but generates problematic results in cases where agents are uncertain over improper scoring rules. I have argued

---

[32] This is the main worry for those who accept a wide-scope enkrasia principle. The view that we are never permissibly axiologically uncertain cannot help us to avoid the problems raised here if epistemic consequentialists endorse narrow scope versions of principles like EVE. This version of EVE says that if an agent has credences such that $EU(A_2) < EU(A_1)$ then regardless of the rational status of these credences she should not adopt attitude A_1. As I stated in section 12.2, narrow scope principles reflect the view that the actual attitudes we adopt can place constraints on the attitudes that it is rational for us to adopt. If we accept the narrow scope version of EVE, then even if agents are irrationally uncertain about axiological facts, this uncertainty could constrain what attitudes it is rational for her to adopt. If this is the case, then epistemic consequentialists will continue to face the problem of axiological uncertainty.

[33] One could argue that a non-ideal agent's certainty cannot be rationally justified here because, as a non-ideal agent, she cannot have employed a method that would produce certainty that is counterfactually secure: it would have to be the result of something like guesswork. But a defender of the view that axiological uncertainty can be rational could argue that this view implies that ideal rationality violates an ought implies can requirement, since the agent ought to be rationally certain, but—given her cognitive limitations—she *cannot* be rationally certain. So the agent finds herself in a rational dilemma where she cannot be rationally certain *or* rationally uncertain in axiological facts.

that the first two of these positions are counterintuitive, while the third position may fail to support epistemic consequentialist arguments for principles like probabilism and conditionalization. And so the problem of axiological uncertainty that arises for epistemic enkrasia principles produces a similar set of difficulties for epistemic consequentialists.

References

Berker, S. 2013. 'Epistemic Teleology and the Separateness of Propositions'. *The Philosophical Review*, 122(3): 337–93.

Broome, J. 2007. 'Wide or Narrow Scope?' *Mind* 116(462): 359–70.

Elga, A. 2013. 'The Puzzle of the Unmarked Clock and the New Rational Reflection Principle'. *Philosophical Studies* 164(1): 127–39.

Gneiting, T. and Raftery, A. E. 2007. 'Strictly Proper Scoring Rules, Prediction and Estimation'. *Journal of the American Statistics Association* 102: 359–78.

Greaves, H. and Wallace, D. 2006. 'Justifying Conditionalization: Conditionalization Maximizes Expected Epistemic Utility'. *Mind* 115: 607–32.

Joyce, J. 2009. 'Accuracy and Coherence: Prospects for an Alethic Epistemology of Partial Belief'. In F. Huber and C. Schmidt-Petri (eds), *Degrees of Belief*. Synthese 342. Dordrecht: Springer, pp. 263–97.

Leitgeb, H. and Pettigrew, R. 2010. 'An Objective Justification of Bayesianism I: Measuring Inaccuracy', *Philosophy of Science* 77: 201–35.

MacAskill, W. 2014. 'Normative Uncertainty'. DPhil dissertation, Oxford University.

Pettigrew, R. 2013. 'A New Epistemic Utility Argument for the Principal Principle'. *Episteme* 10: 19–35.

Sepielli, A. 2014. 'What to Do When You Don't Know What to Do When You Don't Know What to Do . . .'. *Noûs*, 48(3): 521–44.

Titelbaum, M. 2015. 'Rationality's Fixed Point (Or: In Defense of Right Reason)'. In Tamar Szabó Gendler and J. Hawthorne (eds), *Oxford Studies in Epistemology 5*. Oxford: Oxford University Press, pp. 253–94.

Wedgwood, R. 2013. 'Akrasia and Uncertainty'. *Organon F*, 20(4): 483–505.

13
Epistemic Free Riding

Jeffrey Dunn

13.1 Introduction

In epistemology and philosophy of science there has been a growing interest in group inquiry and ways that it might differ fundamentally from individual inquiry. The interest in this topic is understandable. Science is predominately collaborative work. If we want to understand the epistemic success of science we need to understand group inquiry, and it is an important part of this to learn whether it differs from individual inquiry. Philip Kitcher (1990) initiated the focus on scenarios where the norms or best epistemic practices for individuals working alone might come apart from the norms or best epistemic practices for individuals working in groups. Kitcher shows how it is possible for individual scientists who care only about things such as fame and money to nevertheless structure their inquiry in a way that is conducive to finding the truth. Others have carried this work further, looking at various ways that group inquiry can differ in important ways from individual inquiry.[1] Uniting much of this work under one heading, Mayo-Wilson et al. (2011) have recently investigated different versions of what they call the *Independence Thesis*, roughly, the claim that rational individuals can form irrational groups and that rational groups might be composed of irrational individuals.

In this chapter, my goal is to show that some surprising empirical evidence about group problem-solving reveals that groups will often face cases where it is epistemically best for each individual to do one thing, even though this is ultimately epistemically worse for the group. Thus, I will be presenting an epistemic analogue of a free riding scenario. Free riding is familiar in the practical domain, but has seldom been discussed in the epistemic domain, so it is of some interest to investigate whether there are such scenarios. More than that, however, I'll show how the particular epistemic free riding scenario I will discuss directly vindicates a particularly interesting version of the Independence Thesis.

---

[1] See, for instance, Strevens (2003), Zollman (2007), Muldoon and Weisberg (2009), Zollman (2010), and Muldoon (2013).

The arguments that I will give here presuppose a kind of epistemic consequentialism. In particular, I'll be taking for granted that what one epistemically ought to believe can be determined by looking at the expected accuracy of believing in that way.[2] Below I discuss in more detail the particular form of epistemic consequentialism my arguments rely on, but I don't defend the consequentialist viewpoint here. Rather, this chapter should be seen as illustrating one interesting consequence of adopting the consequentialist picture.

Here's the plan. In section 13.2 I'll give a precise characterization of free riding scenarios. After this, in section 13.3, I'll consider the only other example in the literature (of which I'm aware) of epistemic free riding and explain why it doesn't actually seem to be a case of epistemic free riding. In section 13.4 I'll present the empirical evidence that I'll argue leads to an epistemic free riding scenario. In section 13.5 I'll give a formal model to rigorously show that the scenario I'm considering does constitute a free riding problem. In section 13.6 I'll consider the wider significance of the existence of epistemic free riding and how it relates to the Independence Thesis. Finally, in section 13.7, I'll explain how the epistemic free riding scenario gives rise to an interesting puzzle about the explanation for some of our natural doxastic dispositions in cases of group inquiry.

13.2 Characterizing Free Riding Scenarios

What characterizes a free riding scenario? I will follow Philip Pettit (1986) in maintaining that a free riding scenario arises when two conditions are met.[3] First, there is some behavior such that if everyone behaved in this way, the outcome would be Pareto-inferior to the outcome where everyone does not behave in that way.[4] Call this the *Pareto condition*. Second, that behavior can nevertheless be justified in terms of self-interest: the free rider really stands to gain from behaving as he does. Call this the *self-interest condition*. These two features together are what make free riding scenarios especially pernicious. The satisfaction of the Pareto condition shows that the behavior is of the sort that is damaging to everyone if everyone engages in it, and yet the satisfaction of the self-interest condition shows that everyone can justify behaving in that way on the basis of self-interest.

In many presentations of practical free riding, a dominance argument is given to show that the self-interest condition is met. A dominance argument for some action is one that demonstrates that, no matter what the state of the world is, it is best for

---

[2] As I'll note, there are ways of running the argument here that don't take accuracy as the sole epistemic good. However, any way of running the argument relies on some form of consequentialism.

[3] Pettit goes on in that article to distinguish between two types of scenarios where both conditions are met. He dubs one type of scenario as giving rise to *free riding* and the other to *foul dealing*. I won't make those finer distinctions here.

[4] An outcome, O1, is Pareto-inferior to outcome, O2, iff in O1 no one is better off and at least some are worse off compared to O2.

you to perform that action. The argument for why it is in your self-interest to defect in a prisoner's dilemma is a dominance argument: no matter what your partner does, you always do better if you defect. More formally, if C_i (D_i) is the strategy of player i cooperating (defecting), and if '$>_i$' means 'is preferred by i', we have: $(D_1, C_2) >_1 (C_1, C_2)$ and $(D_1, D_2) >_1 (C_1, D_2)$, where you are player 1 and your partner is player 2.

Inspection of many standard examples of free riding, however, reveals that the justification for free riding behavior is not always a strict dominance argument. Suppose that there is a group of recreational fishermen who work a small lake, and, to prevent overfishing, a quota for the season has been set for each person. If everyone sticks to his quota, this will ensure that there is enough fish to have productive fishing seasons year after year. However, there is a safety buffer built into the quotas so that if everyone catches his quota, this does not put the fish population on the brink of disaster. Suppose, then, that everyone adheres to his quota. Then, it is in my interest to ignore the quota, for if I alone exceed my quota, this will not deplete the fish population to dangerous levels. I ensure myself a bigger catch than others this year while still ensuring a replenished supply of fish for next season. Suppose that no one is sticking to his quota. Then, it is again in my interest to ignore the quota, for if everyone is exceeding the quota the population will be decimated whether I stick to it or not. I may as well get as many fish while I can. What about the intermediate situations, where some but not all are sticking to the quota? It is hard to see why it is not in my interest to ignore the quota here, too. For, on the one hand, suppose that there are enough fishermen sticking to the quota that the fish population will survive until next year. In that case, it is unlikely that *my* taking a few more fish will tip the balance. On the other hand, suppose that there are enough fishermen ignoring the quota that the fish population will not survive. In that case, *my* sticking to the quota isn't going to help and so I may as well ignore it. Thus, it seems that no matter the state of the world, it is best for me if I ignore the quota. This seems to be a dominance argument to justify free riding.

On reflection, however, it isn't actually a dominance argument. For surely there is some amount of fish such that if less than that amount is caught then the fish population in the small lake survives and if more than that amount is caught then the fish population does not survive. Given this, there is some state of the world where *my* decision about whether to ignore the quota or not is the decision that determines whether or not the fish population survives. And if my decision to ignore the quota is the one that decimates the fish population for years to come, then it is not in my interest to ignore the quota in that state of the world.[5] Thus, we don't have a dominance argument for free riding. Nevertheless, the reasoning in the previous paragraph still

---

[5] This can be put more formally using the same notation as above. Suppose there are five fishermen. What the argument in the text suggests is that while

$(D_1, C_2, C_3, C_4, C_5) >_1 (C_1, C_2, C_3, C_4, C_5)$

and while

provides a compelling reason for me to free ride. The reason for this is that it is extremely difficult to tell whether I am the crucial one to push the fish population to dangerous levels. Further, if there is a large number of other fishermen, it is extremely unlikely that I am in this situation. This suggests that a free riding scenario can obtain even when there is no *dominance* argument for free riding behavior. The free rider need not prefer the outcome where he defects to the outcome where he cooperates no matter the state of the world. What matters, instead, is that the free rider must be able to justify free riding behavior in terms of self-interest. A dominance argument is a particularly clear way to do this, but it is not the only way.[6]

The example of the fishermen is a practical free riding scenario: the value is prudential and the things being evaluated are actions. In what follows, I'll give an example of epistemic free riding. An epistemic free riding scenario is formally identical to a practical one. The key difference is that the value is *epistemic* and the things being evaluated are *beliefs*.

In some sense, it is extremely easy to construct an epistemic free riding scenario. Suppose that there are 100 of us in a group and if over half of us believe that the earth is flat, then an oracle will tell us 1,000 important truths about the world. If accuracy of belief is the only thing of epistemic value, then failing to believe that the earth is flat seems to be an instance of epistemic free riding. If you fail to believe the earth is flat, you stand to have 1,000 true beliefs and no false beliefs by free riding on the fact that others in the group will believe the earth is flat. This meets the formal conditions for a free riding problem and it is recognizably epistemic. However, there is not much interest in such a case, because the conditions for it to obtain are so unrealistic. Practical free riding is interesting precisely because the conditions for it to occur often arise. Analogously, epistemic free riding will be interesting only if the conditions for it to occur often arise. This toy example does not show us *that*. In contrast, I will present a case of epistemic free riding that is realistic and often arises. Before getting to such a case, however, we need to look at the only other example in the literature of epistemic free riding.

13.3 List and Pettit on Epistemic Free Riding

Christian List and Philip Pettit (2004) purport to give us an example of epistemic free riding that, unlike the oracle scenario, is more realistic. Their scenario makes use of the Condorcet Jury Theorem (CJT). Consider a case where a group is trying to decide

---

$(D_1, D_2, D_3, D_4, D_5) >_1 (C_1, D_2, D_3, D_4, D_5)$
there may be some specific ways that the other fishermen can defect or cooperate where the following holds:
$(D_1, D_2, D_3, C_4, C_5) <_1 (C_1, D_2, D_3, C_4, C_5)$.
This will be the case, for instance, if the fish don't survive the next season in $(D_1, D_2, D_3, C_4, C_5)$ but do survive in $(C_1, D_2, D_3, C_4, C_5)$.

[6] For some thoughts on this, see Pettit (1986), p. 369.

the answer to a question with two possible answers (e.g., guilty or not guilty). The CJT says that if each member is more likely than not to choose the correct answer, and if each member decides independently of the other members, then the probability that the majority vote is accurate approaches 1 as the number of group members increases.[7] This initially striking mathematical result points toward one way that groups can sometimes be more accurate than any individual member of the group.

So, how can this lead to a free riding scenario? List and Pettit ask us to imagine a situation where we are taking votes sequentially and in public. Further, we are to assume that we all know that we are each equally likely to get the verdict correct, that this probability is greater than 0.5, and that we believe each person is voting in accordance with his or her belief. In this case, and if we each know about the CJT result, then we each know that it is more likely that the majority vote is correct than that any one member is correct. Thus, if I am voting third and I have heard two *yea* votes, then no matter what I independently believe to be correct, I stand a better chance of voting correctly if I vote *yea*. And the same thing is true for each person after me. However, in so-doing, we each make the group significantly less likely to get the right answer, since it is now a group with only two independently voting members.[8]

An important question is whether this scenario really is a case of epistemic free riding. As List and Pettit present the example, the members of the group value voting accurately themselves. Since the value in question concerns accurately answering a question, we are plausibly in the epistemic domain. But it is doubtful that it meets the conditions for a free riding scenario. The self-interest condition states that there must be an argument for why it is in the self-interest of the free rider to free ride. Note first that this scenario is not one where there is a dominance argument for voting non-independently. Suppose that *yea* is the correct answer but that, improbably, a large majority is voting *nay*. If agent 1 values voting correctly herself we have: $(N_1, N_2, \ldots, N_n) <_1 (Y_1, N_2, \ldots, N_n)$. This shows that there is no dominance argument for voting with the group. Rather, it is some sort of expected value calculation that must be doing work. But, as noted by List and Pettit, such an argument works only if we assume that everyone else is voting independently. But if one is reasonably confident that everyone else is free riding and voting non-independently, then one has no reason to go with the group since the majority vote is no longer more likely to be correct than one's own.

The scenario also fails to satisfy the Pareto condition. By the very setup of the case, it is not possible for everyone to engage in free riding behavior, which in this case

---

[7] It ends up being important exactly how these different conditions are formally specified to understand the exact content of the theorem. Further, there are extra conditions one can add to strengthen the result. However, these details won't matter for our purposes. A good source for more information on CJTs is Hawthorne (MS).

[8] If the first two votes are split, then the same situation obtains for the person who votes fifth so long as the next two votes agree with each other. In the economics literature, these are known as *informational cascades*. For seminal work in this area see Banerjee (1992) and Bikhchandani et al. (1992).

is to simply vote the way the group votes rather than independently. For the first voter, this is impossible. So, in this scenario, we cannot even evaluate whether it is true that everyone engaging in free riding would be Pareto-inferior to everyone not free riding.[9] Thus, this scenario—though interesting in many ways—isn't an instance of epistemic free riding.

List and Pettit have an alternative scenario, however. In this alternative scenario the members of a group only care that the majority vote is accurate. This is the sole outcome with epistemic value. It's not altogether clear why the group getting the correct answer is of any epistemic value to me, a group member. But put this aside. Perhaps we can make this assumption plausible by assuming that group members will adopt as their own belief whatever the majority votes for. Each member, then, wants the majority vote to be accurate, but each member would also like to save herself the time-consuming effort of coming to an independent view on the issue. It looks, at least initially, as if voting non-independently is an instance of free riding. First, it seems as though the self-interest condition is satisfied. For, ignoring the case where my vote is pivotal and pushes the majority vote to one side or the other, I can save myself significant effort by voting non-independently without changing how the group votes. If we're going to get the same answer regardless of my vote, I might as well save myself the effort of thinking through the issue. And second, the Pareto condition might appear to be satisfied, since we're a much more accurate group when we all vote independently than when we do not.

As with the scenario above, this is an interesting case. However, I also doubt that this is a case of epistemic free riding. The first reason is familiar: initial appearances to the contrary, the Pareto condition cannot really be satisfied in this case, since it is impossible for everyone to vote non-independently. To vote with the group, rather than based on an independent analysis of the issue requires that the group is voting some way, and it is hard to see how this can happen unless at least one person votes independently.

The second worry is novel, however. The worry is that the argument that non-independent voting is in my self-interest concerns more than just epistemic value. The argument also involves prudential value like the time and effort it takes to come to an independent answer. For this reason, the scenario is not a case of (purely) *epistemic* free riding.

I do not want to discount the interesting nature of these two scenarios presented by List and Pettit. They certainly bear a family resemblance to classical free riding

---

[9] One might try to defend List and Pettit by slightly weakening the Pareto condition. The Pareto condition currently says: behavior b meets the Pareto condition iff the outcome that results from *everyone* choosing b is Pareto inferior to the outcome where no one chooses b. One might weaken it to say instead: behavior b meets the Pareto* condition iff the outcome that results from *most* choosing b is Pareto inferior to the outcome where no one chooses b. One problem with the Pareto* condition is that it is vague: how many in a group must choose b for it to be the case that most of the group members chose b? But perhaps a modification of the Pareto condition along these lines could be made to work. Still, the scenario would fail the self-interest condition.

problems, they in some way concern epistemic matters, and they strike me as interesting in their own right. Nevertheless, I doubt that we have been given a realistic scenario that truly can be said to be a case of epistemic free riding. This is important especially if we want to use a free riding scenario to vindicate an *epistemic* version of the Independence Thesis. In what follows, I aim to present such a case. It is, I claim, a realistic scenario, it is purely about epistemic value (not prudential value), and it meets both the Pareto and self-interest conditions.

13.4 Empirical Evidence

To get to the scenario I want to focus on, we need to briefly consider some psychological research on group inquiry. There is evidence for the claim that groups that have members who debate a question *and* genuinely hold dissenting views about the debated question (that is, they are not simply playing the devil's advocate) are more accurate than both individual inquirers and other groups that lack one of these qualities. One important consequence of this is that heterogenous groups—groups where there are individuals that hold different views about the correct answer to a question—are more likely to eventually reach the correct answer to the question than homogenous groups—groups where everyone shares the same view on the answer.

The evidence for this surprising claim comes from several sources. First, there is evidence that groups can often outperform any individual member in reasoning tasks. Consider a study by Moshman and Geil (1998). In the study, the participants were divided into three experimental conditions: individual control, interactive condition, individual/interactive condition. In the individual control, the participants were asked to solve the Wason Selection Task on their own. In the interactive condition, participants were asked to solve the task in groups with five to six members. In the individual/interactive condition, participants were first asked to solve the task alone, and then (without having the correct answer revealed to them) solve the task in a group. The results are striking. In the individual control condition, consistent with other studies on the Wason Selection Task, the success rate was approximately 9 percent. In the interactive condition, the success rate jumped to 70 percent. Finally, in the individual/interactive condition, when these individuals worked in *groups*, the success rate was 80 percent. So, groups can often be more accurate than individuals working alone.

However, there is an important caveat to this general result. There is evidence that for groups to do better than individuals, group members must be debating and arguing with each other in a genuine way. As Mercier and Sperber (2011) write: "many experiments have shown that *debates* are essential to any improvement of performance in group settings" (p. 63, my emphasis). Schulz-Hardt et al. (2006) present a good example of the kind of experiment demonstrating this. The study involved groups attempting to solve *hidden profile* problems. These are problems where the correct solution requires full information, but no one group member possesses full information. For instance, the problem might be to select the best apartment. In a hidden profile problem, the full set of information clearly picks out one apartment as best, but each group member only has partial information. Groups discuss the problem and then decide on a group answer. Schulz-Hardt et al. manipulated the information available to each group member to test the effect of diversity of opinion on the eventual solution the groups put forward. Groups where all group members had full information reached the correct decision 100 percent of the time. Groups with homogenous preferences for options before discussion reached the correct decision 7 percent of the time. Groups where group members had diverse preferences before discussion—but no member who initially preferred the correct option—reached the correct decision 26 percent of the time. Finally, groups where group members had diverse preferences before discussion—and at least one member who initially preferred the correct option—reached the correct decision 62 percent of the time. Overall, groups with heterogenous views reached the correct decision 43 percent of the time.[10]

In an early review article of the literature on group problem-solving, Hastie (1986, pp. 151–2) identifies three characteristics that produce high levels of group performance. The first is that the individuals vary in their competency to answer the problem, and that the problem has a "eureka solution," which is a solution that may not be obvious initially but is demonstrable once discovered. Second, individual judgment accuracy is perturbed by unsystematic errors. This characteristic allows that simple averaging of group members' answers is more likely to be correct than any individual judgment. The third characteristic that leads to high-level group performance is group members who possess different evidence. It is plausible that some combination of these characteristics often obtain in cases that we care about. The first and third conditions are likely to obtain in certain scientific settings, for instance, when a group of physicists is discussing the proper interpretation of some data from the Large Hadron Collider. Though the correct interpretation is by no means *simple*, it is demonstrable, once found. Further, it is likely that different physicists bring slightly different bodies of evidence to bear on the problem. The first and second conditions are plausibly met in the key cases used to motivate conciliatory views of peer disagreement in the recent epistemology literature, such as a case where a group of us disagree about our share of the check at a restaurant (Christensen, 2007).

The data so far canvassed suggest that groups of inquirers that engage in genuine debate about possible answers to a question are ultimately more accurate in answering the question than groups of inquirers that do not engage in such debate. But the results

---

[10] See also Perret-Clermont et al. (2004) (who focus on childhood development), Schulz-Hardt et al. (2006) (for a helpful summary of this research on adults), and Kuhn et al. (1997). Other evidence for the claim that debate is needed for groups to outperform individuals is summarized in Mercier and Sperber (2011) and Mercier (2012, 2011). The claim also fits well with what Sunstein (2002) calls the "law of group polarization." For skepticism about the robustness of this phenomenon, see Gigone and Hastie (1997).

are more surprising than this. It turns out that contrived debate using various devil's advocacy techniques does not yield the advantages for group inquiry that is yielded by genuine debate among group members who genuinely hold dissenting views. Schulz-Hardt et al. (2002), for instance, investigated whether various groups that consisted of genuinely disagreeing members perform similarly to groups where dissent is contrived using various devil's advocacy techniques. They found that groups that had genuine disagreement were less biased in seeking only confirmatory information. Greitemeyer et al. (2006) set out to show that, contrary to the results just described, contrived dissent *can* yield advantages for group reasoning. They instructed various group members to defend different points of view, even if that point of view was not one the group member really believed. Though group members did play the appropriate roles, and as a result a more balanced menu of evidence was discussed, the group answers did not improve. In contrast, in the genuinely heterogenous groups, group answers did improve markedly.[11]

Putting all this evidence together provides a strong reason to think that, at least in many kinds of cases, group members who are investigating some question will, in the long run, end up with more accurate beliefs about the answer to that question if they initially maintain their divergent beliefs and vigorously defend them. Of course, if the group members are to reap the benefits of this group discussion, they must eventually converge on one answer. But they are more likely to believe the true answer if, initially, they stick to the answer they think is true in spite of the disagreement with their peers.[12]

13.5 Epistemic Free Riding

From this empirical data we can construct an epistemic free riding scenario. Suppose that I am in a relatively large group of experts on some topic attempting to answer some question in that topic. Before we start discussing the question, we realize that opinion is approximately evenly split between the possible answers. Plausibly, once the fact that there is this split of opinion among experts is added to my evidence, my evidence now supports each answer to a roughly equal degree. So, if I want to respect this evidence, I should reduce my confidence in my preferred answer and adopt a roughly similar credence for all the possible answers being entertained. However, if all the group members do this, then we will all go into the debate with the same agnostic belief state with respect to our question. We will have turned ourselves

---

[11] Strauss et al. (2011) summarize this study as well as other related ones. Indirect support for the claim that genuine dissent is required for the advantages of group inquiry is provided by the well-known phenomenon of belief bias whereby people are better at identifying flaws in arguments when the conclusions are those with which they disagree and worse at identifying flaws in arguments when the conclusions are those with which they agree (Evans et al. 1983).

[12] There's an obvious potential challenge here for conciliatory views of disagreement, views according to which (roughly) one ought to suspend judgment on a proposition disputed by one's peers. This challenge is considered in Dunn (MS).

from a heterogenous group where different answers have advocates to a homogenous group where opinions are the same, thus reducing the chance that we will reach the correct answer to the question at the end of debate. Thus, if we are looking only at epistemic value, we'd each prefer to be in a group containing mostly members who remain steadfast in their initial opinions during the debate. This way we maximize our chance of landing on an accurate consensus answer to our question. However, since our evidence now supports withholding belief, we each have a good reason to now withhold belief and not remain steadfast in our pre-debate opinions.

That's the basic scenario, but to really make good on the claim that it is a case of epistemic free riding, it needs to be made more precise. To make it more precise we need to specify several things. First, we need to say something about epistemic value. Second, we need to say something about epistemic acts. And third, we need to say something about how epistemic acts are evaluated with respect to epistemic value.

As to the first point, I'll assume that accuracy is the sole final epistemic value.[13] I'll also assume that accuracy comes in degrees. For example, although a credence of 0.5 in P and a credence of 0 in P are both inaccurate when P is true, a credence of 0.5 in P is more accurate than a credence of 0. To measure this precisely we can use a scoring rule. Let the question of interest have a finite number m of mutually exclusive and jointly exhaustive possible answers in $\Omega = \{1, \ldots, m\}$. Let a belief state with respect to this question $\mathbf{c}$, be a probability vector $\{c_1, \ldots, c_m\}$ such that $c_1, \ldots, c_m \geq 0$, $c_1 + \ldots + c_m = 1$. So, for instance, c_1 is the credence assigned to answer 1, c_2 the credence assigned to answer 2, etc. A scoring rule is a function from a credence function $\mathbf{c}$ and true state of the world i into the real numbers. A scoring rule thus awards a score to a credence function based on only two things: the level of credence assigned to the various answers and the state of the world. Scoring rules are thus well equipped to be measures of *accuracy*.

There are many scoring rules that can be used. I'll use the popular Brier score, which is:

$$B(\mathbf{c}, i) = \sum_{j=1}^{m} (\delta_{ij} - c_j)^2,$$

where $\delta_{ij} = 1$ if $i = j$ and $\delta_{ij} = 0$ otherwise. Note that the Brier score has a minimum value of zero and a maximum value that increases with increasing m. If it is important to compare scores between questions that have different numbers of possible answers we can normalize the Brier score by taking $B(\mathbf{c}, i)/m$ where m is the number of possible answers to the question. According to the Brier score, lower numbers are better. Thus, we can see the Brier score as measuring inaccuracy: less is better.

That covers epistemic value. As for epistemic acts, I'll suppose that agents can perform epistemic acts at times and that the only epistemic acts available to an agent

---

[13] The argument doesn't require this; one could still run the argument if one thinks there is, say, epistemic value in following the evidence, and epistemic value in knowing. Taking accuracy as the only epistemic value, however, allows the argument to be continuous with other formal work that appeals to scoring rules (e.g., Joyce (1998) and the work that follows in this tradition).

at a time are the belief states that the agent can come to occupy at that time.[14] Since in this context we'll be focusing on specific questions that groups are attempting to answer, we'll focus solely on the acts available to the agent that concern her belief state *with respect to the question of interest*.

Finally, I'll make the fairly common assumption that epistemic acts will be evaluated in virtue of their *expected* accuracy. Why *expected* accuracy rather than just accuracy? First note that it is compatible with thinking that the sole final epistemic value is accuracy to say that acts are evaluated in virtue of their expected accuracy. Accuracy is still driving the evaluation. Analogously, an investor that evaluates investments in terms of their expected monetary value could still think that the only thing with final value is money. Moreover, this view seems to sit well with at least some of our intuitive verdicts: when a tremendous amount of misleading evidence points towards the falsity of a true proposition, it seems the better epistemic act is to believe the proposition is false.

Given this set up, we can now think more specifically about the scenario of group inquiry. To keep things as simple as possible, we'll consider a scenario where a group of experts is interested in answering a question that has only two possible answers: $\{P, \bar{P}\}$.[15] We'll also suppose that there are only three belief states that an agent can adopt: $\{c_P = 1, c_{\bar{P}} = 0\}$, $\{c_P = 0, c_{\bar{P}} = 1\}$, and $\{c_P = 0.5, c_{\bar{P}} = 0.5\}$. These correspond, respectively, to believing P, believing $\bar{P}$, and withholding belief with respect to P. Denote these with 'c^P', '$c^{\bar{P}}$', 'c^W'. We suppose that before meeting with each other there are approximately equal numbers of members who believe P and who believe $\bar{P}$. So, before meeting, each group member starts out opinionated.

Let's now consider two different dispositions the agents that make up these groups might have. One kind of agent could have the disposition to be *conciliatory*. A conciliatory agent withholds belief in the disputed proposition upon learning there is a disagreement among the group members. A different kind of agent could have the disposition to be *steadfast*. A steadfast agent sticks with her antecedent view of the disputed question, even upon learning of the disagreement. Given this, there are three kinds of groups some agent, S, might find herself in:

(i) S could be in a group where everyone is conciliatory upon learning the opinions of the others. In that case, it is plausible that S being steadfast doesn't make her group have the required heterogeneity to get the benefits of group debate.
(ii) S could be in a group where she is the pivotal member in the sense that if S is steadfast, then the group will have the requisite heterogeneity to get the benefits of debate, but if S is conciliatory then they will not.
(iii) Finally, S could be in a group that has enough other members who are steadfast that the group will get the benefit of heterogeneity independent of what S does.

[14] Greaves (2013) makes this a condition of something being an epistemic act.
[15] I'll let '$\bar{P}$' abbreviate the negation of P.

As in the classic free riding scenarios discussed above, we ignore the pivotal case. Thus, if we are evaluating whether it is epistemically best for S to be steadfast or conciliatory, there are two relevant states of the group: the state where the group has enough steadfast members to have the required heterogeneity to get the benefits of debate and the state where the other group members are all conciliatory. Since S herself can be either steadfast or conciliatory, this will yield a 2 × 2 decision matrix.

We want to evaluate the best option for an agent in the group, S, with respect to expected accuracy. There are two key points at which we'll evaluate S's expected accuracy. First, upon realizing there is a disagreement, S will either remain steadfast and stick with her antecedent view or she will be conciliatory and withhold belief. The group will then discuss and debate the issue and then adopt some consensus answer to the question. We then come to the second evaluation point. We'll assume that each agent adopts the group's consensus answer as her own at the end of the debate. Obviously, each agent's initial decision about whether to be steadfast or conciliatory has an effect on her initial expected accuracy. But since her decision here can also in part determine whether she is in a heterogenous or homogenous group, it can also influence how likely it is that the group consensus is correct. This yields the following decision matrix for S (where a, b, c, and d are the epistemic payoffs for S):

	All other group members are conciliatory	Enough other group members are steadfast
S is conciliatory	a	b
S is steadfast	c	d

It is important to remember that in this chart, "S is conciliatory" stands for a pair of acts—the act of giving up one's initial beliefs and becoming conciliatory as soon as one learns that other members of the group disagree, and the later act of aligning one's beliefs with whatever the group ends up deciding is correct. Likewise, "S is steadfast" stands for a pair of acts—the act of sticking to one's initial beliefs when one learns that other members of the group disagree, and so initially being steadfast, and then the later act of aligning one's beliefs with whatever the group ends up deciding is correct.

I maintain that the epistemic act of being conciliatory is often an act of free riding. This is so just in case the self-interest condition is met as well as the Pareto condition. Given the way we've set things up, the self-interest condition is met so long as $a < c$ and $b < d$ (recall that these are expected *inaccuracy* scores and so lower values are better). We can see whether the Pareto condition is met by determining whether $d < a$.[16]

---

[16] Roughly, the Pareto condition is met iff the case where all free ride is worse than the case where all do not free ride. One might notice, however, that outcome d is not necessarily a case where *all* do not free ride; it is instead a scenario where *some* do not free ride. However, as will be clear shortly, the value of d in this model will be the same in the case where all are steadfast and in the case where enough are steadfast.

Let C and S correspond to S's initial epistemic acts of either being conciliatory or being steadfast. Let GC and GS correspond to the later epistemic act of adopting the group consensus when S is in either a conciliatory or a steadfast group. Letting $EB(X)$ denote the expected Brier inaccuracy of epistemic act X, we have:

$$a = EB(C) + EB(GC)$$
$$b = EB(C) + EB(GS)$$
$$c = EB(S) + EB(GC)$$
$$d = EB(S) + EB(GS)$$

To see if the Pareto and self-interest conditions obtain, we need to say something about $EB(X)$, the expected value of taking epistemic act X. Let i range over the possible answers to the question (in our case: P and $\bar{P}$). Let $\mathbf{c}^n$ range over the possible belief states that can be adopted (in our case: '$\mathbf{c}^P$', '$\mathbf{c}^{\bar{P}}$', '$\mathbf{c}^W$'). The acts and possible belief states can each be subscripted with a time to indicate at what time the act is an option. Finally, let p be a probability function that tracks what the agent's evidence supports now. Then, we have:

$$EB(X_t) = \sum_i \sum_n p(i \wedge \mathbf{c}_t^n | X_t) \times B(\mathbf{c}_t^n, i).$$

Several points deserve note. First, the weight for this expectation is a probability function, p, that tracks what the agent's evidence supports, but which need not be identical to the agent's own belief state. There are several reasons for this. First, there is a technical reason: the agent's belief state with respect to the question, $\mathbf{c}$, is only defined over possible answers to the question. So it doesn't have enough structure to tell us, say, how likely it is that the group consensus is accurate given that the group members hold heterogenous views. Second, there is a philosophical reason: we are interested in whether there might be situations where what an agent should believe comes apart from what the evidence supports. So, it is useful to distinguish what the evidence supports from what the agent believes. Finally, another philosophical reason: one way to maximize expected value (of any kind) is to maximize relative to how one's own degrees of belief weight the different possibilities; but another way to maximize expected value is to maximize relative to more objective weights that track what your evidence supports. It is this latter way that we are interested in here. So, we are asking what is going to maximize epistemic value for an agent, given what her evidence supports.

The second thing to note about $EB(X)$ is that it does not represent a fully general way to calculate the expected epistemic value of adopting a belief state. It builds in, for instance, that we are evaluating act X only with respect to the expected accuracy that X has now rather than with respect to the expected accuracy into the future. This is acceptable in this context since by ignoring the case where the agent is pivotal to whether the group is heterogenous or homogenous, her initial decision doesn't have an effect on her later decision to adopt the group consensus.

Finally, by using a conditional probability, $EB(X)$ also takes a stand in the dispute between evidential and causal decision theory, preferring evidential decision theory. This feature might be objectionable, but in light of what was said in the previous paragraph, it won't be a problem in this case.[17]

Let us now consider whether the self interest condition is satisfied. To do this, we need to see whether $a < c$ and $b < d$. The second term in each of these inequalities is the same, so our question reduces to whether $EB(C) < EB(S)$.

So, we'd like to work out (I've dropped the time subscript for ease of reading):

$$EB(S) = \sum_i \sum_n p(i \wedge c^n|S) \times B(c^n, i)$$

$$EB(C) = \sum_i \sum_n p(i \wedge c^n|C) \times B(c^n, i).$$

These can be simplified. Since choosing act C at the beginning of inquiry will result in having belief state c^W at the beginning of inquiry, it follows that $p(c^W|C) = 1$ and so $p(i \wedge c^W|C) = p(i|C)$ and $p(i \wedge c^P|C) = p(i \wedge c^{\bar{P}}|C) = 0$. Further it is plausible that my choosing to be conciliatory does not affect the probability that answer i is true. Thus, $p(i|C) = p(i)$. Accordingly, $EB(C)$ can be simplified to:

$$EB(C) = \sum_i p(i) \times B(c^W, i),$$

where the value of i can be either P or $\bar{P}$.

A very similar line of argument simplifies $EB(S)$ to either of the following, depending on whether the agent in question either initially believed P or $\bar{P}$:

$$EB(S) = \sum_i p(i) \times B(c^P, i)$$

$$EB(S) = \sum_i p(i) \times B(c^{\bar{P}}, i).$$

If our scoring rule is symmetric, as the Brier score is, in that it assigns the same penalty to $c(P) = n$ when P is true as it assigns to $c(P) = 1 - n$ when P is false, then these two expected scores will be equal.

So long as we use a proper scoring rule,[18] as the Brier score is, these expectations will be minimized for $c_i = p(i)$. So, what is the value of $p(P)$ (and thus also $p(\bar{P})$) in this situation? It is plausible to hold that it is at or near 0.5. This is because at the time of the decision we have a number of qualified individuals, half of whom believe P and the other half who believe $\bar{P}$. Recall that $p(P)$ is measuring the evidential support for

---

[17] For more on the distinction between evidential and causal decision theory in the epistemic realm, see Greaves (2013) and Konek and Levinstein (forthcoming).

[18] A proper scoring rule is a scoring rule for credences that has the following property: the credence function that has the best expected score from the perspective of any coherent credence function, c, is c itself. For more on this see Seidenfeld (1985).

P, and your evidence is that a roughly equal number of experts believe P as believe $\bar{P}$. The conciliatory view in the peer disagreement literature contains arguments that support this claim.[19] With such a value for $p(P)$, one minimizes expected inaccuracy by adopting c^W, which assigns P a credence of 0.5 and $\bar{P}$ a credence of 0.5. Accordingly, $EB(C) < EB(S)$. From this it follows that the self-interest condition is met.

Turn now to the Pareto condition. Here we want to know whether $d < a$, that is, whether $EB(S) + EB(GS) < EB(C) + EB(GC)$. From what was just shown we know that $EB(C) < EB(S)$. The question, then, is whether $EB(GS) < EB(GC)$ to a degree great enough to make $d < a$. To answer this question we need to pay closer attention to our scoring rule. If we normalize the Brier score, $EB(C) = 0.25$ and $EB(S) = 0.5$. Thus, we want to know under what conditions, $EB(GS) + 0.25 < EB(GC)$.

Let 't_{GS}', 'f_{GS}', and 'w_{GS}' denote the probability that a group reaches a true answer, a false answer, or withholds belief conditional on the group being steadfast (and similarly with 'GC' replacing 'GS'). Note that there are two ways to adopt a true (false) belief after the debate: (1) adopt c^P when P is true (false) or (2) adopt $c^{\bar{P}}$ when P is false (true). However, as noted, the Brier score is symmetric and so yields the same score for each of these cases. In particular, the score for a true belief is 0, the score for a false belief is 1, and the score for withholding belief is 1/4. Since at the end of inquiry the agent is going to adopt the group consensus, we know that $EB(GS) = t_{GS} \times 0 + f_{GS} \times 1 + w_{GS} \times 1/4$. From this it follows that $d < a$ if and only if:

$$f_{GC} + w_{GC}/4 - 1/4 > f_{GS} + w_{GS}/4.$$

If groups are forced to decide at the end of inquiry (and thus not withhold belief), then this holds so long as $f_{GC} - 1/4 > f_{GS}$. One simple scenario where this obtains is where $f_{GC} = t_{GC} = 0.5$ and where $f_{GS} = 0.24$ and $t_{GS} = 0.76$. But even if we allow groups to withhold belief at the end of inquiry, there is still a wide range of cases where the inequality holds and so the Pareto condition is met. For instance, here is such a scenario:

$$t_{GC} = 0.4 \quad w_{GC} = 0.2 \quad f_{GC} = 0.4$$
$$t_{GS} = 0.7 \quad w_{GS} = 0.15 \quad f_{GS} = 0.15.$$

Since we have good empirical reason to believe that diverse heterogenous groups are often much more likely to be accurate than homogenous groups, we have reason to believe that in actual cases of group inquiry, both the Pareto and self-interest conditions can be met. Thus, the option of being conciliatory and withholding belief upon realizing that there is a mix of opinion on a question is often an epistemic act of free riding.

Stripping off the formalism, here is the basic picture. In cases of group inquiry, think of group members as able to garner epistemic value at two times: at the beginning of inquiry and then at the end. Once a split of opinion is noticed, each group member

---

[19] This view is sometimes called the 'Equal Weight View' (Elga, 2007).

expects to be most accurate at the beginning by withholding belief on the answer to the disputed question. Each group member also plans to adopt the consensus answer at the end of inquiry. But no one group member can do much to affect the consensus answer at the later time, so since each group member can get a boost in epistemic value *now* by withholding belief, each is reasonable in withholding belief. However, if each follows this advice then the group will be homogenous in their opinions and are less likely than they otherwise would be to reach an accurate consensus answer at the end of inquiry. So although each group member prefers that she withholds belief at the beginning of inquiry, she hopes everyone else will not.

This is surprising in some ways. In the practical domain, actions that count as free riding actions are usually thought of negatively. Not paying one's taxes or fishing above a quota are classic examples of free riding. In this epistemic case, however, the free riding action is one that is often looked on in a favorable light. Someone who modestly withholds belief once she realizes that there is a dispute amongst her peers is generally thought to exhibit some sort of intellectual virtue. The model here together with the empirical evidence suggest that it is nevertheless an act of epistemic free riding.

Before closing this section, let me note something about several simplifying idealizations made in the model. First, we considered a question with only two possible answers. However, the model is able to handle scenarios where questions have more than two possible answers. In the Schulz-Hardt et al. (2006) study cited above, the experimental data is gathered for groups solving a question with four possible answers and it is relatively straightforward to show that free riding can occur in such scenarios. Second, I have here only allowed for three kinds of beliefs to be adopted in any proposition: $c(P) = 1$, $c(P) = 0.5$, or $c(P) = 0$. This makes the calculations much simpler, but again, the model permits consideration of cases where agents can adopt any value for their credences.

13.6 Significance of Epistemic Free Riding

In the introduction to this chapter I mentioned the Independence Thesis (Mayo-Wilson et al., 2011), which claims that rational individuals can form irrational groups and that rational groups might be composed of irrational individuals. In this section I'd like to consider this thesis more closely and its relation to the epistemic free riding scenario just presented.

One way that one might argue for a tension between group and individual rationality is by pointing out that what it is rational for me to believe given that I am working alone is different than what it is rational for me to believe given that I am part of a group. But this claim is not surprising. Since large groups of people can investigate more topics than individuals, I should presumably form stronger beliefs on more varied topics when part of a group than when working alone. There isn't any real conflict between group and individual rationality here, any more than there is a conflict between rationality in situations where there is not much evidence and rationality in situations when there is lots of evidence.

In the scenario I have presented, in contrast, we are presented with a genuine conflict between the group and individual perspective. To see why, suppose we say that an individual is rational iff she minimizes her own expected inaccuracy over time and say that a group is rational iff the average expected inaccuracy of the group is minimized. I don't mean to endorse these definitions of group and individual rationality, but they will help to illustrate the sense in which the free riding scenario here vindicates a certain version of the Independence Thesis. So, granting those definitions, the free riding scenario above shows that rational individuals can make up an irrational group. When I'm in a group setting, it really is epistemically better for me (and every other group member) to withhold belief upon learning of our disagreement. So, from the perspective of individual rationality, each group member should withhold. However, if I'm focused purely on the group performance I should prefer that we all remain steadfast in the face of disagreement. So, the free riding scenario suggests that rational groups will contain irrational members.[20] Thus, what is rational for an individual *qua* group member is different than what is rational for an individual *qua* individual.

Note further that this is a purely epistemic vindication of the Independence Thesis. Some have argued for a tension between group and individual rationality by focusing on the way that communication networks between researchers are structured, or the projects that different group members choose to spend their time pursuing.[21] While these topics are clearly important for the philosophy of science and relevant to epistemology, they are not purely about the belief states adopted by researchers. Thus, these discussions of the Independence Thesis run the risk of being characterized as not genuinely about *epistemic* rationality. Not so here. Here we are focused purely on the epistemic acts of adopting various belief states, which are then evaluated solely in terms of accuracy. It is thus a vindication of a purely epistemic Independence Thesis.

13.7 A Puzzle

I've argued that being conciliatory in group inquiry when one learns that there is disagreement is often to be an epistemic free rider. That is, it is in each person's epistemic self-interest to be conciliatory, even though the effect of everyone acting in this way is epistemically detrimental for everyone.

Against this backdrop, it is interesting to note that there is evidence that humans are naturally disposed to stand their ground in disagreements and not be conciliatory.

---

[20] The free riding scenario doesn't quite show that rational groups contain irrational members, since I haven't said anything about which kind of group will minimize expected accuracy, but it does suggest that whichever group it is, it will contain irrational members.

[21] See, for instance, Zollman (2007), Muldoon and Weisberg (2009), and Mayo-Wilson et al. (2011).

Minson et al. (MS), for instance, give considerable evidence for what they call *disagreement neglect*—the phenomenon where disagreeing parties ignore disagreement and simply stick to their own views. Summarizing their results and the results of other researchers, they write:

> Discounting of peer input has been demonstrated with American, Israeli, French, and multinational samples. In our study, both American and Japanese participants as well as ingroup and outgroup dyad members gave roughly twice as much weight to their own judgments as those of their partner, suggesting that the phenomenon is indeed a feature of basic human judgment. (p. 16)

It is worth noting that this goes against a claim that Thomas Kelly (2005) makes in an early paper on peer disagreement. In that paper Kelly claims that the empirical evidence suggests that most people are conciliatory in cases of disagreement: "There is a considerable amount of empirical evidence which suggests that an awareness of disagreement tends to lead us to significantly moderate our opinions" (pp. 170–1). In support of this, Kelly cites the classic studies by Solomon Asch from the 1950s.[22] These studies involve situations where there is a group of people, and all the group members are posed the same simple question, which they each must answer, sequentially and in front of the other group members. For instance, the question might be which two of three lines on the board are equal length. In the experiment, all the group members are confederates of the experimenter except one. The confederates all give a clearly incorrect answer to the question. Asch's results show that this can have a strong influence on the answer that the experimental subject gives. Though Kelly is correct that this does reveal a certain kind of conciliatory tendency, it is not strong evidence that in all cases of disagreement, humans have such a tendency. Instead, this shows a kind of conciliatory behavior when one is strongly outnumbered in a group situation. However, as Minson et al. (MS) note, we see a kind of non-conciliatory behavior when the groups are more evenly split. In fact, some of Asch's own modifications of his experiments show this. For instance, when Asch instructs just one of the confederates to give the correct answer, the experimental subject is much less likely to go along with majority (and obviously incorrect) opinion.[23] Thus, in the cases of interest—the cases where there is a roughly even split of opinion and so conciliatory attitudes are plausibly supported by the evidence—humans appear to be naturally non-conciliatory.

This mirrors, in an interesting way, what we see in the practical domain. There are many practical opportunities to free ride, to take an action that is in one's own self-interest even though if everyone took that action it would be bad for everyone. Nevertheless, it is commonplace that most of us are not disposed to act in our self-interest in these cases. Consider an example. Most of us recognize that when we are in a national park there is no self-interested reason not to just leave our garbage

---

[22] See, for instance, Asch (1955, 1956). [23] See, for instance, Asch (1955).

in the park, rather than carrying it out. Nevertheless, most of us are also disposed not to just leave our garbage in the park, perhaps out of some notion of fairness or responsibility. So there's a puzzle here: why are we disposed to act against our own self-interest in such cases? The case of epistemic free riding in group inquiry presents us with an analogous puzzle.

In the practical domain, different hypotheses have been given to try to explain this puzzle. Some of the more interesting hypotheses are evolutionary. According to these hypotheses, we are disposed to not be free riders because of some evolutionary advantage obtained by such a disposition. There are more and less controversial versions of this hypothesis.

The more controversial versions posit group-level selection. According to this view, a strategy that is disadvantageous to the individual may nevertheless be selected for in a population since it renders that population stronger than a population that plays the free riding strategy. Though intuitively clear, such a view has trouble explaining why such non-free-riding populations are not overrun by mutants who happen to play the free riding strategy. If such a strategy really is beneficial to the individual, it should eventually win out in a population.

The less controversial versions do not posit group-level selection. Brian Skyrms (1996) develops this kind of idea in the framework of evolutionary game theory. In Skyrms's model the selection is not taking place at the group level. Rather, each individual is modeled as reproducing in proportion to the resources she herself gathers. Skyrms shows that under a wide variety of different strategies that those in your own population might be playing, those who play the free riding strategy will tend to die out. This is primarily due to the fact that many of the alternative strategies do not engage in cooperative behavior with free riders. Here although individual instances of free riding may be beneficial to the individual, the free riding disposition is not, in general, one that survives.

One possible explanation for how we avoid the problem of epistemic free riding, then, models itself on these evolutionary hypotheses: perhaps there is some evolutionary pressure towards the disposition to remain steadfast rather than to be conciliatory in cases of disagreement. This would fit well with the fact that we do appear to have such a disposition.

It is possible to give a plausible-sounding group-level selection story:

Groups that are quickly conciliatory in cases of disagreement are not as good at finding correct answers to questions of importance. Thus, groups with such conciliatory tendencies in the past would have been less successful in answering important questions related to survival such as where to plant crops, where to hunt, and how many resources to stockpile for difficult times. This would lead groups who were non-conciliatory to have an evolutionary advantage over groups with conciliatory tendencies. We are thus naturally disposed to stick to our initial views and defend them because such a disposition keeps most of us from being epistemic free riders and thus allows us to each play our part in group inquiry.

Unfortunately, this story depends on the controversial idea of group-level selection.

It is harder to see how a Skyrms-like story could be told for the disposition to remain steadfast in cases of disagreement. What we would need is some evidence that those who are disposed to be conciliatory are given less opportunity to cooperate with others in inquiry, and so end up gathering less accurate beliefs over the long haul despite the fact that in any one situation they can do better than those who are steadfast. It is hard, however, to see how to make such a story plausible.

13.8 Conclusion

In this chapter I've argued that there are realistic cases of group inquiry where the problem of epistemic free riding can arise. These cases are structurally analogous to the more familiar cases of practical free riding. A certain kind of belief might be in your own epistemic self-interest even though if everyone in the group believed that way, it would be epistemically worse for everyone.

There is good reason to care about such cases. First, the existence of such cases adds to the growing literature suggesting that group inquiry may in some cases be fundamentally different than individual inquiry. Second, cases of epistemic free riding show that even pure inquirers—those who care only about finding the truth—may sometimes have overriding reason to believe propositions that they are not justified in believing. Third, the fact that being conciliatory in a debate is often an instance of free riding raises an interesting question about why humans nevertheless appear to be naturally disposed to be steadfast in the face of controversy.

References

Asch, S. (1955). Opinions and social pressure. *Scientific American*, 193(5), 31–5.

Asch, S. (1956). Studies of independence and conformity: A minority of one against a unanimous majority. *Psychological Monographs: General and Applied*, 70(9), 1–70.

Banerjee, A. (1992). A simple model of herd behavior. *The Quarterly Journal of Economics*, 107(3), 797–817.

Bikhchandani, S., Hirshleifer, D., and Welch, I. (1992). A theory of fads, fashion, custom, and cultural change as informational cascades. *Journal of Political Economy*, 100(5), 992–1026.

Christensen, D. (2007). Epistemology of disagreement: The good news. *Philosophical Review*, 116, 187–217.

Dunn, J. (MS). Peer disagreement and group inquiry.

Elga, A. (2007). Reflection and disagreement. *Noûs*, 41(3), 478–502.

Evans, J. S. B. T., Barston, J. L., and Pollard, P. (1983). On the conflict between logic and belief in syllogistic reasoning. *Memory & Cognition*, 11(3), 295–306.

Gigone, D. and Hastie, R. (1997). Proper analysis of the accuracy of group judgments. *Psychological Bulletin*, 121(1), 149–67.

Greaves, H. (2013). Epistemic decision theory. *Mind*, 122, 915–52.

Greitemeyer, T., Schulz-Hardt, S., Brodbeck, F. C., and Frey, D. (2006). Information sampling and group decision making: The effects of an advocacy decision procedure and task experience. *Journal of Experimental Psychology: Applied*, 12(1), 31–42.

Hastie, R. (1986). Experimental evidence on group accuracy. In B. Grofman and G. Owen (eds), *Information Pooling and Group Decision Making: Proceedings of the Second University of California, Irvine Conference on Political Economy*. Bingley: Emerald Group Publishing Limited, 129–57.

Hawthorne, J. A. (MS). Voting in search of the public good: The probabilistic logic of majority judgments. Available at: https://www.researchgate.net/profile/James_Hawthorne2/publication/228917887_Voting_in_Search_of_the_Public_Good_The_ Probabilistic_Logic _of_Majority_Judgements/links/00b7d51bb34fb364a5000000.pdf.

Joyce, J. (1998). A nonpragmatic vindication of probabilism. *Philosophy of Science*, 65(4), 575–603.

Kelly, T. (2005). The epistemic significance of disagreement. In T. S. Gendler and J. Hawthorne (eds), *Oxford Studies in Epistemology, 1*. Oxford: Oxford University Press, 167–196.

Kitcher, P. (1990). The division of cognitive labor. *The Journal of Philosophy*, 87(1), 5–22.

Konek, J. and Levinstein, B. (forthcoming). The foundations of epistmemic decision theory. *Mind*.

Kuhn, D., Shaw, V., and Felton, M. (1997). Effects of dyadic interaction on argumentive reasoning. *Cognition and Instruction*, 15(3), 287–315.

List, C. and Pettit, P. (2004). An epistemic free riding problem? In P. Catton and G. Macdonald (eds), *Karl Popper: Critical Appraisals*. Abingdon: Routledge, 128–58.

Mayo-Wilson, C., Zollman, K. J., and Danks, D. (2011). The independence thesis: When individual and social epistemology diverge. *Philosophy of Science*, 78(4), 653–77.

Mercier, H. (2011). Reasoning serves argumentation in children. *Cognitive Development*, 26(3), 177–91.

Mercier, H. (2012). Looking for arguments. *Argumentation*, 26(3), 305–24.

Mercier, H. and Sperber, D. (2011). Why do humans reason? Arguments for an argumentative theory. *Behavioral and Brain Sciences*, 34, 57–111.

Minson, J. A., Mercier, H., Deguchi, M., and Yama, H. (MS). Disagreement neglect: Failure to benefit from divergent judgments is moderated by group belonging and culture. Available at: http://citeseerx.ist.psu.edu/viewdoc/download?doi=10.1.1.408. 2124&rep1&type=pdf.

Moshman, D. and Geil, M. (1998). Collaborative reasoning: Evidence for collective rationality. *Thinking and Reasoning*, 4(2), 231–48.

Muldoon, R. (2013). Diversity and the division of cognitive labor. *Philosophy Compass*, 8(2), 117–25.

Muldoon, R. and Weisberg, M. (2009). Epistemic landscapes and the division of cognitive labor. *Philosophy of Science*, 76(2), 225–52.

Perret-Clermont, A.-N., Carugati, F., and Oates, J. (2004). A sociocognitive perspective on learning and cognitive development. In J. Oates and A. Grayson (eds), *Cognitive and Language Development in Children*. Oxford: Blackwell, 303–32.

Pettit, P. (1986). Free riding and foul dealing. *The Journal of Philosophy*, 83(7) 361–79.

Schulz-Hardt, S., Brodbeck, F., Mojzisch, A., Kerschreiter, R., and Frey, D. (2006). Group decision making in hidden profile situations: Dissent as a facilitator for decision quality. *Journal of Personality and Social Psychology*, 91(6), 1080-93.

Schulz-Hardt, S., Jochims, M., and Frey, D. (2002). Productive conflict in group decision making: Genuine and contrived dissent as strategies to counteract biased information seeking. *Organizational Behavior and Human Decision Processes*, 88(2), 563-86.

Seidenfeld, T. (1985). Calibration, coherence, and scoring rules. *Philosophy of Science*, 52, 274-94.

Skyrms, B. (1996). *Evolution of the Social Contract*. Cambridge: Cambridge University Press.

Strauss, S. G., Parker, A. M., and Bruce, J. B. (2011). The group matters: A review of processes and outcomes in intelligence analysis. *Group Dynamics: Theory, Research, and Practice*, 15(2), 128-46.

Strevens, M. (2003). The role of the priority rule in science. *Journal of Philosophy*, 100(2), 55-79.

Sunstein, C. (2002). The law of group polarization. *Journal of Political Philosophy*, 10(2), 175-95.

Zollman, K. J. (2007). The communication structure of epistemic communities. *Philosophy of Science*, 74(5), 574-87.

Zollman, K. J. (2010). The epistemic benefit of transient diversity. *Erkenntnis*, 72(1), 17-35.

Index

accuracy measure:
  Brier score 8–9, 129, 131, 134–5, 139, 152, 165–6, 203n, 242, 248–9, 253–4, 279n, 297, 300–2, 319
  logarithmic score 130, 242, 279n, 297–8, 300–1
  weighted 89–90, 133–6, 138
  see also scoring rule
accuracy-centered epistemology 142, 177, 240–52, 260–5
  see also accuracy-first account, all-accuracy account, credal consequentialism
accuracy-first account 7, 130–3, 150
  see also accuracy-centered epistemology, all-accuracy account, credal consequentialism
accuracy, self vs. de facto 249, 256
Ahlstrom-Vij, Kristoffer 2n, 12n, 23n, 49n, 114
aim of belief 31–2, 127–8, 281
alethic value 85, 88–90, 94, 105–6, 108, 111
all-accuracy account 130–3, 150
  see also accuracy-centered epistemology, accuracy-first account, credal consequentialism
Anscombe, G.E.M. 225
Arntzenius, Frank 107n, 275n, 280
Asch, Solomon 327

Bayesianism 81, 105n, 123, 149–50, 153–5, 223, 245, 270, 275, 284n
Berker, Selim 7, 12, 14, 38n, 48–9, 54–6, 59n, 61, 63, 87, 90, 91, 93, 114, 118–20, 183n, 221n, 237, 260, 270n, 290n
bets 252–5, 260–3

Caie proposition 247, 254, 262
Caie, Michael 107, 240, 245–51, 255, 259, 264
Carr, Jennifer 12, 15, 87n, 89n, 107, 228, 279n
causal decision theory 183–96, 226, 323
causal expectation values 184–8
chance paradox 251, 264
Chisholm, Roderick 71, 81
coherentism 3–4
conditionalization 9–10, 81, 105, 107, 125, 129, 132, 149, 153–4, 170–2, 183, 221, 225, 275–7, 282–3, 305–6
Condorcet Jury Theorem 313–14
Conee, Earl 4, 77–8
consequentialism:
  act 48n, 66, 92; *see also* act utilitarianism

  credal 182, 196–9, 216–17; *see also* accuracy-centered epistemology, accuracy-first account, all-accuracy account
  epistemic 2–6, 23, 26, 28–9, 32, 34, 39–41, 48–9, 54–6, 61, 70, 76, 90, 113–14, 121, 240, 245–6, 249–52, 255–7, 286, 290, 295, 308, 311
  rule 2, 3, 6, 48n, 66, 114, 118; *see also* rule utilitarianism
  sophisticated 114–15, 118, 120, 122
  subjective vs. objective 115–18, 290
continuity 97, 242
counterfactual 90, 142, 185, 204, 222
credal options 27–8, 127, 197, 210–16, 225, 228, 258–9, 263, 278–9
  see also epistemic acts
credence
  as basis of action 263–4
  choosing vs. using 256–7, 262
  initial 102–3, 105, 108–9, 154n, 208, 277, 284
  sham 258–9, 263–5

de Finetti, Bruno 253–5
debate 316–18
decision problem 126–8, 188, 211–12, 214, 246, 321
decision rule 9, 165–7, 278, 284n, 286
  chance estimation 243, 250–1; *see also* dominance, chancy expected
  value of learning 243; *see also* dominance, credal expected
decision theory:
  relation to epistemology 7, 91, 108, 149, 183–4, 222, 240, 245–6, 252–7, 260–5, 286–7
  naive 227
Dennett, Daniel 49, 50–3, 57, 61, 67
dependence hypothesis 185, 188, 197, 250
direction of fit 225–30, 256–7
disagreement neglect 327
dominance 94–6, 153–4, 157, 190–2, 199, 220–5, 243, 311–12
  causal 222–3, 225–6
  chancy expected 155; *see also* chance estimation decision rule
  credal expected 154; *see also* value of learning decision rule
  naive 221–3, 225, 227

dominance (*cont.*)
  strict 153
  worst case 155
doxastic voluntarism 89n, 91, 126–7, 279
Dreier, James 286–7
Dunn, Jeffrey 2n, 12n, 23n, 49n, 114, 171n, 172n

Easwaran, Kenny 10, 25, 150, 159, 162n, 165, 167n
epistemic acts 108, 228–9, 245, 252, 256, 319–20
  see also credal options
epistemic dilemma 157, 159, 261, 278–9, 308n
epistemic permissivism 269–73, 283
  Jamesian Argument for 273, 276
epistemic risk 121, 272, 282
epistemic trade-offs 11–12, 38–9, 49, 54–6, 61–3, 91–3, 118–20, 182–3, 223–5, 234–5, 259–60, 274–5
epistemic utility 7–8, 91, 116, 123, 125–6, 129–30, 133–6, 138–43, 149, 151–2, 165, 182, 196, 202–3, 240, 245–6, 270, 274–5, 284, 301–2, 319
  subjective vs. objective 115–18, 141–2, 169, 197n, 290, 294n, 296–302, 306–7
epistemic value monism 4–5, 25, 30
  see also veritism
error theory 230–2, 233–7
estimation 241, 252, 255–8, 264
ethics, analogies with epistemology 59n, 114–22, 168–9, 182–3, 237, 286–7, 299
evidence 4, 11–13, 24, 50, 60, 77–9, 81, 101–5, 108–10, 116–17, 121, 150, 155, 167, 171–2, 217, 232, 242, 252, 257–8, 273, 279n, 282–4, 294–5, 317–20, 322
evidential norms 168–72, 217
evidential probability 232, 285n, 322
  see also rational probability function
evidentialism 4, 77, 283, 291
evolutionary game theory 328–9
expected utility 9–11, 116–17, 123–5, 127, 170, 183–99, 257, 274–5, 301–2
  see also causal decision theory
expert 61, 106–7, 119, 202, 308, 318, 324
explanation:
  explanatory goals 136, 140, 142–3
  kairetic account 137–8
  sensitivity 138–40
  stability 137–8, 143
  value of 132–6, 285
extensionality 132n, 152, 173–5, 242
  for norms 174–7

Feldman, Richard 4, 77–8
Field, Hartry 272
final ends 240, 253, 256

Firth, Roderick 11, 38n, 54n, 91, 119, 221n
Fitelson, Brandon 10, 25, 150, 159, 162n, 165
Foot, Philippa 2, 25, 36n
free riding 310–13
  epistemic 313–14, 315, 318–25
Fumerton, Richard 11–12

Geil, Molly 316
Gettier problems 33–4, 73
Gibbard, Allan 127–8
Goldman, Alvin 3, 4, 7, 10, 25n, 26, 37n, 55n, 71–83, 120, 220
Good, I. J. 124–5, 244
Greaves, Hilary 10, 12, 91, 108–11, 221–5, 240, 245–6, 250, 256, 259–60, 320
group inquiry 310, 316–18
group-level selection 328–9
groups, homogenous vs. heterogenous 316–18, 324–5

Harper, William 260–1
Hastie, Reid 317
hedonism 28, 119
heuristic 232–7
Howson, Colin 171–2

immodesty 275–7, 280–2
Independence Thesis 310, 325–6
indifference principle 155, 162–3, 170, 221, 225
infinite options 157, 192, 195–6, 200–1, 203–4, 207, 210–16
informational cascades 314
intuitive judgments 34–8, 73, 82, 117, 123, 157, 231–2, 234–6

James, William 121, 269, 282–3
Jenkins, Carrie 12, 38n, 221n
Joyce, James 7–9, 26, 94, 97, 133n, 150, 152, 165, 177–9, 220–1
justification 3–4, 15, 43–5, 54–6, 59, 63–4, 70–83, 85–8, 113–14, 119, 121, 142, 283n, 295n

Kelly, Thomas 271–2, 327
Kitcher, Philip 5, 310
Konek, Jason 182, 225–30, 241, 256–7, 259
Kopec, Matthew 283–4
Kornblith, Hilary 58, 60
Korsgaard, Christine 2
Kvanvig, Jonathan 272

laws of nature 137
learning, value of 124–5, 129–30, 243–4
Leitgeb, Hannes 9–10, 153n, 154n, 274n, 279n, 295–6
Levinstein, Benjamin 152, 182, 225–30, 241, 256–7, 259, 272, 279

INDEX

Lewis, David 154, 185n, 281
List, Christian 313–16
Lynch, Michael 29, 31, 33–4, 41

McKay, Ryan 49, 50–3, 57, 61, 67
maximization 1–2, 3, 26, 30, 44, 113, 119, 123, 129, 182–3, 188–96, 198–9, 208, 212–15, 224, 242, 245–6, 290
   of expected accuracy 7, 9–10, 24, 30, 108, 116–17, 251, 257, 274–5, 280, 295, 306, 311, 320
   when no maximal option 189–96
Mayo-Wilson, Conor 310
Mercier, Hugo 316
minimization of expected inacccuracy, *see* maximization of expected accuracy
Moore, G. E. 5, 23–4, 36–7, 119n
Moshman, David 316
Moss, Sarah 278–9

naturalism, epistemic 5, 70, 72, 74–5, 81, 83
normative force objection 228–30

ordinal ranking 190–1
ought-implies-can 189n, 279, 295n, 308n

peer disagreement 272, 317–18, 324
Pettigrew, Richard 25n, 91, 150–67, 177–8, 241n, 284n, 295n
Pettit, Philip 311, 313–16
positive illusions 51–3
practical rationality, analogies with epistemology 108, 119–22, 217, 245, 261–2, 270–9, 286, 299, 313, 325, 327–8
pragmatic value 48, 49, 56–67
previsions 253–5, 260–2, 264
Principal Principle 100, 154–5, 162–3, 170, 173, 175–6, 178, 221, 225, 244, 250–1, 305–6
principle of indifference, *see* indifference principle
prisoner's dilemma 312
probabilism 7, 107, 153, 161–2, 220, 221, 223–5, 240, 245, 252, 275n, 305–6
propriety 8, 97–8, 129, 134, 170, 242, 244, 254, 275–7, 280, 297–301, 306, 323

questions 123–5, 142

Railton, Peter 115–16
ratifiability 240, 252, 257–8, 260–5
rational probability function 95–103
   see also evidential probability

rationality:
   diachronic principles of 86, 103–7, 153–4, 189n, 198n, 208–9, 275, 282
   individual vs. group 325–6
reflection principle 149n, 221, 225, 294n
reliabilism 3–4, 5, 6, 7, 11, 12, 26n, 55n, 59, 63, 70–1, 75, 77, 80–1, 91, 114–16, 118–19, 122, 221n, 291
resilience 138, 142

satisficing 1, 5, 26n, 44
Scanlon, T. M. 2
Schoenfield, Miriam 153n, 284n
Schulz-Hardt, Stefan 316–17
scoring rule 8, 89, 95–8, 152, 242, 274–82, 284, 297–301, 319
   see also accuracy measure
scoring rule arguments 153–6, 220–1, 240–5
   compatible with each other 156–64
   compatible with veritism 165–7
side-constraint 25, 39, 158–9
Skyrms, Brian 124n, 137n, 142n, 244, 328
Sperber, Dan 316
Stich, Stephen 75–6
stoicism objection 227–8
Strevens, Michael 137, 178
subvaluationism 194–5
supervaluationism 194–5
Swanson, Eric 276n, 280

Talbot, Brian 228–9
teleology 3, 14–15, 24, 44, 48, 91, 114, 279n, 290n
threshold 1, 5, 7, 27, 190–1
Titelbaum, Michael 283–4, 291, 300
truth-directedness 97, 152, 173, 242, 299, 301

Urbach, Peter 171–2
utilitarianism:
   act 1, 2, 3, 5, 12, 28, 66, 92; *see also* act consequentialism
   ideal 119
   rule 3, 6; *see also* rule consequentialism

veritism 4, 26–34, 130–3, 149–52, 165, 177–8, 220
   see also epistemic value monism
virtue:
   epistemic or intellectual 59, 63, 189n, 325
   moral 66, 118

Wallace, David 10, 221, 275n
Weirich, Paul 260–1
well-being 48–9, 56–7
Williamson, Timothy 73, 102, 171n, 232, 279, 285
Woodward, James 137